HACKERS
LSAT
Reading
Comprehension

Hackers Language
Research Institute

About Hackers

Founded in 1998 by linguistics professor Dr. David Cho, Hackers Education Group has become one of the most successful and trusted educational companies. We are proud to provide innovative and effective learning solutions, including books, classes, and online lectures.

Our team of experts strives to incorporate effective instructional techniques into all of our products and services. Our unique prep programs for standardized tests such as the TOEFL, TOEIC, TEPS, IELTS, GRE, SAT, and LSAT are praised by students, and our books are consistently at the top of bestseller lists.

Hackers Language Research Institute
23, Gangnam-daero 61-gil, Seocho-gu, Seoul, Korea
Inquiries   publishing@hackers.com

ISBN   978-89-6542-389-8 (13740)

Printed in South Korea

2 3 4 5 6 7 8 9 10   26 25 24 23 22

Complete LSAT Preparation!
HACKERS ACADEMIA (www.Hackers.ac)
• Accurate diagnostic tests
• Systematic curriculum
• Guided study sessions

Preface

Thank you for purchasing *HACKERS LSAT Reading Comprehension*. All of us at Hackers Education Group are confident that this publication will be an invaluable resource as you prepare for the LSAT.

This comprehensive guide to the Reading Comprehension (RC) section was created by a team of experienced instructors and writers with extensive knowledge of the LSAT. It includes clear explanations of core concepts such as passage analysis, effective strategies for solving each RC question type, and useful tips to improve performance on test day.

A key feature of *HACKERS LSAT Reading Comprehension* is that each RC question type is presented in its own section with the following elements:

- **An easy-to-understand flow chart that outlines the question-solving process**
- **A step-by-step walkthrough of how to determine the correct answer choice**
- **Information about common tricks used to make incorrect answer choices attractive**
- **Example and practice questions taken from previous administrations of the LSAT**
- **Detailed explanations of these questions and their correct/incorrect answer choices**

Another important feature of this book is the inclusion of a complete RC practice test composed of actual LSAT passages and questions. Of course, the answer key for the practice test contains thorough explanations of the questions and answer choices.

Thank you again for choosing *HACKERS LSAT Reading Comprehension*, and we wish you all the best as you take the first step in achieving your dream of a career in the legal profession.

Contents

Chapter 6: Process Family

Chapter 7: Comparative Reading Family

Chapter 8: Putting It All Together

Chapter 9: Pacing and Test Day Preparedness

Chapter 10: Practice Test

Chapter 11: Question Index

Chapter 1 : Welcome to the LSAT

HACKERS
LSAT *Reading Comprehension*

Chapter 1

Welcome to the
LSAT

Chapter 1: Welcome to the LSAT

HACKERS
LSAT *Reading Comprehension*

Introduction

The LSAT is a standardized test that is required for admission to every American Bar Association-approved law school in the United States, as well as a growing number of law schools in other countries.

The LSAT is offered in digital format only. The exam consists of four 35-minute sections: three scored sections and one

	Section	Time	# of Questions
Scored	Logical Reasoning	35 minutes	24-26
Scored	Analytical Reasoning	35 minutes	22-24
Scored	Reading Comprehension	35 minutes	26-28
Unscored	Experimental	35 minutes	22-28

unscored experimental section. The three scored sections of the exam consist of the Logical Reasoning section, the Analytical Reasoning section (also known as Logic Games), and the Reading Comprehension section. The unscored experimental section is an additional Logical Reasoning, Analytical Reasoning, or Reading Comprehension section that is used by the Law School Admission Council (LSAC) for research purposes. As the scored sections of the LSAT are presented in random order, it is impossible to identify the experimental section while taking the test. Test-takers will be permitted to take a 10-minute break at the conclusion of the second 35-minute section.

The LSAT is designed to test the skills required to succeed as a law student and lawyer. These include the ability to construct and analyze arguments (Logical Reasoning), organize abstract information and evaluate relationships between variables (Analytical Reasoning), and understand complex written materials (Reading Comprehension). The LSAT does not directly test vocabulary, grammar, or knowledge of particular subjects, making it very difficult to cram for.

The LSAT is the most significant factor in the admissions process. A high LSAT score will increase your chances of being accepted by a prestigious law school and thus affect your future employment opportunities. In addition, your LSAT score will determine whether you qualify for certain scholarships and how much you are eligible to receive. This book will help you achieve the LSAT score needed to embark on your legal career.

Scoring of the LSAT

Each question on the LSAT is worth one point. If you answer a question correctly, you will receive one point. If you skip a question or answer it incorrectly, you will not receive a point. This means that there is no penalty for guessing, so it is to your advantage to answer every single question.

The number of questions answered correctly determines your raw score. This is converted into a scaled score of 120 to 180, based on the performance of everyone else who participated in the same test administration. A standardized curve is used to assign a scaled score. The number of correctly answered questions needed to achieve a particular scaled score varies.

Raw Score (# of correct answers)		Scaled Score
Lowest	Highest	
97	102	176~180
93	96	171~175
87	92	166~170
80	86	161~165
71	79	156~160
61	70	151~155
52	60	146~150
42	51	141~145
33	41	136~140
26	32	131~135
20	25	126~130
16	19	121~125
0	15	120

Test Administrations

The LSAT testing year runs from July 1 to June 30. The exact number of test administrations varies depending on the year and region. Some administrations are disclosed administrations, meaning that in addition to their score, test-takers are able to access the questions that appear on the exam, an answer key, and a score conversion chart.

LSAC limits the number of administrations that an individual may participate in. The current policy is as follows:

- no more than three LSATs may be taken within a single testing year
- no more than five LSATs may be taken within the current and past five testing years
- no more than seven LSATs may be taken in total

As many law schools only take into consideration an applicant's highest LSAT score, it is usually worthwhile to retake the LSAT with the aim of getting a higher score. However, it is important to keep in mind that law schools receive all of an applicant's valid LSAT scores. Be sure to check the admissions policies of any law schools you plan to apply to.

Reading Comprehension Section Basics

The Reading Comprehension (RC) section of the LSAT tests one's ability to read and understand complex passages, identify viewpoints, analyze arguments, and draw inferences. In addition to strong reading skills and the ability to retain and recall information, test-takers must be able to analyze the structure of a passage and track the different viewpoints presented. It is the focus on viewpoints that distinguishes the LSAT RC section from other reading comprehension tests.

Each RC section includes four passages—three long single passages and one Comparative Reading passage that is made up of two short passages with overlapping subject matter. The long single passages can be classified as Informational, Argumentative, or Debate passages. The two short passages that comprise the Comparative Reading passage are almost always Argumentative. The passages in the RC section are adapted from published sources.

All RC passage topics fall into four general subject areas: law, humanities, natural sciences, and social sciences. The RC section typically includes one passage from each of these subject areas. Specific topics that have appeared in recent administrations of the LSAT include the legal rationale behind a famous Supreme Court case, archeological evidence of the early domestication of animals, plate tectonics, the early Indus Valley civilization, the conventions behind the classical era of filmmaking, and the philosophical underpinnings of the concept of free will. Test-takers are not required to have any prior knowledge of the topics discussed in RC passages. Each passage contains all of the information necessary to correctly answer the accompanying questions.

RC passages are typically 50 to 65 lines long and are followed by five to eight questions. Each question is composed of a prompt (a question task regarding the ideas and logical relationships expressed in the passage) and five answer choices, of which only one is correct. To succeed on the RC section, it is important to anticipate important elements from the passage that are commonly asked about in the questions, as well as understand exactly what information each question type is asking you to extract from the passage. Although any part of a passage could contain the information necessary to answer a question, there are certain elements that are routinely tested. This book discusses these in detail.

The difficulty level of the RC section does not progress as noticeably as that of the other LSAT sections. It is possible that the fourth passage in an RC section will be somewhat more complex than the first one, but this will not always be the case. Therefore, test-takers should treat each passage the same with regard to pacing. Pacing strategies are discussed at length later in this book.

Here is an example of an excerpt from a typical RC passage with a question:

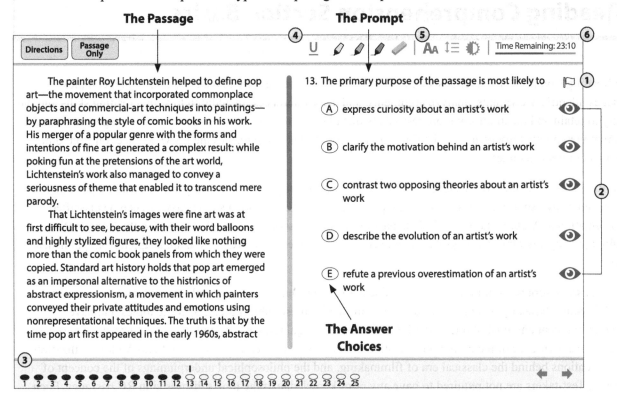

The example above is presented as it would appear on the Digital LSAT. The key features of the interface have been numbered and are explained below.

① **Mark for Review:** Clicking on the flag icon will mark the question for review. A small flag will appear above the corresponding question bubble in the progress bar.

② **Eliminate Answer Choice:** Clicking on one of the eye icons will cause the corresponding answer choice's text to fade and a diagonal slash to appear through both the eye icon and the bubble to the left of the answer choice.

③ **Progress Bar:** Clicking on a bubble above a number in the progress bar will open the corresponding question. The progress bar shows which questions have been answered. A white bubble indicates that a question has not been answered, while a black bubble indicates that it has been answered.

④ **Highlight & Underline:** Clicking on the U icon allows sections of text (in the passage, prompt, or answer choices) to be underlined. Clicking on one of the three colored pen icons allows sections of text to be highlighted. Clicking on the eraser icon allows the underlining or highlighting to be removed.

⑤ **Adjust Appearance:** Clicking on these icons allows the font size, line spacing, and screen brightness to be adjusted.

⑥ **Timer:** Clicking on the numbers toggles the display of the time remaining on and off.

In the pen-and-paper version of the LSAT, line numbers were provided for passages, and certain questions included specific line references. For example:

The word "mysteries" (line 15) refers to

In the digital version of the LSAT, line numbers are not included. Instead, the referenced text in the passage is highlighted. In addition, the prompt often includes a description of where the text can be found in the passage. For example:

The word "mysteries" (second sentence of the first paragraph) refers to

The line numbering system will be used throughout this book as it is most suitable for non-digital formats. Note that the system used to reference text in the passage does not affect the method used to answer a question.

The best way to approach an RC question is to first analyze the passage, then read the prompt, and then move on to the answer choices. Once you have selected the correct answer choice, proceed to the next question's prompt.

Analyze the Passage → **Read the Prompt** → **Find the Correct Answer**

Passages

Passage Types

Being able to identify the passage type is never a requirement to answer a question. However, doing so can sometimes make it easier to analyze the passage. As mentioned previously, there are four types of passages in the RC section. Comparative Reading passages—which were added to the RC section in 2007—always appear once per section, but there is no fixed pattern for Informational, Argumentative, or Debate passages, each of which may appear more than once or not at all.

Below is a brief summary of the key features of each of the four passage types. These will be discussed in detail in Chapter 2.

Informational Passages convey information about a specific topic without presenting an argument. For example, an Informational passage might describe a phenomenon, explain a process, or outline a sequence of events. The information is presented in a neutral manner, meaning that the author's viewpoint is not present. As a result, this type of passage is never accompanied by questions regarding the author's viewpoint or attitude. The main point of an Informational passage is always a descriptive statement that summarizes the key information in the passage.

> A *viewpoint* is the opinion of a person or group. This key concept will be explained in detail later in this section.

Argumentative Passages present an argument in support of a conclusion reached by the author. Therefore, the author's viewpoint is always present. There may be passing references to other viewpoints, but the bulk of the passage is dedicated to advancing the author's conclusion. This is the main point of the passage.

Debate Passages feature multiple viewpoints that often directly conflict with one another. The author's viewpoint may or may not be present. If it is present, the author's conclusion will be the main point of the passage. The author may support one of the competing viewpoints, rebut one of the viewpoints, reconcile all of the viewpoints, or present an independent conclusion about the subject matter. If the author's viewpoint is not present, the main point will be a neutral description of the viewpoints in the passage.

Comparative Reading Passages include two short passages labeled "Passage A" and "Passage B." The subject matter of these dual passages is always connected, but the extent of the connection varies—these passages may overlap completely or be only tangentially related. The dual passages are almost always Argumentative passages. The process for analyzing a Comparative Reading passage differs slightly from that for the other types. This process will be discussed in detail later in this book.

Analyzing the Passage

Due to time constraints, you should only read through the entire passage once. This means that when you are answering questions, you need to be able to quickly locate the relevant content without having to reread the entire passage. In order to be able to do this, it is important to analyze the passage during the initial read-through.

Marking the passage is an important part of the analysis process. It involves underlining and highlighting key information for easy reference. The Digital LSAT interface includes an underlining tool and three highlighting tools (yellow, red, and orange). There are many ways to mark a passage, and it is important to find a system that works well for you. In this book, the following system will be used:

- Underline keywords
- Underline the main point of the passage
- Highlight each viewpoint other than the author's the same color and label each with A), B), or C).

The process of analyzing a passage that is used in this book involves four steps:

- Identify keywords
- Identify and summarize the main point
- Identify paragraph functions and summarize content
- Identify viewpoints and summarize relationships

All four stages should be done during the initial read-through of the passage. For instructional purposes, the analyses throughout this book are very detailed (particularly the summaries of the content). To begin with, your analyses should have the same level of detail. However, as you become more comfortable with the reading passages, you should look for ways to make the process less time-consuming. For example, if the main point of the passage is stated clearly in one sentence, you might skip summarizing it in the notes (as underlining it is sufficient). You should also look for ways to simplify and shorten the content summaries. Ideally, once you get to the point of taking the LSAT, you should be in a position to keep track of much of the information from the initial analysis in your head without having to take extensive notes.

Let's look at the analysis process in detail.

Identify Keywords

Keywords are terms that signal important elements of a passage. Underlining keywords makes it easier to identify these elements. In addition, it can help you locate the necessary information when answering questions. The following table includes examples of keywords that you are likely to encounter and information about their roles:

Role	Keywords		Description
Introduce Author's Viewpoint	Fortunately Correctly Thankfully	Regretfully Paradoxically	These indicate that the author's viewpoint is about to be presented.
Introduce Other Viewpoints	Critics Opinion Traditional Modern	Theory Asserts Claims Predicts	These indicate that a viewpoint other than the author's is about to be presented.
Indicate Author's Attitude	Correct Appropriate Supported Likely Probable Reasonable	Incorrect Inappropriate Unsupported Unlikely Improbable Unreasonable	These show the author's attitude toward a specific topic or viewpoint.
Present Contrasting Information	But However Although Still Yet	Despite Nonetheless By contrast On the other hand	These rebut or add nuance to a previous point. If they occur in a section of text where a viewpoint is being presented, they likely signal that a different viewpoint is about to be introduced.
Present Additional Information	Additionally Also Furthermore Moreover By the same token/idea	First/Firstly Second/Secondly Finally/Lastly Similarly	These introduce additional information to support a previous point. If they occur in a section of text where a viewpoint is being presented, they likely signal that what follows is a continuation of that viewpoint.
Present an Example	For example Because For instance	Since After all Evidently	These introduce an example that illustrates a previous point. If they occur in a section of text where a viewpoint is being presented, they likely signal that what follows is a continuation of that viewpoint.

Identify & Summarize the Main Point

It is important to identify and summarize the main point of the passage. All passages include a main point. The type of main point is dependent on whether or not the author's viewpoint is present. If the author's viewpoint is present, the main point will be a conclusion—a claim that is supported by evidence in the passage. If the author's viewpoint is not present, the main point will be a neutral, descriptive statement that summarizes the important information in the passage.

For an example of a main point that expresses a viewpoint, consider a passage that discusses the impact of Andre Jackson's art on modern realism. A main point in the form of a conclusion might read as follows:

Andre Jackson's art had a major impact on modern realism after his death.

This is a claim made by the author of the passage, and the bulk of the passage would be devoted to providing evidence to support it. You would expect to see this type of main point in an Argumentative passage or a Debate passage that includes the author's viewpoint.

Compare this with a main point in the form of a descriptive statement:

Some art historians believe that Andre Jackson's art had a major impact on modern realism.

This is a neutral statement that simply describes what is discussed in the passage. You would see this type of main point in an Informational passage.

A Debate passage that does not include the author's viewpoint might have the following as a main point:

> **Some art historians believe that Andre Jackson's art had a major impact on modern realism, while others dispute this.**

The main point may appear anywhere in a passage. However, there are some patterns you can anticipate seeing. In an Argumentative passage, the main point is often in the last sentence of the first paragraph. In an Informational passage, the main point is likely to appear in the first or last paragraph. In a Debate passage that includes the author's viewpoint, the main point commonly appears in the last paragraph.

Keep in mind that for passages that include the author's viewpoint, the main point is always explicitly stated in one or two sentences. However, for those that do not, the main point may be explicitly stated, or it may need to be synthesized from information located throughout the passage. In the latter case, it is particularly important to be able to summarize the main point clearly and succinctly in your notes.

Additional guidance on classifying passage types and identifying the main points is provided in Chapter 2.

Identify Paragraph Functions & Summarize Content

You must also identify the function of each paragraph and briefly summarize its content. There is a wide variety of possible paragraph functions depending on the type of passage and the subject matter. The most common are as follows:

- Stating the main point
- Providing background or contextual information
- Providing evidence to support the main point
- Presenting a single viewpoint or multiple viewpoints

A common structure for an Informational passage is for the first paragraph to include a broad overview of the topic and a statement that summarizes what will be discussed (the main point). Each subsequent paragraph provides additional details that elaborate on this statement.

A common structure for an Argumentative passage is for the first paragraph to provide background information about the topic and state the author's conclusion (the main point). The paragraphs that follow present evidence—in the form of supporting details or examples—to support this conclusion.

A common structure for a Debate passage is for the first paragraph to provide background information about the topic and introduce the opposing viewpoints. The next couple of paragraphs will each present a different viewpoint regarding the topic. The final paragraph will then provide the author's viewpoint (the main point).

That being said, there are many possible passage structures. This makes the accurate identification of each paragraph's function a vital part of understanding the passage as a whole.

When summarizing the content of a paragraph, do not attempt to include every detail. Focus on the key information. Remember, the purpose of the summary is to help you quickly locate the relevant information in the passage when answering questions.

Identify Viewpoints & Summarize Relationships

The term *viewpoint* is one that has come up throughout this chapter and will continue to do so throughout the book. It is a key concept that serves as the basis for many RC questions. In the broadest sense, a viewpoint is simply an opinion. It could include a conclusion about a central theme of the passage that is supported by extensive evidence, an assertion about a minor point that is made in passing, or an attitude toward something that is discussed in the passage. In effect, a viewpoint incorporates everything that a person or group referenced in the passage argues for or feels about a particular subject.

Many passages are accompanied by multiple questions related to viewpoint. Therefore, you should take note of any viewpoints you encounter while reading through the passage. The author's viewpoint is the most important to consider when present because it is the main point of the passage. This will be underlined, so there is no need to highlight it. All other viewpoints should be marked using the highlighter function.

Take note of how the various viewpoints relate to the subject matter being discussed and to each other. For example, if the author strongly disagrees with another viewpoint in the passage, you will likely encounter a question related to this.

Analyze the passage below. Mark the <u>keywords</u>, <u>main point</u>, and <u>viewpoints</u> other than the author's. Note the function of each paragraph. Summarize the main point, paragraph content, and viewpoints.

Because the market system enables entrepreneurs and investors who develop new technology to reap financial rewards from their risk of capital, it may seem that the primary result of this activity is that some
(5) people who have spare capital accumulate more. But in spite of the fact that the profits derived from various technological developments have accrued to relatively few people, the developments themselves have served overall as a remarkable democratizing force. In fact,
(10) under the regime of the market, the gap in benefits accruing to different groups of people has been narrowed in the long term.

This tendency can be seen in various well-known technological developments. For example, before the
(15) printing press was introduced centuries ago, few people had access to written materials, much less to scribes and private secretaries to produce and transcribe documents. Since printed materials have become widely available, however, people without special
(20) position or resources—and in numbers once thought impossible—can take literacy and the use of printed texts for granted. With the distribution of books and periodicals in public libraries, this process has been extended to the point where people in general can have
(25) essentially equal access to a vast range of texts that would once have been available only to a very few. A more recent technological development extends this process beyond printed documents. A child in school with access to a personal computer and modem—
(30) which is becoming fairly common in technologically advanced societies—has computing power and database access equal to that of the best-connected scientists and engineers at top-level labs of just fifteen years ago, a time when relatively few people had
(35) personal access to any computing power. Or consider the uses of technology for leisure. In previous centuries only a few people with abundant resources had the ability and time to hire professional entertainment, and to have contact through travel and written
(40) communication—both of which were prohibitively expensive—with distant people. But now broadcast technology is widely available, and so almost anyone can have an entertainment cornucopia unimagined in earlier times. Similarly, the development of
(45) inexpensive mail distribution and telephone connections and, more recently, the establishment of the even more efficient medium of electronic mail have greatly extended the power of distant communication.

This kind of gradual diffusion of benefits across
(50) society is not an accident of these particular technological developments, but rather the result of a general tendency of the market system. Entrepreneurs and investors often are unable to maximize financial success without expanding their market, and this
(55) involves structuring their prices to the consumers so as to make their technologies genuinely accessible to an ever-larger share of the population. In other words, because market competition drives prices down, it tends to diffuse access to new technology across
(60) society as a result.

Main Point

Paragraph 1

Paragraph 2

Paragraph 3

Identify Viewpoints

Drill: Analyze a Passage — Answers

Because the market system enables entrepreneurs and investors who develop new technology to reap financial rewards from their risk of capital, it may seem that the primary result of this activity is that some
(5) people who have spare capital accumulate more. But in spite of the fact that the profits derived from various technological developments have accrued to relatively few people, the developments themselves have served overall as a remarkable democratizing force. In fact,
(10) under the regime of the market, the gap in benefits accruing to different groups of people has been narrowed in the long term.

This tendency can be seen in various well-known technological developments. For example, before the
(15) printing press was introduced centuries ago, few people had access to written materials, much less to scribes and private secretaries to produce and transcribe documents. Since printed materials have become widely available, however, people without special
(20) position or resources—and in numbers once thought impossible—can take literacy and the use of printed texts for granted. With the distribution of books and periodicals in public libraries, this process has been extended to the point where people in general can have
(25) essentially equal access to a vast range of texts that would once have been available only to a very few. A more recent technological development extends this process beyond printed documents. A child in school with access to a personal computer and modem—
(30) which is becoming fairly common in technologically advanced societies—has computing power and database access equal to that of the best-connected scientists and engineers at top-level labs of just fifteen years ago, a time when relatively few people had
(35) personal access to any computing power. Or consider the uses of technology for leisure. In previous centuries only a few people with abundant resources had the ability and time to hire professional entertainment, and to have contact through travel and written
(40) communication—both of which were prohibitively expensive—with distant people. But now broadcast technology is widely available, and so almost anyone can have an entertainment cornucopia unimagined in earlier times. Similarly, the development of
(45) inexpensive mail distribution and telephone connections and, more recently, the establishment of the even more efficient medium of electronic mail have greatly extended the power of distant communication.

This kind of gradual diffusion of benefits across
(50) society is not an accident of these particular technological developments, but rather the result of a general tendency of the market system. Entrepreneurs and investors often are unable to maximize financial success without expanding their market, and this
(55) involves structuring their prices to the consumers so as to make their technologies genuinely accessible to an ever-larger share of the population. In other words, because market competition drives prices down, it tends to diffuse access to new technology across
(60) society as a result.

Main Point

The main point is stated in the last two sentences of the first paragraph. It is that technological developments have narrowed the gap in benefits accruing to different groups in the long term.

Paragraph 1

The first paragraph briefly mentions a viewpoint other than the author's (technological development leads to people with capital accumulating more) before stating the main point.

Paragraph 2

The second paragraph provides evidence to support the main point in the form of several examples (printing press, personal computer, broadcast technology, email, and telephone). Each example describes an instance in which technological developments narrowed the gap between rich and poor.

Paragraph 3

The third paragraph provides additional evidence to support the main point. It states that the market system allows for technological developments, which lead to the gap between rich and poor narrowing. In short, the market system provides incentives for this gap to narrow.

Identify Viewpoints

The author's viewpoint is present and is the focus of the passage. The viewpoint that technological development leads to people with capital accumulating more is mentioned in passing.

Reading Comprehension questions can be divided into five families:

Synthesis Family	Information Family	Inference Family	Process Family	Comparative Reading Family
• Main Point • Structure • Purpose • Function of a Paragraph • Function of a Statement	• Detail • Existence • Meaning	• Implication • Viewpoint • Attitude • Principle	• Application • Strengthen • Weaken • Evaluation • Extension	• Relationship • Agree/Disagree • Comparative

Each RC passage is accompanied by five to eight questions. To answer these correctly, it is important to understand the task that a prompt is asking you to perform. Below is a summary of the five question families and the question types that belong to each.

Synthesis Family

Answering Synthesis Family questions involves identifying the main structural components of the passage. The correct answer choice for many of these questions can be anticipated during the initial read-through of the passage.

> 23.7% of Reading Comprehension Questions

Main Point (MP) – Answering MP questions involves determining the main point of the passage. The correct answer choice will either be a restatement of the author's conclusion or a summary of the most important information in the passage.

MP prompts typically include the following boldfaced expressions:

1. Which one of the following most accurately states **the main point** of the passage?
2. Which one of the following most accurately expresses **the main idea** of the passage?
3. Which one of the following best summarizes **the central idea** of the passage?

Structure (STR) – Answering STR questions involves understanding the structure of the passage or of part of the passage. The correct answer choice will be a sequential list of the functions of each paragraph of either the whole passage or a multi-paragraph section of the passage.

STR prompts typically include the following boldfaced expressions:

1. Which one of the following most accurately describes **the structure** of the passage?
2. Which one of the following most accurately corresponds to **the organization** of the passage?
3. Which one of the following sequences best describes **the presentation of the material** in the passage?

Purpose (P) – Answering P questions involves identifying the overall purpose of the passage.

P prompts typically include the following boldfaced expressions:

1. The author's **primary purpose** in writing the passage is to
2. The passage is **primarily concerned with**
3. Which of the following best states **the primary purpose** of the passage

Function of a Paragraph (FP) – Answering FP questions involves determining how a paragraph is used in the context of the passage.

FP prompts typically include the following boldfaced expressions:

1. **The primary function** of the first **paragraph** is to
2. The discussion in the second **paragraph** is **primarily intended** to
3. Which one of the following best describes **the primary purpose** of the third **paragraph**?

Function of a Statement (FS) – Answering FS questions involves determining how a statement, phrase, or concept is used in the context of the passage.

FS prompts typically include the following boldfaced expressions:

1. **The primary function of the reference** to X (line #) is to
2. The author **mentions X primarily in order to**
3. Which one of the following most accurately expresses **the primary purpose of the sentence** in line #?

Information Family

Answering Information Family questions involves identifying specific information in the passage or the contextual meaning of a referenced word or phrase.

> 14.9% of Reading Comprehension Questions

Detail (D) – Answering D questions involves locating a particular detail that is explicitly stated in the passage.

D prompts typically include the following boldfaced expressions:

1. **The passage indicates** which one of the following as a factor in X?
2. **According to the passage**, what is the advantage of X?
3. Which one of the following does **the passage mention as** an example of X?

Existence (EX) – Answering EX questions involves determining whether or not a detail is explicitly stated in the passage. The prompts for these questions are often very similar to those for D questions.

EX prompts typically include the following boldfaced expressions:

1. Which one of the following does the author **mention in the passage?**
2. Which one of the following is **stated by the passage**?
3. **The passage asserts** which one of the following about X?

Meaning (M) – Answering M questions involves determining the contextual meaning of a word or phrase used in the passage.

M prompts usually include the following boldfaced expressions:

1. Which one of the following most accurately expresses what **the author means** by "X" in line #?
2. Which one of the following most accurately expresses what is **meant when the author refers to the phrase "X"** (line #)?
3. Which one of the following **could replace the phrase** "X" in line # without substantively altering the author's meaning?

Inference Family

Answering Inference Family questions involves synthesizing information to reach a conclusion that is strongly supported by the passage but not explicitly stated.

<table>
<tr><td>29.8% of Reading Comprehension Questions</td></tr>
</table>

Implication (IMP) – Answering IMP questions involves identifying an inference that is supported by information in the passage.

IMP prompts usually include the following boldfaced expressions:

1. The passage **suggests** which one of the following about X?
2. Which one of the following can be **most reasonably inferred** from the information in the passage?
3. The information in the passage **provides the most support** for which one of the following statements?

Viewpoint (V) – Answering V questions involves identifying an inference that is compatible with the viewpoint of a specific person (including the author) or group in the passage.

V prompts usually include the following boldfaced expressions:

1. According to the passage, X **believes** that
2. Which one of the following statements would the author of the passage **most likely agree with**?
3. Which one of the following **views** would proponents of X **most likely hold**?

Attitude (ATT) – Answering ATT questions involves determining how the author feels about a topic or viewpoint. Although both V questions and ATT questions may be about the author's viewpoint, ATT questions focus on feelings, values, or attitudes.

ATT prompts usually include the following boldfaced expressions:

1. According to the passage, **the author's attitude** toward X can most accurately be described as
2. It can be most reasonably inferred that **the author views** X as
3. Which one of the following most accurately characterizes **the author's stance** toward X?

Principle (PR) – Answering PR questions involves identifying a general principle that an argument is based on.

PR prompts usually include the following boldfaced expressions:

1. Which one of the following **principles** most likely **underlies the author's reasoning** throughout the passage?
2. Which one of the following **principles** is most clearly operative in the author's argument?
3. Based on the passage, X should be handled according to which one of the following **principles**?

Process Family

Answering Process Family questions involves applying a process to information in the passage.

<table>
<tr><td>12.1% of Reading Comprehension Questions</td></tr>
</table>

Application (APP) – Answering APP questions involves identifying a situation, argument, or approach that is analogous to one in the passage.

APP prompts usually include the following boldfaced expressions:

1. Which one of the following **best exemplifies** X discussed in the passage?
2. Based on the passage, which one of the following **relationships is most analogous to** X?
3. Which one of the following is **most similar** to that discussed in the last paragraph?

Strengthen (S) – Answering S questions involves identifying a statement that strengthens an argument in the passage.

S prompts usually include the following boldfaced expressions:

1. Which one of the following, if true, would **most strengthen** the author's primary conclusion?
2. Which one of the following, if true, **most supports** the author's claim about X?
3. Which one of the following, if true, **lends the most credence to** X?

Weaken (W) – Answering W questions involves identifying a statement that weakens an argument in the passage.

W prompts usually include the following boldfaced expressions:

1. Which one of the following, if true, **most weakens** the author's primary conclusion?
2. Which one of the following, if true, would **most seriously challenge** X?
3. Which one of the following, if true, would **undermine** the claim that X?

Evaluation (E) – Answering E questions involves identifying a question that can be answered using the information in the passage or one for which the answer would strengthen or weaken an argument in the passage.

E prompts usually include the following boldfaced expressions:

1. **An answer** to which one of the following **questions** would be **most relevant to** X?
2. **Data** from to which one of the following sources would be **most relevant to evaluating** X?
3. **Information** in the passage **most helps to answer** which one of the following **questions**?

Extension (EXT) – Answering EXT questions involves identifying a statement that may be added to the last paragraph of the passage.

EXT prompts usually include the following boldfaced expressions:

1. Based on the information in the passage, which one of the following sentences could **most logically be added to the end of the passage**?
2. Given the the information in the passage, which one of the following **most logically completes the last paragraph**?
3. Which one of the following sentences could **most logically be appended to** the passage as **a concluding sentence**?

Comparative Reading Family

Answering Comparative Reading Family questions generally involves determining the relationship between the dual passages that comprise a Comparative Reading passage. However, there may occasionally be questions about only one of the two passages.

> 19.5% of Reading Comprehension Questions

Relationship (R) – Answering R questions involves determining the structural relationship between the two passages. R questions always ask about both passages.

R prompts usually include the following boldfaced expressions:

1. Which one of the following most accurately describes **the relationship between passage A and passage B**?
2. Which one of the following most accurately describes a way in which **the two passages are related** to one another?
3. **The relationship between the two passages** can best be described as

Agree/Disagree (A/D) – Answering A/D questions involves identifying a statement that the authors of both passages would agree with or that one author would agree with and the other would disagree with. A/D questions always ask about both passages.

A/D prompts usually include the following boldfaced expressions:

1. It is most likely that **the authors of the passages** would **disagree** with each other about the truth of which one of the following statements?
2. Which one of the following is a statement central to **the argument made by** the author of **passage A** that would **most likely be rejected by** the author of **passage B**?
3. **The authors of the two passages** would **most likely agree** with which one of the following statements?

Comparative (C) – C questions are variants of question types from other families that have been modified for use in Comparative Reading passages. C questions may ask about both passages or about only one passage.

C prompts can include the following boldfaced expressions:

1. A discussion of which one of the following is **central to both passages**?
2. The authors of **both passages attempt to answer** which one of the following **questions**?
3. Which one of the following most accurately describes **the stance** expressed by the author of **passage A toward** X?
4. **The meaning of the phrase "X"** (line #) as it is used **in passage B** is most closely **related to** which one of the following concepts **in passage A**?
5. Which one of the following **conforms to** X advocated **by** the authors of **both passages**?
6. The authors of **both passages attempt to answer** which one of the following **questions**?
7. Which one of the following is **addressed by** the author of **passage A but not by** the author of **passage B**?

Special Case—EXCEPT Questions

The word EXCEPT is sometimes added to a question prompt. For example:

The author of the passage would likely agree with each of the following statements EXCEPT

This is a V EXCEPT question. The correct answer choice will be a statement the author would not agree with, and the four incorrect answer choices would be statements the author would agree with.

Although EXCEPT questions are rare, they can be based on any question type.

Drill: Identify the Question Type

Determine the question type for each of the prompts below.

Main Point	Detail	Attitude	Evaluation
Structure	Existence	Principle	Extension
Purpose	Meaning	Application	Relationship
Function of a Paragraph	Implication	Strengthen	Agree/Disagree
Function of a Statement	Viewpoint	Weaken	Comparative

1. Which one of the following statements most accurately describes the function of the first paragraph?

   Question Type: _____

2. According to the passage, which one of the following is true?

   Question Type: _____

3. The author's attitude toward the Victorian Era can be categorized as

   Question Type: _____

4. Which one of the following, if true, most strengthens the author's position on game theory?

   Question Type: _____

5. Which one of the following relationships is most analogous to that between a conservationist and philanthropist?

   Question Type: _____

6. Which one of the following most accurately states the main idea of the passage?

   Question Type: _____

7. Which one of the following most accurately describes a way in which the two passages are related to each other?

   Question Type: _____

8. Given the context of the passage, which one of the following sentences most logically completes the last paragraph?

   Question Type: _____

9. The author mentions the proliferation of Atlantic cod primarily in order to

   Question Type: _____

10. The passage offers information to answer which one of the following questions?

    Question Type: _____

11. Which one of the following can most reasonably be inferred from the information in the passage?

    Question Type: _____

12. It can be inferred that the authors of both passages would agree with each other on which one of the following?

    Question Type: _____

13. The author's primary purpose in writing the passage is to

    Question Type: _____

14. Which one of the following statements would the author of the passage be most likely to agree with?

    Question Type: _____

15. Which one of the following describes a benefit mentioned in the passage that people get from socializing with others?

    Question Type: _____

16. Which one of the following phrases could replace the word "vague" in line 45 without substantively altering the author's meaning?

    Question Type: _____

17. Which one of the following, if true, most weakens the author's criticism?

    Question Type: _____

18. Based on the passage, a screenwriter is most likely to claim that a successful script will satisfy which one of the following principles?

    Question Type: _____

19. Which one of the following most accurately describes the organization of the first paragraph?

    Question Type: _____

Drill: Identify the Question Type — Answers

1. Function of a Paragraph (FP)

2. Existence (EX)

3. Attitude (ATT)

4. Strengthen (S)

5. Application (APP)

6. Main Point (MP)

7. Relationship (R)

8. Extension (EXT)

9. Function of a Statement (FS)

10. Evaluation (E)

11. Implication (IMP)

12. Agree/Disagree (A/D)

13. Purpose (P)

14. Viewpoint (V)

15. Detail (D)

16. Meaning (M)

17. Weaken (W)

18. Principle (PR)

19. Structure (STR)

If you were not able to accurately identify every question type, don't worry. Plenty of examples are given in the subsequent chapters of this book on individual question types. Note that the LSAT test-makers sometimes use variants and tricks to make questions harder. These are also discussed later in the book.

Answer Choices

Each RC question includes four incorrect answer choices and one correct answer choice. There will never be a case in which two answer choices are correct, but one answer choice is a better choice than the other.

Correct Answer Choices

Correct answer choices are correct because they are consistent with the information presented in the passage and match the task assigned by the prompt. The recommended approach for answering RC questions is as follows:

Anticipate

After analyzing the passage and reading the prompt (in that order), anticipate the correct answer choice if possible. For some question types, such as Main Point, the correct answer choice is easy to anticipate. For others, such as Attitude, anticipating the correct answer choice is more difficult. Note that for certain question types, it is impossible to anticipate the correct answer choice because the prompt includes insufficient context. For these questions, proceed directly to eliminating answer choices.

Separate

You should then read through the answer choices to identify those that match the answer choice you anticipated. Separate the answer choices into candidates—those that correspond to your anticipated answer choice—and losers. If you end up with only one candidate, this is most likely the correct answer choice. If you have several candidates, you need to proceed to the next step.

Eliminate

If you have more than one candidate, you need to eliminate potentially correct answer choices until only one remains. This process, which varies for each question type, is explored in greater detail in later chapters. If you end up eliminating all the answer choices, you must reread the prompt and work through the remaining steps of the process again.

Incorrect Answer Choices

Incorrect answer choices are incorrect because they misrepresent or omit information in the passage, or do not match the task assigned by the question prompt. Each RC question type utilizes specific tricks to make incorrect answer choices attractive to test-takers. Some incorrect answer choice tricks are used for only one question type. These are discussed in detail in the relevant chapters of this book. However, certain tricks are commonly used for variety of question types:

Wrong Task: Accurate statements that do not address the task specified in the prompt

Wrong Viewpoint: Accurate statements about a viewpoint other than the one specified in the prompt

Wrong Part of Passage: Accurate statements about a part of the passage not specified in the prompt

Too Strong: Claims that are too strong to be supported by the passage

Contradictory Information: Statements that contradict information in the passage

Irrelevant Information: Statements that present new information that is not relevant to the task specified in the prompt

Incomplete Information: Accurate statements that omit details necessary to address the task specified in the prompt

Guessing

Unlike some other standardized tests, there is no penalty for guessing on the LSAT. Therefore, test-takers should make sure to select an answer choice for every question. A common LSAT myth is that certain answer choices are more commonly correct than others—for example, that (D) or (B) has the highest probability of being correct for the final few questions of the RC section. This is not true. There is no optimal guessing strategy except to make sure that you leave no questions blank.

If you are not completely certain about an answer choice or are torn between two or more answer choices, do not spend so much time on the question that you have to rush through the subsequent ones. Make your best guess, mark the question for review, and move on. If you have extra time after answering the remaining questions, you can return to those you had to guess on and try to determine the correct answer choices with more certainty. The advantage of this strategy is that if you do not have enough time to return to these questions, you have already selected answer choices and, therefore, have a chance of getting points for them.

Key Takeaways

Synthesis Family	Information Family	Inference Family	Process Family	Comparative Reading Family
The main structural elements of the passage must be identified.	Specific information in the passage or the contextual meaning of a word or phrase must be identified.	Inferences supported by the information in the passage must be identified.	A process must be applied to information in the passage.	The relationship between two passages must be identified. Some questions ask about only one passage.

Analyze the Passage
Mark the keywords, main point, and viewpoints. Note the function of each paragraph. Summarize the main point, paragraph content, and viewpoints.

Read the Prompt
Read the prompt and identify the question type. Understanding exactly what the prompt is asking you to do is essential.

Anticipate
Anticipate potential correct answer choices if possible. For some question types, such as Main Point, this will be easy to do. For others, such as Attitude, this will be difficult. For certain questions this will be impossible.

Separate
Read through the answer choices, looking for ones that match your anticipated answer choices. Separate candidates and losers.

Eliminate
Eliminate candidates until you are left with only one. If all candidates are eliminated, reread the prompt and work through the remaining steps of the process again.

Passage Types

Informational: A passage that conveys information about a specific topic without presenting an argument (author's viewpoint is never present)

Argumentative: A passage that presents an argument to support a conclusion made by the author (author's viewpoint is always present)

Debate: A passage that features multiple viewpoints that often directly conflict (author's viewpoint may or may not be present)

Comparative Reading: A set of two short passages that are connected in terms of subject matter

Incorrect Answer Choice Tricks

Wrong Task: Accurate statements that do not address the task specified in the prompt

Wrong Viewpoint: Accurate statements about a viewpoint other than the one specified in the prompt

Wrong Part of Passage: Accurate statements about a part of the passage not specified in the prompt

Too Strong: Claims that are too strong to be supported by the passage

Contradictory Information: Statements that contradict information in the passage

Irrelevant Information: Statements that present new information that is not relevant to the task specified in the prompt

Incomplete Information: Accurate statements that omit details necessary to address the task specified in the prompt

HACKERS
LSAT *Reading Comprehension*

Chapter 2

Deconstructing
the Passage

Chapter 2: Deconstructing the Passage

HACKERS
LSAT *Reading Comprehension*

Introduction

Informational Passages

As discussed in Chapter 1, it is not necessary to identify the type of passage to answer questions. However, doing so may make it easier to analyze the passage.

There are two basic passage formats in the RC section—the long single passages that are classified as Informational, Argumentative, or Debate passages and the set of two short passages that is classified as a Comparative Reading passage. One Comparative Reading passage appears in each RC section.

> There is no relationship between subject matter and passage type. Each of the four types of passages can be about any topic appropriate to the RC section.

Informational Passages

The purpose of an Informational passage is simply to convey information about a particular topic. For example, it may describe a natural phenomenon, explain a scientific process, or outline a historical event. A distinguishing feature of this passage type is that the author's viewpoint is always absent. The information is presented in a neutral manner, and the author does not make any claims and does not argue for or against any ideas or viewpoints in the passage.

Passage Features

Main Point

The main point of an Informational passage is a neutral statement that summarizes the key information in the passage. The main point may or may not be explicitly stated. If it is, you can usually find it in the first or last paragraph of the passage. If the main point is not explicitly stated, you may have to synthesize it from information throughout the passage.

Keep in mind that the main point of an Informational passage is always a descriptive statement—it is never a statement that can function as the conclusion of an argument. Consider the following examples:

> **Lyric poetry is the most expressive form of poetry in Western literature.**
> **Lyric poetry is a form of poetry found in Western literature.**

The first statement makes the claim that lyric poetry is the most expressive form of poetry. As this is an assertion, it could not be the main point of an Informational passage. It could, however, serve this purpose in an Argumentative passage. The second statement is neutral and descriptive. As it does not state a position that could be argued for or against, it could function as the main point of an Informational passage.

Paragraph Functions

Most commonly, the first paragraph of the passage provides background information to introduce the subject matter and set the scope of the discussion. If the main point is explicitly stated, it is usually located in this paragraph or the last one. The other paragraphs present additional details related to the topic.

Viewpoints

As an Informational passage does not include an argument, the author's viewpoint is never present. Other viewpoints may be mentioned in passing and even explored in detail. However, the author never directly or indirectly expresses an opinion about them. The absence of the author's viewpoint and the author's refusal to evaluate other viewpoints is a defining feature of an Informational passage.

Question Types

Main Point (MP), Function of a Paragraph (FP), Function of a Statement (FS), Detail (D), Existence (EX), and Meaning (M) questions are very common for this passage type. However, given that Informational passages do not include the author's viewpoint, you will never see Attitude (ATT) questions. Viewpoint (V), Structure (STR), and Purpose (P) questions are rare.

Analyze the passage below. Identify and mark the <u>keywords</u>, <u>main point</u>, and <u>viewpoints</u> other than the author's. Note the function of each paragraph. Summarize the main point, paragraph content, and viewpoints.

Passage 1

During most of the nineteenth century, many French women continued to be educated according to models long established by custom and religious tradition. One recent observer has termed the failure
(5) to institute real and lasting educational reform at the end of the eighteenth century a "missed opportunity"—for in spite of the egalitarian and secular aims of the French Revolution in 1789, a truly nondiscriminatory education system for both
(10) women and men would not be established in the country until the 1880s. However, legislators had put forth many proposals for educational reform in the years just after the revolution; two in particular attempted to institute educational systems for women
(15) that were, to a great extent, egalitarian.

The first of these proposals endeavored to replace the predominantly religious education that women originally received in convents and at home with reformed curricula. More importantly, the proposal
(20) insisted that, because education was a common good that should be offered to both sexes, instruction should be available to everyone. By the same token, teachers would be drawn from both sexes. Thus the proposal held it essential that schools for both men
(25) and women be established promptly throughout the country and that these schools be public, a tangible sign of the state's interest in all of its citizens. One limitation of this proposal, however, was that girls, unlike boys, were to leave school at age eight in
(30) order to be educated at home in the skills necessary for domestic life and for the raising of families. The second proposal took a more comprehensive approach. It advocated equal education for women and men on the grounds that women and men enjoy
(35) the same rights, and it was the only proposal of the time that called for coeducational schools, which were presented as a bulwark against the traditional gender roles enforced by religious tradition. In other respects, however, this proposal also continued to
(40) define women in terms of their roles in the domestic sphere and as mothers.

That neither proposal was able to envision a system of education that was fully equal for women, and that neither was adopted into law even as such,
(45) bespeaks the immensity of the cultural and political obstacles to egalitarian education for women at the time. Nevertheless, the vision of egalitarian educational reform was not entirely lost. Nearly a century later, in the early 1880s, French legislators
(50) recalled the earlier proposals in their justification of new laws that founded public secondary schools for women, abolished fees for education, and established compulsory attendance for all students. In order to pass these reforms, the government needed to
(55) demonstrate that its new standards were rooted in a

long philosophical, political, and pedagogical tradition. Various of the resulting institutions also made claim to revolutionary origin, as doing so allowed them to appropriate the legitimacy conferred
(60) by tradition and historical continuity.

Main Point

Paragraph 1

Paragraph 2

Paragraph 3

Identify Viewpoints

Passage 2

A lichen consists of a fungus living in symbiosis (i.e., a mutually beneficial relationship) with an alga. Although most branches of the complex evolutionary family tree of fungi have been well established, the
(5) evolutionary origins of lichen-forming fungi have been a mystery. But a new DNA study has revealed the relationship of lichen-forming fungi to several previously known branches of the fungus family tree. The study reveals that, far from being oddities,
(10) lichen-forming fungi are close relatives of such common fungi as brewer's yeast, morel mushrooms, and the fungus that causes Dutch elm disease. This accounts for the visible similarity of certain lichens to more recognizable fungi such as mushrooms.

(15)   In general, fungi present complications for the researcher. Fungi are usually parasitic or symbiotic, and researchers are often unsure whether they are examining fungal DNA or that of the associated organism. But lichen-forming fungi are especially
(20) difficult to study. They have few distinguishing characteristics of shape or structure, and they are unusually difficult to isolate from their partner algae, with which they have a particularly delicate symbiosis. In some cases the alga is wedged between
(25) layers of fungal tissue; in others, the fungus grows through the alga's cell walls in order to take nourishment, and the tissues of the two organisms are entirely enmeshed and inseparable. As a result, lichen-forming fungi have long been difficult to
(30) classify definitively within the fungus family. By default they were thus considered a separate grouping of fungi with an unknown evolutionary origin. But, using new analytical tools that allow them to isolate the DNA of fungi in parasitic or symbiotic
(35) relationships, researchers were able to establish the DNA sequence in a certain gene found in 75 species of fungi, including 10 species of lichen-forming fungi. Based on these analyses, the researchers found 5 branches on the fungus family tree to which
(40) varieties of lichen-forming fungi belong. Furthermore, the researchers stress that it is likely that as more types of lichen-forming fungi are analyzed, they will be found to belong to still more branches of the fungus family tree.

(45)   One implication of the new research is that it provides evidence to help overturn the long-standing evolutionary assumption that parasitic interactions inevitably evolve over time to a greater benignity and eventually to symbiosis so that the parasites will not
(50) destroy their hosts. The addition of lichen-forming fungi to positions along branches of the fungus family tree indicates that this assumption does not hold for fungi. Fungi both harmful and benign can now be found both early and late in fungus
(55) evolutionary history. Given the new layout of the fungus family tree resulting from the lichen study, it appears that fungi can evolve toward mutualism and then just as easily turn back again toward parasitism.

Main Point

Paragraph 1

Paragraph 2

Paragraph 3

Identify Viewpoints

Passage 1

During most of the nineteenth century, many French women continued to be educated according to models long established by custom and religious tradition. One recent observer has termed the failure
(5) to institute real and lasting educational reform at the end of the eighteenth century a "missed opportunity"—for in spite of the egalitarian and secular aims of the French Revolution in 1789, a truly nondiscriminatory education system for both
(10) women and men would not be established in the country until the 1880s. However, legislators had put forth many proposals for educational reform in the years just after the revolution; two in particular attempted to institute educational systems for women
(15) that were, to a great extent, egalitarian.

The first of these proposals endeavored to replace the predominantly religious education that women originally received in convents and at home with reformed curricula. More importantly, the proposal
(20) insisted that, because education was a common good that should be offered to both sexes, instruction should be available to everyone. By the same token, teachers would be drawn from both sexes. Thus the proposal held it essential that schools for both men
(25) and women be established promptly throughout the country and that these schools be public, a tangible sign of the state's interest in all of its citizens. One limitation of this proposal, however, was that girls, unlike boys, were to leave school at age eight in
(30) order to be educated at home in the skills necessary for domestic life and for the raising of families. The second proposal took a more comprehensive approach. It advocated equal education for women and men on the grounds that women and men enjoy
(35) the same rights, and it was the only proposal of the time that called for coeducational schools, which were presented as a bulwark against the traditional gender roles enforced by religious tradition. In other respects, however, this proposal also continued to
(40) define women in terms of their roles in the domestic sphere and as mothers.

That neither proposal was able to envision a system of education that was fully equal for women, and that neither was adopted into law even as such,
(45) bespeaks the immensity of the cultural and political obstacles to egalitarian education for women at the time. Nevertheless, the vision of egalitarian educational reform was not entirely lost. Nearly a century later, in the early 1880s, French legislators
(50) recalled the earlier proposals in their justification of new laws that founded public secondary schools for women, abolished fees for education, and established compulsory attendance for all students. In order to pass these reforms, the government needed to
(55) demonstrate that its new standards were rooted in a long philosophical, political, and pedagogical tradition. Various of the resulting institutions also made claim to revolutionary origin, as doing so allowed them to appropriate the legitimacy conferred

(60) by tradition and historical continuity.

Main Point

The main point must be synthesized from the first and last paragraphs. It is that two proposals for educational reform in France were put forward in the late 18th century to make the educational system more egalitarian for women, but these proposals were not adopted into law. However, egalitarian educational reform was implemented in France a century later using these earlier proposals as justification.

Paragraph 1

The first paragraph briefly puts forward the viewpoint that failed educational reform was a missed opportunity in late 18th century France. It then states part of the main point of the paragraph; namely, that two egalitarian legislative proposals were introduced.

Paragraph 2

This paragraph discusses the two proposals introduced in the previous paragraph in detail. The first was to include women in the type of education usually reserved for men. The second was for the establishment of coeducational schools to place men and women on more equal footing. The limiting factor of both proposals was that there was a focus on the domestic sphere for women.

Paragraph 3

The last paragraph states the second part of the main point. It specifies that although both proposals ultimately failed, they served as justification a century later for several reforms that made education more egalitarian for women.

Identify Viewpoints

The first paragraph mentions in passing the viewpoint of one recent observer who believes that the initial failure to reform the French educational system was a missed opportunity. The author's viewpoint is not present.

Passage 2

A lichen consists of a fungus living in symbiosis (i.e., a mutually beneficial relationship) with an alga. Although most branches of the complex evolutionary family tree of fungi have been well established, the
(5) evolutionary origins of lichen-forming fungi have been a mystery. But a new DNA study has revealed the relationship of lichen-forming fungi to several previously known branches of the fungus family tree. The study reveals that, far from being oddities,
(10) lichen-forming fungi are close relatives of such common fungi as brewer's yeast, morel mushrooms, and the fungus that causes Dutch elm disease. This accounts for the visible similarity of certain lichens to more recognizable fungi such as mushrooms.

(15) In general, fungi present complications for the researcher. Fungi are usually parasitic or symbiotic, and researchers often unsure whether they are examining fungal DNA or that of the associated organism. But lichen-forming fungi are especially
(20) difficult to study. They have few distinguishing characteristics of shape or structure, and they are unusually difficult to isolate from their partner algae, with which they have a particularly delicate symbiosis. In some cases the alga is wedged between
(25) layers of fungal tissue; in others, the fungus grows through the alga's cell walls in order to take nourishment, and the tissues of the two organisms are entirely enmeshed and inseparable. As a result, lichen-forming fungi have long been difficult to
(30) classify definitively within the fungus family. By default they were thus considered a separate grouping of fungi with an unknown evolutionary origin. But, using new analytical tools that allow them to isolate the DNA of fungi in parasitic or symbiotic
(35) relationships, researchers were able to establish the DNA sequence in a certain gene found in 75 species of fungi, including 10 species of lichen-forming fungi. Based on these analyses, the researchers found 5 branches on the fungus family tree to which
(40) varieties of lichen-forming fungi belong. Furthermore, the researchers stress that it is likely that as more types of lichen-forming fungi are analyzed, they will be found to belong to still more branches of the fungus family tree.

(45) One implication of the new research is that it provides evidence to help overturn the long-standing evolutionary assumption that parasitic interactions inevitably evolve over time to a greater benignity and eventually to symbiosis so that the parasites will not
(50) destroy their hosts. The addition of lichen-forming fungi to positions along branches of the fungus family tree indicates that this assumption does not hold for fungi. Fungi both harmful and benign can now be found both early and late in fungus
(55) evolutionary history. Given the new layout of the fungus family tree resulting from the lichen study, it appears that fungi can evolve toward mutualism and then just as easily turn back again toward parasitism.

Main Point

The main point is stated in the third sentence of the first paragraph. It is that a new DNA study has established the relationship between lichen-forming fungi and several previously known branches of the fungus family tree.

Paragraph 1

This paragraph provides definitions of *symbiosis* and *lichen*, and explains that the origins of lichen-forming fungi have been a mystery. It then states the main point of the passage and specifies that it is now known that lichen-forming fungi are closely related to and share similarities with common fungi.

Paragraph 2

This paragraph provides background information about why fungi are so difficult to study (parasitic or symbiotic) and specifies that lichen-forming fungi are particularly problematic because they are enmeshed with the host algae. It then explains how new tools have allowed researchers to isolate the DNA of fungi in symbiotic or parasitic relationships, revealing the branches of the fungus family tree that some varieties of lichen-forming fungi belong to.

Paragraph 3

This paragraph presents an implication of the new research; namely, that it overturns the assumption that harmful parasitic interactions evolve into benign symbiotic relationships. This is because both harmful and benign fungi can be found in the early and late stages of fungus evolutionary history. It then suggests that fungi can go from symbiotic relationships (mutualism) to parasitic ones.

Identify Viewpoints

The author's viewpoint is not present. There are no other viewpoints in the passage.

Argumentative Passages

The purpose of an Argumentative passage is to present a conclusion reached by the author and to provide evidence to support it. Rather than discussing a topic objectively, the author makes a claim and presents supporting details and examples to advance it. As a result, the author's viewpoint is always present. There may be other viewpoints as well, but the focus of the passage is on the author's. It is important to keep track of the relationship between the author's viewpoint and any others in the passage.

Passage Features

Main Point

The main point of an Argumentative passage is a conclusion made by the author. It is explicitly stated and often appears in the first paragraph of the passage. To identify the main point, you must look for a statement that can function as the conclusion of an argument. Unlike the main point of an Informational passage, the main point of an Argumentative passage is never a neutral statement. Consider the following examples:

> **String theory is one of many theories considered to have practical applications to a quantum theory of gravity.**
> **String theory is currently the best candidate for a quantum theory of gravity.**

The first statement could function as the main point of an Informational passage. It is a neutral, descriptive statement that does not make an assertion. In contrast, the second statement presents a specific position that must be supported by evidence. Therefore, it could serve as the main point of an Argumentative passage.

Paragraph Functions

Most commonly, the first paragraph of the passage includes an introduction to the topic in the form of background information or an opposing viewpoint. The last sentence or two of the first paragraph states the author's conclusion, which is the main point of the passage. Subsequent paragraphs provide evidence to support the main point in the form of supporting details or examples.

Viewpoints

An Argumentative passage always includes the author's viewpoint. This is because the author's conclusion is the main point, and the bulk of the content in the passage is devoted to supporting this main point. Other viewpoints may be discussed, but the author's viewpoint is the most important. Pay close attention to the relationship between the author's viewpoint and the others. If the author expresses an opinion about another viewpoint or attempts to rebut it, take note.

Question Types

Argumentative passages may be accompanied by any question type. Given that the author's viewpoint is always present, Viewpoint (V), Attitude (ATT), and Principle (PR) questions frequently accompany this type of passage. Likewise, the fact that an argument is always present makes it likely that Weaken (W) and Strengthen (S) questions will be encountered. You will also see many Inference Family questions.

Drill: Analyze Argumentative Passages

Analyze the passage below. Identify and mark the <u>keywords</u>, <u>main point</u>, and viewpoints other than the author's. Note the function of each paragraph. Summarize the main point, paragraph content, and viewpoints.

Passage 1

The Cultural Revolution of 1966 to 1976, initiated by Communist Party Chairman Mao Zedong in an attempt to reduce the influence of China's intellectual elite on the country's institutions, has had
(5) lasting repercussions on Chinese art. It intensified the absolutist mind-set of Maoist Revolutionary Realism, which had dictated the content and style of Chinese art even before 1966 by requiring that artists "truthfully" depict the realities of socialist life in
(10) China. Interest in nonsocial, nonpolitical subjects was strictly forbidden, and, during the Cultural Revolution, what constituted truth was entirely for revolutionary forces to decide—the only reality artists could portray was one that had been thoroughly
(15) colored and distorted by political ideology.

Ironically, the same set of requirements that constricted artistic expression during the Cultural Revolution has had the opposite effect since; many artistic movements have flourished in reaction to the
(20) monotony of Revolutionary Realism. One of these, the Scar Art movement of the 1980s, was spearheaded by a group of intellectual painters who had been trained in Maoist art schools and then exiled to rural areas during the Cultural Revolution.
(25) In exile, these painters were for perhaps the first time confronted with the harsh realities of rural poverty and misery—aspects of life in China that their Maoist mentors would probably have preferred they ignore. As a result of these experiences, they developed a
(30) radically new approach to realism. Instead of depicting the version of reality sanctioned by the government, the Scar Art painters chose to represent the "scarred reality" they had seen during their exile. Their version of realist painting emphasized the day-
(35) to-day hardships of rural life. While the principles of Revolutionary Realism had insisted that artists choose public, monumental, and universal subjects, the Scar artists chose instead to focus on the private, the mundane, and the particular; where the principles of
(40) Revolutionary Realism had demanded that they depict contemporary Chinese society as outstanding or perfect, the Scar artists chose instead to portray the bleak realities of modernization.

As the 1980s progressed, the Scar artists' radical
(45) approach to realism became increasingly co-opted for political purposes, and as this political cast became stronger and more obvious, many artists abandoned the movement. Yet a preoccupation with rural life persisted, giving rise to a related development known
(50) as the Native Soil movement, which focused on the native landscape and embodied a growing nostalgia for the charms of peasant society in the face of modernization. Where the Scar artists had reacted to the ideological rigidity of the Cultural Revolution by
(55) emphasizing the damage inflicted by modernization,

the Native Soil painters reacted instead by idealizing traditional peasant life. Unfortunately, in the end Native Soil painting was trivialized by a tendency to romanticize certain qualities of rural Chinese society
(60) in order to appeal to Western galleries and collectors.

Main Point

Paragraph 1

Paragraph 2

Paragraph 3

Identify Viewpoints

Passage 2

Sometimes there is no more effective means of controlling an agricultural pest than giving free rein to its natural predators. A case in point is the cyclamen mite, a pest whose population can be
(5) effectively controlled by a predatory mite of the genus *Typhlodromus*. Cyclamen mites infest strawberry plants; they typically establish themselves in a strawberry field shortly after planting, but their populations do not reach significantly damaging
(10) levels until the plants' second year. *Typhlodromus* mites usually invade the strawberry fields during the second year, rapidly subdue the cyclamen mite populations, and keep them from reaching significantly damaging levels.

(15) *Typhlodromus* owes its effectiveness as a predator to several factors in addition to its voracious appetite. Its population can increase as rapidly as that of its prey. Both species reproduce by parthenogenesis—a mode of reproduction in which unfertilized eggs
(20) develop into fertile females. Cyclamen mites lay three eggs per day over the four or five days of their reproductive life span; *Typhlodromus* lay two or three eggs per day for eight to ten days. Seasonal synchrony of *Typhlodromus* reproduction with the
(25) growth of prey populations and ability to survive at low prey densities also contribute to the predatory efficiency of *Typhlodromus*. During winter, when cyclamen mite populations dwindle to a few individuals hidden in the crevices and folds of leaves
(30) in the crowns of the strawberry plants, the predatory mites subsist on the honeydew produced by aphids and white flies. They do not reproduce except when they are feeding on the cyclamen mites. These features, which make *Typhlodromus* well-suited for
(35) exploiting the seasonal rises and falls of its prey, are common among predators that control prey populations.

Greenhouse experiments have verified the importance of *Typhlodromus* predation for keeping
(40) cyclamen mites in check. One group of strawberry plants was stocked with both predator and prey mites; a second group was kept predator-free by regular application of parathion, an insecticide that kills the predatory species but does not affect the cyclamen
(45) mite. Throughout the study, populations of cyclamen mites remained low in plots shared with *Typhlodromus*, but their infestation attained significantly damaging proportions on predator-free plants.

(50) Applying parathion in this instance is a clear case in which using a pesticide would do far more harm than good to an agricultural enterprise. The results were similar in field plantings of strawberries, where cyclamen mites also reached damaging levels when
(55) predators were eliminated by parathion, but they did not attain such levels in untreated plots. When cyclamen mite populations began to increase in an untreated planting, the predator populations quickly responded to reduce the outbreak. On average,
(60) cyclamen mites were about 25 times more abundant in the absence of predators than in their presence.

Main Point

Paragraph 1

Paragraph 2

Paragraph 3

Paragraph 4

Identify Viewpoints

Passage 1

The Cultural Revolution of 1966 to 1976, initiated by Communist Party Chairman Mao Zedong in an attempt to reduce the influence of China's intellectual elite on the country's institutions, has had
(5) lasting repercussions on Chinese art. It intensified the absolutist mind-set of Maoist Revolutionary Realism, which had dictated the content and style of Chinese art even before 1966 by requiring that artists "truthfully" depict the realities of socialist life in
(10) China. Interest in nonsocial, nonpolitical subjects was strictly forbidden, and, during the Cultural Revolution, what constituted truth was entirely for revolutionary forces to decide—the only reality artists could portray was one that had been thoroughly
(15) colored and distorted by political ideology.

Ironically, the same set of requirements that constricted artistic expression during the Cultural Revolution has had the opposite effect since; many artistic movements have flourished in reaction to the
(20) monotony of Revolutionary Realism. One of these, the Scar Art movement of the 1980s, was spearheaded by a group of intellectual painters who had been trained in Maoist art schools and then exiled to rural areas during the Cultural Revolution.
(25) In exile, these painters were for perhaps the first time confronted with the harsh realities of rural poverty and misery—aspects of life in China that their Maoist mentors would probably have preferred they ignore. As a result of these experiences, they developed a
(30) radically new approach to realism. Instead of depicting the version of reality sanctioned by the government, the Scar Art painters chose to represent the "scarred reality" they had seen during their exile. Their version of realist painting emphasized the day-
(35) to-day hardships of rural life. While the principles of Revolutionary Realism had insisted that artists choose public, monumental, and universal subjects, the Scar artists chose instead to focus on the private, the mundane, and the particular; where the principles of
(40) Revolutionary Realism had demanded that they depict contemporary Chinese society as outstanding or perfect, the Scar artists chose instead to portray the bleak realities of modernization.

As the 1980s progressed, the Scar artists' radical
(45) approach to realism became increasingly co-opted for political purposes, and as this political cast became stronger and more obvious, many artists abandoned the movement. Yet a preoccupation with rural life persisted, giving rise to a related development known
(50) as the Native Soil movement, which focused on the native landscape and embodied a growing nostalgia for the charms of peasant society in the face of modernization. Where the Scar artists had reacted to the ideological rigidity of the Cultural Revolution by
(55) emphasizing the damage inflicted by modernization, the Native Soil painters reacted instead by idealizing traditional peasant life. Unfortunately, in the end Native Soil painting was trivialized by a tendency to romanticize certain qualities of rural Chinese society
(60) in order to appeal to Western galleries and collectors.

Main Point

> The main point is stated in the first sentence of the first paragraph. It is that the Chinese Cultural Revolution under Mao Zedong had a profound influence on Chinese art.

Paragraph 1

> This paragraph states the main point of the passage. It provides background information regarding Maoist Revolutionary Realism and the relationship between Chinese Communist political ideology and Chinese art.

Paragraph 2

> This paragraph presents a specific example to support the main point. It discusses how artists developed the principles behind the Scar Art movement in response to the restrictiveness of the Cultural Revolution.

Paragraph 3

> This paragraph presents a second example of the influence of the Cultural Revolution on art. It discusses the abandonment of the Scar Art movement and how the preoccupation with rural life developed into the Native Soil movement, which would later become trivialized by commercialism.

Identify Viewpoints

> The author's viewpoint is present and is the focus of the passage. There are no other viewpoints in this passage.

Passage 2

Sometimes there is no more effective means of controlling an agricultural pest than giving free rein to its natural predators. A case in point is the cyclamen mite, a pest whose population can be
(5) effectively controlled by a predatory mite of the genus *Typhlodromus*. Cyclamen mites infest strawberry plants; they typically establish themselves in a strawberry field shortly after planting, but their populations do not reach significantly damaging
(10) levels until the plants' second year. *Typhlodromus* mites usually invade the strawberry fields during the second year, rapidly subdue the cyclamen mite populations, and keep them from reaching significantly damaging levels.
(15) *Typhlodromus* owes its effectiveness as a predator to several factors in addition to its voracious appetite. Its population can increase as rapidly as that of its prey. Both species reproduce by parthenogenesis—a mode of reproduction in which unfertilized eggs
(20) develop into fertile females. Cyclamen mites lay three eggs per day over the four or five days of their reproductive life span; *Typhlodromus* lay two or three eggs per day for eight to ten days. Seasonal synchrony of *Typhlodromus* reproduction with the
(25) growth of prey populations and ability to survive at low prey densities also contribute to the predatory efficiency of *Typhlodromus*. During winter, when cyclamen mite populations dwindle to a few individuals hidden in the crevices and folds of leaves
(30) in the crowns of the strawberry plants, the predatory mites subsist on the honeydew produced by aphids and white flies. They do not reproduce except when they are feeding on the cyclamen mites. These features, which make *Typhlodromus* well-suited for
(35) exploiting the seasonal rises and falls of its prey, are common among predators that control prey populations.

Greenhouse experiments have verified the importance of *Typhlodromus* predation for keeping
(40) cyclamen mites in check. One group of strawberry plants was stocked with both predator and prey mites; a second group was kept predator-free by regular application of parathion, an insecticide that kills the predatory species but does not affect the cyclamen
(45) mite. Throughout the study, populations of cyclamen mites remained low in plots shared with *Typhlodromus*, but their infestation attained significantly damaging proportions on predator-free plants.
(50) Applying parathion in this instance is a clear case in which using a pesticide would do far more harm than good to an agricultural enterprise. The results were similar in field plantings of strawberries, where cyclamen mites also reached damaging levels when
(55) predators were eliminated by parathion, but they did not attain such levels in untreated plots. When cyclamen mite populations began to increase in an untreated planting, the predator populations quickly responded to reduce the outbreak. On average,
(60) cyclamen mites were about 25 times more abundant in the absence of predators than in their presence.

Main Point

The main point is in the first sentence of the first paragraph. It is that not interfering with an agricultural pest's natural predators is the most effective form of pest control in some cases.

Paragraph 1

The paragraph states the main point and introduces the example of the relationship between the cyclamen mite (a strawberry plant pest) and the *Typhlodromus* mite (a cyclamen mite predator) to support it.

Paragraph 2

This paragraph expands on the example by presenting factors that make *Typhlodromus* an effective predator: it reproduces as rapidly as its prey and has a voracious appetite. In addition, *Typhlodromus* and cyclamen mites reproduce by parthenogenesis, lay multiple eggs over a period of a few days, and have seasonally synchronized reproduction. *Typhlodromus* can utilize other food sources to survive periods with low prey density.

Paragraph 3

This paragraph discusses experiments showing the effectiveness of *Typhlodromus* as a predator. Plants with both types of mites and plants with only cyclamen mites (*Typhlodromus* were eliminated using a pesticide called parathion) were compared. The cyclamen mites achieved damaging levels on plants without *Typhlodromus*.

Paragraph 4

This paragraph continues the discussion of the experiments. It shows that similar results were achieved in field plantings. Cyclamen mites reached damaging levels in plots treated with parathion but not in untreated plots.

Identify Viewpoints

The author's viewpoint is present and is the focus of the passage. There are no other viewpoints in this passage.

Debate Passages

The purpose of a Debate passage is to explore multiple viewpoints in detail. These viewpoints address the same subject matter but are often in direct conflict with each other. The author's viewpoint may or may not be present.

Passage Features

Main Point

If the author's viewpoint is present, the main point of the passage will be the author's conclusion. The author's conclusion is usually explicitly stated in one or two sentences.

If the author's viewpoint is absent, the main point will be a general statement that summarizes the viewpoints discussed in the passage. It may be explicitly stated, or it may have to be inferred by synthesizing information from throughout the passage.

Paragraph Functions

Most commonly, the first paragraph provides background information to introduce the topic and makes it clear that there are conflicting viewpoints. The remaining paragraphs each introduce a different viewpoint. It is difficult to predict where the main point will appear in a Debate passage. However, if the author's viewpoint is present, the main point will most commonly appear in the final paragraph.

Viewpoints

A Debate passage always includes at least two opposing viewpoints, and it may include as many as four or five. Each viewpoint advances a position with regards to the topic, and some may directly counter the points made by others. If the author's viewpoint is present, the author may support one of the other viewpoints, rebut one of the other viewpoints, attempt to reconcile all of the viewpoints, or even propose an entirely new position. Keeping track of the various viewpoints that appear in a Debate passage and how they relate to each other is important.

Question Types

Debate passages may be accompanied by any question type. There is usually content that could serve as the basis of Viewpoint (V) questions and, if the author's viewpoint is present, Attitude (ATT) questions.

Drill: Analyze Debate Passages

Analyze the passage below. Identify and mark the <u>keywords</u>, <u>main point</u>, and viewpoints other than the author's. Note the function of each paragraph. Summarize the main point, paragraph content, and viewpoints.

Passage 1

The Canadian Auto Workers' (CAW) Legal Services Plan, designed to give active and retired autoworkers and their families access to totally prepaid or partially reimbursed legal services, has
(5) been in operation since late 1985. Plan members have the option of using either the plan's staff lawyers, whose services are fully covered by the cost of membership in the plan, or an outside lawyer. Outside lawyers, in turn, can either sign up with the plan as a
(10) "cooperating lawyer" and accept the CAW's fee schedule as payment in full, or they can charge a higher fee and collect the balance from the client. Autoworkers appear to have embraced the notion of prepaid legal services: 45 percent of eligible union
(15) members were enrolled in the plan by 1988. Moreover, the idea of prepaid legal services has been spreading in Canada. A department store is even offering a plan to holders of its credit card.

While many plan members seem to be happy to
(20) get reduced-cost legal help, many lawyers are concerned about the plan's effect on their profession, especially its impact on prices for legal services. Some point out that even though most lawyers have not joined the plan as cooperating lawyers, legal fees
(25) in the cities in which the CAW plan operates have been depressed, in some cases to an unprofitable level. The directors of the plan, however, claim that both clients and lawyers benefit from their arrangement. For while the clients get ready access to
(30) reduced-price services, lawyers get professional contact with people who would not otherwise be using legal services, which helps generate even more business for their firms. Experience shows, the directors say, that if people are referred to a firm and
(35) receive excellent service, the firm will get three to four other referrals who are not plan subscribers and who would therefore pay the firm's standard rate.

But it is unlikely that increased use of such plans will result in long-term client satisfaction or in a
(40) substantial increase in profits for law firms. Since lawyers with established reputations and client bases can benefit little, if at all, from participation, the plans function largely as marketing devices for lawyers who have yet to establish themselves. While
(45) many of these lawyers are no doubt very able and conscientious, they will tend to have less expertise and to provide less satisfaction to clients. At the same time, the downward pressure on fees will mean that the full-fee referrals that proponents say will come
(50) through plan participation may not make up for a firm's investment in providing services at low plan rates. And since lowered fees provide little incentive for lawyers to devote more than minimal effort to cases, a "volume discount" approach toward the
(55) practice of law will mean less time devoted to complex cases and a general lowering of quality for clients.

Main Point

Paragraph 1

Paragraph 2

Paragraph 3

Identify Viewpoints

Passage 2

The poet Louise Glück has said that she feels comfortable writing within a tradition often characterized as belonging only to male poets. About her own experience reading poetry, Glück notes that
(5) her gender did not keep her from appreciating the poems of Shakespeare, Blake, Keats, and other male poets. Rather she believed this was the tradition of her language and that it was for this reason her poetic inheritance. She thus views the canon of poets in
(10) English as a literary family to which she clearly belongs. Whereas many contemporary women poets have rejected this tradition as historically exclusionary and rhetorically inadequate for women, Glück embraces it with respect and admiration.
(15) Glück's formative encounters with poetry also provided her with the theoretical underpinnings of her respect for this tradition; she notes that in her youth she could sense many of the great themes and subjects of poetry even before experiencing them in
(20) her own life. These subjects—loss, the passage of time, desire—are timeless, available to readers of any age, gender, or social background. Glück makes no distinction between these subjects as belonging to female or male poets alone, calling them "the great
(25) human subjects." If the aim of a poem is to explore the issue of human mortality, for example, then issues of gender distinction fade behind the presence of this universal reality.
Some of Glück's critics claim that this idea of the
(30) universal is suspect and that the idea that gender issues are transcended by addressing certain subjects may attribute to poetry an innocence that it does not have. They maintain that a female poet writing within a historically male-dominated tradition will on some
(35) level be unable to avoid accepting certain presuppositions, which, in the critics' view, are determined by a long-standing history of denigration and exclusion of female artists. Furthermore, they feel that this long-standing history cannot be confronted
(40) using tools—in Glück's case, poetic forms—forged by the traditions of this history. Instead critics insist that women poets should strive to create a uniquely female poetry by using new forms to develop a new voice.
(45) Glück, however, observes that this ambition, with its insistence on an essentially female perspective, is as limiting as her critics believe the historically male-dominated tradition to be. She holds that to the extent that there are some gender differences that have been
(50) shaped by history, they will emerge in the differing ways that women and men write about the world— indeed, these differences will be revealed with more authority in the absence of conscious intention. She points out that the universal subjects of literature do
(55) not make literature itself timeless and unchanging. Literature, she maintains, is inescapably historical, and every work, both in what it includes and in what it omits, inevitably speaks of its social and historical context.

Main Point

Paragraph 1

Paragraph 2

Paragraph 3

Paragraph 4

Identify Viewpoints

Passage 1

The Canadian Auto Workers' (CAW) Legal Services Plan, designed to give active and retired autoworkers and their families access to totally prepaid or partially reimbursed legal services, has
(5) been in operation since late 1985. Plan members have the option of using either the plan's staff lawyers, whose services are fully covered by the cost of membership in the plan, or an outside lawyer. Outside lawyers, in turn, can either sign up with the plan as a
(10) "cooperating lawyer" and accept the CAW's fee schedule as payment in full, or they can charge a higher fee and collect the balance from the client. Autoworkers appear to have embraced the notion of prepaid legal services: 45 percent of eligible union
(15) members were enrolled in the plan by 1988. Moreover, the idea of prepaid legal services has been spreading in Canada. A department store is even offering a plan to holders of its credit card.

While many plan members seem to be happy to
(20) get reduced-cost legal help, A)many lawyers are concerned about the plan's effect on their profession, especially its impact on prices for legal services. Some point out that even though most lawyers have not joined the plan as cooperating lawyers, legal fees
(25) in the cities in which the CAW plan operates have been depressed, in some cases to an unprofitable level. B)The directors of the plan, however, claim that both clients and lawyers benefit from their arrangement. For while the clients get ready access to
(30) reduced-price services, lawyers get professional contact with people who would not otherwise be using legal services, which helps generate even more business for their firms. Experience shows, the directors say, that if people are referred to a firm and
(35) receive excellent service, the firm will get three to four other referrals who are not plan subscribers and who would therefore pay the firm's standard rate.

But it is unlikely that increased use of such plans will result in long-term client satisfaction or in a
(40) substantial increase in profits for law firms. Since lawyers with established reputations and client bases can benefit little, if at all, from participation, the plans function largely as marketing devices for lawyers who have yet to establish themselves. While
(45) many of these lawyers are no doubt very able and conscientious, they will tend to have less expertise and to provide less satisfaction to clients. At the same time, the downward pressure on fees will mean that the full-fee referrals that proponents say will come
(50) through plan participation may not make up for a firm's investment in providing services at low plan rates. And since lowered fees provide little incentive for lawyers to devote more than minimal effort to cases, a "volume discount" approach toward the
(55) practice of law will mean less time devoted to complex cases and a general lowering of quality for clients.

Main Point

The main point is stated in the first sentence of the last paragraph. It is that the CAW Legal Services Plan and other prepaid legal services plans are unlikely to result in long-term client satisfaction or an increase in profits for law firms. This is the author's conclusion.

Paragraph 1

The first paragraph provides background information to introduce the topic. It offers a detailed overview of the Canadian Auto Workers' (CAW) Legal Services Plan and states that prepaid legal services plans, in general, are becoming more popular.

Paragraph 2

This paragraph presents two competing viewpoints. Many lawyers think that the CAW's plan depresses legal fees to an unprofitable level for lawyers. The directors of the plan, however, claim that lawyers who provide these low-cost services get more referrals that would pay their law firm's standard rate.

Paragraph 3

This paragraph states the main point of the passage. It then provides evidence to support this claim.

Identify Viewpoints

The two main viewpoints explored in this passage are that of lawyers opposed to prepaid legal services plans and the directors of the CAW plan. The author's viewpoint is also present. The author rebuts the viewpoint of the directors.

Passage 2

A)The poet Louise Glück has said that she feels comfortable writing within a tradition often characterized as belonging only to male poets. About her own experience reading poetry, Glück notes that
(5) her gender did not keep her from appreciating the poems of Shakespeare, Blake, Keats, and other male poets. Rather she believed this was the tradition of her language and that it was for this reason her poetic inheritance. She thus views the canon of poets in
(10) English as a literary family to which she clearly belongs. Whereas many contemporary women poets have rejected this tradition as historically exclusionary and rhetorically inadequate for women, Glück embraces it with respect and admiration.
(15) A)Glück's formative encounters with poetry also provided her with the theoretical underpinnings of her respect for this tradition; she notes that in her youth she could sense many of the great themes and subjects of poetry even before experiencing them in
(20) her own life. These subjects—loss, the passage of time, desire—are timeless, available to readers of any age, gender, or social background. Glück makes no distinction between these subjects as belonging to female or male poets alone, calling them "the great
(25) human subjects." If the aim of a poem is to explore the issue of human mortality, for example, then issues of gender distinction fade behind the presence of this universal reality.
B)Some of Glück's critics claim that this idea of the
(30) universal is suspect and that the idea that gender issues are transcended by addressing certain subjects may attribute to poetry an innocence that it does not have. They maintain that a female poet writing within a historically male-dominated tradition will on some
(35) level be unable to avoid accepting certain presuppositions, which, in the critics' view, are determined by a long-standing history of denigration and exclusion of female artists. Furthermore, they feel that this long-standing history cannot be confronted
(40) using tools—in Glück's case, poetic forms—forged by the traditions of this history. Instead critics insist that women poets should strive to create a uniquely female poetry by using new forms to develop a new voice.
(45) A)Glück, however, observes that this ambition, with its insistence on an essentially female perspective, is as limiting as her critics believe the historically male-dominated tradition to be. She holds that to the extent that there are some gender differences that have been
(50) shaped by history, they will emerge in the differing ways that women and men write about the world—indeed, these differences will be revealed with more authority in the absence of conscious intention. She points out that the universal subjects of literature do
(55) not make literature itself timeless and unchanging. Literature, she maintains, is inescapably historical, and every work, both in what it includes and in what it omits, inevitably speaks of its social and historical context.

Main Point

The main point is stated in the last sentence of the first paragraph. It is that many contemporary women poets have rejected the English poetry tradition as being exclusionary and inadequate for women, but Glück embraces it with respect and admiration. This is a neutral statement that summarizes the two viewpoints present.

Paragraph 1

This paragraph introduces Glück's viewpoint, which is that she belongs to the English poetry tradition, even though it is characterized as belonging to male poets. It also states the main point of the passage.

Paragraph 2

This paragraph explores Glück's viewpoint in detail. It states that Glück believes that poems express themes that are available to readers of any age, gender, and background. These themes do not belong exclusively to male or female poets. Therefore, the issue of gender distinctions fades behind the universalism of poetry.

Paragraph 3

This paragraph summarizes the viewpoint of Glück's critics. They feel that women are limited by writing in a male-dominated tradition and that female poets should strive to create poetry that is uniquely female.

Paragraph 4

This paragraph puts forward Glück's rebuttal of her critics' claims. She observes that the insistence on a female perspective is limiting. She also believes that gender differences emerge more strongly without conscious intention. She also points out that literature always reflects its social and historical context.

Identify Viewpoints

The two main viewpoints in this passage are those of Glück and her critics. The author's viewpoint is absent.

Comparative Reading Passages

A Comparative Reading passage includes a set of two short passages that discuss related subject matter. As a result, this type of passage is very easy to identify. Every RC section includes one Comparative Reading passage.

Passage Features

Structure

Each of the passages that make up a Comparative Reading passage typically has a structure similar to that of a standard Argumentative passage, although you may occasionally encounter one that resembles an Informational passage or that is hard to categorize. Regardless, these passages always address similar—and, in some cases, identical—subject matter. They are shorter and less complex than standard passages, making it easier to identify.

Passage Analysis

The process for analyzing a Comparative Reading passage is different from the one used to analyze standard Informational, Argumentative, and Debate passages. Many of the questions that accompany a Comparative Reading passage ask about the relationship between the dual passages. Therefore, this should be the focus of your analysis.

During the initial read-through of a Comparative Reading passage, each of the dual passages should be marked as usual. Underline the keywords, and the main points, and highlight all viewpoints other than the author's. However, instead of taking note of paragraph functions and summarizing content, you should look for the similarities and dissimilarities between the two passages. Focus on the major points of agreement and disagreement, and pay close attention to the relationship between the authors' conclusions. Summarizing the content of each paragraph is not as important for Comparative Reading passages compared to standard passages because the dual passages are much shorter and simpler. This means that it is usually easier to locate information in the passages without referring to notes.

Question Types

Comparative Reading passages will always be accompanied by questions from the Comparative Reading Family. Relationship (R) and Agree/Disagree (A/D) questions that focus on the relationship between the two passages and the points on which the authors agree and disagree are certain to appear. There will also be Comparative (C) questions, which include question types from the other families that have been adapted for Comparative Reading passages. Many of these will ask about both passages. However, some will ask about only one of the two passages.

Identify and mark the <u>keywords</u>, <u>main point</u>, and viewpoints other than the author's. Then, summarize the main points and take note of any similarities and dissimilarities between the two passages.

The following passages concern a plant called purple loosestrife. Passage 1A is excerpted from a report issued by a prairie research council; passage 1B from a journal of sociology.

Passage 1A

Purple loosestrife (Lythrum salicaria), an aggressive and invasive perennial of Eurasian origin, arrived with settlers in eastern North America in the early 1800s and has spread across the continent's
(5) midlatitude wetlands. The impact of purple loosestrife on native vegetation has been disastrous, with more than 50 percent of the biomass of some wetland communities displaced. Monospecific blocks of this weed have maintained themselves for at least 20 years.
(10) Impacts on wildlife have not been well studied, but serious reductions in waterfowl and aquatic furbearer productivity have been observed. In addition, several endangered species of vertebrates are threatened with further degradation of their
(15) breeding habitats. Although purple loosestrife can invade relatively undisturbed habitats, the spread and dominance of this weed have been greatly accelerated in disturbed habitats. While digging out the plants can temporarily halt their spread, there has been little
(20) research on long-term purple loosestrife control. Glyphosate has been used successfully, but no measure of the impact of this herbicide on native plant communities has been made.

With the spread of purple loosestrife growing
(25) exponentially, some form of integrated control is needed. At present, coping with purple loosestrife hinges on early detection of the weed's arrival in areas, which allows local eradication to be carried out with minimum damage to the native plant community.

Passage 1B

(30) The war on purple loosestrife is apparently conducted on behalf of nature, an attempt to liberate the biotic community from the tyrannical influence of a life-destroying invasive weed. Indeed, purple loosestrife control is portrayed by its practitioners as
(35) an environmental initiative intended to save nature rather than control it. Accordingly, the purple loosestrife literature, scientific and otherwise, dutifully discusses the impacts of the weed on endangered species—and on threatened biodiversity
(40) more generally. Purple loosestrife is a pollution, according to the scientific community, and all of nature suffers under its pervasive influence.

Regardless of the perceived and actual ecological effects of the purple invader, it is apparent that
(45) popular pollution ideologies have been extended into the wetlands of North America. Consequently, the scientific effort to liberate nature from purple loosestrife has failed to decouple itself from its philosophical origin as an instrument to control nature

(50) to the satisfaction of human desires. Birds, particularly game birds and waterfowl, provide the bulk of the justification for loosestrife management. However, no bird species other than the canvasback has been identified in the literature as endangered by
(55) purple loosestrife. The impact of purple loosestrife on furbearing mammals is discussed at great length, though none of the species highlighted (muskrat, mink) can be considered threatened in North America. What is threatened by purple loosestrife is the
(60) economics of exploiting such preferred species and the millions of dollars that will be lost to the economies of the United States and Canada from reduced hunting, trapping, and recreation revenues due to a decline in the production of the wetland
(65) resource.

Main Point of Passage 1A

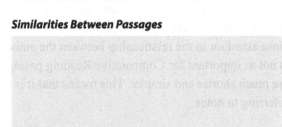

Main Point of Passage 1B

Similarities Between Passages

Dissimilarities Between Passages

Passage 2A

Recent studies have shown that sophisticated computer models of the oceans and atmosphere are capable of simulating large-scale climate trends with remarkable accuracy. But these models make use of
(5) large numbers of variables, many of which have wide ranges of possible values. Because even small differences in those values can have a significant impact on what the simulations predict, it is important to determine the impact when values differ even
(10) slightly.

Since the interactions between the many variables in climate simulations are highly complex, there is no alternative to a "brute force" exploration of all possible combinations of their values if predictions
(15) are to be reliable. This method requires very large numbers of calculations and simulation runs. For example, exhaustive examination of five values for each of only nine variables would require 2 million calculation-intensive simulation runs. Currently
(20) available individual computers are completely inadequate for such a task.

However, the continuing increase in computing capacity of the average desktop computer means that climate simulations can now be run on privately
(25) owned desktop machines connected to one another via the Internet. The calculations are divided among the individual desktop computers, which work simultaneously on their share of the overall problem. Some public resource computing projects of this kind
(30) have already been successful, although only when they captured the public's interest sufficiently to secure widespread participation.

Passage 2B

Researchers are now learning that many problems in nature, human society, science, and engineering are
(35) naturally "parallel"; that is, that they can be effectively solved by using methods that work simultaneously in parallel. These problems share the common characteristic of involving a large number of similar elements such as molecules, animals, even
(40) people, whose individual actions are governed by simple rules but, taken collectively, function as a highly complex system.

An example is the method used by ants to forage for food. As Lewis Thomas observed, a solitary ant is
(45) little more than a few neurons strung together by fibers. Its behavior follows a few simple rules. But when one sees a dense mass of thousands of ants, crowded together around their anthill retrieving food or repelling an intruder, a more complex picture
(50) emerges; it is as if the whole is thinking, planning, calculating. It is an intelligence, a kind of live computer, with crawling bits for wits.

We are now living through a great paradigm shift in the field of computing, a shift from sequential
(55) computing (performing one calculation at a time) to massive parallel computing, which employs thousands of computers working simultaneously to solve one computation-intensive problem. Since many computation-intensive problems are inherently
(60) parallel, it only makes sense to use a computing

model that exploits that parallelism. A computing model that resembles the inherently parallel problem it is trying to solve will perform best. The old paradigm, in contrast, is subject to the speed limits
(65) imposed by purely sequential computing.

Main Point of Passage 2A

Main Point of Passage 2B

Similarities Between Passages

Dissimilarities Between Passages

The following passages concern a plant called purple loosestrife. Passage 1A is excerpted from a report issued by a prairie research council; passage 1B from a journal of sociology.

Passage 1A

Purple loosestrife (Lythrum salicaria), an aggressive and invasive perennial of Eurasian origin, arrived with settlers in eastern North America in the early 1800s and has spread across the continent's
(5) midlatitude wetlands. The impact of purple loosestrife on native vegetation has been disastrous, with more than 50 percent of the biomass of some wetland communities displaced. Monospecific blocks of this weed have maintained themselves for at least 20 years.
(10) Impacts on wildlife have not been well studied, but serious reductions in waterfowl and aquatic furbearer productivity have been observed. In addition, several endangered species of vertebrates are threatened with further degradation of their
(15) breeding habitats. Although purple loosestrife can invade relatively undisturbed habitats, the spread and dominance of this weed have been greatly accelerated in disturbed habitats. While digging out the plants can temporarily halt their spread, there has been little
(20) research on long-term purple loosestrife control. Glyphosate has been used successfully, but no measure of the impact of this herbicide on native plant communities has been made.

With the spread of purple loosestrife growing
(25) exponentially, some form of integrated control is needed. At present, coping with purple loosestrife hinges on early detection of the weed's arrival in areas, which allows local eradication to be carried out with minimum damage to the native plant community.

Passage 1B

(30) The war on purple loosestrife is apparently conducted on behalf of nature, an attempt to liberate the biotic community from the tyrannical influence of a life-destroying invasive weed. Indeed, purple loosestrife control is portrayed by its [A] practitioners as
(35) an environmental initiative intended to save nature rather than control it. Accordingly, [A] the purple loosestrife literature, scientific and otherwise, dutifully discusses the impacts of the weed on endangered species—and on threatened biodiversity
(40) more generally. Purple loosestrife is a pollution, according to the [A] scientific community, and all of nature suffers under its pervasive influence. Regardless of the perceived and actual ecological effects of the purple invader, it is apparent that
(45) popular pollution ideologies have been extended into the wetlands of North America. Consequently, the scientific effort to liberate nature from purple loosestrife has failed to decouple itself from its philosophical origin as an instrument to control nature
(50) to the satisfaction of human desires. Birds, particularly game birds and waterfowl, provide the bulk of the justification for loosestrife management.

However, no bird species other than the canvasback has been identified in the literature as endangered by
(55) purple loosestrife. The impact of purple loosestrife on furbearing mammals is discussed at great length, though none of the species highlighted (muskrat, mink) can be considered threatened in North America. What is threatened by purple loosestrife is the
(60) economics of exploiting such preferred species and the millions of dollars that will be lost to the economies of the United States and Canada from reduced hunting, trapping, and recreation revenues due to a decline in the production of the wetland
(65) resource.

Main Point of Passage 1A

The main point is stated in the first and last paragraphs. It is that purple loosestrife has a disastrous impact on native vegetation and some form of integrated control is needed.

Main Point of Passage 1B

The main point is stated in the last paragraph. It is that purple loosestrife has a negative economic impact rather than an environmental one.

Similarities Between Passages

Both discuss purple loosestrife and its effect on wetlands.
Both discuss efforts to control purple loosestrife.
Both discuss the impact of purple loosestrife on furbearing animals.

Dissimilarities Between Passages

Passage 1A claims the purple loosestrife is an environmental threat and must be controlled, while Passage 1B does not consider it an environmental threat and argues that efforts to control it have economic motives.
Passage 1A states that waterfowl, aquatic furbearers, and endangered vertebrates are threatened by the effect of purple loosestrife on habitats, while Passage 1B states that only one bird species is threatened by purple loosestrife and that none of the furbearing mammals impacted by purple loosestrife are threatened.

Passage 2A

Recent studies have shown that sophisticated computer models of the oceans and atmosphere are capable of simulating large-scale climate trends with remarkable accuracy. But these models make use of

(5) large numbers of variables, many of which have wide ranges of possible values. Because even small differences in those values can have a significant impact on what the simulations predict, it is important to determine the impact when values differ even

(10) slightly.

Since the interactions between the many variables in climate simulations are highly complex, there is no alternative to a "brute force" exploration of all possible combinations of their values if predictions

(15) are to be reliable. This method requires very large numbers of calculations and simulation runs. For example, exhaustive examination of five values for each of only nine variables would require 2 million calculation-intensive simulation runs. Currently

(20) available individual computers are completely inadequate for such a task.

However, the continuing increase in computing capacity of the average desktop computer means that climate simulations can now be run on privately

(25) owned desktop machines connected to one another via the Internet. The calculations are divided among the individual desktop computers, which work simultaneously on their share of the overall problem. Some public resource computing projects of this kind

(30) have already been successful, although only when they captured the public's interest sufficiently to secure widespread participation.

Passage 2B

Researchers are now learning that many problems in nature, human society, science, and engineering are

(35) naturally "parallel"; that is, that they can be effectively solved by using methods that work simultaneously in parallel. These problems share the common characteristic of involving a large number of similar elements such as molecules, animals, even

(40) people, whose individual actions are governed by simple rules but, taken collectively, function as a highly complex system.

An example is the method used by ants to forage for food. As Lewis Thomas observed, a solitary ant is

(45) little more than a few neurons strung together by fibers. Its behavior follows a few simple rules. But when one sees a dense mass of thousands of ants, crowded together around their anthill retrieving food or repelling an intruder, a more complex picture

(50) emerges; it is as if the whole is thinking, planning, calculating. It is an intelligence, a kind of live computer, with crawling bits for wits.

We are now living through a great paradigm shift in the field of computing, a shift from sequential

(55) computing (performing one calculation at a time) to massive parallel computing, which employs thousands of computers working simultaneously to solve one computation-intensive problem. Since many computation-intensive problems are inherently

(60) parallel, it only makes sense to use a computing model that exploits that parallelism. A computing model that resembles the inherently parallel problem it is trying to solve will perform best. The old paradigm, in contrast, is subject to the speed limits

(65) imposed by purely sequential computing.

Main Point of Passage 2A

The main point is stated in the second and third paragraphs. It is that climate simulations require brute force exploration of possible values, which may be done on privately owned computers that are connected via the Internet (parallel computing).

Main Point of Passage 2B

The main point is stated in the third paragraph. It is that there is a paradigm shift to parallel computing because it is the best way to solve computation-intensive problems that arise in many fields.

Similarities Between Passages

Both passages suggest that parallel computing is increasing in use and has the ability to solve computation-intensive problems.

Dissimilarities Between Passages

Passage 2A focuses on one computation-intensive problem (climate modeling) that can be solved using parallel computing, while Passage 2B discusses the characteristics of certain problems that make parallel computing the best way to solve them. Passage 2A discusses climate simulations as an example of a computation-intensive problem, while Passage 2B presents ant foraging as an example of a complex parallel system in nature.

Key Takeaways

Informational Passages	Argumentative Passages
Purpose • The purpose is to convey information about a topic. **Main Point** • The main point is a neutral summary of the information in the passage. • It may or may not be explicitly stated. **Common Paragraph Functions** • The first paragraph introduces the topic. • Subsequent paragraphs provide details about the topic. • The main point often appears in the first or last paragraph if explicitly stated. **Viewpoints** • The author's viewpoint is never present. • Other viewpoints may be present. **Question Types** • MP, FP, FS, D, EX, and M questions are common. • ATT questions do not appear. • V, STR, and P questions are rare.	**Purpose** • The purpose is to state and support the author's conclusion. **Main Point** • The main point is a conclusion made by the author. • It is explicitly stated. **Common Paragraph Functions** • The first paragraph introduces the topic. • Subsequent paragraphs provide evidence to support the main point. • The main point often appears at the end of the first paragraph. **Viewpoints** • The author's viewpoint is always present. • Other viewpoints may be present. **Question Types** • V, ATT, PR, S, and W questions are common.
Debate Passages	**Comparative Reading Passages**
Purpose • The purpose is to present multiple viewpoints on an issue. **Main Point** • If the author's viewpoint is present, the main point will be the author's conclusion and will be explicitly stated. The author may support one of the other viewpoints, rebut one of the other viewpoints, attempt to reconcile all of the viewpoints, or even propose an entirely new position. • If the author's viewpoint is absent, the main point will be a general statement that summarizes the viewpoints. • It may or may not be explicitly stated. **Common Paragraph Functions** • The first paragraph introduces the topic. • Subsequent paragraphs present different viewpoints. **Viewpoints** • The author's viewpoint may or may not be present. • Other viewpoints are always present. **Question Types** • V and ATT questions are common.	**Structure** • The passage usually includes two short passages that are usually Argumentative. **Passage Analysis** • Mark the passages as usual. • Summarize the main point of each passage. • Take note of the similarities and dissimilarities between the two passages. • Focus on the major points of agreement and disagreement. • Pay close attention to the authors' conclusions and how they are supported. **Question Types** • Comparative Reading Family questions always appear. • Most questions ask about the relationship between the dual passages. • Some C questions ask about only one of the two passage.

HACKERS
LSAT *Reading Comprehension*

Chapter 3

Synthesis
Family

Chapter 3: Synthesis Family

Overview

Example Passages and Questions

In this chapter, you will learn how to identify and solve Synthesis Family questions.

Synthesis Family questions ask you to identify the key structural elements of the passage and understand how they relate to each other. The process of analyzing a passage during the initial read-through that was discussed in Chapter 1 involves identifying many of these elements and relationships. Therefore, you will have located the information necessary to answer many Synthesis Family questions before you even read the prompts.

The five question types in this family—Main Point (MP), Structure (STR), Purpose (P), Function of a Paragraph (FP), and Function of a Statement (FS)—are examined in detail in separate sections. Each section includes step-by-step instructions on how to solve the question type and detailed analyses of example questions. In addition, you will get to tackle practice questions taken from previous administrations of the LSAT. The methods for solving these practice questions are explained thoroughly in the answer keys.

Example Passages and Questions

The example questions analyzed in the How-to-Solve subsections reference the following passages, and you should refer back to them as necessary. The analysis of each passage has already been done for you.

For Example Questions 1–4

The Canadian Auto Workers' (CAW) Legal Services Plan, designed to give active and retired autoworkers and their families access to totally prepaid or partially reimbursed legal services, has
(5) been in operation since late 1985. Plan members have the option of using either the plan's staff lawyers, whose services are fully covered by the cost of membership in the plan, or an outside lawyer. Outside lawyers, in turn, can either sign up with the plan as a
(10) "cooperating lawyer" and accept the CAW's fee schedule as payment in full, or they can charge a higher fee and collect the balance from the client. Autoworkers appear to have embraced the notion of prepaid legal services: 45 percent of eligible union
(15) members were enrolled in the plan by 1988. Moreover, the idea of prepaid legal services has been spreading in Canada. A department store is even offering a plan to holders of its credit card.

While many plan members seem to be happy to
(20) get reduced-cost legal help, A)many lawyers are concerned about the plan's effect on their profession, especially its impact on prices for legal services. Some point out that even though most lawyers have not joined the plan as cooperating lawyers, legal fees
(25) in the cities in which the CAW plan operates have been depressed, in some cases to an unprofitable level. B)The directors of the plan, however, claim that both clients and lawyers benefit from their arrangement. For while the clients get ready access to
(30) reduced-price services, lawyers get professional contact with people who would not otherwise be using legal services, which helps generate even more business for their firms. Experience shows, the directors say, that if people are referred to a firm and
(35) receive excellent service, the firm will get three to four other referrals who are not plan subscribers and who would therefore pay the firm's standard rate.

But it is unlikely that increased use of such plans will result in long-term client satisfaction or in a
(40) substantial increase in profits for law firms. Since lawyers with established reputations and client bases can benefit little, if at all, from participation, the plans function largely as marketing devices for lawyers who have yet to establish themselves. While
(45) many of these lawyers are no doubt very able and conscientious, they will tend to have less expertise and to provide less satisfaction to clients. At the same time, the downward pressure on fees will mean that the full-fee referrals that proponents say will come
(50) through plan participation may not make up for a firm's investment in providing services at low plan rates. And since lowered fees provide little incentive for lawyers to devote more than minimal effort to cases, a "volume discount" approach toward the
(55) practice of law will mean less time devoted to

complex cases and a general lowering of quality for clients.

Main Point

The main point is stated in the first sentence of the last paragraph. It is that the CAW Legal Services Plan and other prepaid legal services plans are unlikely to result in long-term client satisfaction or an increase in profits for law firms. This is the author's conclusion.

Paragraph 1

The first paragraph provides background information to introduce the topic. It offers a detailed overview of the Canadian Auto Workers' (CAW) Legal Services Plan and states that prepaid legal services plans, in general, are becoming more popular.

Paragraph 2

This paragraph presents two competing viewpoints. Many lawyers think that the CAW's plan depresses legal fees to an unprofitable level for lawyers. The directors of the plan, however, claim that lawyers who provide these low-cost services get more referrals that would pay their law firm's standard rate.

Paragraph 3

This paragraph states the main point of the passage. It then provides evidence to support this claim.

Identify Viewpoints

The two main viewpoints explored in this passage are that of lawyers opposed to prepaid legal services plans and the directors of the CAW plan. The author's viewpoint is also present. The author rebuts the viewpoint of the directors.

1. Which one of the following most accurately expresses the main point of the passage?

   (A) In the short term, prepaid legal plans such as the CAW Legal Services Plan appear to be beneficial to both lawyers and clients, but in the long run lawyers will profit at the expense of clients.
   (B) The CAW Legal Services Plan and other similar plans represent a controversial, but probably effective, way of bringing down the cost of legal services to clients and increasing lawyers' clientele.
   (C) The use of prepaid legal plans such as that of the CAW should be rejected in favor of a more equitable means of making legal services more generally affordable.
   (D) In spite of widespread consumer support for legal plans such as that offered by the CAW, lawyers generally criticize such plans, mainly because of their potential financial impact on the legal profession.
   (E) Although they have so far attracted many subscribers, it is doubtful whether the CAW Legal Services Plan and other similar prepaid plans will benefit lawyers and clients in the long run.

2. Which one of the following sequences most accurately and completely corresponds to the presentation of the material in the passage?

   (A) a description of a recently implemented set of procedures and policies; a summary of the results of that implementation; a proposal of refinements in those policies and procedures
   (B) an evaluation of a recent phenomenon; a comparison of that phenomenon with related past phenomena; an expression of the author's approval of that phenomenon
   (C) a presentation of a proposal; a discussion of the prospects for implementing that proposal; a recommendation by the author that the proposal be rejected
   (D) a description of an innovation; a report of reasoning against and reasoning favoring that innovation; argumentation by the author concerning that innovation
   (E) an explanation of a recent occurrence; an evaluation of the practical value of that occurrence; a presentation of further data regarding that occurrence

3. The primary purpose of the passage is to

   (A) compare and contrast legal plans with the traditional way of paying for legal services
   (B) explain the growing popularity of legal plans
   (C) trace the effect of legal plans on prices of legal services
   (D) caution that increased use of legal plans is potentially harmful to the legal profession and to clients
   (E) advocate reforms to legal plans as presently constituted

4. Which one of the following most accurately represents the primary function of the author's mention of marketing devices (line 43)?

   (A) It points to an aspect of legal plans that the author believes will be detrimental to the quality of legal services.
   (B) It is identified by the author as one of the primary ways in which plan administrators believe themselves to be contributing materially to the legal profession in return for lawyers' participation.
   (C) It identifies what the author considers to be one of the few unequivocal benefits that legal plans can provide.
   (D) It is reported as part of several arguments that the author attributes to established lawyers who oppose plan participation.
   (E) It describes one of the chief burdens of lawyers who have yet to establish themselves and offers an explanation of their advocacy of legal plans.

For Example Questions 5–6

The Cultural Revolution of 1966 to 1976, initiated by Communist Party Chairman Mao Zedong in an attempt to reduce the influence of China's intellectual elite on the country's institutions, has had
(5) lasting repercussions on Chinese art. It intensified the absolutist mind-set of Maoist Revolutionary Realism, which had dictated the content and style of Chinese art even before 1966 by requiring that artists "truthfully" depict the realities of socialist life in
(10) China. Interest in nonsocial, nonpolitical subjects was strictly forbidden, and, during the Cultural Revolution, what constituted truth was entirely for revolutionary forces to decide—the only reality artists could portray was one that had been thoroughly
(15) colored and distorted by political ideology.

Ironically, the same set of requirements that constricted artistic expression during the Cultural Revolution has had the opposite effect since; many artistic movements have flourished in reaction to the
(20) monotony of Revolutionary Realism. One of these, the Scar Art movement of the 1980s, was spearheaded by a group of intellectual painters who had been trained in Maoist art schools and then exiled to rural areas during the Cultural Revolution.
(25) In exile, these painters were for perhaps the first time confronted with the harsh realities of rural poverty and misery—aspects of life in China that their Maoist mentors would probably have preferred they ignore. As a result of these experiences, they developed a
(30) radically new approach to realism. Instead of depicting the version of reality sanctioned by the government, the Scar Art painters chose to represent the "scarred reality" they had seen during their exile. Their version of realist painting emphasized the day-
(35) to-day hardships of rural life. While the principles of Revolutionary Realism had insisted that artists choose public, monumental, and universal subjects, the Scar artists chose instead to focus on the private, the mundane, and the particular; where the principles of
(40) Revolutionary Realism had demanded that they depict contemporary Chinese society as outstanding or perfect, the Scar artists chose instead to portray the bleak realities of modernization.

As the 1980s progressed, the Scar artists' radical
(45) approach to realism became increasingly co-opted for political purposes, and as this political cast became stronger and more obvious, many artists abandoned the movement. Yet a preoccupation with rural life persisted, giving rise to a related development known
(50) as the Native Soil movement, which focused on the native landscape and embodied a growing nostalgia for the charms of peasant society in the face of modernization. Where the Scar artists had reacted to the ideological rigidity of the Cultural Revolution by
(55) emphasizing the damage inflicted by modernization, the Native Soil painters reacted instead by idealizing traditional peasant life. Unfortunately, in the end Native Soil painting was trivialized by a tendency to romanticize certain qualities of rural Chinese society
(60) in order to appeal to Western galleries and collectors.

Main Point

The main point is stated in the first sentence of the first paragraph. It is that the Chinese Cultural Revolution under Mao Zedong had a profound influence on Chinese art.

Paragraph 1

This paragraph states the main point of the passage. It provides background information regarding Maoist Revolutionary Realism and the relationship between Chinese Communist political ideology and Chinese art.

Paragraph 2

This paragraph presents a specific example to support the main point. It discusses how artists developed the principles behind the Scar Art movement in response to the restrictiveness of the Cultural Revolution.

Paragraph 3

This paragraph presents a second example of the influence of the Cultural Revolution on art. It discusses the abandonment of the Scar Art movement and how the preoccupation with rural life developed into the Native Soil movement, which would later become trivialized by commercialism.

Identify Viewpoints

The author's viewpoint is present and is the focus of the passage. There are no other viewpoints in this passage.

5. Which one of the following titles most accurately captures the main point of the passage?

(A) "Painting and Politics: A Survey of Political Influences on Contemporary Chinese Art"
(B) "How Two Movements in Chinese Painting Transformed the Cultural Revolution"
(C) "Scarred Reality: A Look into Chinese Rural Life in the Late Twentieth Century"
(D) "The Rise of Realism in Post-Maoist Art in China"
(E) "The Unforeseen Artistic Legacy of China's Cultural Revolution"

6. The primary function of the first paragraph is to

(A) introduce the set of political and artistic ideas that spurred the development of two artistic movements described in the subsequent paragraphs
(B) acknowledge the inescapable melding of political ideas and artistic styles in China
(C) explain the transformation of Chinese society that came about as a result of the Cultural Revolution
(D) present a hypothesis about realism in Chinese art that is refuted by the ensuing discussion of two artistic movements
(E) show that the political realism practiced by the movements discussed in the ensuing paragraphs originated during the Cultural Revolution

Main Point

SYNTHESIS FAMILY

Main Point
Structure
Purpose
Function of a Paragraph
Function of a Statement

Main Point

≈ 2.63 questions per test

Example Prompts

Which one of the following most accurately states *the main point* of the passage?

Which one of the following most accurately expresses *the main idea* of the passage?

Which one of the following best summarizes *the central idea* of the passage?

Take These Steps

Is the author's viewpoint present?

Yes →

Identify the author's conclusion. In an Argumentative passage, this will be a strong claim regarding the subject matter. In a Debate passage, this may be a statement that supports or rebuts another viewpoint, reconciles all viewpoints, or presents an independent claim regarding the subject matter. The main point will be explicitly stated.

No →

Identify a neutral, descriptive statement. In an Informational passage, this statement will summarize the key details. In a Debate passage, this statement will summarize all viewpoints. The main point may be explicitly stated or it may need to be synthesized from sentences throughout the passage.

Once you have identified the main point, anticipate a correct answer choice that fully and accurately restates it. The correct answer choice may include additional information that is accurate according to the passage but is not necessary to restate the main point.

Answer Choices

Correct Answer Choices	Incorrect Answer Choices
Accurate restatements of the author's conclusion (author's viewpoint present)	Descriptive statements (author's viewpoint present) or conclusions (author's viewpoint absent)
Accurate restatements of the summary of the important information in the passage (author's viewpoint absent)	Wrong task
	Wrong viewpoint
	Contradictory information
	Irrelevant information
	Incomplete information

Main Point (MP) questions ask you to find the answer choice that accurately restates the main point of the passage. If the author's viewpoint is present, the main point will be the author's conclusion. If the author's viewpoint is absent, the main point will be a summary of the most important information in the passage.

MP question prompts include terms such as *main point*, *main idea*, or *central idea*. Other terms with similar meanings may be used as well. MP questions can appear in any passage type. They are very common, with the majority of question sets beginning with a question of this type.

You will likely have identified the main point during your initial read-through of the passage. In this case, you should simply anticipate a correct answer choice that restates it. For instructional purposes, however, we will proceed based on the assumption that you have not already identified the main point when you encounter an MP question.

How to Solve MP Questions

The first step in solving an MP question is to determine whether the author's viewpoint is present. Identifying the passage type can make this easier. For Argumentative passages, the author's viewpoint is always present. For Informational passages, the author's viewpoint is always absent. However, if you are dealing with a Debate passage or have not been able to identify the passage type, you will need to look more closely at the text. As discussed in Chapter 1, the author's viewpoint can be signaled by keywords that are used to pass judgment. These include (among others) *fortunately*, *correctly*, *thankfully*, *regretfully*, and *paradoxically*. If you see keywords such as these, you can be fairly certain that the author's viewpoint is present. You should also check for statements that pass judgment and cannot be attributed to a person or group mentioned in the passage. If you find such language, the passage will likely include the author's viewpoint.

If the Author's Viewpoint is Present

When the author's viewpoint is present, the main point will be a conclusion reached by the author. If it is an Argumentative passage, the author will make a claim with regard to the subject matter, and the bulk of the passage will be devoted to supporting this claim. Most commonly, the main point appears at the end of the first paragraph of an Argumentative passage. If it is a Debate passage, the author may support or rebut one of the viewpoints, attempt to reconcile all viewpoints, or present an independent claim regarding the topic. The author's conclusion is most commonly located in the last paragraph of a Debate passage. However, it often appears elsewhere in the passage. Regardless of whether it is an Argumentative or Debate passage, the main point will be explicitly stated.

Once you have identified the main point, you should anticipate a correct answer choice that fully and accurately restates it. Note that the correct answer choice may include additional details from the passage that are not necessary to restate the main point. This is acceptable, provided that these details are accurate according to the passage.

Let's look at Example Question 1 (page 61):

Which one of the following most accurately expresses the main point of the passage?

(A) In the short term, prepaid legal plans such as the CAW Legal Services Plan appear to be beneficial to both lawyers and clients, but in the long run lawyers will profit at the expense of clients.

(B) The CAW Legal Services Plan and other similar plans represent a controversial, but probably effective, way of bringing down the cost of legal services to clients and increasing lawyers' clientele.

(C) The use of prepaid legal plans such as that of the CAW should be rejected in favor of a more equitable means of making legal services more generally affordable.

(D) In spite of widespread consumer support for legal plans such as that offered by the CAW, lawyers generally criticize such plans, mainly because of their potential financial impact on the legal profession.

(E) Although they have so far attracted many subscribers, it is doubtful whether the CAW Legal Services Plan and other similar prepaid plans will benefit lawyers and clients in the long run.

This is a Debate passage, and the author's viewpoint is present. The author's conclusion appears in the first sentence of the last paragraph. It rebuts the information that precedes it and asserts that prepaid legal plans are unlikely to result in long-term client satisfaction or an increase in profits for law firms. We should anticipate a correct answer choice that accurately expresses this conclusion.

(A) In the short term, prepaid legal plans such as the CAW Legal Services Plan appear to be beneficial to both lawyers and clients, but in the long run lawyers will profit at the expense of clients.

This answer choice includes contradictory information. The author does not argue that lawyers will benefit at the expense of clients but rather that neither lawyers nor clients will benefit. This is a loser.

(B) The CAW Legal Services Plan and other similar plans represent a controversial, but probably effective, way of bringing down the cost of legal services to clients and increasing lawyers' clientele.

This answer choice refers to the wrong viewpoint. It restates the viewpoint of the directors of the plan, which the author is directly rebutting. This is another loser.

(C) The use of prepaid legal plans such as that of the CAW should be rejected in favor of a more equitable means of making legal services more generally affordable.

This matches our anticipated answer choice. The author rejects prepaid legal plans because they do not benefit lawyers or clients. This is a candidate.

(D) In spite of widespread consumer support for legal plans such as that offered by the CAW, lawyers generally criticize such plans, mainly because of their potential financial impact on the legal profession.

This answer choice includes incomplete information. The answer choice accurately states that many consumers are happy with prepaid legal services plans and that lawyers oppose them for financial reasons. However, it does not include a key idea from the main point—that these plans are unlikely to benefit clients. This is a loser.

(E) Although they have so far attracted many subscribers, it is doubtful whether the CAW Legal Services Plan and other similar prepaid plans will benefit lawyers and clients in the long run.

This also matches our anticipated answer choice. The second clause accurately restates the author's conclusion that prepaid legal services plans will not benefit lawyers or clients. The first clause includes additional information that is supported by the information in the last three lines of the first paragraph of the passage. This is a candidate.

We have two candidates, (C) and (E), so we need to eliminate one. Looking back at (C), we can see that it is the weaker candidate. First, although the author strongly implies that prepaid legal services plans should be rejected, he does not explicitly state this. Second, this answer choice actually includes irrelevant information. The author does not argue that prepaid legal plans should be replaced by an equitable alternative that makes legal services more affordable. Therefore, (E) is the correct answer choice.

If the Author's Viewpoint is Absent

When the author's viewpoint is absent, the main point will be a neutral, descriptive statement. If it is an Informational passage, the main point will simply summarize the most important details in the passage. If it is a Debate passage, the main point will summarize all of the viewpoints in the passage. In either case, the main point may be explicitly stated or it may need to be synthesized from information presented throughout the passage.

Once you have identified the main point of the passage, you should anticipate a correct answer choice that fully and accurately restates it. As is the case when the author's viewpoint is present, the correct answer choice may include additional information that is accurate according to the passage.

Title Questions

Title questions are an MP question variant. The prompt of a Title question asks you to perform the same basic task as that of a regular MP question—select the answer choice that best expresses the main point of the passage. However, the answer choices are all possible titles of the passage.

The process for answering a regular MP question and Title question is the same. The only difference is that sometimes the correct answer choice for a Title question will be a question that can be answered by the main point rather than a direct restatement of the main point.

Let's look at Example Question 5 (page 63):

Which one of the following titles most accurately captures the main point of the passage?

(A) "Painting and Politics: A Survey of Political Influences on Contemporary Chinese Art"
(B) "How Two Movements in Chinese Painting Transformed the Cultural Revolution"
(C) "Scarred Reality: A Look into Chinese Rural Life in the Late Twentieth Century"
(D) "The Rise of Realism in Post-Maoist Art in China"
(E) "The Unforeseen Artistic Legacy of China's Cultural Revolution"

This is an Argumentative passage, so the author's viewpoint is present. The author's conclusion is stated in the first sentence of the first paragraph. It is that the Chinese Cultural Revolution under Mao Zedong had profound influences on Chinese art. As the answer choices are not in the form of a question, we should anticipate a correct answer choice that accurately expresses this conclusion.

(A) "Painting and Politics: A Survey of Political Influences on Contemporary Chinese Art"

This answer choice includes irrelevant information. The passage focuses on the influence of only one political movement. It is not a survey of multiple political influences on Chinese art. This is a loser.

(B) "How Two Movements in Chinese Painting Transformed the Cultural Revolution"

This answer choice includes contradictory information. The passage states that the Cultural Revolution influenced two artistic movements. It does not discuss two movements that influenced the Cultural Revolution. This is another loser.

(C) "Scarred Reality: A Look into Chinese Rural Life in the Late Twentieth Century"

This answer choice includes incomplete information. The passages discuss two artistic movements in detail—the Scar Art movement and the Native Soil movement. This answer choice only refers to the first art movement. This is also a loser.

(D) "The Rise of Realism in Post-Maoist Art in China"

This answer choice also includes incomplete information. The Scar Art movement discussed in the passage was a form of realism. However, the Native Soil movement was not. Therefore, this answer choice is a loser.

(E) "The Unforeseen Artistic Legacy of China's Cultural Revolution"

This matches our anticipated answer choice. It accurately summarizes the main point of the passage—that the Cultural Revolution had a profound influence on Chinese Art. The term *unforeseen* is supported by the information in the first sentence of the second paragraph (particularly, the use of the terms *ironically* and *opposite effect*). This is a candidate.

As (E) is the only candidate, it is the correct answer choice.

Looking at the Answer Choices

The correct answer choice is always a statement that fully and accurately restates the main point of the passage. If the author's viewpoint is present, the main point will be the author's conclusion. If the author's viewpoint is absent, the main point will be a summary of the key details in the passage (Informational passage) or a summary of all viewpoints (Debate passage). The correct answer choice may include additional details that are accurate according to the passage.

If the author's viewpoint is present, an incorrect answer choice may be a neutral, descriptive statement rather than a restatement of the authors' conclusion. If the author's viewpoint is absent, it may be a statement that makes a claim rather than a neutral, descriptive one. It is also common for an answer choice to be incorrect because it addresses the wrong task. For example, it may accurately restate a supporting detail rather than the main point. Incorrect answer choices may also present viewpoints other than the author's, restate part of the main point but omit key information, or present contradictory or irrelevant information.

Structure

SYNTHESIS FAMILY

Main Point
Structure
Purpose
Function of a Paragraph
Function of a Statement

Structure

≈ 0.88 questions per test

Example Prompts

| Which one of the following most accurately describes *the structure* of the passage? | Which one of the following most accurately corresponds to *the organization* of the passage? | Which one of the following sequences best describes *the presentation of the material* in the passage? |

Take These Steps

Determine whether the prompt asks you to focus on the passage as a whole or on a multi-paragraph section of the passage.

Refer back to your initial analysis to determine the functions of the relevant paragraphs.

Anticipate a correct answer choice that presents a sequence of paragraph function descriptions that matches the structure of the passage or section. If a paragraph has more than one function, each may be described separately in the correct answer choice.

Answer Choices

Correct Answer Choices	Incorrect Answer Choices
Sequences of paragraph function descriptions that match the organizational structure of all or part of the passage	Sequences that present the paragraph functions in the incorrect order
	Wrong part of passage
	Too strong
	Contradictory information
	Irrelevant information
	Incomplete information

Structure (STR) questions ask you to find the answer choice that describes the structure of all or part of the passage. To answer this type of question, you must have a clear understanding of the function of each paragraph in the passage and how the paragraphs relate to each other.

STR question prompts usually include terms such as *structure*, *organization*, or *presentation of the material*. Other terms with similar meanings may be used as well. STR questions can appear in any passage type. However, they are most common in Argumentative and Debate passages that include the author's viewpoint.

How to Solve STR Questions

The first step in solving an STR question is to determine whether the prompt asks about the structure of the entire passage or of a multi-paragraph section of the passage. Once you have done this, you must identify the function of the relevant paragraphs in the passage. To do this, refer to the analysis of the passage you performed during your initial read-through.

As discussed in Chapter 1, each paragraph of an RC passage has one or more functions. These include (among others):

- Stating the main point
- Providing background or contextual information
- Providing evidence to support the main point
- Presenting a single viewpoint or multiple viewpoints
- Providing additional information related to the topic

An STR question requires that you be more specific regarding the function of a paragraph. For example, in a typical Argumentative passage, there will likely be several paragraphs that provide support for the main point. To accomplish this, one paragraph might explain a scientific process, one might provide a description of a phenomenon, and one might evaluate recent research.

Each answer choice of an STR question is a sequence of specific paragraph function descriptions. You should anticipate a correct answer choice that describes the paragraph functions you identified in the correct order.

Note that some paragraphs may have more than one function. For example, the first paragraph of an Argumentative passage may provide background information and then state the author's conclusion. The correct answer choice will likely describe each of these functions separately.

Let's look at Example Question 2 (page 61):

Which one of the following sequences most accurately and completely corresponds to the presentation of the material in the passage?

(A) a description of a recently implemented set of procedures and policies; a summary of the results of that implementation; a proposal of refinements in those policies and procedures

(B) an evaluation of a recent phenomenon; a comparison of that phenomenon with related past phenomena; an expression of the author's approval of that phenomenon

(C) a presentation of a proposal; a discussion of the prospects for implementing that proposal; a recommendation by the author that the proposal be rejected

(D) a description of an innovation; a report of reasoning against and reasoning favoring that innovation; argumentation by the author concerning that innovation

(E) an explanation of a recent occurrence; an evaluation of the practical value of that occurrence; a presentation of further data regarding that occurrence

This prompt refers to the passage as a whole. This passage has three paragraphs. The first paragraph provides background information about the CAW Legal Services Plan and prepaid legal plans in general. The second paragraph presents a viewpoint in favor of these plans and a viewpoint opposed to these plans. The last paragraph states the author's conclusion, which directly rebuts the earlier viewpoint in favor of these plans. We should anticipate a correct answer choice that describes these functions in this order.

(A) a description of a recently implemented set of procedures and policies; a summary of the results of that implementation; a proposal of refinements in those policies and procedures

This answer choice includes irrelevant information. The passage does not specify that the CAW Legal Services Plan and other prepaid legal services plans were recently implemented. In addition, the results of the plans are not summarized—they are argued for and against. Finally, there is no proposal to refine these plans. This is a loser.

(B) an evaluation of a recent phenomenon; a comparison of that phenomenon with related past phenomena; an expression of the author's approval of that phenomenon

This answer choice includes a combination of irrelevant and contradictory information. First, the passage does not indicate that prepaid legal services plans are a recent phenomenon. It also does not begin with an evaluation of these plans, and it does not compare them with a previous one. Finally, the author does not approve of prepaid legal services plans. This is another loser.

(C) a presentation of a proposal; a discussion of the prospects for implementing that proposal; a recommendation by the author that the proposal be rejected

This answer choice includes irrelevant information and a statement that is too strong. First, the passage does not begin by presenting a proposal; instead, it describes the legal services plans. Second, there is no discussion of the prospects for implementing these plans, just a discussion about their effects. Finally, the last function described in the answer choice makes too strong of a claim. The author is not recommending that the proposal be rejected but, rather, suggesting that the plans will have an overall negative effect. While it may be implied that the author would reject these plans, it is not explicitly stated in the passage. Therefore, this is a loser.

(D) a description of an innovation; a report of reasoning against and reasoning favoring that innovation; argumentation by the author concerning that innovation

This matches our anticipated answer choice. The passage begins with a description of prepaid legal services plans. It then describes a debate between opponents and proponents of these plans. Finally, the author rebuts those who support the plans. This is a candidate.

(E) an explanation of a recent occurrence; an evaluation of the practical value of that occurrence; a presentation of further data regarding that occurrence

This answer choice includes contradictory information. The first two functions described in this answer choice seem to match the passage, which begins with an overview of the legal services plan and then presents two opposing evaluations of the plans. However, the last part of this answer choice is inaccurate. The final paragraph of the passage does not present new data—it presents the authors' conclusion regarding the plans. This is a loser.

As (D) is the only candidate, it is the correct answer choice.

Looking at the Answer Choices

The correct answer choice is always a sequence of paragraph function descriptions that corresponds exactly to the structure of the passage or of multi-paragraph section of the passage. If a paragraph has multiple functions, these will likely be described separately in the correct answer choice.

Incorrect answer choices may describe the functions of the passage accurately but present them in the wrong order. They may also include irrelevant or contradictory information, or make too strong of a claim.

Purpose

...purpose (P) questions ask you to find the answer choice that accurately states the author's overall purpose, or goal, in writing the passage. If the author's viewpoint is present, the purpose of the passage w... conclusion. If the author's viewpoint is absent, the purpose will be simply to present information...

SYNTHESIS FAMILY

Main Point
Structure
Purpose
Function of a Paragraph
Function of a Statement

Purpose
≈ 0.88 questions per test

Example Prompts

| The author's *primary purpose* in writing the passage is to | The passage is *primarily concerned with* | Which one of the following best states *the primary purpose* of the passage? |

Is the author's viewpoint present?

Yes ← | → No

Take These Steps

Identify the author's conclusion. The purpose of the passage will be to advance this conclusion. Anticipate a correct answer choice that combines an appropriate action verb with an accurate description of the conclusion. The action verb will be one related to making a claim, such as *argue*, *suggest*, or *propose*. The description will fully and accurately describe the author's conclusion in general terms.

Identify a neutral statement that summarizes the key information in the passage. The purpose of the passage will be to present this information. Anticipate a correct answer choice that combines an appropriate action verb with an accurate description of the summary. The action verb will be one related to presenting information, such as *describe*, *present*, or *summarize*. The description will fully and accurately describe the summary in general terms.

Answer Choices

Correct Answer Choices	Incorrect Answer Choices
Accurate expressions of the author's purpose in writing the passage	Statements with inappropriate action verbs
Statements that combine an appropriate action verb related to making a claim and a description of the author's conclusion (author's viewpoint present)	Statements with appropriate action verbs but incorrect main points
	Contradictory information
	Irrelevant information
Statements that combine an appropriate action verb related to presenting information and a description of the summary of the key information in the passage (author's viewpoint absent)	Incomplete information

Purpose (P) questions ask you to find the answer choice that accurately states the author's overall purpose, or goal, in writing the passage. If the author's viewpoint is present, the purpose of the passage will be to advance a conclusion. If the author's viewpoint is absent, the purpose will be simply to present information.

P question prompts usually include terms such as *purpose* or *concerned with*. Other terms with similar meanings may be used as well. P questions can appear in any passage type.

How to Solve P Questions

Like MP questions, P questions are based on the main point of the passage. However, the correct answer choice of a P question does not restate the main point; instead, it includes an action verb and a general description of the main point. Consider the following examples:

> **While some anthropologists view the Out-of-Africa hypothesis as being more firmly rooted in evidence, others claim that there is new evidence that a hybrid Out-of-Africa/Multiregional Evolution model more accurately explains early human development and migration.**

> **To discuss several theories proposed by anthropologists concerning early human evolution and migration**

The first example is a possible correct answer choice for an MP question. It fully restates the main point of the passage.

The second example is a possible correct answer choice for a P question. It includes an action verb (*discuss*) that is followed by a general description of the main point (*several theories proposed . . .*). The correct answer choice of a P question always has this basic structure. The action verb plays an important role in determining whether an answer choice is correct or incorrect. Some action verbs may only be used if the author's viewpoint is present, while others may only be

| Appropriate Action Verb |
| + |
| Description of Main Point |
| = |
| Correct Answer Choice |

used if the author's viewpoint is absent. An answer choice that includes an inappropriate action verb can usually quickly be sorted into the loser category. Note that it may occasionally be difficult to determine whether an action verb is appropriate. For example, *explain* is an action verb that is usually used when the author's viewpoint is absent. However, in rare cases, it may be used when the author's viewpoint is present. Consider the following example:

> **To explain how these legal services plans harm both clients and law firms**

The inclusion of *harm* in the description of the main point makes this answer choice a description of a claim. This type of answer choice is rare, but you should be aware of it and read through the answer choices carefully before eliminating them.

The first step in solving a P question is to determine whether the author's viewpoint is present. The instructions included in the How-to-Solve section for MP questions apply here. Look for keywords or other expressions that pass judgment and that cannot be attributed to a person or group mentioned in the passage. If you find such language, the passage likely includes the author's viewpoint.

If the Author's Viewpoint is Present

When the author's viewpoint is present, the purpose of the passage will be to advance the author's conclusion.

Therefore, you need to identify the claim made by the author. This process is explained in the MP question section of this chapter. You should then anticipate a correct answer choice that combines an appropriate action verb with an accurate description of the conclusion. The action verb will almost always be one related to making a claim, such as *show*, *argue*, *suggest*, *conclude*, *propose*, *advocate*, *criticize*, *condemn*, or *confirm*. In most cases, if an answer choice does not include this category of action verb, it can be sorted into the loser category.

Let's look at Example Question 3 (page 61):

The primary purpose of the passage is to

(A) compare and contrast legal plans with the traditional way of paying for legal services
(B) explain the growing popularity of legal plans
(C) trace the effect of legal plans on prices of legal services
(D) caution that increased use of legal plans is potentially harmful to the legal profession and to clients
(E) advocate reforms to legal plans as presently constituted

As mentioned earlier in this chapter, this is a Debate passage, and the author's viewpoint is present. The author's conclusion is that prepaid legal services plans are unlikely to result in long-term client satisfaction or an increase in profits for law firms. This is stated in the first sentence of the last paragraph. We should anticipate a correct answer choice that combines an appropriate action verb with a description of this conclusion. As the author is critical of prepaid legal plans and feels that they are detrimental to lawyers and clients, the correct answer choice will likely be something along the lines of "to criticize prepaid legal services plans because they negatively affect both clients and lawyers."

(A) compare and contrast legal plans with the traditional way of paying for legal services

Compare and *contrast* are inappropriate action verbs for a passage that makes a claim. The purpose of the passage is not to compare the legal services plans to traditional ways of paying for legal services. In fact, there is not much discussion of the traditional way of paying for legal services in the passage at all. Therefore, this is a loser.

(B) explain the growing popularity of legal plans

Explain is another inappropriate action verb. While the growing popularity of legal services plans is mentioned in the first paragraph of the passage, the purpose of the passage as a whole is not to explain this popularity. This is also a loser.

(C) trace the effect of legal plans on prices of legal services

Trace is another inappropriate action verb. The effects of legal services plans on prices of legal services are not traced in the passage. This is another loser.

(D) caution that increased use of legal plans is potentially harmful to the legal profession and to clients

This matches our anticipated answer choice. *Caution* is an appropriate action verb for a passage that makes a claim. In addition, this answer choice seems to include an accurate description of the author's conclusion. We will keep this as a candidate.

(E) advocate reforms to legal plans as presently constituted

Advocate is also an appropriate action verb. However, the description of the main point includes irrelevant information. The author does not discuss reforming the legal plans. This is a loser.

As (D) is the only candidate, it is the correct answer choice.

If the Author's Viewpoint is Absent

If the author's viewpoint is absent, the purpose of the passage will be simply to present information on a topic, and the main point will be a neutral summary of the key information in the passage. Therefore, you must look for action verbs related to presenting information, such as *describe, convey, present, examine, summarize, review, survey, explain*, and *compare*. Anticipate a correct answer choice that includes an appropriate action verb and an accurate description of the summary.

Looking at the Answer Choices

The correct answer choice is always an expression of the author's purpose in writing the passage. It includes an appropriate action verb and an accurate description of the main point. If the author's viewpoint is present, the action verb will be one related to making a claim. If the author's viewpoint is absent, the action verb will be one related to presenting information.

Incorrect answer choices often include inappropriate action verbs. This usually makes it easy to sort incorrect answer choices into the loser category, although you should always read through the entire answer choice carefully. Incorrect answer choices may also include appropriate action verbs but inaccurately describe the main point. The description may include contradictory, irrelevant, or incomplete information.

Function of a Paragraph

Main Point
Structure
Purpose
Function of a Paragraph
Function of a Statement

Function of a Paragraph
≈ 0.5 questions per test

Example Prompts

The primary function of the first *paragraph* is to

The discussion in the second *paragraph* is *primarily intended* to

Which one of the following best describes *the primary purpose* of the third *paragraph*?

Take These Steps

Refer back to your initial analysis to determine the function of the referenced paragraph. Review the functions of the other paragraphs to make sure you understand the role of the referenced paragraph in the context of the passage.

Anticipate a correct answer choice that includes an appropriate action verb and an accurate description of the function of the referenced paragraph.

Answer Choices

Correct Answer Choices	**Incorrect Answer Choices**
Statements that accurately express the function of the referenced paragraph	Statements with inappropriate action verbs
	Statements that describe the content of the paragraph but not its function
	Wrong part of passage
	Contradictory information
	Irrelevant information
	Incomplete information

Function of a Paragraph (FP) questions ask you to find the answer choice that accurately describes the function of a paragraph.

FP question prompts include terms such as *function*, *purpose*, or *concerned with*. Other terms with similar meanings may be used as well. They also reference a specific paragraph, which distinguishes FP question prompts from P question prompts. FP questions can appear in any passage type.

How to Solve FP Questions

The first step in solving an FP question is to identify the function of the paragraph referenced in the prompt. If you analyzed the passage during the initial read-though, you will have a clear idea of each paragraph's function before you even look at the questions. As discussed in the STR question section of this chapter, there are a number of possible paragraph functions.

Once you have identified the function of the referenced paragraph, review the functions of the other paragraphs—particularly the ones that precede or follow the one specified in the prompt. Make sure you are clear on the relationship between the referenced paragraph and the others. You should then anticipate a correct answer choice that accurately describes the function of the paragraph in the context of the passage. FP question answer choices combine an action verb (similar to the action verbs in P question answer choices) and a description of the function of the paragraph (similar to the function descriptions in STR question answer choices, only more detailed).

Note that the presence or absence of the author's viewpoint is less significant in FP questions than in P questions with regard to the action verb. This is because the question is asking about the function of an individual paragraph rather than the passage as a whole. Therefore, the correct answer choice of an FP question in an Argumentative passage may include an action verb suitable for presenting information (*describe*, *convey*, *present*, etc.), and the correct answer choice of an FP question in an Informational passage may include an action verb suitable for making a claim (*argue*, *suggest*, *conclude*, etc.). Always keep in mind that the action verb must be compatible with the function of the referenced paragraph in the context of the passage.

Let's look at Example Question 6 (page 63):

The primary function of the first paragraph is to

(A) introduce the set of political and artistic ideas that spurred the development of two artistic movements described in the subsequent paragraphs
(B) acknowledge the inescapable melding of political ideas and artistic styles in China
(C) explain the transformation of Chinese society that came about as a result of the Cultural Revolution
(D) present a hypothesis about realism in Chinese art that is refuted by the ensuing discussion of two artistic movements
(E) show that the political realism practiced by the movements discussed in the ensuing paragraphs originated during the Cultural Revolution

The first paragraph states the main point of the passage, which is that the Chinese Cultural Revolution had a profound influence on Chinese art. The main point is supported in subsequent paragraphs by the examples of the Scar Art movement and the Native Soil movement. The first paragraph also provides background information regarding the relationship between Chinese Communist political ideology and Chinese art. The purpose of the first paragraph seems to be to introduce an ideology that influenced the development of the Scar Art and Native Soil movements. We should anticipate a correct answer choice that expresses this.

(A) introduce the set of political and artistic ideas that spurred the development of two artistic movements described in the subsequent paragraphs

This matches our anticipated answer choice. We know that the subsequent paragraphs present two specific art movements—the Scar Art movement and the Native Soil movement. The first paragraph introduces the political and artistic context from which these two movements developed. This is a candidate.

(B) acknowledge the inescapable melding of political ideas and artistic styles in China

This answer choice includes incomplete information. While the first paragraph does make it clear that politics and art were melded in China, the focus is on the influence of a specific political movement (the Cultural Revolution) on later art movements. This is not included in this answer choice. This is a loser.

(C) explain the transformation of Chinese society that came about as a result of the Cultural Revolution

The answer choice includes irrelevant information. The first paragraph states that Chinese art was transformed by the Cultural Revolution. There is no discussion of society as a whole being transformed. This is a loser.

(D) present a hypothesis about realism in Chinese art that is refuted by the ensuing discussion of two artistic movements

This answer choice includes contradictory information. There is no hypothesis about realism in the first paragraph (which means, obviously, that this hypothesis is not refuted in the later paragraphs). This is another loser.

(E) show that the political realism practiced by the movements discussed in the ensuing paragraphs originated during the Cultural Revolution

This answer choice also includes contradictory information. The first paragraph does not state that the Scar Art and Native Soil movements developed during the Cultural Revolution. The subsequent paragraphs make it clear that these movements developed after the Cultural Revolution had ended. This is another loser.

As (A) is the only candidate, it is the correct answer choice.

Looking at the Answer Choices

The correct answer choice is always a statement that accurately expresses the function of the referenced paragraph. It includes an appropriate action verb and an accurate description of the function.

Incorrect answer choices may include inappropriate action verbs, but this is more difficult to determine than it is for P questions because the suitability of an action verb is not dependent on whether or not the author's viewpoint is present. In addition, incorrect answer choices may simply describe the paragraph's content without describing its function. Sometimes, they are based on the wrong part of the passage or include contradictory, irrelevant, or incomplete information.

Function of a Statement

SYNTHESIS FAMILY

Main Point
Structure
Purpose
Function of a Paragraph
Function of a Statement

Function of a Statement

≈ 0.66 questions per test

Example Prompts

The primary function of the reference to _____ (line #) is to

The author *mentions* _____ *primarily in order to*

Which one of the following most accurately expresses *the primary purpose of the sentence* in line #?

Take These Steps

Locate the referenced statement in the passage, and then read the sentence it appears in and the ones that come before and after. Refer to the analysis of the passage you performed during the initial read-through to determine the function of the paragraph in which the statement appears.

Anticipate a correct answer choice that accurately expresses the function of the referenced statement in relation to the immediate and broader context.

Answer Choices

Correct Answer Choices	Incorrect Answer Choices
Statements that accurately express the function of the referenced statement	Statements with inappropriate action verbs
	Statements that describe the function without reference to the context
	Wrong viewpoints
	Wrong part of passage
	Contradictory information
	Irrelevant information
	Incomplete information

Function of a Statement (FS) questions ask you to find the answer choice that accurately states the function, or purpose, of a particular statement in the passage.

FS question prompts include terms such as *in order to*, *function*, or *purpose*. Other terms with similar meanings may be used as well. They also include a reference to a specific statement in the passage. FS questions can appear in any passage type.

How to Solve FS Questions

The first step in solving an FS question is to locate the referenced statement. Some FS question prompts include the referenced statement, some specify where it is in the passage, and some do both. Once you have located the statement, read the sentence it appears in and the ones that come before and after to better understand the immediate context. You should also take note of the function of the paragraph in which the referenced text appears to get a sense of the broader context. Anticipate a correct answer choice that accurately expresses the function of the referenced statement in relation to the context.

FS question answer choices include an action verb plus a description of the statement's function. The action verb can be useful when separating answer choices. If an answer choice includes an action verb that is incompatible with the function you identified, it is most likely incorrect. As with FP questions, the presence or absence of the author's viewpoint is not a consideration with regard to the action verb.

Let's look at Example Question 4 (page 61):

Which one of the following most accurately represents the primary function of the author's mention of marketing devices (line 43)?

(A) It points to an aspect of legal plans that the author believes will be detrimental to the quality of legal services.

(B) It is identified by the author as one of the primary ways in which plan administrators believe themselves to be contributing materially to the legal profession in return for lawyers' participation.

(C) It identifies what the author considers to be one of the few unequivocal benefits that legal plans can provide.

(D) It is reported as part of several arguments that the author attributes to established lawyers who oppose plan participation.

(E) It describes one of the chief burdens of lawyers who have yet to establish themselves and offers an explanation of their advocacy of legal plans.

The first step is to locate the referenced statement in the passage, which is easy to do because its location is specified in the prompt. Then, read the sentence it appears in and the ones before and after it. The preceding sentence includes the main point of the passage, which is the authors' conclusion that the CAW Legal Services Plan and other prepaid legal service plans are unlikely to result in long-term client satisfaction or an increase in profits for law firms. The sentence with the referenced statement points out that experienced lawyers will not participate in these plans, so they function largely as marketing devices for inexperienced lawyers. The sentence that follows states that these inexperienced lawyers have less expertise and provide less satisfaction to clients. The function of this paragraph is to state the author's conclusion and provide evidence to support it. Based on the context, the term *marketing devices* is used to draw attention to an aspect of the legal services plans that will lead to a negative outcome for clients. We should anticipate a correct answer choice that expresses this function of the statement.

(A) **It points to an aspect of legal plans that the author believes will be detrimental to the quality of legal services.**

This matches our anticipated answer choice. By acting as marketing devices that connect clients with inexperienced lawyers with less expertise, legal services plans result in lower quality legal services for clients. This is a candidate.

(B) **It is identified by the author as one of the primary ways in which plan administrators believe themselves to be contributing materially to the legal profession in return for lawyers' participation.**

This answer choice refers to the wrong viewpoint. It incorrectly attributes marketing devices to plan administrators. The position of the plan administrators is discussed in the second paragraph. This is a loser.

(C) **It identifies what the author considers to be one of the few unequivocal benefits that legal plans can provide.**

This answer choice includes contradictory information. The author mentions marketing devices to show that clients will connect with inexperienced lawyers, which will result in less client satisfaction. Therefore, the referenced statement points to something detrimental to clients rather than beneficial. This is another loser.

(D) **It is reported as part of several arguments that the author attributes to established lawyers who oppose plan participation.**

This answer choice refers to the wrong viewpoint. The viewpoint of lawyers who oppose the plan is discussed in the second paragraph. This paragraph presents the viewpoint of the author. This is also a loser.

(E) **It describes one of the chief burdens of lawyers who have yet to establish themselves and offers an explanation of their advocacy of legal plans.**

The answer choice includes irrelevant information. There is nothing in the statement itself or the surrounding context to suggest that marketing devices are a burden for new lawyers or that new lawyers support the legal plans. This is a loser.

As (A) is the only candidate, it is the correct answer choice.

Looking at the Answer Choices

The correct answer choice is always a statement that accurately expresses the function of the referenced statement. This function can often be determined by looking at the immediate context, but sometimes the wider context of the passage as a whole must be considered. The correct answer choice includes an appropriate action verb and an accurate description of the statement's function.

Incorrect answer choices may include inappropriate action verbs as well as contradictory, irrelevant, or incomplete information. They may also be based on a viewpoint other than the one that relates to the referenced statement. In addition, some incorrect answer choices will simply describe the statement's content without any reference to its function in the context.

Practice Sets: Synthesis Family

Analyze the passages below. Mark the keywords, main points, and viewpoints other than the author's. Note the function of each paragraph. Summarize the main points, paragraph content, and viewpoints. Then answer the questions that follow each passage.

Surviving sources of information about women doctors in ancient Greece and Rome are fragmentary: some passing mentions by classical authors, scattered references in medical works, and about 40
(5) inscriptions on tombs and monuments. Yet even from these fragments we can piece together a picture. The evidence shows that in ancient Greece and Rome there were, in fact, female medical personnel who were the ancient equivalent of what we now call
(10) medical doctors. So the history of women in medicine by no means begins in 1849 with Dr. Elizabeth Blackwell, the first woman to earn an M.D. in modern times, or even in 1321 with Francesca de Romana's licensure to practice general medicine, the
(15) earliest known officially recorded occurrence of this sort.

The very nature of the scant evidence tells us something. There is no list of women doctors in antiquity, no direct comment on the fact that there
(20) were such people. Instead, the scattering of references to them indicates that, although their numbers were probably small, women doctors were an unremarkable part of ancient life. For example, in The Republic (421 B.C.), the earliest known source attesting to the
(25) existence of women doctors in Greece, Plato argues that, for the good of the state, jobs should be assigned to people on the basis of natural aptitude, regardless of gender. To support his argument he offers the example that some women, as well as some
(30) men, are skilled in medicine, while others are not. Here, Plato is not trying to convince people that there ought to be women doctors. Rather, he is arguing for an ideal distribution of roles within the state by pointing to something that everyone could already
(35) see—that there were female doctors as well as male.

Moreover, despite evidence that some of these women doctors treated mainly female patients, their practice was clearly not limited to midwifery. Both Greek and Latin have distinct terms for midwife and
(40) doctor, and important texts and inscriptions refer to female practitioners as the latter. Other references provide evidence of a broad scope of practice for women doctors. The epitaph for one named Domnina reads: "You delivered your homeland from disease."
(45) A tribute to another describes her as "savior of all through her knowledge of medicine."

Also pointing to a wider medical practice are the references in various classical medical works to a great number of women's writings on medical
(50) subjects. Here, too, the very nature of the evidence tells us something, for Galen, Pliny the elder, and other ancient writers of encyclopedic medical works

quote the opinions and prescriptions of male and female doctors indiscriminately, moving from one to
(55) the other and back again. As with the male doctors they cite, these works usually simply give excerpts from the female authority's writing without biographical information or special comment.

Main Point

Paragraph 1

Paragraph 2

Paragraph 3

Paragraph 4

Identify Viewpoints

1. Which one of the following most accurately states the main point of the passage?

   (A) There is a range of textual evidence indicating that the existence and professional activity of women doctors were an accepted part of everyday life in ancient Greece and Rome.

   (B) Some scholars in ancient Greece and Rome made little distinction in their writings between learned women and learned men, as can especially be seen in those scholars' references to medical experts and practitioners.

   (C) Although surviving ancient Greek and Roman texts about women doctors contain little biographical or technical data, important inferences can be drawn from the very fact that those texts pointedly comment on the existence of such doctors.

   (D) Ancient texts indicate that various women doctors in Greece and Rome were not only practitioners but also researchers who contributed substantially to the development of medical science.

   (E) Scholars who have argued that women did not practice medicine until relatively recently are mistaken, insofar as they have misinterpreted textual evidence from ancient Greece and Rome.

2. The primary function of the third paragraph of the passage is to

   (A) provide additional support for the argument presented in the first paragraph

   (B) suggest that the implications of the argument presented in the first paragraph are unnecessarily broad

   (C) acknowledge some exceptions to a conclusion defended in the second paragraph

   (D) emphasize the historical importance of the arguments presented in the first two paragraphs

   (E) describe the sources of evidence that are cited in the first two paragraphs in support of the author's main conclusion

3. The tribute quoted in lines 45–46 is offered primarily as evidence that at least some women doctors in ancient times were

   (A) acknowledged as authorities by other doctors
   (B) highly educated
   (C) very effective at treating illness
   (D) engaged in general medical practice
   (E) praised as highly as male doctors

Individual family members have been assisted in resolving disputes arising from divorce or separation, property division, or financial arrangements, through court-connected family mediation programs, which
(5) differ significantly from court adjudication. When courts use their authority to resolve disputes by adjudicating matters in litigation, judges' decisions are binding, subject only to appeal. Formal rules govern the procedure followed, and the hearings are
(10) generally open to the public. In contrast, family mediation is usually conducted in private, the process is less formal, and mediators do not make binding decisions. Mediators help disputing parties arrive at a solution themselves through communication and
(15) cooperation by facilitating the process of negotiation that leads to agreement by the parties.

Supporters of court adjudication in resolving family disputes claim that it has numerous advantages over family mediation, and there is some validity to
(20) this claim. Judges' decisions, they argue, explicate and interpret the broader social values involved in family disputes, and family mediation can neglect those values. Advocates of court adjudication also argue that since the dynamics of power in disputes
(25) are not always well understood, mediation, which is based on the notion of relatively equal parties, would be inappropriate in many situations. The court system, on the other hand, attempts to protect those at a disadvantage because of imbalances in bargaining
(30) power. Family mediation does not guarantee the full protection of an individual's rights, whereas a goal of the court system is to ensure that lawyers can secure all that the law promises to their clients. Family mediation also does not provide a formal record of
(35) the facts and principles that influence the settlement of a dispute, so if a party to a mediated agreement subsequently seeks modification of the judgment, the task of reconstructing the mediation process is especially difficult. Finally, mediated settlements
(40) divert cases from judicial consideration, thus eliminating the opportunity for such cases to refine the law through the ongoing development of legal precedent.

But in the final analysis, family mediation is
(45) better suited to the unique needs of family law than is the traditional court system. Proponents of family mediation point out that it constitutes a more efficient and less damaging process than litigation. By working together in the mediation process, family members
(50) can enhance their personal autonomy and reduce government intervention, develop skills to resolve future disputes, and create a spirit of cooperation that can lead to greater compliance with their agreement. The family mediation process can assist in resolving
(55) emotional as well as legal issues and thus may reduce stress in the long term. Studies of family mediation programs in several countries report that the majority of participants reach a full or partial agreement and express positive feelings about the process, perceiving
(60) it to be more rational and humane than the court system.

Main Point

Paragraph 1

Paragraph 2

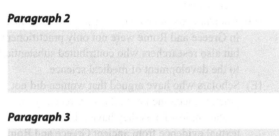

Paragraph 3

Identify Viewpoints

4. Which one of the following most accurately expresses the main point of the passage?

   (A) Recent studies show that family mediation is preferred by family members for resolving family disputes because it is more rational and humane than the court adjudication process.
   (B) Even though a majority of participants in family mediation programs are satisfied with the settlements they reach, the use of court adjudication in resolving family disputes has several advantages over the use of mediation.
   (C) When given the option, family members involved in disputes have typically elected to use family mediation rather than court adjudication to settle their disputes.
   (D) While court adjudication of family disputes has certain advantages, family mediation serves the needs of family members better because it enhances autonomy and encourages greater communication and cooperation in reaching an agreement.
   (E) Although supporters of court adjudication argue that family mediation does not contribute to the development and refinement of legal precedent, they fail to recognize that most family disputes can be resolved without appeal to legal precedents.

5. Which one of the following most accurately expresses the primary purpose of the sentence at lines 30–33?

   (A) to illustrate that court adjudication can have certain benefits that family mediation may lack
   (B) to present material that reveals the inherent limitations of the court adjudication model
   (C) to prove that the assumptions implicit in court adjudication and family mediation are irreconcilable
   (D) to present an alternative judicial option that combines the benefits of both court adjudication and family mediation
   (E) to suggest that lawyers are essential for the protection of individual rights during disputes

6. The author's primary purpose in the passage is to

   (A) document the evolution of a particular body of law and its various conflict-resolution processes
   (B) describe how societal values are embedded in and affect the outcome of two different processes for resolving disputes
   (C) explain why one method of conflict resolution is preferable to another for a certain class of legal disputes
   (D) show how and why legal precedents in a certain branch of the law can eventually alter the outcomes of future cases
   (E) demonstrate that the court system too often disregards the needs of individuals involved in disputes

The painter Roy Lichtenstein helped to define pop
art—the movement that incorporated commonplace
objects and commercial-art techniques into paintings—
by paraphrasing the style of comic books in his work.
(5) His merger of a popular genre with the forms and
intentions of fine art generated a complex result: while
poking fun at the pretensions of the art world,
Lichtenstein's work also managed to convey a
seriousness of theme that enabled it to transcend mere
(10) parody.
　　That Lichtenstein's images were fine art was at
first difficult to see, because, with their word balloons
and highly stylized figures, they looked like nothing
more than the comic book panels from which they were
(15) copied. Standard art history holds that pop art emerged
as an impersonal alternative to the histrionics of
abstract expressionism, a movement in which painters
conveyed their private attitudes and emotions using
nonrepresentational techniques. The truth is that by the
(20) time pop art first appeared in the early 1960s, abstract
expressionism had already lost much of its force. Pop
art painters weren't quarreling with the powerful early
abstract expressionist work of the late 1940s but with a
second generation of abstract expressionists whose
(25) work seemed airy, high-minded, and overly lyrical.
Pop art paintings were full of simple black lines and
large areas of primary color. Lichtenstein's work was
part of a general rebellion against the fading emotional
power of abstract expressionism, rather than an aloof
(30) attempt to ignore it.
　　But if rebellion against previous art by means of
the careful imitation of a popular genre were all that
characterized Lichtenstein's work, it would possess
only the reflective power that parodies have in relation
(35) to their subjects. Beneath its cartoonish methods, his
work displayed an impulse toward realism, an urge to
say that what was missing from contemporary painting
was the depiction of contemporary life. The stilted
romances and war stories portrayed in the comic books
(40) on which he based his canvases, the stylized
automobiles, hot dogs, and table lamps that appeared in
his pictures, were reflections of the culture Lichtenstein
inhabited. But, in contrast to some pop art,
Lichtenstein's work exuded not a jaded cynicism about
(45) consumer culture, but a kind of deliberate naivete,
intended as a response to the excess of sophistication
he observed not only in the later abstract expressionists
but in some other pop artists. With the comics—
typically the domain of youth and innocence—as his
(50) reference point, a nostalgia fills his paintings that gives
them, for all their surface bravado, an inner sweetness.
His persistent use of comic-art conventions
demonstrates a faith in reconciliation, not only between
cartoons and fine art, but between parody and true
(55) feeling.

Main Point

Paragraph 1

Paragraph 2

Paragraph 3

Identify Viewpoints

7. Which one of the following most accurately states the main point of the passage?

(A) Lichtenstein's use of comic book elements in his paintings, considered simply a parodic reaction to the high-mindedness of later abstract expressionism, is also an attempt to re-create the emotionally powerful work of earlier abstract expressionists.

(B) Lichtenstein's use of comic book elements is not solely a parodic reaction to the high-mindedness of later abstract expressionism but also demonstrates an attempt to achieve realistic and nostalgic effects simultaneously in his paintings.

(C) Lichtenstein's use of comic book elements obscures the emotional complexity contained in his paintings, a situation that has prevented his work from being recognized as fine art in the expressionist tradition.

(D) Lichtenstein's use of comic book elements appears to mark his paintings as parodic reactions to the whole of abstract expressionism when they are instead a rebellion against the high-mindedness of the later abstract expressionists.

(E) Lichtenstein's use of comic book elements in his paintings, though a response to the excessive sophistication of the art world, is itself highly sophisticated in that it manages to reconcile pop art and fine art.

8. The author most likely lists some of the themes and objects influencing and appearing in Lichtenstein's paintings (lines 38–43) primarily to

(A) Show that the paintings depict aspects of contemporary life
(B) Support the claim that Lichtenstein's work was parodic in intent
(C) Contrast Lichtenstein's approach to art with that of abstract expressionism
(D) Suggest the emotions that lie at the heart of Lichtenstein's work
(E) Endorse Lichtenstein's attitude toward consumer culture

9. The primary purpose of the passage is most likely to

(A) express curiosity about an artist's work
(B) clarify the motivation behind an artist's work
(C) contrast two opposing theories about an artist's work
(D) describe the evolution of an artist's work
(E) refute a previous overestimation of an artist's work

The moral precepts embodied in the Hippocratic oath, which physicians standardly affirm upon beginning medical practice, have long been considered the immutable bedrock of medical ethics,
(5) binding physicians in a moral community that reaches across temporal, cultural, and national barriers. Until very recently the promises expressed in that oath—for example to act primarily for the benefit and not the harm of patients and to conform to various standards
(10) of professional conduct including the preservation of patients' confidences—even seemed impervious to the powerful scientific and societal forces challenging it. Critics argue that the oath is outdated; its fixed moral rules, they say, are incompatible with more flexible
(15) modern ideas about ethics. It also encourages doctors to adopt an authoritarian stance that depreciates the privacy and autonomy of the patient. Furthermore, its emphasis on the individual patient without regard for the wider social context frustrates the physician's
(20) emerging role as gatekeeper in managed care plans and impedes competitive market forces, which, some critics believe, should determine the quality, price, and distribution of health care as they do those of other commodities. The oath is also faulted for its
(25) omissions: its failure to mention such vital contemporary issues as human experimentation and the relationships of physicians to other health professionals. Some respected opponents even cite historical doubts about the oath's origin and
(30) authorship, presenting evidence that it was formulated by a small group of reformist physicians in ancient Greece and that for centuries it was not uniformly accepted by medical practitioners.

This historical issue may be dismissed at the
(35) outset as irrelevant to the oath's current appropriateness. Regardless of the specific origin of its text—which, admittedly, is at best uncertain—those in each generation who critically appraise its content and judge it to express valid
(40) principles of medical ethics become, in a more meaningful sense, its authors. More importantly, even the more substantive, morally based arguments concerning contemporary values and newly relevant issues cannot negate the patients' need for assurance
(45) that physicians will pursue appropriate goals in treatment in accordance with generally acceptable standards of professionalism. To fulfill that need, the core value of beneficence—which does not actually conflict with most reformers' purposes—should be
(50) retained, with adaptations at the oath's periphery by some combination of revision, supplementation, and modern interpretation. In fact, there is already a tradition of peripheral reinterpretation of traditional wording; for example, the oath's vaguely and
(55) archaically worded proscription against "cutting for the stone" may once have served to forbid surgery, but with today's safer and more effective surgical techniques it is understood to function as a promise to practice within the confines of one's expertise,
(60) which remains a necessary safeguard for patients' safety and well-being.

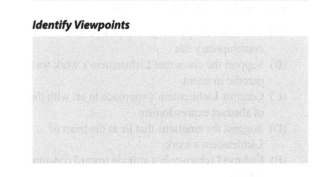

Main Point

Paragraph 1

Paragraph 2

Identify Viewpoints

10. Which one of the following most accurately states the main point of the passage?

   (A) The Hippocratic oath ought to be reevaluated carefully, with special regard to the role of the physician, to make certain that its fundamental moral rules still apply today.
   (B) Despite recent criticisms of the Hippocratic oath, some version of it that will continue to assure patients of physicians' professionalism and beneficent treatment ought to be retained.
   (C) Codes of ethics developed for one society at a particular point in history may lose some specific application in later societies but can retain a useful fundamental moral purpose.
   (D) Even the criticisms of the Hippocratic oath based on contemporary values and newly relevant medical issues cannot negate patients' need for assurance.
   (E) Modern ideas about ethics, especially medical ethics, obviate the need for and appropriateness of a single code of medical ethics like the Hippocratic oath.

11. Which one of the following most accurately describes the organization of the material presented in the passage?

   (A) A general principle is described, criticisms of the principle are made, and modifications of the principle are made in light of these criticisms.
   (B) A set of criticisms is put forward, and possible replies to those criticisms are considered and dismissed.
   (C) The history of a certain code of conduct is discussed, criticisms of the code are mentioned and partially endorsed, and the code is modified as a response.
   (D) A general principle is formulated, a partial defense of that principle is presented, and criticisms of the principle are discussed and rejected.
   (E) The tradition surrounding a certain code of conduct is discussed, criticisms of that code are mentioned, and a general defense of the code is presented.

12. The author's primary purpose in the passage is to

   (A) affirm society's continuing need for a code embodying certain principles
   (B) chastise critics within the medical community who support reinterpretation of a code embodying certain principles
   (C) argue that historical doubts about the origin of a certain code are irrelevant to its interpretation
   (D) outline the pros and cons of revising a code embodying certain principles
   (E) propose a revision of a code embodying certain principles that will increase the code's applicability to modern times

13. Which one of the following would be most suitable as a title for this passage if it were to appear as an editorial piece?

   (A) "The Ancients versus the Moderns: Conflicting Ideas About Medical Ethics"
   (B) "Hypocritical Oath: Why 'Managed Care' Proponents are Seeking to Repeal an Ancient Code"
   (C) "Genetic Fallacy in the Age of Gene-Splicing: Why the Origins of the Hippocratic Oath Don't Matter"
   (D) "The Dead Hand of Hippocrates: Breaking the Hold of Ancient Ideas on Modern Medicine"
   (E) "Prescription for the Hippocratic Oath: Facelift or Major Surgery?"

Until recently, biologists were unable to explain the fact that pathogens—disease-causing parasites—have evolved to incapacitate, and often overwhelm, their hosts. Such behavior is at odds with the
(5) prevailing view of host-parasite relations—that, in general, host and parasite ultimately develop a benign coexistence. This view is based on the idea that parasites that do not harm their hosts have the best chance for long-term survival: they thrive because
(10) their hosts thrive. Some biologists, however, recently have suggested that if a pathogen reproduced so extensively as to cause its host to become gravely sick, it could still achieve evolutionary success if its replication led to a level of transmission into new
(15) hosts that exceeded the loss of pathogens resulting from the host's incapacitation. This scenario suggests that even death-causing pathogens can achieve evolutionary success.

One implication of this perspective is that a
(20) pathogen's virulence—its capacity to overcome a host's defenses and incapacitate it—is a function of its mode of transmission. For example, rhinoviruses, which cause the common cold, require physical proximity for transmission to occur. If a rhinovirus
(25) reproduces so extensively in a solitary host that the host is too unwell to leave home for a day, the thousands of new rhinoviruses produced that day will die before they can be transmitted. So, because it is transmitted directly, the common cold is unlikely to
(30) disable its victims.

The opposite can occur when pathogens are transported by a vector—an organism that can carry and transmit an infectious agent. If, for example, a pathogen capable of being transported by a mosquito
(35) reproduces so extensively that its human host is immobilized, it can still pass along its genes if a mosquito bites the host and transmits this dose to the next human it bites. In such circumstances the virulence is likely to be more severe, because the
(40) pathogen has reproduced to such concentration in the host that the mosquito obtains a high dose of the pathogen, increasing the level of transmission to new hosts.

While medical literature generally supports the
(45) hypothesis that vector-borne pathogens tend to be more virulent than directly transmitted pathogens—witness the lethal nature of malaria, yellow fever, typhus, and sleeping sickness, all carried by biting insects—a few directly transmitted pathogens such as
(50) diphtheria and tuberculosis bacteria can be just as lethal. Scientists call these "sit and wait" pathogens, because they are able to remain alive outside their hosts until a new host comes along, without relying on a vector. Indeed, the endurance of these pathogens,
(55) many of which can survive externally for weeks or months before transmission into a new host—compared, for instance, to an average rhinovirus life span of hours—makes them among the most dangerous of all pathogens.

Main Point

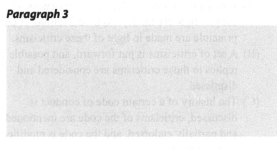

Paragraph 1

Paragraph 2

Paragraph 3

Paragraph 4

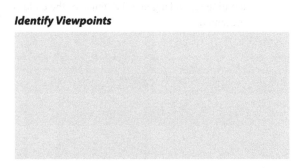

Identify Viewpoints

14. Which one of the following most accurately summarizes the main idea of the passage?

   (A) A new hypothesis about the host-incapacitating behavior of some pathogens suggests that directly transmitted pathogens are just as virulent as vector-borne pathogens, due to the former's ability to survive outside a host for long periods of time.

   (B) A new hypothesis about the host-incapacitating behavior of some pathogens suggests that, while most pathogens reproduce so extensively as to cause their hosts to become gravely sick or even to die, some eventually develop a benign coexistence with their hosts.

   (C) A new hypothesis about the host-incapacitating behavior of some pathogens suggests that they are able to achieve reproductive success because they reproduce to a high level of concentration in their incapacitated hosts.

   (D) A new hypothesis about the host-incapacitating behavior of some pathogens suggests that they are generally able to achieve reproductive success unless their reproduction causes the death of the host.

   (E) A new hypothesis about the host-incapacitating behavior of some pathogens suggests that pathogen virulence is generally a function of their mode of transmission, with vector-borne pathogens usually more virulent than directly transmitted pathogens, except for those directly transmitted pathogens able to endure outside their hosts.

15. Which one of the following most accurately describes the organization of the passage?

   (A) introduction of a scientific anomaly; presentation of an explanation for the anomaly; mention of an implication of the explanation; discussion of two examples illustrating the implication; discussion of exceptions to the implication

   (B) introduction of a scientific anomaly; presentation of an explanation for the anomaly; discussion of two examples illustrating the explanation; discussion of exceptions to the explanation; mention of an implication of the explanation

   (C) introduction of a scientific anomaly; presentation of an explanation for the anomaly; discussion of two examples illustrating the explanation; mention of an implication of the explanation; discussion of examples illustrating the implication

   (D) introduction of a scientific anomaly; presentation of an implication of the anomaly; discussion of two examples illustrating the implication; discussion of exceptions to the implication

   (E) introduction of a scientific anomaly; discussion of two examples illustrating the anomaly; presentation of an explanation for the anomaly; discussion of examples illustrating the explanation

16. The primary purpose of the passage is to

   (A) compare examples challenging the prevailing view of host-parasite relations with examples supporting it

   (B) argue that the prevailing view of host-parasite relations is correct but is based on a mistaken rationale

   (C) offer a modification to the prevailing view of host-parasite relations

   (D) attack evidence that supports the prevailing view of host-parasite relations

   (E) examine the origins of the prevailing view of host-parasite relations

For Questions 1–3

Surviving sources of information about women doctors in ancient Greece and Rome are fragmentary: some passing mentions by classical authors, scattered references in medical works, and about 40
(5) inscriptions on tombs and monuments. Yet even from these fragments we can piece together a picture. The evidence shows that in ancient Greece and Rome there were, in fact, female medical personnel who were the ancient equivalent of what we now call
(10) medical doctors. So the history of women in medicine by no means begins in 1849 with Dr. Elizabeth Blackwell, the first woman to earn an M.D. in modern times, or even in 1321 with Francesca de Romana's licensure to practice general medicine, the
(15) earliest known officially recorded occurrence of this sort.

The very nature of the scant evidence tells us something. There is no list of women doctors in antiquity, no direct comment on the fact that there
(20) were such people. Instead, the scattering of references to them indicates that, although their numbers were probably small, women doctors were an unremarkable part of ancient life. For example, in *The Republic* (421 B.C.), the earliest known source attesting to the
(25) existence of women doctors in Greece, Plato argues that, for the good of the state, jobs should be assigned to people on the basis of natural aptitude, regardless of gender. To support his argument he offers the example that some women, as well as some
(30) men, are skilled in medicine, while others are not. Here, Plato is not trying to convince people that there ought to be women doctors. Rather, he is arguing for an ideal distribution of roles within the state by pointing to something that everyone could already
(35) see—that there were female doctors as well as male.

Moreover, despite evidence that some of these women doctors treated mainly female patients, their practice was clearly not limited to midwifery. Both Greek and Latin have distinct terms for midwife and
(40) doctor, and important texts and inscriptions refer to female practitioners as the latter. Other references provide evidence of a broad scope of practice for women doctors. The epitaph for one named Domnina reads: "You delivered your homeland from disease."
(45) A tribute to another describes her as "savior of all through her knowledge of medicine."

Also pointing to a wider medical practice are the references in various classical medical works to a great number of women's writings on medical
(50) subjects. Here, too, the very nature of the evidence tells us something, for Galen, Pliny the elder, and other ancient writers of encyclopedic medical works quote the opinions and prescriptions of male and female doctors indiscriminately, moving from one to
(55) the other and back again. As with the male doctors they cite, these works usually simply give excerpts from the female authority's writing without biographical information or special comment.

Main Point

The main point is stated in the third sentence of the first paragraph. It is that there were female medical personnel equivalent to doctors in ancient Greece and Rome.

Paragraph 1

This paragraph states the main point of the paragraph. It also provides background information regarding the fragmentary nature of the records related to female medical personnel prior to the earliest official records.

Paragraph 2

This paragraph supports the main point by pointing out that the scant evidence of women doctors indicates that the existence of women doctors was an unremarkable and accepted part of ancient life. It then provides the example of *The Republic* to illustrate this.

Paragraph 3

This paragraph provides further evidence for the main point by explaining that female doctors' practices were not limited to midwifery. It supports this with references to texts and inscriptions.

Paragraph 4

This paragraph includes another supporting detail to support the main point. It states that classical medical works included many references to female doctors and their methods of treatment.

Identify Viewpoints

The author's viewpoint is present and is the focus of the passage. There are no other viewpoints.

1. **Correct Answer (A).** *Prep Test 49, Section 3, Passage 3, Question 14.*

Which one of the following most accurately states the main point of the passage?

This is an MP question. It is an Argumentative passage, so the author's viewpoint is present. The author's conclusion is stated in the third sentence of the first paragraph. The author claims that there were female medical personnel equivalent to doctors in ancient Greece and Rome. We should anticipate a correct answer choice that accurately expresses this conclusion.

(A) **There is a range of textual evidence indicating that the existence and professional activity of women doctors were an accepted part of everyday life in ancient Greece and Rome.**

This matches our anticipated answer choice. It states that there were female doctors in ancient Greece and Rome. It includes the additional detail that these doctors were an accepted part of everyday life, which is supported by the use of the term *unremarkable* in the second paragraph. This is a candidate.

(B) **Some scholars in ancient Greece and Rome made little distinction in their writings between learned women and learned men, as can especially be seen in those scholars' references to medical experts and practitioners.**

This answer choice addresses the wrong task. It includes accurate information but restates a supporting detail rather than the main point. This is a loser.

(C) **Although surviving ancient Greek and Roman texts about women doctors contain little biographical or technical data, important inferences can be drawn from the very fact that those texts pointedly comment on the existence of such doctors.**

This answer choice includes contradictory information. First, the author is not concluding that inferences can be drawn. The author is concluding that female doctors did in fact exist. Second, the texts do not pointedly comment on this existence of women doctors. They do the opposite—they speak about male and female doctors indiscriminately. This is another loser.

(D) **Ancient texts indicate that various women doctors in Greece and Rome were not only practitioners but also researchers who contributed substantially to the development of medical science.**

This answer choice includes irrelevant information. The passage does not state that women doctors contributed substantially to the development of medical science. This is a loser.

(E) **Scholars who have argued that women did not practice medicine until relatively recently are mistaken, insofar as they have misinterpreted textual evidence from ancient Greece and Rome.**

This answer choice includes irrelevant information. The author provides two examples of female doctors from later periods in the first paragraph and implies that some people might think these were the first women to practice medicine. However, there is no reference to any scholars who hold this opinion and no mention of these scholars misinterpreting textual evidence. This is a loser.

As (A) is the only candidate, it is the correct answer choice.

2. **Correct Answer (A).** *Prep Test 49, Section 3, Passage 3, Question 16.*

The primary function of the third paragraph of the passage is to

This is an FP question. The function of the third paragraph is to provide evidence for the main point of the passage, which is the author's conclusion that there were women doctors in Ancient Greece and Rome. We should anticipate a correct answer choice that includes an appropriate action verb and an accurate description of this function.

(A) provide additional support for the argument presented in the first paragraph

This matches our anticipated answer choice. The argument presented in the first paragraph is the author's conclusion, and the third paragraph provides evidence to support it. This is a candidate.

(B) suggest that the implications of the argument presented in the first paragraph are unnecessarily broad

This answer choice includes contradictory information. The third paragraph does not suggest that the argument is unnecessarily broad. In fact, this passage relies on explicitly making the broad claim that women were medical practitioners and not just midwives. This is another loser.

(C) acknowledge some exceptions to a conclusion defended in the second paragraph

This answer choice includes irrelevant information. The claim in the second paragraph is that women doctors were an uncontroversial part of ancient life. There are no exceptions to this conclusion addressed in the third paragraph or anywhere in the passage. This is a loser.

(D) emphasize the historical importance of the arguments presented in the first two paragraphs

This answer choice includes irrelevant information. The third paragraph does not emphasize the historical importance of arguments presented in the previous paragraphs. This is another loser.

(E) describe the sources of evidence that are cited in the first two paragraphs in support of the author's main conclusion

This answer choice is based on the wrong part of the passage. The sources of evidence cited in the first two paragraphs are described in those paragraphs, not in the third paragraph. This is a loser.

As (A) is the only candidate, it is the correct answer choice.

3. Correct Answer (D). *Prep Test 49, Section 3, Passage 3, Question 19.*

The tribute quoted in lines 45–46 is offered primarily as evidence that at least some women doctors in ancient times were

This is an FS question. After locating the referenced statement, we should read the sentence it appears in and the ones before and after it. However, the sentence after the one with the referenced statement starts another paragraph, so it will probably be less important in terms of context. The sentence before does not provide much context either. So, it is probably important to understand the function of the paragraph the referenced statement appears in. The function of the third paragraph is to provide support for the authors' conclusion by showing that the women doctors were not only midwives but also general medical practitioners. The referenced statement is part of the evidence provided for this claim. Therefore, the function of the referenced statement is to support the claim that women doctors were general medical practitioners and not solely midwives. We should anticipate a correct answer choice with an appropriate action verb that expresses this function.

(A) acknowledged as authorities by other doctors

This answer choice focuses on the content of the referenced statement rather than its function. The woman in question does seem to be acknowledged by other doctors as an authority, or at least this can be inferred. However, the quote is not included to provide evidence of this. This is why it is important to understand the referenced statement in the context of the paragraph and the passage as a whole. Why did the author include this quote? Not to show how great this one female doctor was but to provide textual evidence that women did not practice only midwifery. This is a loser.

(B) highly educated

Again, this answer choice focuses on the content rather than the function. The quote implies that the woman was highly educated, but the quote was not offered as evidence of this. This is another loser.

(C) very effective at treating illness

Like the last two answers, this answer choice focuses on the content. While this may be implied by the quote, this was not the reason the quote was included in the paragraph. This is a loser.

(D) engaged in general medical practice

This matches our anticipated answer choice. The quote is included to offer an example of a female doctor who was not solely a midwife, which supports the argument in the passage that women were general medical practitioners. This is a candidate.

(E) praised as highly as male doctors

Again, this answer choice focuses on the content. The quote implies that women doctors were praised as highly as male ones, but it was not included to provide evidence of this. This is a loser.

As (D) is the only candidate, it is the correct answer choice.

For Questions 4–6

Individual family members have been assisted in resolving disputes arising from divorce or separation, property division, or financial arrangements, through court-connected family mediation programs, which
(5) differ significantly from ^A)^ court adjudication. When courts use their authority to resolve disputes by adjudicating matters in litigation, judges' decisions are binding, subject only to appeal. Formal rules govern the procedure followed, and the hearings are
(10) generally open to the public. In contrast, ^B)^ family mediation is usually conducted in private, the process is less formal, and mediators do not make binding decisions. Mediators help disputing parties arrive at a solution themselves through communication and
(15) cooperation by facilitating the process of negotiation that leads to agreement by the parties.

^A)^ Supporters of court adjudication in resolving family disputes claim that it has numerous advantages over family mediation, and there is some validity to
(20) this claim. Judges' decisions, they argue, explicate and interpret the broader social values involved in family disputes, and family mediation can neglect those values. Advocates of court adjudication also argue that since the dynamics of power in disputes
(25) are not always well understood, mediation, which is based on the notion of relatively equal parties, would be inappropriate in many situations. The court system, on the other hand, attempts to protect those at a disadvantage because of imbalances in bargaining
(30) power. Family mediation does not guarantee the full protection of an individual's rights, whereas a goal of the court system is to ensure that lawyers can secure all that the law promises to their clients. Family mediation also does not provide a formal record of
(35) the facts and principles that influence the settlement of a dispute, so if a party to a mediated agreement subsequently seeks modification of the judgment, the task of reconstructing the mediation process is especially difficult. Finally, mediated settlements
(40) divert cases from judicial consideration, thus eliminating the opportunity for such cases to refine the law through the ongoing development of legal precedent.

But in the final analysis, family mediation is
(45) better suited to the unique needs of family law than is the traditional court system. ^B)^ Proponents of family mediation point out that it constitutes a more efficient and less damaging process than litigation. By working together in the mediation process, family members
(50) can enhance their personal autonomy and reduce government intervention, develop skills to resolve future disputes, and create a spirit of cooperation that can lead to greater compliance with their agreement. The family mediation process can assist in resolving
(55) emotional as well as legal issues and thus may reduce stress in the long term. Studies of family mediation programs in several countries report that the majority of participants reach a full or partial agreement and express positive feelings about the process, perceiving
(60) it to be more rational and humane than the court system.

Main Point

The main point is explicitly stated in the first sentence of the third paragraph. It is that family mediation is better suited to the needs of family law. This is the author's conclusion.

Paragraph 1

The first paragraph provides background information to introduce the topic and the two opposing viewpoints. It explains the need for a system to resolve disputes between family members and contrasts two existing systems. It describes court adjudication as formal and binding and family mediation as less formal and non-binding.

Paragraph 2

This paragraph presents the viewpoint of the supporters of court adjudication and provides evidence in favor of this form of dispute resolution.

Paragraph 3

This paragraph states the main point of the passage, which is the author's conclusion that family mediation is preferable. It then presents the viewpoint of proponents of family mediation and provides support for this position.

Identify Viewpoints

The two main viewpoints explored in this passage are those of the supporters of court adjudication and the proponents of family mediation. The author's viewpoint is also present. The author supports the position of proponents of family mediation.

4. **Correct Answer (D).** *Prep Test 47, Section 2, Passage 3, Question 12.*

> **Which one of the following most accurately expresses the main point of the passage?**

This is an MP question. It is a Debate passage, and the author's viewpoint is present. The author's conclusion appears in the first sentence of the third paragraph. It is that family mediation is better suited for family law than the traditional court system (court adjudication). We should anticipate a correct answer choice that accurately expresses this conclusion.

> **(A) Recent studies show that family mediation is preferred by family members for resolving family disputes because it is more rational and humane than the court adjudication process.**

This is a descriptive statement rather than a conclusion. This answer choice simply states a fact—that family mediation is preferred by family members. This is a loser.

> **(B) Even though a majority of participants in family mediation programs are satisfied with the settlements they reach, the use of court adjudication in resolving family disputes has several advantages over the use of mediation.**

This answer choice refers to the wrong viewpoint. This answer choice presents the viewpoint of proponents of court adjudication rather than that of the author, who favors family mediation. This is another loser.

> **(C) When given the option, family members involved in disputes have typically elected to use family mediation rather than court adjudication to settle their disputes.**

This is another descriptive statement rather than a conclusion. This is also a loser.

> **(D) While court adjudication of family disputes has certain advantages, family mediation serves the needs of family members better because it enhances autonomy and encourages greater communication and cooperation in reaching an agreement.**

This matches our anticipated answer choice. It states that family mediation is better for family members and provides evidence from the third paragraph to support this conclusion. The first clause acknowledges that court adjudication of family disputes has certain advantages. The author does not deny the advantages of court adjudication that are stated in the second paragraph but instead claims that family mediation is better suited for family law. Although the term *family law* is not used, the answer is framed in terms of *family disputes* and *family members*. This is a candidate.

> **(E) Although supporters of court adjudication argue that family mediation does not contribute to the development and refinement of legal precedent, they fail to recognize that most family disputes can be resolved without appeal to legal precedents.**

This answer choice includes incomplete information. It does not address the author's claim that family mediation is better for family law than court adjudication. This is a loser.

As (D) is the only candidate, it is the correct answer choice.

5. **Correct Answer (A).** *Prep Test 47, Section 2, Passage 3, Question 13.*

> **Which one of the following most accurately expresses the primary purpose of the sentence at lines 30–33?**

This is an FS question. Therefore, we should locate the referenced statement. In this case, the entire sentence is referenced, so we should read it and the ones that come before and after it. The referenced statement claims that family mediation does not fully protect an individual's rights, whereas courts ensure that lawyers can secure these rights for their clients. The sentence before states that the court system attempts to protect those at a disadvantage, while the sentence after points out that family mediation does not provide a formal record, making it difficult to modify agreements. All three sentences are examples of how court adjudication is best suited for family disputes. This is because the function of this paragraph is to present the viewpoint of supporters of court adjudication. Therefore, the function of the referenced statement is to provide an example of an advantage of court adjudication over family mediation. We should anticipate a correct answer choice that includes an appropriate action verb and an accurate description of this function.

(A) to illustrate that court adjudication can have certain benefits that family mediation may lack

This matches our anticipated answer choice. This is a candidate.

(B) to present material that reveals the inherent limitations of the court adjudication model

This answer choice includes contradictory information. The statement is an example of a benefit of the court adjudication model. This is a loser.

(C) to prove that the assumptions implicit in court adjudication and family mediation are irreconcilable

This answer choice includes irrelevant information. There is no mention of the assumptions implicit to either model or how these assumptions are irreconcilable. This is another loser.

(D) to present an alternative judicial option that combines the benefits of both court adjudication and family mediation

This answer choice also includes irrelevant information. The statement shows a benefit of court adjudication only. There is also no attempt to present an alternative judicial option anywhere in the passage. This is also a loser.

(E) to suggest that lawyers are essential for the protection of individual rights during disputes

This answer choice focuses on the statement's content rather than its function. This is another loser.

As (A) is the only candidate, it is the correct answer choice.

6. **Correct Answer (C).** *Prep Test 47, Section 2, Passage 3, Question 18.*

The author's primary purpose in the passage is to

This is a P question, and the author's viewpoint is present in the passage. The author's conclusion appears in the first sentence of the third paragraph. It is that family mediation is better suited for family law than is the traditional court system (court adjudication). We should anticipate a correct answer choice that combines an appropriate action verb with a description of this conclusion. As the author believes that family mediation is better suited to handling disputes in family law, the correct answer choice will likely be something along the lines of "to show how one model for conflict resolution is superior to another."

(A) document the evolution of a particular body of law and its various conflict-resolution processes

Document is an inappropriate action verb for a passage that makes a claim. The purpose of the passage is not to document the development of a body of law. This is a loser.

(B) describe how societal values are embedded in and affect the outcome of two different processes for resolving disputes

Describe is another inappropriate action verb. The author is not attempting to describe how social values affect dispute resolution processes. This is another loser.

(C) explain why one method of conflict resolution is preferable to another for a certain class of legal disputes

This matches our anticipated answer choice. *Explain* is used in conjunction with *preferable* to accurately represent the author's conclusion. This is a candidate.

(D) show how and why legal precedents in a certain branch of the law can eventually alter the outcomes of future cases

Show is an appropriate action word. However, this answer choice includes irrelevant information. The passage does not discuss legal precedents or how they can alter the outcome of future cases. This is a loser.

(E) demonstrate that the court system too often disregards the needs of individuals involved in disputes

Demonstrates is an appropriate action word. However, this answer choice includes incomplete information. It does not specify that the author prefers family mediation over the court adjudication system. This is a loser.

As (C) is the only candidate, it is the correct answer choice.

For Questions 7–9

The painter Roy Lichtenstein helped to define pop art—the movement that incorporated commonplace objects and commercial-art techniques into paintings—by paraphrasing the style of comic books in his work.
(5) His merger of a popular genre with the forms and intentions of fine art generated a complex result: while poking fun at the pretensions of the art world, Lichtenstein's work also managed to convey a seriousness of theme that enabled it to transcend mere
(10) parody.

That Lichtenstein's images were fine art was at first difficult to see, because, with their word balloons and highly stylized figures, they looked like nothing more than the comic book panels from which they were
(15) copied. Standard art history holds that pop art emerged as an impersonal alternative to the histrionics of abstract expressionism, a movement in which painters conveyed their private attitudes and emotions using nonrepresentational techniques. The truth is that by the
(20) time pop art first appeared in the early 1960s, abstract expressionism had already lost much of its force. Pop art painters weren't quarreling with the powerful early abstract expressionist work of the late 1940s but with a second generation of abstract expressionists whose
(25) work seemed airy, high-minded, and overly lyrical. Pop art paintings were full of simple black lines and large areas of primary color. Lichtenstein's work was part of a general rebellion against the fading emotional power of abstract expressionism, rather than an aloof
(30) attempt to ignore it.

But if rebellion against previous art by means of the careful imitation of a popular genre were all that characterized Lichtenstein's work, it would possess only the reflective power that parodies have in relation
(35) to their subjects. Beneath its cartoonish methods, his work displayed an impulse toward realism, an urge to say that what was missing from contemporary painting was the depiction of contemporary life. The stilted romances and war stories portrayed in the comic books
(40) on which he based his canvases, the stylized automobiles, hot dogs, and table lamps that appeared in his pictures, were reflections of the culture Lichtenstein inhabited. But, in contrast to some pop art, Lichtenstein's work exuded not a jaded cynicism about
(45) consumer culture, but a kind of deliberate naivete, intended as a response to the excess of sophistication he observed not only in the later abstract expressionists but in some other pop artists. With the comics— typically the domain of youth and innocence—as his
(50) reference point, a nostalgia fills his paintings that gives them, for all their surface bravado, an inner sweetness. His persistent use of comic-art conventions demonstrates a faith in reconciliation, not only between cartoons and fine art, but between parody and true
(55) feeling.

Main Point

The main point is stated in the last sentence of the first paragraph. It is that Lichtenstein's merger of a popular genre (comic books) with fine art meant that his work not only poked fun at the pretensions of the art world but also transcended parody because it conveyed a seriousness of theme.

Paragraph 1

The paragraph provides background information (definition of pop art) and states the main point of the passage.

Paragraph 2

This paragraph provides information about abstract impressionism, the art movement that pop artists in general and Lichtenstein in particular rebelled against.

Paragraph 3

This paragraph provides support for the main point that Lichtenstein's work was not mere parody but had a seriousness of theme. This paragraph describes Lichtenstein's impulse toward realism, deliberate naivete towards consumer culture, and nostalgia that gives his works inner sweetness.

Identify Viewpoints

The author's viewpoint is present and is the focus of the passage. There are no other viewpoints in this passage.

7. Correct Answer (B). *Prep Test 42, Section 3, Passage 2, Question 8.*

Which one of the following most accurately states the main point of the passage?

This is an MP question. It is an Argumentative passage, so the author's viewpoint is present. The author's conclusion is stated in the last sentence of the first paragraph. It is that Lichtenstein's merger of a popular genre (comic books) with fine art meant that his work not only poked fun at the pretensions of the art world but also transcended parody because it conveyed a seriousness of theme. We should anticipate a correct answer choice that accurately expresses this conclusion.

(A) Lichtenstein's use of comic book elements in his paintings, considered simply a parodic reaction to the high-mindedness of later abstract expressionism, is also an attempt to re-create the emotionally powerful work of earlier abstract expressionists.

This answer choice includes contradictory information. Lichtenstein's work was not an attempt to recreate the emotionally powerful work of abstract expressionists but rather a response to abstract expressionists. This is a loser.

(B) Lichtenstein's use of comic book elements is not solely a parodic reaction to the high-mindedness of later abstract expressionism but also demonstrates an attempt to achieve realistic and nostalgic effects simultaneously in his paintings.

This matches our anticipated answer choice. Although the conclusion uses the phrase *seriousness of theme*, the third paragraph defines this as Lichtenstein's impulse toward realism, deliberate naivete, and nostalgia. The inclusion of two of these is sufficient to make this answer choice a candidate.

(C) Lichtenstein's use of comic book elements obscures the emotional complexity contained in his paintings, a situation that has prevented his work from being recognized as fine art in the expressionist tradition.

This answer choice makes too strong of a claim. Lichtenstein's use of comic book elements made the fine art value of his work difficult to see, but that does not mean it prevented his work from being recognized as fine art. Additionally, while these elements may have also made it somewhat harder to see the emotions present in his work, it is far too strong to say that the elements obscured these emotions. This is another loser.

(D) Lichtenstein's use of comic book elements appears to mark his paintings as parodic reactions to the whole of abstract expressionism when they are instead a rebellion against the high-mindedness of the later abstract expressionists.

This answer choice includes incomplete information. While it contains some elements of the main point—Lichtenstein's work not being solely parody—it does not address the idea of seriousness of theme. This is a loser.

(E) Lichtenstein's use of comic book elements in his paintings, though a response to the excessive sophistication of the art world, is itself highly sophisticated in that it manages to reconcile pop art and fine art.

This answer choice makes too strong of a claim. Although the passage suggests that Lichtenstein's work reconciled pop and fine art, it does not indicate why Lichtenstein's work is highly sophisticated. This is another loser.

As (B) is the only candidate, it is the correct answer choice.

8. **Correct Answer (A).** *Prep Test 42, Section 3, Passage 2, Question 10.*

> **The author most likely lists some of the themes and objects influencing and appearing in Lichtenstein's paintings (lines 38–43) primarily to**

This is an FS question. Therefore, we should read the sentence with the referenced statement and the ones that come before and after it. The sentence before states that Lichtenstein displayed an impulse toward realism and an urge to show that depictions of contemporary life were missing from contemporary paintings. The referenced sentence includes examples of various themes and objects that reflect the culture Lichtenstein inhabited. The sentence after moves on to discuss Lichtenstein's naivete and lack of jaded cynicism about consumer culture. The function of the referenced statement seems to be to demonstrate Lichtenstein's realism and his urge to include depictions of contemporary life. We should anticipate a correct answer choice that expresses this function.

(A) show that the paintings depict aspects of contemporary life

This matches our anticipated answer choice. The referenced sentence includes a list of themes and objects that are all related to contemporary life. Therefore, its function is to show that Lichtenstein's work depicts aspects of contemporary life. This is a candidate.

(B) support the claim that Lichtenstein's work was parodic in intent

This answer choice includes contradictory information. The author does not claim that Lichtenstein's work was parodic in intent. Rather, the author asserts that it transcended parody. The passage focuses on the aspects other than parody that make Lichtenstein's work important. This is a loser.

(C) contrast Lichtenstein's approach to art with that of abstract expressionism

Contrast is an inappropriate action verb. This list is not provided to contrast Lichtenstein's work with that of abstract impressionists, but rather to show the realism of his work. This is a loser.

(D) suggest the emotions that lie at the heart of Lichtenstein's work

This answer choice is based on the wrong part of the passage. It is related to a description of Lichtenstein's work as having an inner sweetness that appears later in the passage. The referenced claim does not have any connection to this. This is another loser.

(E) endorse Lichtenstein's attitude toward consumer culture

Endorse is an inappropriate action verb. The function of the referenced statement is not to endorse Lichtenstein's attitude toward consumer culture. In fact, the author has not expressed an opinion about Lichtenstein's attitude anywhere in the passage. This is also a loser.

As (A) is the only candidate, it is the correct answer choice.

9. **Correct Answer (B).** *Prep Test 42, Section 3, Passage 2, Question 13.*

> **The primary purpose of the passage is most likely to**

This is a P question. The authors' viewpoint is present. The author's conclusion appears in the last sentence of the first paragraph. It is that Lichtenstein's merger of a popular genre (comic books) with fine art meant that his work not only poked fun at the pretensions of the art world but also transcended parody because it conveyed a seriousness of theme. It is difficult to anticipate a correct answer choice for this question because the author's conclusion is so general. The claim being made about Lichtenstein's work is almost a description of Lichtenstein's artistic goals and the methods he used to achieve them. Given this, the correct answer choice will likely be more general than we would usually expect to see for a passage that includes the author's viewpoint. In addition, action verbs may be less useful as an indicator of whether an answer choice is a loser or candidate as well. When an answer is difficult to anticipate, you should proceed directly to eliminating answer choices.

(A) express curiosity about an artist's work

The term *express curiosity* is not appropriate, as the author makes a confident evaluation of Lichtenstein's work. This is a loser.

(B) clarify the motivation behind an artist's work

This seems like the purpose of the passage. The author's conclusion provides insight into the reasons for Lichtenstein's artistic style. There is also additional information about Lichtenstein's motivations throughout the passage. The purpose of the passage as a whole can be seen to explore why Lichtenstein painted the way he did. This is a candidate.

(C) contrast two opposing theories about an artist's work

This answer choice includes contradictory information. The passage includes only the author's viewpoint and it develops only one theory about Lichtenstein's work. This is another loser.

(D) describe the evolution of an artist's work

This answer choice includes irrelevant information. The passage does not discuss the evolution of Lichtenstein's work. It focuses on the reasons he painted the way he did and why his work is significant. This is another loser.

(E) refute a previous overestimation of an artist's work

This answer choice includes contradictory information. The author implies that Lichtenstein's work has been underestimated as mere parody, not overestimated. This is a loser.

As (B) is the only candidate, it is the correct answer choice.

For Questions 10–13

The moral precepts embodied in the Hippocratic oath, which A)physicians standardly affirm upon beginning medical practice, have long been considered the immutable bedrock of medical ethics,
(5) binding physicians in a moral community that reaches across temporal, cultural, and national barriers. Until very recently the promises expressed in that oath—for example to act primarily for the benefit and not the harm of patients and to conform to various standards
(10) of professional conduct including the preservation of patients' confidences—even seemed impervious to the powerful scientific and societal forces challenging it. B)Critics argue that the oath is outdated; its fixed moral rules, they say, are incompatible with more flexible
(15) modern ideas about ethics. It also encourages doctors to adopt an authoritarian stance that depreciates the privacy and autonomy of the patient. Furthermore, its emphasis on the individual patient without regard for the wider social context frustrates the physician's
(20) emerging role as gatekeeper in managed care plans and impedes competitive market forces, which, B)some critics believe, should determine the quality, price, and distribution of health care as they do those of other commodities. The oath is also faulted for its
(25) omissions: its failure to mention such vital contemporary issues as human experimentation and the relationships of physicians to other health professionals. B)Some respected opponents even cite historical doubts about the oath's origin and
(30) authorship, presenting evidence that it was formulated by a small group of reformist physicians in ancient Greece and that for centuries it was not uniformly accepted by medical practitioners.

This historical issue may be dismissed at the
(35) outset as irrelevant to the oath's current appropriateness. Regardless of the specific origin of its text—which, admittedly, is at best uncertain—those in each generation who critically appraise its content and judge it to express valid
(40) principles of medical ethics become, in a more meaningful sense, its authors. More importantly, even the more substantive, morally based arguments concerning contemporary values and newly relevant issues cannot negate the patients' need for assurance
(45) that physicians will pursue appropriate goals in treatment in accordance with generally acceptable standards of professionalism. To fulfill that need, the core value of beneficence—which does not actually conflict with most reformers' purposes—should be
(50) retained, with adaptations at the oath's periphery by some combination of revision, supplementation, and modern interpretation. In fact, there is already a tradition of peripheral reinterpretation of traditional wording; for example, the oath's vaguely and
(55) archaically worded proscription against "cutting for the stone" may once have served to forbid surgery, but with today's safer and more effective surgical techniques it is understood to function as a promise to practice within the confines of one's expertise,
(60) which remains a necessary safeguard for patients' safety and well-being.

Main Point

The main point is explicitly stated in the fourth sentence of the second paragraph. It is that the core of the Hippocratic oath should be retained, with minor adaptations to the oath's non-core values by way of revision, supplementation, and modern interpretation. This is the author's conclusion.

Paragraph 1

The first paragraph introduces two opposing viewpoints and provides background information. First, the traditional position of physicians regarding the Hippocratic oath—that it is a key element of medical ethics—is stated. Then, background information about the role of the oath in the medical community is provided. Finally, the opinions of critics of the oath are presented.

Paragraph 2

The second paragraph begins by dismissing a criticism of the oath—that its historical origins are in doubt. It then states the main point, which is that the oath should be retained with minor changes to its non-core values. This paragraph also provides an example to support the main point. The author points out that what was once interpreted as a prohibition against surgery has been reinterpreted to mean that doctors should practice within the confines of their expertise.

Identify Viewpoints

There are two main viewpoints in this passage—the traditional view of the Hippocratic oath and that of modern critics of the oath. The author's viewpoint is also present. The author believes that the oath should be retained with minor changes to its non-core values. The author is rebutting the viewpoint of critics of the oath.

10. **Correct Answer (B).** *Prep Test 45, Section 2, Passage 2, Question 7.*

> **Which one of the following most accurately states the main point of the passage?**

This is an MP question. It is a Debate passage, and the author's viewpoint is present. The author's conclusion appears in the fourth sentence of the second paragraph. It is that that the core of the Hippocratic Oath should be retained, with minor adaptations to the oath's non-core values by way of revision, supplementation, and modern interpretation. The author is rebutting a previous viewpoint. We should anticipate a correct answer choice that accurately expresses this conclusion.

> **(A) The Hippocratic oath ought to be reevaluated carefully, with special regard to the role of the physician, to make certain that its fundamental moral rules still apply today.**

This matches our anticipated answer choice. It says that the oath must be reevaluated in a way that ensures its core values are not altered. This is a candidate.

> **(B) Despite recent criticisms of the Hippocratic oath, some version of it that will continue to assure patients of physicians' professionalism and beneficent treatment ought to be retained.**

This also matches our anticipated answer choice. It is very similar to answer choice (A). This is a candidate as well.

> **(C) Codes of ethics developed for one society at a particular point in history may lose some specific application in later societies but can retain a useful fundamental moral purpose.**

The term *codes of ethics* seems overly broad. In addition, this answer choice includes incomplete information. It does not address the author's claim that the core values of the Hippocratic Oath must be retained and that only minor changes should be made to its non-core values. This is a loser.

> **(D) Even the criticisms of the Hippocratic oath based on contemporary values and newly relevant medical issues cannot negate patients' need for assurance.**

This answer choice addresses the wrong task. This information is not related to the main point of the passage. It is a detail provided to support the main point. This is another loser.

> **(E) Modern ideas about ethics, especially medical ethics, obviate the need for and appropriateness of a single code of medical ethics like the Hippocratic oath.**

This answer choice includes contradictory information. The author's conclusion is that the oath must be retained with only minor changes. This is also a loser.

We have two candidates, (A) and (B), so we need to eliminate one. Looking back at (A), we can see that it is the weaker candidate. The term *ought to be reevaluated* is too strong. The author does not actually say that the oath should be reevaluated, just that its non-core values can be altered. Answer choice (B) better matches the main point of the passage. It mentions the criticism of the oath, puts forward the view that some version of it should be retained, and includes the author's main reason for why it should be retained. Therefore, (B) is the correct answer choice.

11. **Correct Answer (E).** *Prep Test 45, Section 2, Passage 2, Question 8.*

> **Which one of the following most accurately describes the organization of the material presented in the passage?**

This is an STR question. The passage has two paragraphs. The first paragraph introduces the traditional position of physicians regarding the Hippocratic Oath, provides background information about the role of the oath in the medical community, and presents the opinions of critics of the oath. The second paragraph presents the author's viewpoint, which is that the oath should be retained, and provides evidence to support this claim. We should anticipate a correct answer choice that describes these functions in this order.

(A) A general principle is described, criticisms of the principle are made, and modifications of the principle are made in light of these criticisms.

This answer choice includes contradictory information. The first two functions match the passage. The Hippocratic Oath can be considered a rule or a principle, and the first paragraph describes it and then provides criticisms of it. However, the third function is stated inaccurately. The author does not modify the oath in response to these criticisms. The discussion about surgery in the second paragraph is an example of how the oath can be reinterpreted, but this is not discussed by critics. This is a loser.

(B) A set of criticisms is put forward, and possible replies to those criticisms are considered and dismissed.

This answer choice includes contradictory and incomplete information. No reference is made to the discussion of the oath in the first paragraph. In addition, the author does not dismiss possible replies to the criticisms of the oath. This is a loser.

(C) The history of a certain code of conduct is discussed, criticisms of the code are mentioned and partially endorsed, and the code is modified as a response.

This answer choice includes contradictory information. It is very similar to (A). The code is not modified as a response to the criticisms. This is another loser.

(D) A general principle is formulated, a partial defense of that principle is presented, and criticisms of the principle are discussed and rejected.

This answer choice presents the functions in the wrong order. The defense of the oath appears in the passage after the criticisms are discussed. This is a loser.

(E) The tradition surrounding a certain code of conduct is discussed, criticisms of that code are mentioned, and a general defense of the code is presented.

This matches our anticipated answer choice. The tradition surrounding the Hippocratic Oath is discussed, critical viewpoints are given, and then the author presents a general defense of the oath. This is the correct answer choice.

---

12. Correct Answer (A). *Prep Test 45, Section 2, Passage 2, Question 10.*

The author's primary purpose in the passage is to

This is a P question, and the author's viewpoint is present. The author's conclusion appears in the fourth sentence of the second paragraph. It is that the core of the Hippocratic Oath should be retained, with minor adaptations to the oath's non-core values by way of revision, supplementation, and modern interpretation. We should anticipate a correct answer choice that combines an appropriate action verb with a description of this conclusion. The correct answer choice will likely be something along the lines of "to support the need for a traditional ethical code."

(A) affirm society's continuing need for a code embodying certain principles

This matches our anticipated answer choice. *Affirm* is an appropriate action verb for a passage that makes a claim, and the description of the author's conclusion is accurate. This is a candidate.

(B) chastise critics within the medical community who support reinterpretation of a code embodying certain principles

Chastise is an inappropriate action verb, and it is too strong. The author acknowledges that the code as written is not a perfect model for medical ethics, as shown by the discussion of slight alterations through revision, supplementation, and modern interpretation. This answer choice focuses on rebutting the critics instead of supporting the oath. This is a loser.

(C) argue that historical doubts about the origin of a certain code are irrelevant to its interpretation

Argue is an appropriate action verb, but the description of the author's conclusion is incomplete. It focuses on a small part of the author's argument that is presented in the first sentence of the second paragraph and fails to address the author's belief that the oath must be retained. This is another loser.

(D) outline the pros and cons of revising a code embodying certain principles

Outline is an inappropriate action verb. Although the passage includes arguments for and against the oath, the author is clearly in favor of the oath. As this is not conveyed in this answer choice, it is a loser.

(E) propose a revision of a code embodying certain principles that will increase the code's applicability to modern times

Propose is an appropriate action verb, but the description of the author's conclusion includes irrelevant information. No specific revision is proposed by the author here. This is also a loser.

As (A) is the only candidate, it is the correct answer choice.

13. **Correct Answer (E).** *Prep Test 45, Section 2, Passage 2, Question 14.*

> **Which one of the following would be most suitable as a title for this passage if it were to appear as an editorial piece?**

This is a Title question–a variant of an MP question. We should approach it the same way we would an MP question. The only difference is that the answer choices are possible titles to the passage rather than direct restatements of the main point. The author's conclusion is that the core of the Hippocratic Oath should be retained, with minor adaptations to the oath's non-core values by way of revision, supplementation, and modern interpretation. We should anticipate a correct answer choice that expresses this conclusion.

(A) "The Ancients versus the Moderns: Conflicting Ideas About Medical Ethics"

This answer choice includes contradictory information. The author does not actually believe that core medical ethics have changed from ancient to modern times. This is a loser.

(B) "Hypocritical Oath: Why 'Managed Care' Proponents are Seeking to Repeal an Ancient Code"

This answer choice includes irrelevant information. There is no discussion of managed care proponents in the passage. This is a loser.

(C) "Genetic Fallacy in the Age of Gene-Splicing: Why the Origins of the Hippocratic Oath Don't Matter"

This answer choice also includes irrelevant information. Gene-splicing is not discussed in the passage. This is another loser.

(D) "The Dead Hand of Hippocrates: Breaking the Hold of Ancient Ideas on Modern Medicine"

This answer choice refers to the wrong viewpoint. The author generally supports the oath. This is also a loser.

(E) "Prescription for the Hippocratic Oath: Facelift or Major Surgery?"

This matches our anticipated answer choice. The author is willing to consider minor changes to the non-core values of the Hippocratic Oath. In addition, the author is rebutting critics of the oath who want major changes. Therefore, the author is in favor of giving the oath a facelift rather than major surgery. This is the correct answer choice.

For Questions 14–16

Until recently, [A)]biologists were unable to explain the fact that pathogens—disease-causing parasites—have evolved to incapacitate, and often overwhelm, their hosts. Such behavior is at odds with the

(5) prevailing view of host-parasite relations—that, in general, host and parasite ultimately develop a benign coexistence. This view is based on the idea that parasites that do not harm their hosts have the best chance for long-term survival: they thrive because

(10) their hosts thrive. [B)]Some biologists, however, recently have suggested that if a pathogen reproduced so extensively as to cause its host to become gravely sick, it could still achieve evolutionary success if its replication led to a level of transmission into new

(15) hosts that exceeded the loss of pathogens resulting from the host's incapacitation. This scenario suggests that even death-causing pathogens can achieve evolutionary success.

One implication of this perspective is that a

(20) pathogen's virulence—its capacity to overcome a host's defenses and incapacitate it—is a function of its mode of transmission. For example, rhinoviruses, which cause the common cold, require physical proximity for transmission to occur. If a rhinovirus

(25) reproduces so extensively in a solitary host that the host is too unwell to leave home for a day, the thousands of new rhinoviruses produced that day will die before they can be transmitted. So, because it is transmitted directly, the common cold is unlikely to

(30) disable its victims.

The opposite can occur when pathogens are transported by a vector—an organism that can carry and transmit an infectious agent. If, for example, a pathogen capable of being transported by a mosquito

(35) reproduces so extensively that its human host is immobilized, it can still pass along its genes if a mosquito bites the host and transmits this dose to the next human it bites. In such circumstances the virulence is likely to be more severe, because the

(40) pathogen has reproduced to such concentration in the host that the mosquito obtains a high dose of the pathogen, increasing the level of transmission to new hosts.

While medical literature generally supports the

(45) hypothesis that vector-borne pathogens tend to be more virulent than directly transmitted pathogens—witness the lethal nature of malaria, yellow fever, typhus, and sleeping sickness, all carried by biting insects—a few directly transmitted pathogens such as

(50) diphtheria and tuberculosis bacteria can be just as lethal. Scientists call these "sit and wait" pathogens, because they are able to remain alive outside their hosts until a new host comes along, without relying on a vector. Indeed, the endurance of these pathogens,

(55) many of which can survive externally for weeks or months before transmission into a new host—compared, for instance, to an average rhinovirus life span of hours—makes them among the most dangerous of all pathogens.

Main Point

The main point is stated in the first and second paragraphs. It is that some biologists believe that pathogens that cause their host to become seriously ill can achieve evolutionary success if their replication results in more individual pathogens being transmitted than are lost due to the incapacitation of the original host, and this is dependent on the mode of transmission.

Paragraph 1

This paragraph introduces an aspect of pathogens (incapacitating hosts) that scientists have been unable to explain and a theory to explain it. The theory is part of the main point.

Paragraph 2

This paragraph discusses an important implication of the theory, which is that a pathogen's virulence is a function of its transmission. This is part of the main point. The paragraph then illustrates this theory with the example of rhinoviruses, which would not be transmitted to as many hosts if they were highly virulent.

Paragraph 3

This paragraph provides a second example to illustrate the implication discussed in the previous paragraph. In this case, a pathogen that is transmitted by a vector is more likely to be highly virulent because this would increase the level of transmission.

Paragraph 4

This paragraph discusses how some pathogens that are transmitted directly are able to survive outside their host for extended periods. These are just as virulent as vector-borne pathogens.

Identify Viewpoints

The first viewpoint is that of biologists in the past, who were unable to explain why pathogens evolved to incapacitate their hosts. The second viewpoint is that of some current biologists now who have an explanation for this phenomenon. The second viewpoint is explored throughout the passage. The author's viewpoint is not present.

Which one of the following most accurately summarizes the main idea of the passage?

This is an MP question. It is an Informational passage, and the author's viewpoint is absent. The main point of the passage is that biologists believe that pathogens that cause their host to become seriously ill can achieve evolutionary success if their replication results in more individual pathogens being transmitted to a new host than are lost due to the incapacitation of the original host, and this is dependent on the mode of transmission. We should anticipate a correct answer choice that expresses this descriptive statement.

(A) A new hypothesis about the host-incapacitating behavior of some pathogens suggests that directly transmitted pathogens are just as virulent as vector-borne pathogens, due to the former's ability to survive outside a host for long periods of time.

This answer choice includes contradictory information. The passage states that there are some directly transmitted pathogens that are as virulent (able to incapacitate a host) as vector-borne pathogens, but this does not mean that all directly transmitted pathogens are as virulent. In addition, the second paragraph mentions the rhinovirus, which is directly transmitted and not very virulent. This is a loser.

(B) A new hypothesis about the host-incapacitating behavior of some pathogens suggests that, while most pathogens reproduce so extensively as to cause their hosts to become gravely sick or even to die, some eventually develop a benign coexistence with their hosts.

This answer choice makes too strong of a claim. The passage does not suggest that most pathogens are very virulent. This is another loser.

(C) A new hypothesis about the host-incapacitating behavior of some pathogens suggests that they are able to achieve reproductive success because they reproduce to a high level of concentration in their new incapacitated hosts.

This answer choice addresses the wrong task. The main point of the passage is about all pathogens that incapacitate their host. This information is relevant to vector-borne pathogens only. This answer choice presents a supporting idea rather than the main point. It is a loser.

(D) A new hypothesis about the host-incapacitating behavior of some pathogens suggests that they are generally able to achieve reproductive success unless their reproduction causes the death of the host.

Again, this answer choice also addresses the wrong task. It presents a supporting detail from the passage rather than the main point. The passage is about all pathogens, and it specifies that some pathogens can be transmitted when their host is dead. This is also a loser.

(E) A new hypothesis about the host-incapacitating behavior of some pathogens suggests that pathogen virulence is generally a function of their mode of transmission, with vector-borne pathogens usually more virulent than directly transmitted pathogens, except for those directly transmitted pathogens able to endure outside their hosts.

This matches our anticipated answer choice. This new hypothesis shows how pathogen virulence is linked to the mode of transmission. The answer choice also includes accurate details about vector-borne pathogens and those that can survive outside their host. This is a candidate

As (E) is the only candidate, it is the correct answer choice.

Which one of the following most accurately describes the organization of the passage?

This is an STR question. The passage has four paragraphs. The first paragraph introduces a new explanation by biologists as to how pathogens could have evolved to incapacitate their hosts. The second paragraph explores an important implication of this hypothesis–that virulence is linked to the mode of transmission. It also provides an example of this implication. The third paragraph shows how vector-borne pathogens can survive even when they are especially virulent. Finally, the last paragraph shows how virulence and mode of transmission are not always linked and provides a few examples of virulent pathogens that are directly transmitted. We should anticipate a correct answer choice that describes these functions in this order.

(A) introduction of a scientific anomaly; presentation of an explanation for the anomaly; mention of an implication of the explanation; discussion of two examples illustrating the implication; discussion of exceptions to the implication

This matches our anticipated answer choice. The first paragraph presents an anomaly (how pathogens could have evolved to incapacitate hosts) and a recent hypothesis to explain this anomaly. The second paragraph discusses an implication of this anomaly and provides an example of it. The third paragraph provides another example of the implication. The final paragraph discusses cases in which the implication does not apply. This is a candidate.

(B) introduction of a scientific anomaly; presentation of an explanation for the anomaly; discussion of two examples illustrating the explanation; discussion of exceptions to the explanation; mention of an implication of the explanation

This answer choice presents the sequence in the wrong order. The implication of the biologist's explanation is given before the examples. In addition, it includes contradictory information. The examples illustrate the implication, not the explanation. This is a loser.

(C) introduction of a scientific anomaly; presentation of an explanation for the anomaly; discussion of two examples illustrating the explanation; mention of an implication of the explanation; discussion of examples illustrating the implication

This answer choice presents the sequence in the wrong order and includes contradictory information. As with the previous answer choice, the examples illustrate the implication of the explanation, not the explanation itself. Additionally, the last function should be exceptions to the implication, not examples of the implication. This is another loser.

(D) introduction of a scientific anomaly; presentation of an implication of the anomaly; discussion of two examples illustrating the implication; discussion of exceptions to the implication

This answer choice includes incomplete and contradictory information. It does not mention the biologist's explanation of the anomaly. In addition, the passage does not discuss an implication of the anomaly but rather an implication of the explanation of the anomaly. This is also a loser.

(E) introduction of a scientific anomaly; discussion of two examples illustrating the anomaly; presentation of an explanation for the anomaly; discussion of examples illustrating the explanation

This answer choice includes incomplete and contradictory information. It does not mention the explanation of the anomaly, the implication of the explanation, nor the exceptions to the implication. In addition, the passage does not include examples that illustrate the explanation. This is another loser.

As (A) is the only candidate, it is the correct answer choice.

16. Correct Answer (C). *Prep Test 47, Section 2, Passage 4, Question 26.*

The primary purpose of the passage is to

This is a P question, and the author's viewpoint is absent. The main point of the passage is that biologists believe that pathogens that cause their host to become seriously ill can achieve evolutionary success if their replication results in more individual pathogens being transmitted to a new host than are lost due to the incapacitation of the original host, and this is dependent on the mode of transmission. We should anticipate a correct answer choice that combines an appropriate action verb with a description of this neutral summary of the key information in the passage. The correct answer choice will likely be something along the lines of "to describe a new theory on host-parasite relations and its implications."

(A) compare examples challenging the prevailing view of host-parasite relations with examples supporting it

Compare is an appropriate action verb for a passage that does not make a claim. However, the description of the main point is not accurate. The author does not compare examples that challenge a hypothesis, but rather presents the hypothesis itself. The last paragraph presents examples of exceptions to the hypothesis, but this is not done to challenge the hypothesis. This is a loser.

(B) argue that the prevailing view of host-parasite relations is correct but is based on a mistaken rationale

Argue is an inappropriate action verb. The author is not arguing for or against the new hypothesis, but merely describing the hypothesis and its implications. This is another loser.

(C) offer a modification to the prevailing view of host-parasite relations

This matches our anticipated answer choice. *Offer* is an appropriate action verb. The author is offering a modification, or a new hypothesis, that goes against the prevailing view of host-parasite relations. This is a candidate.

(D) attack evidence that supports the prevailing view of host-parasite relations

Attack is an inappropriate action verb. The author is not attacking evidence supporting the prevailing view but rather presenting a new view. This is a loser.

(E) examine the origins of the prevailing view of host-parasite relations

Examine is an appropriate action verb. However, the author is not examining the origins of the prevailing view of host-parasite relations. The passage presents a new view. This is another loser.

As (C) is the only candidate, it is the correct answer.

Key Takeaways

23.7% of RC Questions

Main Point (MP) – 9.7% of RC Questions
Structure (STR) – 3.3% of RC Questions
Purpose (P) – 3.3% of RC Questions
Function of a Paragraph (FP) – 1.9% of RC Questions
Function of a Statement (FS) – 5.5% of RC Questions

Question Tasks

MP: Identify the main point of the paragraph

STR: Determine the structure of all or part of the passage

P: Determine the purpose of the passage

FP: Determine the function of a paragraph

FS: Determine the function of a statement

Identify the key structural elements of the passage and understand how they relate to each other.

Example Prompts

MP: Which one of the following most accurately states the main point of the passage?
MP: Which one of the following most accurately expresses the main idea of the passage?
MP: Which one of the following best summarizes the central idea of the passage?

STR: Which one of the following most accurately describes the structure of the passage?
STR: Which one of the following most accurately corresponds to the organization of the passage?
STR: Which one of the following sequences best describes the presentation of the material in the passage?

P: The author's primary purpose in writing the passage is to
P: The passage is primarily concerned with
P: Which one of the following best states the primary purpose of the passage?

FP: The primary function of the first paragraph is to
FP: The discussion in the second paragraph is primarily intended to
FP: Which one of the following best describes the primary purpose of the third paragraph?

FS: The primary function of the reference to _____ (line #) is to
FS: The author mentions _____ primarily in order to
FS: Which one of the following most accurately expresses the primary purpose of the sentence in lines #?

Correct Answer Choices

MP: Accurate restatements of the author's conclusion (author's viewpoint present)

MP: Accurate restatements of the summary of the important information in the passage (author's viewpoint absent)

STR: Sequences of paragraph function descriptions that matches the organizational structure of all or part of the passage

P: Accurate expressions of the author's purpose in writing the passage

P: Statements that combine an appropriate action verb related to making a claim and a description of the author's conclusion (author's viewpoint present)

P: Statements that combine an appropriate action verb related to presenting information and a description of the summary of the key information in the passage (author's viewpoint absent)

FP: Statements that accurately express the function of the referenced paragraph

FS: Statements that accurately express the function of the referenced statement

Incorrect Answer Choices

Descriptive statements (author's viewpoint present) **or conclusions** (author's viewpoint absent) **(MP)**

Sequences that present the paragraph functions in the incorrect order (STR)

Statements with inappropriate action verbs (P, FP, FS)

Statements with appropriate action verbs but incorrect main points (P)

Statements that describe the content of the paragraph but not its function (FP)

Statements that describe the content of the function without reference to the context (FS)

Wrong Task: Accurate statements that do not address the task specified in the prompt (MP)

Wrong Viewpoint: Accurate statements about a viewpoint other than the one specified in the prompt (MP, FS)

Wrong Part of Passage: Accurate statements about a part of the passage not specified in the prompt (STR, FP, FS)

Too Strong: Claims that are too strong to be supported (STR)

Contradictory Information: Statements that contradict information in the passage (MP, STR, P, FP, FS)

Irrelevant Information: Statements that present new information that is not relevant to the task specified in the prompt (MP, STR, P, FP, FS)

Incomplete Information: Accurate statements that omit necessary details (MP, STR, P, FP, FS)

Chapter 4

Information Family

Chapter 4: Information Family

HACKERS
LSAT *Reading Comprehension*

Overview

Example Passage and Questions

In this chapter, you will learn how to identify and solve Information Family questions.

Information Family questions ask you to identify specific information that is explicitly stated in the passage or to determine the contextual meaning of a referenced term. The analysis performed during the initial read-through of the passage is less helpful in anticipating the correct answer choices for Information Family questions than for Synthesis Family questions. However, the analysis is still important because it may make it easier to locate the information in the passage that is necessary to correctly answer a question.

The three question types in this family—Detail (D), Existence (EX), and Meaning (M)—are examined in detail in separate sections. Each section includes step-by-step instructions on how to solve the question type and detailed analyses of example questions. In addition, you will get to tackle practice questions taken from previous administrations of the LSAT. The methods for solving these practice questions are explained thoroughly in the answer keys.

The example questions analyzed in the How-to-Solve subsections reference the following passage, and you should refer back to it as necessary. The analysis of the passage has already been done for you.

For Example Questions 1–3

A)The poet Louise Glück has said that she feels comfortable writing within a tradition often characterized as belonging only to male poets. About her own experience reading poetry, Glück notes that
(5) her gender did not keep her from appreciating the poems of Shakespeare, Blake, Keats, and other male poets. Rather she believed this was the tradition of her language and that it was for this reason her poetic inheritance. She thus views the canon of poets in
(10) English as a literary family to which she clearly belongs. Whereas many contemporary women poets have rejected this tradition as historically exclusionary and rhetorically inadequate for women, Glück embraces it with respect and admiration.

(15)   A)Glück's formative encounters with poetry also provided her with the theoretical underpinnings of her respect for this tradition; she notes that in her youth she could sense many of the great themes and subjects of poetry even before experiencing them in
(20) her own life. These subjects—loss, the passage of time, desire—are timeless, available to readers of any age, gender, or social background. Glück makes no distinction between these subjects as belonging to female or male poets alone, calling them "the great
(25) human subjects." If the aim of a poem is to explore the issue of human mortality, for example, then issues of gender distinction fade behind the presence of this universal reality.

      B)Some of Glück's critics claim that this idea of the
(30) universal is suspect and that the idea that gender issues are transcended by addressing certain subjects may attribute to poetry an innocence that it does not have. They maintain that a female poet writing within a historically male-dominated tradition will on some
(35) level be unable to avoid accepting certain presuppositions, which, in the critics' view, are determined by a long-standing history of denigration and exclusion of female artists. Furthermore, they feel that this long-standing history cannot be confronted
(40) using tools—in Glück's case, poetic forms—forged by the traditions of this history. Instead critics insist that women poets should strive to create a uniquely female poetry by using new forms to develop a new voice.

(45)   A)Glück, however, observes that this ambition, with its insistence on an essentially female perspective, is as limiting as her critics believe the historically male-dominated tradition to be. She holds that to the extent that there are some gender differences that have been
(50) shaped by history, they will emerge in the differing ways that women and men write about the world—indeed, these differences will be revealed with more authority in the absence of conscious intention. She points out that the universal subjects of literature do
(55) not make literature itself timeless and unchanging.

Literature, she maintains, is inescapably historical, and every work, both in what it includes and in what it omits, inevitably speaks of its social and historical context.

Main Point

The main point is stated in the last sentence of the first paragraph. It is that many contemporary women poets have rejected the English poetry tradition as being exclusionary and inadequate for women, but Glück embraces it with respect and admiration. This is a neutral statement that summarizes the two viewpoints present.

Paragraph 1

This paragraph introduces Glück's viewpoint, which is that she belongs to the English poetry tradition, even though it is characterized as belonging to male poets. It also states the main point of the paragraph.

Paragraph 2

This paragraph explores Glück's viewpoint in detail. It states that Glück believes that poems express themes that are available to readers of any age, gender, and background. These themes do not belong exclusively to male or female poets. Therefore, the issue of gender distinctions fades behind the universalism of poetry.

Paragraph 3

This paragraph summarizes the viewpoint of Glück's critics. They feel that women are limited by writing in a male-dominated tradition and that female poets should strive to create poetry that is uniquely female.

Paragraph 4

This paragraph puts forward Glück's rebuttal of her critics' claims. She observes that the insistence on a female perspective is limiting. She also believes that gender differences emerge more strongly without conscious intention. She also points out that literature always reflects its social and historical context.

Identify Viewpoints

The two main viewpoints in this passage are those of Glück and her critics. The author's viewpoint is absent.

1. According to the passage, Glück believes that art reveals gender differences with more authority when which one of the following is true?

   (A) The artist refuses to accept certain presuppositions about gender.
   (B) The artist uses the tools of that art's tradition.
   (C) The artist does not consciously intend to reveal such differences.
   (D) The artist comments on gender issues through the use of other subject matter.
   (E) The artist embraces that art's tradition with respect.

2. Which one of the following statements about Glück is made in the passage?

   (A) She objects to the use of traditional poetic forms to confront the history of the poetic tradition.
   (B) She recognizes that the idea of the universal in poetry is questionable.
   (C) She claims to accept only male poets as her literary family.
   (D) She claims to write from a gender-neutral perspective.
   (E) She claims to have sensed the great themes and subjects of poetry while in her youth.

3. As it is used in the passage, "inheritance" (line 9) refers most specifically to

   (A) the burden that a historically male-dominated poetic canon places on a contemporary woman poet
   (B) the set of poetic forms and techniques considered acceptable within a linguistic culture
   (C) the poetry written in a particular language, whose achievement serves as a model for other poets writing in that language
   (D) the presumption that contemporary poets can write only on subjects already explored by the poets in that language who are considered to be the most celebrated
   (E) the imposition on a poet, based on the poetry of preceding generations in that language, of a particular writing style

Detail

Detail
Existence
Meaning

Detail

≈ 2.13 questions per test

Example Prompts

The passage indicates which one of the following as a factor in _____ ?

According to the passage, what is the advantage of _____ ?

Which one of the following does *the passage mention as* an example of _____ ?

Take These Steps

Locate the paragraph that discusses the topic of the prompt. Use the summary of the paragraph content created during the initial analysis of the passage to do this. Then, find the relevant information in this paragraph. The wording of the prompt can help narrow the search.

Find the detail requested by the prompt. This will be explicitly stated in the passage. It will usually be stated in one sentence but may be expressed over multiple sentences.

Anticipate a correct answer choice that restates the detail requested by the prompt. The correct answer choice will closely paraphrase the passage and may repeat key terms.

Answer Choices

Correct Answer Choices

Statements that accurately restate a detail asked for in the prompt

Incorrect Answer Choices

Wrong viewpoint

Wrong part of passage

Contradictory information

Irrelevant information

Detail (D) questions ask you to retrieve a specific piece of information that is explicitly stated in the passage.

D question prompts include terms such as *according to the passage*, *cite*, *identify*, *state*, or *mention*. However, the prompts of other question types may include these terms as well. Fortunately, D question prompts can also be identified by the fact that they always ask for a specific detail and indicate that this detail is explicitly stated in the passage. D questions can appear in any passage type.

How to Solve D Questions

The first step in solving a D question is to locate the paragraph in which the topic of the prompt is discussed. Each D question prompt introduces a topic and then asks for a detail related to it. The topic is always discussed in a specific section of the passage—usually within a single paragraph. The analysis performed during the initial read-through of the passage is particularly helpful at this stage. Assuming that you summarized the content of each paragraph when noting its function, you should already know where the key ideas of the passage are discussed. You then need to find the relevant information in the paragraph you identified. D question prompts closely paraphrase the language of the passage and often repeat key terms. This means that you can quickly scan the paragraph to identify the information you need.

You now need to find the detail requested by the prompt. This will always be something explicitly stated in the passage. For example, if the prompt asks why bees gather pollen, the passage will clearly state a reason that bees gather pollen. The detail is usually presented in a single sentence, although it may be expressed in multiple sentences.

Once you have located the detail that is being asked for by the prompt, anticipate a correct answer choice that restates it. The correct answer choice will closely paraphrase the passage text and may repeat key terms.

> D EXCEPT questions are common. When you encounter one, the correct answer choice will not restate a detail requested by the prompt, and the four incorrect answer choices will. When answering a D EXCEPT question, the best approach is to eliminate answer choices that restate a detail requested by the prompt until you find one that does not.

Let's look at Example Question 1 (page 121):

According to the passage, Glück believes that art reveals gender differences with more authority when which one of the following is true?

(A) The artist refuses to accept certain presuppositions about gender.
(B) The artist uses the tools of that art's tradition.
(C) The artist does not consciously intend to reveal such differences.
(D) The artist comments on gender issues through the use of other subject matter.
(E) The artist embraces that art's tradition with respect.

The topic of the prompt is Glück's belief about when art reveals gender differences with more authority. Looking back at our analysis of the passage, gender differences are discussed in the fourth paragraph of the passage. Scanning this paragraph, we can see that the terms *gender*, *differences*, and *authority* are used in the second sentence. We should look here for the detail requested by the prompt, which is a requirement for art to reveal gender differences with more authority. The second sentence explicitly states that this occurs in the absence of conscious intention. We should anticipate a correct answer choice that restates this detail.

(A) The artist refuses to accept certain presuppositions about gender.

This answer choice includes irrelevant information. The passage does not state that Glück refuses to accept certain presuppositions about gender. This is a loser.

(B) The artist uses the tools of that art's tradition.

This answer choice includes information from the wrong part of the passage. The first paragraph of the passage strongly implies that Glück believes this. However, this detail has no connection to the discussion on art revealing gender differences with more authority. This is also a loser.

(C) The artist does not consciously intend to reveal such differences.

This matches our anticipated answer choice. It accurately restates the detail we identified in the passage. This is a candidate.

(D) The artist comments on gender issues through the use of other subject matter.

This answer choice includes irrelevant information. The passage does not state that Glück's work comments on gender issues. This is another loser.

(E) The artist embraces that art's tradition with respect.

This answer choice includes information from the wrong part of the passage. Embracing tradition is discussed in the first paragraph of the passage, but this idea is not connected to the issue of art revealing gender differences with more authority. This is a loser as well.

As (C) is the only candidate, it is the correct answer choice.

Looking at the Answer Choices

The correct answer choice is an accurate restatement of the detail that is asked for by the prompt. This detail is always explicitly stated in the passage.

The most common incorrect answer choice is one that includes a detail from the wrong part of the passage or an idea expressed by a viewpoint other than the one specified in the prompt. These incorrect answer choices accurately restate a detail from the passage, but it is not the one requested by the prompt. Incorrect answer choices that include irrelevant information are common as well. These can be tricky because they may state a detail that is requested by the prompt and that can be inferred from the passage. Remember, if the detail is not explicitly stated in the passage, the answer choice cannot be correct. Finally, some incorrect answer choices include contradictory information.

Existence

INFORMATION FAMILY

Detail
Existence
Meaning

Existence
≈ 0.38 questions per test

Example Prompts

Which one of the following does the author *mention in the passage*?

Which one of the following is *stated by the passage*?

The passage asserts which one of the following about _____?

Take These Steps

It is impossible to anticipate a correct answer choice, so proceed directly to eliminating answer choices.

Read through all of the answer choices to identify any related to a detail that you remember from the passage. Go to the relevant section of the passage to determine if the answer choice accurately restates a detail. Use the paragraph summaries from your analysis of the passage to get a sense of where the information related to the remaining answer choices is located. Go through each of these to determine if they accurately restate a detail from the passage.

If you determine with certainty that an answer choice accurately restates a detail from the passage, simply mark it as the correct answer choice and move on to the next question.

Answer Choices

Correct Answer Choices	Incorrect Answer Choices
Statements that accurately restate a detail from the passage	Too strong
	Contradictory information
	Irrelevant information

Existence (EX) questions ask you to determine whether or not a specific detail appears in the passage.

EX question prompts usually include terms such as *state*, *affirm*, *mention*, *cite*, *identify*, *explicitly*, or *directly*. At first glance, EX questions seem similar to D questions. However, it is easy to distinguish between these two question types. D question prompts include a topic and ask for a specific detail related to it. EX question prompts simply ask which answer choice restates a detail from the passage. As EX question prompts do not include a specific topic, you must consider the entire passage when looking for the correct answer choice. EX questions can appear in any passage type.

How to Solve EX Questions

The correct answer choice of an EX question cannot be anticipated. This is because the prompt requires that you identify a detail in the passage, but does not include any significant information to help you find it. Consider the following examples:

> **Which one of the following does the author mention in the passage?**
> **The passage cites which one of the following as a belief of Jonas Salk?**

The first example clearly includes no information that can be used to narrow down your search to a particular section of the passage. The second one may appear to (perhaps only one section of the passage discusses Jonas Salk), but this type of information is only included in an EX question prompt when it relates to the main topic of a passage. Therefore, the second example prompt would only appear if the entire passage was about Jonas Salk, meaning that it does not include enough information to identify a specific section of the passage.

As a result, the first step in solving an EX question is to proceed directly to eliminating answer choices. You need to look at each answer choice and determine whether or not it accurately restates a detail from the passage. It may be tempting to simply read the answer choices and select the one that seems correct based on your memory of the passage. However, this approach is not recommended—the incorrect answer choices are designed to be similar to the information that appears in the passage, making it easy to select an incorrect one if you do not refer back to the passage.

> EX EXCEPT questions are common. When you encounter one, the correct answer choice will not restate a detail from the passage, and four incorrect answer choices will.

Obviously, going through the entire passage for each answer choice would be time consuming. Fortunately, there are ways to speed up the process. Read through all of the answer choices to identify any that state a detail that you remember from the passage. You can then go directly to the relevant section of the passage to determine whether or not the answer choice accurately restates a detail from the passage. For the remaining answer choices, use the paragraph summaries from your analysis of the passage to get a sense of where the information related to each might be. Go through these answer choices until you find one that restates information from the passage.

Once you have determined with certainty that an answer choice accurately restates a detail from the passage, select it as the correct answer choice and move on to the next question. Do not waste time going through the remaining ones unless you have any doubts about your selection. For instructional purposes, we will go through each answer choice even if we have identified one that restates a detail from the question.

Let's look at Example Question 2 (page 121):

> Which one of the following statements about Glück is made in the passage?

(A) She objects to the use of traditional poetic forms to confront the history of the poetic tradition.

(B) She recognizes that the idea of the universal in poetry is questionable.

(C) She claims to accept only male poets as her literary family.

(D) She claims to write from a gender-neutral perspective.

(E) She claims to have sensed the great themes and subjects of poetry while in her youth.

Although the question prompt specifies that the statements are about Glück, this does not identify a specific section of the passage to look at because the entire passage is about Glück. Even the third paragraph, which presents the viewpoints of Glück's critics, cannot be ignored because it still includes statements about Glück. Therefore, we need to eliminate each answer choice one-by-one.

(A) She objects to the use of traditional poetic forms to confront the history of the poetic tradition.

This answer choice includes irrelevant information. Glück does not advocate for or against confronting the history of the poetic tradition anywhere in the passage. This is a loser.

(B) She recognizes that the idea of the universal in poetry is questionable.

This answer choice also includes irrelevant information. The second paragraph discusses Glück's belief in the universality of poetry. Nowhere in the passage is it suggested that she believes that the universal in poetry is questionable. This is another loser.

(C) She claims to accept only male poets as her literary family.

This answer choice makes too strong of a claim. In the first paragraph, Glück acknowledges that she belongs to the English poetry tradition, even though it is characterized as belonging to male poets. However, this does not necessarily mean that she accepts only male poets as her literary family. This is a loser.

(D) She claims to write from a gender-neutral perspective.

This answer choice seems compatible with the information in the passage. In the second paragraph, Glück states that the themes of poetry are available to readers of any age, gender, or social background. She also says that they belong to both male and female poets, and that gender distinction fades. In the fourth paragraph, she states that an insistence on a female perspective is limiting. As this answer choice is closely related to a couple of key ideas in the passage, we will consider it a candidate.

(E) She claims to have sensed the great themes and subjects of poetry while in her youth.

This is a direct paraphrase of part of the first sentence of the second paragraph, which states that Glück could sense many of the great themes and subjects of poetry in her youth. This is a candidate (and given the closeness of the wording, almost certainly the correct answer choice).

As we have two candidates, we need to eliminate one. Looking back at (D), we can see that it is the weaker answer choice. You could infer that Glück makes this claim, but this detail is not explicitly stated anywhere. Therefore, this answer choice includes irrelevant information and can be eliminated. Answer choice (E) directly restates a claim made by Glück in the passage. Therefore, it is the correct answer choice.

Looking at the Answer Choices

The correct answer choice is an accurate restatement of a detail that appears in the passage. This detail is always explicitly stated.

Incorrect answer choices often include irrelevant information. These answer choices include ideas that are closely related to the content of the passage, making them logical inferences. Remember, if an answer choice does not restate a detail explicitly stated in the passage, it is incorrect. Other common incorrect answer choices include contradictory information or make too strong of a claim.

Meaning

Detail
Existence
Meaning

Meaning
≈ 0.66 questions per test

Example Prompts

Which one of the following most accurately expresses what *the author means* by "_____" in line #?

Which one of the following most accurately expresses what is *meant when the author refers to the phrase* "_____" (line #)?

Which one of the following *could replace the phrase* "_____" in line # without substantively altering the author's meaning?

Take These Steps

Locate the referenced term in the passage. If the term is used throughout the passage, focus on the section of text where it is first introduced.

Determine the contextual meaning of the term. Read the sentence that it appears in, as well as the ones that come before and after. Look for clues to understand the specific meaning of the term in the context. If necessary, look earlier and later in the passage for additional clues.

Anticipate a correct answer choice that expresses the specific contextual meaning of the referenced term.

Answer Choices

Correct Answer Choices	Incorrect Answer Choices
Statements that accurately express the contextual meaning of the referenced term	Statements that express a common meaning of the term that does not match the specific contextual meaning
	Contradictory information
	Irrelevant information

Meaning (M) questions ask you to determine the meaning of a referenced term within the context of the passage. It is important to note that you are not being asked for the dictionary definition of the term; instead, you must identify the particular way in which it is used by the author in the passage.

M question prompts usually include terms such as *refer to*, *replace*, or *mean*. Other terms with similar meanings may be used as well. In addition, M question prompts indicate exactly where the referenced term is located in the passage. M questions can appear in any passage type.

How to Solve M Questions

The first step in solving an M question is to locate the referenced term in the passage. It is easy to do this because the prompt will specify where the term is located. If the term is used throughout the passage, focus on the section of text where it is first introduced. Then, you must determine its contextual meaning. Read the sentence that includes the term, as well as the ones that come before and after. Look for clues to understand the specific meaning of the term within the context. If necessary, look earlier and later in the passage for additional clues. Once you understand exactly how the author is using the term, anticipate a correct answer choice that expresses this meaning.

Let's look at Example Question 3 (page 121):

As it is used in the passage, "inheritance" (line 9) refers most specifically to

(A) the burden that a historically male-dominated poetic canon places on a contemporary woman poet

(B) the set of poetic forms and techniques considered acceptable within a linguistic culture

(C) the poetry written in a particular language, whose achievement serves as a model for other poets writing in that language

(D) the presumption that contemporary poets can write only on subjects already explored by the poets in that language who are considered to be the most celebrated

(E) the imposition on a poet, based on the poetry of preceding generations in that language, of a particular writing style

After locating the term *inheritance* in the third sentence of the first paragraph, we should read this sentence and the ones that come before and after it. Based on the sentence in which *inheritance* appears and the one before it, we can see that Glück believes that the poems of Shakespeare, Blake, Keats, and other male poets are the tradition of her language and that this tradition is her poetic inheritance. The sentence that follows the one in which *inheritance* appears makes it clear that Glück feels that these English poets are a family to which she also belongs. In the context, *inheritance* means the tradition of English poetry that Glück belongs to. We should anticipate a correct answer choice that expresses this meaning.

(A) the burden that a historically male-dominated poetic canon places on a contemporary woman poet

This answer choice includes contradictory information. Glück does not state nor imply that the English poetry tradition is a burden. In fact, Glück embraces this tradition with respect and admiration. This is a loser.

(B) the set of poetic forms and techniques considered acceptable within a linguistic culture

This answer choice includes irrelevant information. The passage does not discuss poetic forms and techniques. It also does not address what is acceptable within a linguistic culture. This is another loser.

(C) the poetry written in a particular language, whose achievement serves as a model for other poets writing in that language

This matches our anticipated answer choice. The first clause expresses the idea that the poems of the earlier poets are the tradition of English poetry, and the second clause is compatible with Glück's claim of belonging to this tradition. This is a candidate.

(D) the presumption that contemporary poets can write only on subjects already explored by the poets in that language who are considered to be the most celebrated

This answer choice includes irrelevant information. There is no presumption that poets can only write on subjects already explored by the poets in that language who are considered most celebrated. This is another loser.

(E) the imposition on a poet, based on the poetry of preceding generations in that language, of a particular writing style

This answer choice includes irrelevant information. The passage does not make any reference to the poetry of proceeding generations imposing a particular writing style on Glück (or any other poet). This is also a loser.

As (C) is the only candidate, it is the correct answer choice.

Looking at the Answer Choices

The correct answer choice is an accurate expression of the contextual meaning of the referenced term. The meaning presented in the correct answer choice must match the specific way in which the term is used by the author in the passage.

Incorrect answer choices may include a correct and common definition of the term that does not match the specific contextual meaning. This is why it is important to determine the particular meaning of the term within the context before looking at the answer choice. It is also common for incorrect answer choices to include irrelevant or contradictory information.

Practice Sets: Information Family

Analyze the passages below. Mark the <u>keywords</u>, <u>main points</u>, and <mark>viewpoints</mark> other than the author's. Note the function of each paragraph. Summarize the main points, paragraph content, and viewpoints. Then answer the questions that follow each passage.

With his first published works in the 1950s, Amos Tutuola became the first Nigerian writer to receive wide international recognition. Written in a mix of standard English, idiomatic Nigerian English, and
(5) literal translation of his native language, Yoruba, Tutuola's works were quick to be praised by many literary critics as fresh, inventive approaches to the form of the novel. Others, however, dismissed his works as simple retellings of local tales, full of
(10) unwelcome liberties taken with the details of the well-known story lines. However, to estimate properly Tutuola's rightful position in world literature, it is essential to be clear about the genre in which he wrote; literary critics have assumed too facilely that
(15) he wrote novels.

No matter how flexible a definition of the novel one uses, establishing a set of criteria that enable Tutuola's works to be described as such applies to his works a body of assumptions the works are not
(20) designed to satisfy. Tutuola is not a novelist but a teller of folktales. Many of his critics are right to suggest that Tutuola's subjects are not strikingly original, but it is important to bear in mind that whereas realism and originality are expected of the
(25) novel, the teller of folktales is expected to derive subjects and frameworks from the corpus of traditional lore. The most useful approach to Tutuola's works, then, is one that regards him as working within the African oral tradition.

(30) Within this tradition, a folktale is common property, an expression of a people's culture and social circumstances. The teller of folktales knows that the basic story is already known to most listeners and, equally, that the teller's reputation depends on
(35) the inventiveness with which the tale is modified and embellished, for what the audience anticipates is not an accurate retelling of the story but effective improvisation and delivery. Thus, within the framework of the basic story, the teller is allowed
(40) considerable room to maneuver—in fact, the most brilliant tellers of folktales transform them into unique works.

Tutuola's adherence to this tradition is clear: specific episodes, for example, are often repeated for
(45) emphasis, and he embellishes familiar tales with personal interpretations or by transferring them to modern settings. The blend of English with local idiom and Yoruba grammatical constructs, in which adjectives and verbs are often interchangeable,
(50) re-creates the folktales in singular ways. And, perhaps most revealingly, in the majority of Tutuola's works, the traditional accents and techniques of the teller of folktales are clearly discernible, for example in the

adoption of an omniscient, summarizing voice at the
(55) end of his narratives, a device that is generally recognized as being employed to conclude most folktales.

Main Point

Paragraph 1

Paragraph 2

Paragraph 3

Paragraph 4

Identify Viewpoints

1. According to the passage, some critics have criticized Tutuola's work on the ground that

   (A) his literary works do not exhibit enough similarities to the African oral tradition from which they are drawn
   (B) his mixture of languages is not entirely effective as a vehicle for either traditional folktales or contemporary novels
   (C) his attempt to fuse elements of traditional storytelling style with the format of the novel is detrimental to his artistic purposes
   (D) his writing borrows substantially from well-known story lines and at the same time alters their details
   (E) his unique works are not actually novels, even though he characterizes them as such

2. The author attributes each of the following to Tutuola EXCEPT:

   (A) repetition of elements in his stories for emphasis
   (B) relocation of traditional stories to modern settings
   (C) attainment of international recognition
   (D) use of an omniscient narrator in his works
   (E) transformation of Yoruba folktales into modern novels

The pronghorn, an antelope-like mammal that lives on the western plains of North America, is the continent's fastest land animal, capable of running 90 kilometers per hour and of doing so for several

(5) kilometers. Because no North American predator is nearly fast enough to chase it down, biologists have had difficulty explaining why the pronghorn developed its running prowess. One biologist, however, has recently claimed that pronghorns run as

(10) fast as they do because of adaptation to predators known from fossil records to have been extinct for 10,000 years, such as American cheetahs and long-legged hyenas, either of which, it is believed, were fast enough to run down the pronghorn.

(15) Like all explanations that posit what is called a relict behavior—a behavior that persists though its only evolutionary impetus comes from long-extinct environmental conditions—this one is likely to meet with skepticism. Most biologists distrust explanations positing relict

(20) behaviors, in part because testing these hypotheses is so difficult due to the extinction of a principal component. They typically consider such historical explanations only when a lack of alternatives forces them to do so. But present-day observations sometimes yield

(25) evidence that supports relict behavior hypotheses.

In the case of the pronghorn, researchers have identified much supporting evidence, as several aspects of pronghorn behavior appear to have been shaped by enemies that no longer exist. For example,

(30) pronghorns—like many other grazing animals—roam in herds, which allows more eyes to watch for predators and diminishes the chances of any particular animal being attacked but can also result in overcrowding and increased competition for food. But, since

(35) pronghorns have nothing to fear from present-day carnivores and thus have nothing to gain from herding, their herding behavior appears to be another adaptation to extinct threats. Similarly, if speed and endurance were once essential to survival, researchers would

(40) expect pronghorns to choose mates based on these athletic abilities, which they do—with female pronghorns, for example, choosing the victor after male pronghorns challenge each other in sprints and chases.

Relict behaviors appear to occur in other animals

(45) as well, increasing the general plausibility of such a theory. For example, one study reports relict behavior in stickleback fish belonging to populations that have long been free of a dangerous predator, the sculpin. In the study, when presented with sculpin, these

(50) stickleback fish immediately engaged in stereotypical antisculpin behavior, avoiding its mouth and swimming behind to bite it. Another study found that ground squirrels from populations that have been free from snakes for 70,000 to 300,000 years still clearly recognize

(55) rattlesnakes, displaying stereotypical antirattlesnake behavior in the presence of the snake. Such fear, however, apparently does not persist interminably. Arctic ground squirrels, free of snakes for about 3 million years, appear to be unable to recognize the

(60) threat of a rattlesnake, exhibiting only disorganized caution even after being bitten repeatedly.

Main Point

Paragraph 1

Paragraph 2

Paragraph 3

Paragraph 4

Identify Viewpoints

3. Based on the passage, the term "principal component" (line 21) most clearly refers to which one of the following?

(A) behavior that persists even though the conditions that provided its evolutionary impetus are extinct
(B) the original organism whose descendants' behavior is being investigated as relict behavior
(C) the pronghorn's ability to run 90 kilometers per hour over long distances
(D) the environmental conditions in response to which relict behaviors are thought to have developed
(E) an original behavior of an animal of which certain present-day behaviors are thought to be modifications

4. Which one of the following describes a benefit mentioned in the passage that grazing animals derive from roaming in herds?

(A) The greater density of animals tends to intimidate potential predators.
(B) The larger number of adults in a herd makes protection of the younger animals from predators much easier.
(C) With many animals searching it is easier for the herd to find food and water.
(D) The likelihood that any given individual will be attacked by a predator decreases.
(E) The most defenseless animals can achieve greater safety by remaining in the center of the herd.

5. The passage mentions each of the following as support for the explanation of the pronghorn's speed proposed by the biologist referred to in line 8 EXCEPT:

(A) fossils of extinct animals believed to have been able to run down a pronghorn
(B) the absence of carnivores in the pronghorn's present-day environment
(C) the present-day preference of pronghorns for athletic mates
(D) the apparent need for a similar explanation to account for the herding behavior pronghorns now display
(E) the occurrence of relict behavior in other species

The first thing any embryo must do before it can develop into an organism is establish early polarity—that is, it must set up a way to distinguish its top from its bottom and its back from its front. The

(5) mechanisms that establish the earliest spatial configurations in an embryo are far less similar across life forms than those relied on for later development, as in the formation of limbs or a nervous system: for example, the signals that the developing fruit fly uses

(10) to know its front end from its back end turn out to be radically different from those that the nematode, a type of worm, relies on, and both appear to be quite different from the polarity signals in the development of humans and other mammals.

(15) In the fruit fly, polarity is established by signals inscribed in the yolklike cytoplasm of the egg before fertilization, so that when the sperm contributes its genetic material, everything is already set to go. Given all the positional information that must be

(20) distributed throughout the cell, it takes a fruit fly a week to make an egg, but once that well-appointed egg is fertilized, it is transformed from a single cell into a crawling larva in a day. By contrast, in the embryonic development of certain nematodes, the

(25) point where the sperm enters the egg appears to provide crucial positional information. Once that information is present, little bundles of proteins called p-granules, initially distributed uniformly throughout the cytoplasm, begin to congregate at one end of the

(30) yolk; when the fertilized egg divides, one of the resulting cells gets all the p-granules. The presence or absence of these granules in cells appears to help determine whether their subsequent divisions will lead to the formation of the worm's front or back

(35) half. A similar sperm-driven mechanism is also thought to establish body orientation in some comparatively simple vertebrates such as frogs, though apparently not in more complex vertebrates such as mammals. Research indicates that in human

(40) and other mammalian embryos, polarity develops much later, as many stages of cell division occur with no apparent asymmetries among cells. Yet how polarity is established in mammals is currently a tempting mystery to researchers.

(45) Once an embryo establishes polarity, it relies on sets of essential genes that are remarkably similar among all life forms for elaboration of its parts. There is an astonishing conservation of mechanism in this process: the genes that help make eyes in flies

(50) are similar to the genes that make eyes in mice or humans. So a seeming paradox arises: when embryos of different species are at the one- or few-cell stage and still appear almost identical, the mechanisms of development they use are vastly different; yet when

(55) they start growing brains or extremities and become identifiable as distinct species, the developmental mechanisms they use are remarkably similar.

Main Point

Paragraph 1

Paragraph 2

Paragraph 3

Identify Viewpoints

6. According to the passage, polarity is established in a human embryo

   (A) after more stages of cell division than in frogs
   (B) before the sperm enters the egg
   (C) after positional information is provided by the massing of p-granules
   (D) by the same sperm-driven mechanism as in the nematode
   (E) in the same way as in simpler vertebrates

7. By "conservation of mechanism" (line 48) the author is probably referring to

   (A) how the same mechanism can be used to form different parts of the same organism
   (B) the fact that no genetic material is wasted in development
   (C) how few genes a given organism requires in order to elaborate its parts
   (D) a highly complex organism's requiring no more genetic material than a simpler one
   (E) the fact that analogous structures in different species are brought about by similar genetic means

8. According to the passage, which one of the following is a major difference between the establishment of polarity in the fruit fly and in the nematode?

   (A) The fruit fly embryo takes longer to establish polarity than does the nematode embryo.
   (B) The mechanisms that establish polarity are more easily identifiable in the nematode than in the fruit fly.
   (C) Polarity signals for the fruit fly embryo are inscribed entirely in the egg and these signals for the nematode embryo are inscribed entirely in the sperm.
   (D) Polarity in the fruit fly takes more stages of cell division to become established than in the nematode.
   (E) Polarity is established for the fruit fly before fertilization and for the nematode through fertilization.

The World Wide Web, a network of electronically
produced and interconnected (or "linked") sites, called
pages, that are accessible via personal computer, raises
legal issues about the rights of owners of intellectual
(5)   property, notably those who create documents for
inclusion on Web pages. Some of these owners of
intellectual property claim that unless copyright law is
strengthened, intellectual property on the Web will not
be protected from copyright infringement. Web users,
(10) however, claim that if their ability to access
information on Web pages is reduced, the Web cannot
live up to its potential as an open, interactive medium
of communication.
      The debate arises from the Web's ability to link
(15) one document to another. Links between sites are
analogous to the inclusion in a printed text of
references to other works, but with one difference: the
cited document is instantly retrievable by a user who
activates the link. This immediate accessibility creates
(20) a problem, since current copyright laws give owners of
intellectual property the right to sue a distributor of
unauthorized copies of their material even if that
distributor did not personally make the copies. If
person A, the author of a document, puts the document
(25) on a Web page, and person B, the creator of another
Web page, creates a link to A's document, is B
committing copyright infringement?
      To answer this question, it must first be
determined who controls distribution of a document on
(30) the Web. When A places a document on a Web page,
this is comparable to recording an outgoing message
on one's telephone answering machine for others to
hear. When B creates a link to A's document, this is
akin to B's giving out A's telephone number, thereby
(35) allowing third parties to hear the outgoing message for
themselves. Anyone who calls can listen to the
message; that is its purpose. While B's link may
indeed facilitate access to A's document, the crucial
point is that A, simply by placing that document on the
(40) Web, is thereby offering it for distribution. Therefore,
even if B leads others to the document, it is A who
actually controls access to it. Hence creating a link to a
document is not the same as making or distributing a
copy of that document. Moreover, techniques are
(45) already available by which A can restrict access to a
document. For example, A may require a password to
gain entry to A's Web page, just as a telephone owner
can request an unlisted number and disclose it only to
selected parties. Such a solution would compromise
(50) the openness of the Web somewhat, but not as much as
the threat of copyright infringement litigation.
Changing copyright law to benefit owners of
intellectual property is thus ill-advised because it
would impede the development of the Web as a public
(55) forum dedicated to the free exchange of ideas.

Main Point

Paragraph 1

Paragraph 2

Paragraph 3

Identify Viewpoints

9. Which one of the following is closest in meaning to the term "strengthened" as that term is used in line 8 of the passage?

   (A) made more restrictive
   (B) made uniform worldwide
   (C) made to impose harsher penalties
   (D) dutifully enforced
   (E) more fully recognized as legitimate

10. According to the passage, present copyright laws

   (A) allow completely unrestricted use of any document placed by its author on a Web page
   (B) allow those who establish links to a document on a Web page to control its distribution to others
   (C) prohibit anyone but the author of a document from making a profit from the document's distribution
   (D) allow the author of a document to sue anyone who distributes the document without permission
   (E) should be altered to allow more complete freedom in the exchange of ideas

Through the last half century, the techniques used by certain historians of African art for judging the precise tribal origins of African sculptures on the basis of style have been greatly refined. However, as
(5) one recent critic of the historians' classificatory assumptions has put it, the idea that the distribution of a particular style is necessarily limited to the area populated by one tribe may be "a dreadful oversimplification . . . a decided falsification of the
(10) very life of art in Africa."

Objects and styles have often been diffused through trade, most notably by workshops of artists who sell their work over a large geographical area. Styles cannot be narrowly defined as belonging
(15) uniquely to a particular area; rather, there are important "centers of style" throughout Africa where families, clans, and workshops produce sculpture and other art that is dispersed over a large, multitribal geographical area. Thus, a family of artists belonging
(20) to a single ethnic group may produce sculpture on commission for several neighboring tribes. While this practice contributes to a marked uniformity of styles across a large area, the commissioned works must nevertheless be done to some extent in the style of
(25) the tribe commissioning the work. This leads to much confusion on the part of those art historians who attempt to assign particular objects to individual groups on the basis of style.

One such center of style is located in the village
(30) of Ouri, in central Burkina Faso, where members of the Konaté family continue a long tradition of sculpture production not only for five major neighboring ethnic groups, but in recent times also for the tourist trade in Ouagadougou. The Konaté
(35) sculptors are able to distinguish the characteristics of the five styles in which they carve, and will point to the foliate patterns that radiate from the eyes of a Nuna ask, or the diamond-shaped mouth of many Ko masks, as characteristics of a particular tribal style
(40) that must be included to satisfy their clients. Nevertheless, their work is consistent in its proportions, composition, color, and technique. In fact, although the Konaté sculptors can identify the styles they carve, the characteristic patterns are so
(45) subtly different that few people outside of the area can distinguish Nuna masks from Ko masks.

Perhaps historians of African art should ask if objects in similar styles were produced in centers of style, where artists belonging to one ethnic group
(50) produced art for all of their neighbors. Perhaps it is even more important to cease attempting to break down large regional styles into finer and finer tribal styles and substyles, and to recognize that artists in Africa often do not produce work only in their own
(55) narrowly defined ethnic contexts. As the case of the Konaté sculptors makes clear, one cannot readily tell which group produced an object by analyzing fine style characteristics.

Main Point

Paragraph 1

Paragraph 2

Paragraph 3

Paragraph 4

Identify Viewpoints

11. According to the passage, which one of the following is a feature that Konaté sculptors can identify as a requirement of a particular tribal style?

    (A) horizontal incisions
    (B) eye position
    (C) top attachments
    (D) bottom decorations
    (E) mouth shape

12. Which one of the following does the author attribute to the Konaté sculptors?

    (A) use of nontraditional materials in sculptures
    (B) production of sculptures in several distinct styles that are nevertheless very similar to one another
    (C) stylistic innovations that have influenced the work of other sculptors in a large geographical area
    (D) adoption of a carving style that was previously used only by members of a different tribe
    (E) introduction of the practice of producing sculptures for neighboring groups

13. Which one of the following most accurately expresses what the author means by "centers of style" (line 16)?

    (A) geographical areas in which masks and similar sculptures are for the most part interchangeable among a number of closely connected tribes who use them
    (B) locations in which works of art are produced by sculptors using a particular style who then instruct other artists throughout large surrounding geographical areas
    (C) locations in which stylistically consistent but subtly varied works of art are produced and distributed to ethnically varied surrounding areas
    (D) large geographical areas throughout which the various tribes produce works of art that differ subtly along ethnic lines but are so similar that they are very difficult for outside observers to distinguish from one another
    (E) locations in which sculptures and similar works of art are traditionally produced by a diverse community of artists who migrate in from various tribes of surrounding areas

For Questions 1–2

With his first published works in the 1950s, Amos Tutuola became the first Nigerian writer to receive wide international recognition. Written in a mix of standard English, idiomatic Nigerian English, and
(5) literal translation of his native language, Yoruba, Tutuola's works were quick to be praised by A)many literary critics as fresh, inventive approaches to the form of the novel. B)Others, however, dismissed his works as simple retellings of local tales, full of
(10) unwelcome liberties taken with the details of the well-known story lines. However, to estimate properly Tutuola's rightful position in world literature, it is essential to be clear about the genre in which he wrote; literary critics have assumed too facilely that
(15) he wrote novels.

No matter how flexible a definition of the novel one uses, establishing a set of criteria that enable Tutuola's works to be described as such applies to his works a body of assumptions the works are not
(20) designed to satisfy. Tutuola is not a novelist but a teller of folktales. B)Many of his critics are right to suggest that Tutuola's subjects are not strikingly original, but it is important to bear in mind that whereas realism and originality are expected of the
(25) novel, the teller of folktales is expected to derive subjects and frameworks from the corpus of traditional lore. The most useful approach to Tutuola's works, then, is one that regards him as working within the African oral tradition.
(30) Within this tradition, a folktale is common property, an expression of a people's culture and social circumstances. The teller of folktales knows that the basic story is already known to most listeners and, equally, that the teller's reputation depends on
(35) the inventiveness with which the tale is modified and embellished, for what the audience anticipates is not an accurate retelling of the story but effective improvisation and delivery. Thus, within the framework of the basic story, the teller is allowed
(40) considerable room to maneuver—in fact, the most brilliant tellers of folktales transform them into unique works.

Tutuola's adherence to this tradition is clear: specific episodes, for example, are often repeated for
(45) emphasis, and he embellishes familiar tales with personal interpretations or by transferring them to modern settings. The blend of English with local idiom and Yoruba grammatical constructs, in which adjectives and verbs are often interchangeable,
(50) re-creates the folktales in singular ways. And, perhaps most revealingly, in the majority of Tutuola's works, the traditional accents and techniques of the teller of folktales are clearly discernible, for example in the adoption of an omniscient, summarizing voice at the
(55) end of his narratives, a device that is generally recognized as being employed to conclude most folktales.

Main Point

The main point is stated in the last sentence of the first and second paragraph. It is that critics have inaccurately assumed that Tutuola wrote novels though he actually belongs to the African oral tradition. This is the author's conclusion.

Paragraph 1

This paragraph provides background information. It states that Tutuola was the first Nigerian writer to gain recognition, and that his works include a mix of languages. Two opposing viewpoints are also introduced. Tutuola's supporters feel his works are fresh approaches to the novel, while critics dismiss his works as simple retellings of local tales. This paragraph also states the first part of the main point.

Paragraph 2

This paragraph provides details to support the author's claim that Tutuola is not a novelist but instead belonged to the African oral tradition. The second part of the main point is stated in this paragraph as well.

Paragraph 3

This paragraph provides background information about the folktale, which is an important part of the African oral tradition.

Paragraph 4

The last paragraph supports the claim that Tutuola's works are part of the African oral tradition. It describes the elements of his works that demonstrate his adherence to this tradition.

Identify Viewpoints

The viewpoints of those who praise Tutuola's works are mentioned briefly, while the viewpoint of those who criticize Tutuola's works is explored in more detail. The author's viewpoint is also present. It rebuts both of the other viewpoints.

1. **Correct Answer (D).** *Prep Test 56, Section 4, Passage 1, Question 4.*

According to the passage, some critics have criticized Tutuola's work on the ground that

This is a D question. The topic of the prompt is the grounds on which critics have criticized Tutuola's work. Looking back at our analysis of the passage, we can see that the viewpoint of critics of Tutuola's work is discussed primarily in the first paragraph. They dismiss his work as simple retellings of local tales that are full of unwelcome liberties taken with the details of the well-known story lines. We should anticipate a correct answer choice that restates this.

(A) his literary works do not exhibit enough similarities to the African oral tradition from which they are drawn

This answer choice presents the wrong viewpoint and includes contradictory information. Critics of his work do not make any reference to the African oral tradition. The author discusses this and argues that his work has many similarities to the African oral tradition. Therefore, this is a loser.

(B) his mixture of languages is not entirely effective as a vehicle for either traditional folktales or contemporary novels

This answer choice presents the wrong viewpoint and includes irrelevant information. The author discusses Tutuola's mixture of languages in the final paragraph and states that this re-creates the folktales in singular ways. This is also a loser.

(C) his attempt to fuse elements of traditional storytelling style with the format of the novel is detrimental to his artistic purposes

This answer choice includes irrelevant information. The fusion of traditional storytelling with the novel format being detrimental is not discussed in the passage. This is a loser.

(D) his writing borrows substantially from well-known story lines and at the same time alters their details

This matches our anticipated answer choice. It is an accurate paraphrase of the detail we identified earlier. This is a candidate.

(E) his unique works are not actually novels, even though he characterizes them as such

This answer choice presents the wrong viewpoint. The critics do not claim that his works are not actually novels. This is the author's position. This is another loser.

As (D) is the only candidate, it is the correct answer choice.

2. **Correct Answer (E).** *Prep Test 56, Section 4, Passage 1, Question 5.*

The author attributes each of the following to Tutuola EXCEPT:

This is an EX EXCEPT question. The prompt mentions Tutuola, but this is the main topic of the passage. We cannot use this topic to narrow down our search to a particular section of the passage. Therefore, we need to go through each answer choice one-by-one. As this is an EXCEPT question, we should anticipate a correct answer choice that states a detail that is not in the passage.

(A) repetition of elements in his stories for emphasis

This is stated in the passage. The author attributes this detail to Tutuola in the fourth paragraph. This is a loser.

(B) relocation of traditional stories to modern settings

This is stated in the passage. The author attributes this detail to Tutuola in the fourth paragraph. This is a loser.

(C) attainment of international recognition

This is stated in the passage. The author attributes this detail to Tutuola in the first paragraph. This is a loser.

(D) use of an omniscient narrator in his works

This is stated in the passage. The author attributes this detail to Tutuola in the fourth paragraph. This is a loser.

(E) transformation of Yoruba folktales into modern novels

This is not stated in the passage. Yoruba folktales are not discussed anywhere in the passage. In addition, the author argues throughout the passage that Tutuola's works are not novels. Therefore, this is the correct answer choice.

For Questions 3–5

The pronghorn, an antelope-like mammal that lives on the western plains of North America, is the continent's fastest land animal, capable of running 90 kilometers per hour and of doing so for several
(5) kilometers. Because no North American predator is nearly fast enough to chase it down, biologists have had difficulty explaining why the pronghorn developed its running prowess. A)One biologist, however, has recently claimed that pronghorns run as
(10) fast as they do because of adaptation to predators known from fossil records to have been extinct for 10,000 years, such as American cheetahs and long-legged hyenas, either of which, it is believed, were fast enough to run down the pronghorn.
(15) Like all explanations that posit what is called a relict behavior—a behavior that persists though its only evolutionary impetus comes from long-extinct environmental conditions—this one is likely to meet with skepticism. B)Most biologists distrust explanations positing relict
(20) behaviors, in part because testing these hypotheses is so difficult due to the extinction of a principal component. They typically consider such historical explanations only when a lack of alternatives forces them to do so. But present-day observations sometimes yield
(25) evidence that supports relict behavior hypotheses.
In the case of the pronghorn, researchers have identified much supporting evidence, as several aspects of pronghorn behavior appear to have been shaped by enemies that no longer exist. For example,
(30) pronghorns—like many other grazing animals—roam in herds, which allows more eyes to watch for predators and diminishes the chances of any particular animal being attacked but can also result in overcrowding and increased competition for food. But, since
(35) pronghorns have nothing to fear from present-day carnivores and thus have nothing to gain from herding, their herding behavior appears to be another adaptation to extinct threats. Similarly, if speed and endurance were once essential to survival, researchers would
(40) expect pronghorns to choose mates based on these athletic abilities, which they do—with female pronghorns, for example, choosing the victor after male pronghorns challenge each other in sprints and chases.
Relict behaviors appear to occur in other animals
(45) as well, increasing the general plausibility of such a theory. For example, one study reports relict behavior in stickleback fish belonging to populations that have long been free of a dangerous predator, the sculpin. In the study, when presented with sculpin, these
(50) stickleback fish immediately engaged in stereotypical antisculpin behavior, avoiding its mouth and swimming behind to bite it. Another study found that ground squirrels from populations that have been free from snakes for 70,000 to 300,000 years still clearly recognize
(55) rattlesnakes, displaying stereotypical antirattlesnake behavior in the presence of the snake. Such fear, however, apparently does not persist interminably. Arctic ground squirrels, free of snakes for about 3 million years, appear to be unable to recognize the
(60) threat of a rattlesnake, exhibiting only disorganized caution even after being bitten repeatedly.

Main Point

The main point is stated in the last sentences of the second paragraph and the first sentence of the third paragraph. It is that there is evidence that the pronghorn's ability to outrun any predator is a relict behavior.

Paragraph 1

The first paragraph provides background information about the pronghorn and introduces the mystery about this animal's ability to run at high speeds. It then introduces the viewpoint of a biologist that this ability is a relict behavior.

Paragraph 2

This paragraph defines relict behavior and briefly explains why some biologists mistrust this explanation. It then presents part of the main point, that there is evidence to support the relict behavior theory in general.

Paragraph 3

This paragraph specifies that there is evidence to support the relict behavior theory in the case of the pronghorn. It then provides examples of aspects of pronghorn behavior that resulted from predators that no longer exist, such as herding and mate selection.

Paragraph 4

This paragraph provides supporting details for the relict behavior theory. It states that relict behavior exists in other animals, which makes it a plausible explanation for the pronghorn's speed. It then presents the examples of stickleback fish and ground squirrels. It also states that relict behavior is not permanent and illustrates this with the example of arctic squirrels.

Identify Viewpoints

The author's viewpoint is present and is the focus of the passage. The author supports the viewpoint of biologists who believe relict behavior explains the pronghorn's speed. The viewpoint of biologists who distrust this theory is mentioned in passing.

3. **Correct Answer (D).** *Prep Test 46, Section 1, Passage 3, Question 17.*

> **Based on the passage, the term "principal component" (line 21) most clearly refers to which one of the following?**

This is an M question. The term *principal component* is located in the second sentence of the second paragraph. Reading this sentence, we can see that *principal component* is something that plays an important role in relict behavior and that is extinct. In the previous sentence, the author specifies that the impetus for relict behavior is long-extinct environmental conditions. Therefore, *principal component* in this context means *long-extinct environmental conditions*. We should anticipate a correct answer choice that restates this.

> **(A) behavior that persists even though the conditions that provided its evolutionary impetus are extinct**

This answer choice includes contradictory information. The passage makes it clear that the principal component is not a behavior—it contributes to the behavior. This is a loser.

> **(B) the original organism whose descendants' behavior is being investigated as relict behavior**

Again, this answer choice includes contradictory information. The principal component contributes to the behavior—it is not an organism that exhibits this behavior. This is another loser.

> **(C) the pronghorn's ability to run 90 kilometers per hour over long distances**

Again, this answer choice includes contradictory information. It is actually almost identical to answer choice (A). In the case of the pronghorn, the behavior that persists is the ability to run 90 kilometers per hour. The principal component contributes to this behavior—it is not the behavior itself. This is also a loser.

> **(D) the environmental conditions in response to which relict behaviors are thought to have developed**

This matches our anticipated answer choice. It accurately expresses the contextual meaning we identified. This is a candidate.

> **(E) an original behavior of an animal of which certain present-day behaviors are thought to be modifications**

This answer choice includes contradictory information. As with answer choices (A) and (C), the principal component is the environmental conditions that produced the behavior, not the behavior itself. This is another loser.

As (D) is the only candidate, it is the correct answer choice.

4. **Correct Answer (D).** *Prep Test 46, Section 1, Passage 3, Question 19.*

> **Which one of the following describes a benefit mentioned in the passage that grazing animals derive from roaming in herds?**

This is a D question. The topic of the prompt is a benefit mentioned in the passage that grazing animals derive from roaming in herds. Looking back at our analysis of the passage, we can see that herding is discussed in the third paragraph. The second sentence of this paragraph states that herding results in more eyes to watch for predators and that this diminishes the chances of any particular animal being attacked. As this is the only benefit of herding mentioned, we should anticipate a correct answer choice that restates this detail.

(A) The greater density of animals tends to intimidate potential predators.

This answer choice includes irrelevant information. The intimidation of potential predators is not discussed in the passage. This is a loser.

(B) The larger number of adults in a herd makes protection of the younger animals from predators much easier.

This answer choice also includes irrelevant information. It may be inferable that the presence of more adults makes the protection of younger animals easier, but this is not explicitly stated. Therefore, this is a loser as well.

(C) With many animals searching it is easier for the herd to find food and water.

This answer choice includes irrelevant information as well. Finding food and water is not mentioned. This is a loser.

(D) The likelihood that any given individual will be attacked by a predator decreases.

This matches our anticipated answer choice. It is an accurate restatement of the detail we identified. This is a candidate.

(E) The most defenseless animals can achieve greater safety by remaining in the center of the herd.

Again, this answer choice includes irrelevant information. The relative safety of animals in the center of the herd is not discussed. This is a loser.

As (D) is the only candidate, it is the correct answer choice.

5. **Correct Answer (B).** *Prep Test 46, Section 1, Passage 3, Question 20.*

The passage mentions each of the following as support for the explanation of the pronghorn's speed proposed by the biologist referred to in line 8 EXCEPT:

This is a D EXCEPT question. Although a specific topic and line number is included in the prompt, we will have to look throughout the passage. This is because the topic and line number refer to the main point of the passage. The support for the explanation of the pronghorn's speed is discussed throughout the passage. Therefore, we need to go through each answer choice one-by-one. As this is an EXCEPT question, we should anticipate a correct answer choice that states a detail that is not in the passage or that does not provide support for the explanation of the pronghorn's speed.

(A) fossils of extinct animals believed to have been able to run down a pronghorn

This is stated in the passage. The author mentions in the first paragraph that there are fossils of extinct animals fast enough to run down a pronghorn that could have lived near pronghorns many years ago. This supports the idea that the pronghorn's speed is a relict behavior. Therefore, this is a loser.

(B) the absence of carnivores in the pronghorn's present-day environment

This is not stated in the passage. The third paragraph states that pronghorns have nothing to fear from present-day carnivores. However, this does not mean that there are no carnivores. It means that pronghorns do not need to fear the ones that exist in their environment. This is a candidate and is almost certainly the correct answer choice, but we will go through the remaining answer choices to be certain.

(C) the present-day preference of pronghorns for athletic mates

This is stated in the third paragraph. Because female pronghorns prefer male pronghorns with greater speed and endurance, these characteristics must have been an evolutionary advantage at some point. This is another loser.

(D) the apparent need for a similar explanation to account for the herding behavior pronghorns now display

This is stated in the passage. The third paragraph presents herding as a behavior that also cannot be explained by current environmental conditions, which necessitates the need for a relict behavior explanation. This is a loser.

(E) the occurrence of relict behavior in other species

This is stated in the passage. The last paragraph presents a couple of examples of relict behavior in the species to support the idea that the pronghorn's speed is also a relict behavior. This is a loser.

As (B) is the only candidate, it is the correct answer choice.

For Questions 6–8

The first thing any embryo must do before it can develop into an organism is establish early polarity— that is, it must set up a way to distinguish its top from its bottom and its back from its front. The
(5) mechanisms that establish the earliest spatial configurations in an embryo are far less similar across life forms than those relied on for later development, as in the formation of limbs or a nervous system: for example, the signals that the developing fruit fly uses
(10) to know its front end from its back end turn out to be radically different from those that the nematode, a type of worm, relies on, and both appear to be quite different from the polarity signals in the development of humans and other mammals.

(15) In the fruit fly, polarity is established by signals inscribed in the yolklike cytoplasm of the egg before fertilization, so that when the sperm contributes its genetic material, everything is already set to go. Given all the positional information that must be
(20) distributed throughout the cell, it takes a fruit fly a week to make an egg, but once that well-appointed egg is fertilized, it is transformed from a single cell into a crawling larva in a day. By contrast, in the embryonic development of certain nematodes, the
(25) point where the sperm enters the egg appears to provide crucial positional information. Once that information is present, little bundles of proteins called p-granules, initially distributed uniformly throughout the cytoplasm, begin to congregate at one end of the
(30) yolk; when the fertilized egg divides, one of the resulting cells gets all the p-granules. The presence or absence of these granules in cells appears to help determine whether their subsequent divisions will lead to the formation of the worm's front or back
(35) half. A similar sperm-driven mechanism is also thought to establish body orientation in some comparatively simple vertebrates such as frogs, though apparently not in more complex vertebrates such as mammals. Research indicates that in human
(40) and other mammalian embryos, polarity develops much later, as many stages of cell division occur with no apparent asymmetries among cells. Yet how polarity is established in mammals is currently a tempting mystery to researchers.

(45) Once an embryo establishes polarity, it relies on sets of essential genes that are remarkably similar among all life forms for elaboration of its parts. There is an astonishing conservation of mechanism in this process: the genes that help make eyes in flies
(50) are similar to the genes that make eyes in mice or humans. So a seeming paradox arises: when embryos of different species are at the one- or few-cell stage and still appear almost identical, the mechanisms of development they use are vastly different; yet when
(55) they start growing brains or extremities and become identifiable as distinct species, the developmental mechanisms they use are remarkably similar.

Main Point

The main point is stated in the second sentence of the first paragraph. It is that the mechanisms that establish the earliest spatial configurations (polarity) are less similar across life forms than those relied on in later stages of development.

Paragraph 1

This paragraph provides a definition of polarity, which is a concept discussed throughout the passage. It also states the main point, and provides several examples (fruit flies, nematodes, and humans and other mammals) to illustrate differences in establishing polarity.

Paragraph 2

This paragraph expands on the examples in the previous paragraph. It discusses in detail how polarity is established in fruit flies, nematodes, and humans and other mammals. It also introduces one additional example (simple vertebrates such as frogs).

Paragraph 3

This paragraph provides additional supporting details for the main point. It explains that once polarity is established, the embryos of different species use similar genes for the elaboration of their parts. It then discusses a paradox that arises; namely, embryos of all species at the early stages look similar but use different genes, while embryos at the later stages look different but use similar genes.

Identify Viewpoints

The author's viewpoint is present and is the focus of the passage. There are no other viewpoints.

6. Correct Answer (A). *Prep Test 48, Section 3, Passage 4, Question 23.*

According to the passage, polarity is established in a human embryo

This is a D question. The topic of the prompt is the establishment of polarity in a human embryo. Looking back at our analysis of the passage, we can see that although humans are introduced in the first paragraph, they are discussed in detail in the second paragraph. The second to last sentence of this paragraph states that research indicates that in human and other mammalian embryos, polarity develops much later, as many stages of cell division occur with no apparent asymmetries among cells. Given that *later* is a comparative term, we should determine what is being compared here. The previous sentence discusses how a sperm-driven mechanism is also thought to establish body orientation in some comparatively simple vertebrates such as frogs. Therefore, we can anticipate a correct answer choice that states that polarity is established in a human embryo later than in simple vertebrates such as frogs.

(A) after more stages of cell division than in frogs

This matches our anticipated answer choice. The passage states that polarity in humans develops later because many stages of cell division occur (which means that more cell division occurs in human embryos before polarity is established than in frog embryos). This is a candidate.

(B) before the sperm enters the egg

This answer choice includes information from the wrong part of the passage. Earlier in the second paragraph, it is stated that fruit flies, nematodes, and frogs seem to all have sperm driven mechanisms of polarity. However, the second to last sentence of this paragraph states that human embryos establish polarity much later. This is a loser.

(C) after positional information is provided by the massing of p-granules

Again, this answer choice includes information from the wrong part of the passage. This is how nematodes establish polarity, not humans. This is another loser.

(D) by the same sperm-driven mechanism as in the nematode

This answer choice also includes contradictory information. The passage states that simple vertebrates use a mechanism similar to that of nematodes, but not complex vertebrates such as mammals. This is a loser.

(E) in the same way as in simpler vertebrates

This answer choice includes contradictory information. It is wrong for the same reason as answer choice (D). This is another loser.

As (A) is the only candidate, it is the correct answer choice.

7. Correct Answer (E). *Prep Test 48, Section 3, Passage 4, Question 24.*

By "conservation of mechanism" (line 48) the author is probably referring to

This is an M question. The phrase *conservation of mechanism* is located in the second sentence of the third paragraph. Reading this sentence, we can see that *conservation of mechanism* relates to how the genes involved in the development of specific body parts are similar among different species. In the previous sentence, the author states that after polarity is established, the genes used to elaborate parts are similar among all life forms. The sentence after the one in which the phrase appears discusses how when embryos of different species start developing brains or extremities, the developmental mechanisms (i.e. genes) are remarkably similar. Therefore, we can easily see that what *conservation of mechanism* refers to is related to the idea that the embryos of different species use similar genes to develop body parts. We should anticipate a correct answer choice that expresses this meaning.

(A) how the same mechanism can be used to form different parts of the same organism

This answer choice includes contradictory information. The passage states that similar genes in different species are used to develop the same parts. It uses the example of eyes in fruit flies, mice, and humans. This is a loser.

(B) the fact that no genetic material is wasted in development

This answer choice provides a common definition of the term *conservation* that does not match how the term *conservation of mechanism* is used in the passage. This is another loser.

(C) how few genes a given organism requires in order to elaborate its parts

This answer choice includes irrelevant information. The passage never mentions the number of genes in a given organism. This is also a loser.

(D) a highly complex organism's requiring no more genetic material than a simpler one

Again, this answer choice includes irrelevant information. The passage does not discuss the relative amounts of genetic material in complex and simple organisms. This is a loser.

(E) the fact that analogous structures in different species are brought about by similar genetic means

This matches our anticipated answer. Analogous structures (eyes) in different species (flies, mice, and humans) are brought about by similar genetic means. This is the correct answer choice.

---

8. **Correct Answer (E).** *Prep Test 48, Section 3, Passage 4, Question 26.*

> **According to the passage, which one of the following is a major difference between the establishment of polarity in the fruit fly and in the nematode?**

This is a D question. The topic of the prompt is a difference between the establishment of polarity in the fruit fly and in the nematode. The examples of the fruit fly and nematode are discussed in detail in the second paragraph. The first sentence of this paragraph states that fruit fly polarity is established by signals inscribed in the yolklike cytoplasm of the egg before fertilization. The transitional term *by contrast* is used to introduce the discussion of nematode polarity. For this type of animal, the point where the sperm enters the egg appears to provide crucial positional information to establish polarity. The main difference seems to be that polarity is established before fertilization in fruit flies and after fertilization in nematodes. We should anticipate a correct answer choice that restates this.

(A) The fruit fly embryo takes longer to establish polarity than does the nematode embryo.

This answer choice includes irrelevant information. The passage does not discuss how long it takes to establish polarity. This is a loser.

(B) The mechanisms that establish polarity are more easily identifiable in the nematode than in the fruit fly.

This answer choice also includes irrelevant information. There is no indication that the mechanisms are easier to identify in one species. This is another loser.

(C) Polarity signals for the fruit fly embryo are inscribed entirely in the egg and these signals for the nematode embryo are inscribed entirely in the sperm.

This does not match our anticipated answer choice, but it seems related. If fruit fly polarity is established before fertilization, then the polarity signals must be in the egg. In contrast, if nematode polarity is established after fertilization, then the polarity signals must be in the sperm. This is a candidate.

(D) Polarity in the fruit fly takes more stages of cell division to become established than in the nematode.

This answer choice includes irrelevant information. The passage does not explicitly state how many stages of cell division are required for polarity to be established in fruit flies or nematodes. This is a loser.

(E) Polarity is established for the fruit fly before fertilization and for the nematode through fertilization.

This matches our anticipated answer choice exactly. This is a candidate as well.

As we have two candidates, we must eliminate one. Looking back at answer choice (C), we can see it is the weaker candidate. The use of the term *entirely* results in too strong of a claim. The passage states that the point where the sperm enters the egg appears to provide crucial positional information. The term *crucial information* does not mean all information. It may be that some non-crucial information is inscribed on the egg. For this reason, we can eliminate (C) and select (E), which directly matches our anticipated answer choice.

For Questions 9–10

The World Wide Web, a network of electronically produced and interconnected (or "linked") sites, called pages, that are accessible via personal computer, raises legal issues about the rights of owners of intellectual
(5) property, notably those who create documents for inclusion on Web pages. A)Some of these owners of intellectual property claim that unless copyright law is strengthened, intellectual property on the Web will not be protected from copyright infringement. B)Web users,
(10) however, claim that if their ability to access information on Web pages is reduced, the Web cannot live up to its potential as an open, interactive medium of communication.

The debate arises from the Web's ability to link
(15) one document to another. Links between sites are analogous to the inclusion in a printed text of references to other works, but with one difference: the cited document is instantly retrievable by a user who activates the link. This immediate accessibility creates
(20) a problem, since current copyright laws give owners of intellectual property the right to sue a distributor of unauthorized copies of their material even if that distributor did not personally make the copies. If person A, the author of a document, puts the document
(25) on a Web page, and person B, the creator of another Web page, creates a link to A's document, is B committing copyright infringement?

To answer this question, it must first be determined who controls distribution of a document on
(30) the Web. When A places a document on a Web page, this is comparable to recording an outgoing message on one's telephone answering machine for others to hear. When B creates a link to A's document, this is akin to B's giving out A's telephone number, thereby
(35) allowing third parties to hear the outgoing message for themselves. Anyone who calls can listen to the message; that is its purpose. While B's link may indeed facilitate access to A's document, the crucial point is that A, simply by placing that document on the
(40) Web, is thereby offering it for distribution. Therefore, even if B leads others to the document, it is A who actually controls access to it. Hence creating a link to a document is not the same as making or distributing a copy of that document. Moreover, techniques are
(45) already available by which A can restrict access to a document. For example, A may require a password to gain entry to A's Web page, just as a telephone owner can request an unlisted number and disclose it only to selected parties. Such a solution would compromise
(50) the openness of the Web somewhat, but not as much as the threat of copyright infringement litigation. Changing copyright law to benefit owners of intellectual property is thus ill-advised because it would impede the development of the Web as a public
(55) forum dedicated to the free exchange of ideas.

Main Point

The main point is stated in the sixth and final sentences of the third paragraph. It is that creating an online link to a document is not the same as copying or distributing the document, so copyright law should not be changed to benefit owners of intellectual property. This is the author's conclusion.

Paragraph 1

This paragraph presents background information about the controversy regarding the inclusion of links to documents on other Web sites. It then presents two opposing viewpoints—those of the owners of intellectual property and web users.

Paragraph 2

This paragraph provides additional background information to explain how including a link to a document on a Web site provides a user with instant access to the document. It then explains how current copyright law addresses a related issue. It also poses the key issue of the debate—whether creating a link is copyright infringement—in the form of a question.

Paragraph 3

This paragraph answers the question posed in the previous paragraph, stating the main point in the process. The author claims that creating an online link to a document is not copyright infringement. The author then explains that there are methods to restrict access to a document and provides an example. Finally, the author states the second part of the main point, which is that copyright law should not be changed to benefit owners of intellectual property.

Identify Viewpoints

The two main viewpoints in this passage are those of owners of intellectual property and web users. The author's viewpoint is also present. The author supports the position of web users.

9. Correct Answer (A). *Prep Test 51.5, Section 4, Passage 3, Question 16.*

Which one of the following is closest in meaning to the term "strengthened" as that term is used in line 8 of the passage?

This is an M question. The term *strengthened* is located in the second sentence of the first paragraph. Reading this sentence, we can see that *strengthened* is used in reference to copyright law. The sentence states that owners of intellectual property claim that if copyright law is not strengthened, then intellectual property on the Web will not be protected. The previous sentence states that there are legal issues regarding the rights of intellectual property owners. The sentence after the one that includes the term states that web users believe that strengthening copyright law will reduce their ability to access information online. Based on this, it is likely that *strengthened* is being used to mean *make copyright law more restrictive*. We should anticipate a correct answer choice that expresses this meaning.

(A) made more restrictive

This matches our anticipated answer choice. The owners of intellectual property want copyright law to be made more restrictive to protect their work. This is a candidate.

(B) made uniform worldwide

This answer choice includes irrelevant information. The uniformity of copyright law, whether in one country or worldwide, is never discussed in the passage. This is a loser.

(C) made to impose harsher penalties

Again, this answer choice includes irrelevant information. Penalties are never discussed in the passage. This is another loser.

(D) dutifully enforced

This answer choice also includes irrelevant information. The enforcement of laws is not mentioned. This is also a loser.

(E) more fully recognized as legitimate

Once more, this answer choice includes irrelevant information. The enforcement or legitimacy of current laws is not at question. This is also a loser.

As (A) is the only candidate, it is the correct answer choice.

10. Correct Answer (D). *Prep Test 51.5, Section 4, Passage 3, Question 22.*

According to the passage, present copyright laws

This is a D question. The topic of the prompt is present copyright laws. Looking back at our analysis of the passage, we can see that current copyright laws are discussed in the second paragraph. The second sentence of that paragraph states that current copyright laws give owners of intellectual property the right to sue a distributor of unauthorized copies of their material even if that distributor did not personally make the copies. As nothing else is mentioned about present copyright laws, we should anticipate a correct answer choice that restates this detail.

(A) allow completely unrestricted use of any document placed by its author on a Web page

This answer choice includes contradictory information. The passage clearly states that owners can sue a distributor of unauthorized copies. The debate is about whether including a link to a document counts as unauthorized distribution. This is a loser.

(B) allow those who establish links to a document on a Web page to control its distribution to others

This answer choice also includes contradictory information. In the sixth sentence of the third paragraph, the author states that even if someone leads others to a document, it is the person that has the document on their Web page who actually controls access to it. This is another loser.

(C) prohibit anyone but the author of a document from making a profit from the document's distribution

This answer choice includes irrelevant information. Profit is never discussed in the passage. This is another loser.

(D) allow the author of a document to sue anyone who distributes the document without permission

This matches our anticipated answer choice. It is a direct paraphrase of the detail we identified in the passage. This is a candidate.

(E) should be altered to allow more complete freedom in the exchange of ideas

This answer choice makes too strong of a claim. In the final sentence of the third paragraph, the author says that copyright law should not be changed to benefit owners of intellectual property because it would limit the free exchange of ideas. This is not the same as claiming that it should be changed to allow more freedom. This is another loser.

As (D) is the only candidate, it is the correct answer choice.

For Questions 11–13

Through the last half century, the techniques used by A) certain historians of African art for judging the precise tribal origins of African sculptures on the basis of style have been greatly refined. However, as
(5) B) one recent critic of the historians' classificatory assumptions has put it, the idea that the distribution of a particular style is necessarily limited to the area populated by one tribe may be "a dreadful oversimplification . . . a decided falsification of the
(10) very life of art in Africa."

Objects and styles have often been diffused through trade, most notably by workshops of artists who sell their work over a large geographical area. Styles cannot be narrowly defined as belonging
(15) uniquely to a particular area; rather, there are important "centers of style" throughout Africa where families, clans, and workshops produce sculpture and other art that is dispersed over a large, multitribal geographical area. Thus, a family of artists belonging
(20) to a single ethnic group may produce sculpture on commission for several neighboring tribes. While this practice contributes to a marked uniformity of styles across a large area, the commissioned works must nevertheless be done to some extent in the style of
(25) the tribe commissioning the work. This leads to much confusion on the part of those art historians who attempt to assign particular objects to individual groups on the basis of style.

One such center of style is located in the village
(30) of Ouri, in central Burkina Faso, where members of the Konaté family continue a long tradition of sculpture production not only for five major neighboring ethnic groups, but in recent times also for the tourist trade in Ouagadougou. The Konaté
(35) sculptors are able to distinguish the characteristics of the five styles in which they carve, and will point to the foliate patterns that radiate from the eyes of a Nuna ask, or the diamond-shaped mouth of many Ko masks, as characteristics of a particular tribal style
(40) that must be included to satisfy their clients. Nevertheless, their work is consistent in its proportions, composition, color, and technique. In fact, although the Konaté sculptors can identify the styles they carve, the characteristic patterns are so
(45) subtly different that few people outside of the area can distinguish Nuna masks from Ko masks.

Perhaps historians of African art should ask if objects in similar styles were produced in centers of style, where artists belonging to one ethnic group
(50) produced art for all of their neighbors. Perhaps it is even more important to cease attempting to break down large regional styles into finer and finer tribal styles and substyles, and to recognize that artists in Africa often do not produce work only in their own
(55) narrowly defined ethnic contexts. As the case of the Konaté sculptors makes clear, one cannot readily tell which group produced an object by analyzing fine style characteristics.

Main Point

The main point is stated in the second sentence of the second paragraph. It is that African artistic styles cannot be narrowly defined to a particular region, but, rather, there are centers of style throughout Africa.

Paragraph 1

This paragraph briefly mentions the viewpoint of certain historians who judge the precise tribal origins of African art. It then states the viewpoint of a recent critic who challenges the prevailing assumptions that style is limited to the area populated by one tribe.

Paragraph 2

This paragraph states the main point of the paragraph, which supports the viewpoint of the recent critic. It then provides an explanation of exactly what a center of style is.

Paragraph 3

This paragraph supports the main point by providing the example of Konaté family of sculptors as a center of style.

Paragraph 4

This last paragraph emphasizes that historians should focus less on tribes and defined ethnic contexts, suggesting that centers of style are more important in assessing art characteristics.

Identify Viewpoints

The author's viewpoint is present and is the focus of the passage. Two opposing viewpoints are mentioned briefly in the first paragraph (certain historians who judge the precise tribal origins of African art and a recent critic who challenges the prevailing assumptions). The author rebuts both of these viewpoints.

11. **Correct Answer (E).** *Prep Test 49, Section 3, Passage 2, Question 9.*

> **According to the passage, which one of the following is a feature that Konaté sculptors can identify as a requirement of a particular tribal style?**

This is a D question. The topic of the prompt is a feature that Konaté sculptors can identify as a requirement of a particular tribal style. Looking back at our analysis of the passage, we can see that the Konaté sculptors are discussed in the third paragraph. The second sentence of that paragraph states that the Konaté sculptors point to the foliate patterns that radiate from the eyes of a Nuna ask, or the diamond-shaped mouth of many Ko masks, as characteristics of a particular tribal style that must be included to satisfy their clients. There are two specific features mentioned (foliate patterns that radiate from the eyes / diamond-shaped mouth), and we should anticipate a correct answer choice that restates one or both of these details.

> **(A) horizontal incisions**

This answer choice includes irrelevant information. There is no mention of horizontal incisions. This is a loser.

> **(B) eye position**

Again, this answer choice includes irrelevant information. The position of the eyes is not a feature discussed in the passage. This is a loser.

> **(C) top attachments**

This answer choice also includes irrelevant information. There is no mention of top attachments. This is a loser as well.

> **(D) bottom decorations**

This answer choice includes irrelevant information. There is no mention of bottom decorations. This is a loser.

> **(E) mouth shape**

This matches one of our anticipated answer choices. The passage refers to a diamond-shaped mouth as a feature of a particular tribal style. This is the correct answer choice.

12. **Correct Answer (B).** *Prep Test 49, Section 3, Passage 2, Question 12.*

> **Which one of the following does the author attribute to the Konaté sculptors?**

This is a D question. The topic of the prompt is something attributed to the Konaté sculptors. We know from the previous question that the Konaté sculptors are discussed in the third paragraph. The author attributes several things to the Konaté sculptors in this paragraph. The Konaté are exemplified as a center of style, they continue a long tradition of producing sculptures for neighboring ethnic groups and the tourist trade, they are able to distinguish and carve in five similar styles, and their work is consistent in terms of stylistic elements such as proportions, composition, color, and technique. We should anticipate a correct answer choice that restates one or more of these details.

> **(A) use of nontraditional materials in sculptures**

This answer choice includes irrelevant information. The use of nontraditional materials is never mentioned. This is a loser.

(B) production of sculptures in several distinct styles that are nevertheless very similar to one another

This matches one of our anticipated answer choices. It is a combination of the third and fourth details we identified. The Konaté sculpt in five different styles and their work is consistent in terms of stylistic elements. This is a candidate.

(C) stylistic innovations that have influenced the work of other sculptors in a large geographical area

This answer choice includes irrelevant information. The passage does not state that the Konaté influenced the work of other sculptors in the area. This is a loser.

(D) adoption of a carving style that was previously used only by members of a different tribe

This answer choice makes too strong of a claim because of the inclusion of the term *only*. The Konaté sculptors do create sculptures in different tribal styles. However, there is nothing to indicate that only tribal members used each tribe's carving style before the Konaté sculptors began doing this. This is a loser.

(E) introduction of the practice of producing sculptures for neighboring groups

This is irrelevant information. There is no indication that the Konaté introduced this practice. This is another loser.

As (B) is the only candidate, it is the correct answer choice.

---

13. **Correct Answer (C).** *Prep Test 49, Section 3, Passage 2, Question 13.*

Which one of the following most accurately expresses what the author means by "centers of style" (line 16)?

This is an M question. The term *centers of style* is used throughout the passage, but it is introduced in the second sentence of the second paragraph. Reading this sentence, we can see that a center of style is where families, clans, and workshops produce sculpture and other art that is dispersed over a large, multitribal geographical area. The previous sentence explains how style cannot be narrowly defined to a particular region. The sentence after the one with the referenced term describes a center of style in more detail. A family of artists can produce sculptures for several neighboring tribes, contributing to a more uniform style, even if that style is still distinct for each ethnic group. We should anticipate a correct answer choice that expresses this meaning.

(A) geographical areas in which masks and similar sculptures are for the most part interchangeable among a number of closely connected tribes who use them

This answer choice includes contradictory information. The passage does not define centers of style simply as geographical areas. In addition, it states that the sculptures produced in a center of style are still distinct for each ethnic group. This is a loser.

(B) locations in which works of art are produced by sculptors using a particular style who then instruct other artists throughout large surrounding geographical areas

This answer choice includes irrelevant information. The passage does not discuss sculptors in a center of style instructing other artists. This is a loser.

(C) locations in which stylistically consistent but subtly varied works of art are produced and distributed to ethnically varied surrounding areas

This matches our anticipated answer choice. In a center of style, the works are produced by a family and distributed to neighboring tribes. These works are similar but subtly varied. This is a candidate.

(D) large geographical areas throughout which the various tribes produce works of art that differ subtly along ethnic lines but are so similar that they are very difficult for outside observers to distinguish from one another

This answer choice includes contradictory information. Centers of style are not large geographical areas according to the passage. In addition, a center of style is a single family, clan, or workshop—not various tribes. This is a loser.

(E) locations in which sculptures and similar works of art are traditionally produced by a diverse community of artists who migrate in from various tribes of surrounding areas

This answer choice includes irrelevant information. There is no discussion of neighboring tribes migrating to a location to produce art. In addition, a center of style is a single family, clan, or workshop. It is not a diverse community of artists from various tribes. This is a loser.

As (C) is the only candidate, it is the correct answer choice.

Key Takeaways

This passage out-anticipated answer choice. In addition of style the work is produced by a family and distributed to neighboring tribes. These works are similar but subtly varied. This is a class

---

14.9% of RC Questions

Detail (D) – 8.0% of RC Questions
Existence (EX) – 1.4% of RC Questions
Meaning (M) – 5.5% of RC Questions

Identify specific information that is explicitly stated in the passage or determine the contextual meaning of a referenced term.

Question Tasks

D: Retrieve a specific piece of information that is explicitly stated in the passage

EX: Determine whether or not a specific detail appears in the passage

M: Determine the meaning of a referenced term within the context of the passage

Example Prompts

D: The passage indicates which one of the following as a factor in _____?
D: According to the passage, what is the advantage of _____?
D: Which one of the following does the passage mention as an example of _____?

EX: Which one of the following does the author mention in the passage?
EX: Which one of the following is stated by the passage?
EX: The passage asserts which one of the following about _____?

M: Which one of the following most accurately expresses what the author means by " _____ " in line #?
M: Which one of the following most accurately expresses what is meant when the author refers to the phrase " _____ " (line #)?
M: Which one of the following could replace the phrase " _____ " in line # without substantively altering the author's meaning?

Correct Answer Choices

D: Statements that accurately restate a detail asked for in the prompt

EX: Statements that accurately restate a detail from the passage

M: Statements that accurately express the contextual meaning of the referenced term

Incorrect Answer Choices

Statements that express a common meaning of the term that does not match the specific contextual meaning (M)

Wrong Viewpoint: Accurate statements about a viewpoint other than the one specified in the prompt (D)

Wrong Part of Passage: Accurate statements about a part of the passage not specified by the prompt (D)

Too Strong: Claims that are too strong to be supported (EX)

Contradictory Information: Statements that contradict information in the passage (D, EX, M)

Irrelevant Information: Statements that present new information that is not relevant to the task specified in the prompt (D, EX, M)

HACKERS
LSAT *Reading Comprehension*

Chapter 5

Inference Family

Chapter 5: Inference Family

Overview

Example Passages and Questions

In this chapter, you will learn how to identify and solve Inference Family questions.

Inference Family questions ask you to synthesize information to reach a conclusion that is strongly supported by the passage but not explicitly stated. The initial analysis of the passage plays an important role in answering Inference Family questions as it makes it possible to quickly locate the relevant information.

The four question types in this family—Implication (IMP), Viewpoint (V), Attitude (ATT), and Principle (PR)— are examined in detail in separate sections. Each section includes step-by-step instructions on how to solve the question type and detailed analyses of example questions. In addition, you will get to tackle practice questions taken from previous administrations of the LSAT. The methods for solving these practice questions are explained thoroughly in the answer keys.

Example Passages and Questions

The example questions analyzed in the How-to-Solve subsections reference the following passages, and you should refer back to them as necessary. The analysis of each passage has already been done for you.

For Example Questions 1–3

The painter Roy Lichtenstein helped to define pop art—the movement that incorporated commonplace objects and commercial-art techniques into paintings—by paraphrasing the style of comic books in his work.
(5) His merger of a popular genre with the forms and intentions of fine art generated a complex result: while poking fun at the pretensions of the art world, Lichtenstein's work also managed to convey a seriousness of theme that enabled it to transcend mere
(10) parody.

That Lichtenstein's images were fine art was at first difficult to see, because, with their word balloons and highly stylized figures, they looked like nothing more than the comic book panels from which they were
(15) copied. Standard art history holds that pop art emerged as an impersonal alternative to the histrionics of abstract expressionism, a movement in which painters conveyed their private attitudes and emotions using nonrepresentational techniques. The truth is that by the
(20) time pop art first appeared in the early 1960s, abstract expressionism had already lost much of its force. Pop art painters weren't quarreling with the powerful early abstract expressionist work of the late 1940s but with a second generation of abstract expressionists whose
(25) work seemed airy, high-minded, and overly lyrical. Pop art paintings were full of simple black lines and large areas of primary color. Lichtenstein's work was part of a general rebellion against the fading emotional power of abstract expressionism, rather than an aloof
(30) attempt to ignore it.

But if rebellion against previous art by means of the careful imitation of a popular genre were all that characterized Lichtenstein's work, it would possess only the reflective power that parodies have in relation
(35) to their subjects. Beneath its cartoonish methods, his work displayed an impulse toward realism, an urge to say that what was missing from contemporary painting was the depiction of contemporary life. The stilted romances and war stories portrayed in the comic books
(40) on which he based his canvases, the stylized automobiles, hot dogs, and table lamps that appeared in his pictures, were reflections of the culture Lichtenstein inhabited. But, in contrast to some pop art, Lichtenstein's work exuded not a jaded cynicism about
(45) consumer culture, but a kind of deliberate naivete, intended as a response to the excess of sophistication he observed not only in the later abstract expressionists but in some other pop artists. With the comics—typically the domain of youth and innocence—as his
(50) reference point, a nostalgia fills his paintings that gives them, for all their surface bravado, an inner sweetness. His persistent use of comic-art conventions demonstrates a faith in reconciliation, not only between cartoons and fine art, but between parody and true
(55) feeling.

Main Point

The main point is stated in the last sentence of the first paragraph. It is that Lichtenstein's merger of a popular genre (comic books) with fine art meant that his work not only poked fun at the pretensions of the art world but also transcended parody because it conveyed a seriousness of theme.

Paragraph 1

The paragraph provides background information (definition of pop art) and states the main point of the passage.

Paragraph 2

This paragraph provides information about abstract impressionism, the art movement that pop artists in general and Lichtenstein in particular rebelled against.

Paragraph 3

This paragraph provides support for the main point that Lichtenstein's work was not mere parody but had a seriousness of theme. This paragraph describes Lichtenstein's impulse toward realism, deliberate naivete towards consumer culture, and nostalgia that gives his works inner sweetness.

Identify Viewpoints

The author's viewpoint is present and is the focus of the passage. There are no other viewpoints in this passage.

1. Based on the passage, which one of the following can most reasonably be inferred about abstract expressionism?

   (A) Over time, it moved from abstraction to realism.
   (B) Over time, it moved from intensity to lyricism.
   (C) Over time, it moved from intellectualism to emotionalism.
   (D) Over time, it moved from obscurity to clarity.
   (E) Over time, it moved from density to sparseness.

2. Based on the passage, which one of the following does the author appear to believe about the rebellious aspect of Lichtenstein's work?

   (A) It was directed less against abstract expressionism exclusively than against overly sophisticated art.
   (B) It was directed less against later abstract expressionism than against commercial art.
   (C) It was directed less against later abstract expressionism exclusively than against abstract expressionism in general.
   (D) It was an objection to the consumerism of the culture.
   (E) It was an objection to the simplicity of line and color used by pop artists.

3. Which one of the following best captures the author's attitude toward Lichtenstein's work?

   (A) enthusiasm for its more rebellious aspects
   (B) respect for its successful parody of youth and innocence
   (C) pleasure in its blatant rejection of abstract expressionism
   (D) admiration for its subtle critique of contemporary culture
   (E) appreciation for its ability to incorporate both realism and naivete

For Example Questions 4–7

Sometimes there is no more effective means of controlling an agricultural pest than giving free rein to its natural predators. A case in point is the cyclamen mite, a pest whose population can be
(5) effectively controlled by a predatory mite of the genus *Typhlodromus*. Cyclamen mites infest strawberry plants; they typically establish themselves in a strawberry field shortly after planting, but their populations do not reach significantly damaging
(10) levels until the plants' second year. *Typhlodromus* mites usually invade the strawberry fields during the second year, rapidly subdue the cyclamen mite populations, and keep them from reaching significantly damaging levels.
(15) *Typhlodromus* owes its effectiveness as a predator to several factors in addition to its voracious appetite. Its population can increase as rapidly as that of its prey. Both species reproduce by parthenogenesis—a mode of reproduction in which unfertilized eggs
(20) develop into fertile females. Cyclamen mites lay three eggs per day over the four or five days of their reproductive life span; *Typhlodromus* lay two or three eggs per day for eight to ten days. Seasonal synchrony of *Typhlodromus* reproduction with the
(25) growth of prey populations and ability to survive at low prey densities also contribute to the predatory efficiency of *Typhlodromus*. During winter, when cyclamen mite populations dwindle to a few individuals hidden in the crevices and folds of leaves
(30) in the crowns of the strawberry plants, the predatory mites subsist on the honeydew produced by aphids and white flies. They do not reproduce except when they are feeding on the cyclamen mites. These features, which make *Typhlodromus* well-suited for
(35) exploiting the seasonal rises and falls of its prey, are common among predators that control prey populations.
Greenhouse experiments have verified the importance of *Typhlodromus* predation for keeping
(40) cyclamen mites in check. One group of strawberry plants was stocked with both predator and prey mites; a second group was kept predator-free by regular application of parathion, an insecticide that kills the predatory species but does not affect the cyclamen
(45) mite. Throughout the study, populations of cyclamen mites remained low in plots shared with *Typhlodromus*, but their infestation attained significantly damaging proportions on predator-free plants.
(50) Applying parathion in this instance is a clear case in which using a pesticide would do far more harm than good to an agricultural enterprise. The results were similar in field plantings of strawberries, where cyclamen mites also reached damaging levels when
(55) predators were eliminated by parathion, but they did not attain such levels in untreated plots. When cyclamen mite populations began to increase in an untreated planting, the predator populations quickly responded to reduce the outbreak. On average,
(60) cyclamen mites were about 25 times more abundant in the absence of predators than in their presence.

Main Point

The main point is in the first sentence of the first paragraph. It is that not interfering with an agricultural pest's natural predators is the most effective form of pest control in some cases.

Paragraph 1

The paragraph states the main point and introduces the example of the relationship between the cyclamen mite (a strawberry plant pest) and the *Typhlodromus* mite (a cyclamen mite predator) to support it.

Paragraph 2

This paragraph expands on the example by presenting factors that make *Typhlodromus* an effective predator: it reproduces as rapidly as its prey and has a voracious appetite. In addition, *Typhlodromus* and cyclamen mites reproduce by parthenogenesis, lay multiple eggs over a period of a few days, and have seasonally synchronized reproduction. *Typhlodromus* can utilize other food sources to survive periods with low prey density.

Paragraph 3

This paragraph discusses experiments showing the effectiveness of *Typhlodromus* as a predator. Plants with both types of mites and plants with only cyclamen mites (*Typhlodromus* were eliminated using a pesticide called parathion) were compared. The cyclamen mites achieved damaging levels on plants without *Typhlodromus*.

Paragraph 4

This paragraph continues the discussion of the experiments. It shows that similar results were achieved in field plantings. Cyclamen mites reached damaging levels in plots treated with parathion but not in untreated plots.

Identify Viewpoints

The author's viewpoint is present and is the focus of the passage. There are no other viewpoints in this passage.

4. Information in the passage most strongly supports which one of the following statements?

(A) Strawberry crops can support populations of both cyclamen mites and *Typhlodromus* mites without significant damage to those crops.

(B) For control of cyclamen mites by another mite species to be effective, it is crucial that the two species have the same mode of reproduction.

(C) Factors that make *Typhlodromus* effective against cyclamen mites also make it effective against certain other pests of strawberry plants.

(D) When *Typhlodromus* is relied on to control cyclamen mites in strawberry crops, pesticides may be necessary to prevent significant damage during the first year.

(E) Strawberry growers have unintentionally caused cyclamen mites to become a serious crop pest by the indiscriminate use of parathion.

5. Suppose that pesticide X drastically slows the reproductive rate of cyclamen mites and has no other direct effect on cyclamen mites or *Typhlodromus*. Based on the information in the passage, which one of the following would most likely have occurred if, in the experiments mentioned in the passage, pesticide X had been used instead of parathion, with all other conditions affecting the experiments remaining the same?

(A) In both treated and untreated plots inhabited by both *Typhlodromus* and cyclamen mites, the latter would have been effectively controlled.

(B) Cyclamen mite populations in all treated plots from which *Typhlodromus* was absent would have been substantially lower than in untreated plots inhabited by both kinds of mites.

(C) In the treated plots, slowed reproduction in cyclamen mites would have led to a loss of reproductive synchrony between *Typhlodromus* and cyclamen mites.

(D) In the treated plots, *Typhlodromus* populations would have decreased temporarily and would have eventually increased.

(E) In the treated plots, cyclamen mite populations would have reached significantly damaging levels more slowly, but would have remained at those levels longer, than in untreated plots.

6. It can be inferred from the passage that the author would be most likely to agree with which one of the following statements about the use of predators to control pest populations?

(A) If the use of predators to control cyclamen mite populations fails, then parathion should be used to control these populations.

(B) Until the effects of the predators on beneficial insects that live in strawberry fields are assessed, such predators should be used with caution to control cyclamen mite populations.

(C) Insecticides should be used to control certain pest populations in fields of crops only if the use of natural predators has proven inadequate.

(D) If an insecticide can effectively control pest populations as well as predator populations, then it should be used instead of predators to control pest populations.

(E) Predators generally control pest populations more effectively than pesticides because they do not harm the crops that their prey feed on.

7. Based on the passage, the author would probably hold that which one of the following principles is fundamental to long-term predatory control of agricultural pests?

(A) The reproduction of the predator population should be synchronized with that of the prey population, so that the number of predators surges just prior to a surge in prey numbers.

(B) The effectiveness of the predatory relationship should be experimentally demonstrable in greenhouse as well as field applications.

(C) The prey population should be able to survive in times of low crop productivity, so that the predator population will not decrease to very low levels.

(D) The predator population's level of consumption of the prey species should be responsive to variations in the size of the prey population.

(E) The predator population should be vulnerable only to pesticides to which the prey population is also vulnerable.

Implication

Implication
Viewpoint
Attitude
Principle

Implication

≈ 3.13 questions per test

Example Prompts

The passage *suggests* which one of the following about _____?

Which one of the following can be *most reasonably inferred* from the information in the passage?

The information in the passage *provides the most support* for which one of the following statements?

Take These Steps

Does the prompt reference a topic from a specific part of the passage?

No

Yes

Proceed directly to eliminating answer choices. Use your initial analysis to figure out where each answer choice's topic is discussed in the passage. Then, read the relevant content to determine whether each answer choice is a logical inference.

Use your initial analysis of the passage to figure out where the topic in the prompt is discussed in the passage. Read through the content to determine if there are any logical inferences to be drawn.

If you are able to identify an inference, anticipate a correct answer choice that accurately expresses it.

If you are unable to identify an inference, eliminate answer choices based on the information in the relevant content.

Answer Choices

Correct Answer Choices

Clear and logical inferences that are supported by specific information in the passage

Incorrect Answer Choices

Wrong part of passage

Too strong

Contradictory information

Irrelevant information

Implication (IMP) questions ask you to identify an inference based on information presented in the passage.

IMP question prompts usually include terms such as *infer*, *imply*, *suggest*, or *most supported by*. In addition, IMP question prompts may occasionally be worded in such a way as to not include these types of terms. Instead, they will present a hypothetical scenario based on the information in the passage. Regardless, an IMP question can be identified by the fact that they ask you to draw a conclusion that is strongly supported by specific evidence in the passage but not explicitly stated. IMP questions can appear in any passage type.

How to Solve IMP Questions

The first step in solving an IMP question is to determine whether or not the prompt asks about a topic that is addressed in a specific part of the passage. Some IMP question prompts include a topic that is discussed throughout the passage, and some do not include one at all. Other IMP question prompts ask about a topic that is discussed in only one part of the passage (usually in a one- or two-paragraph section).

For example, consider a passage about early 20th-century art that focuses on modernism in the third paragraph. An IMP question for this passage might include one of the following prompts:

The passage suggests which one of the following?
The passage suggests which one of the following about early 20th-century art?

The passage suggests which one of the following about modernism?

The first two prompts provide no indication about where the required information is located in the passage. The first does not mention a topic, and the second references the main topic of the passage. However, the third prompt clearly indicates that all of the answer choices are related to the topic of modernism, meaning that only the information in the third paragraph needs to be considered.

The process for solving an IMP question varies depending on whether or not the prompt references a topic from a specific part of the passage.

If the Prompt Does Not Reference a Specific Part of the Passage

When the prompt does not reference a topic from a specific part of the passage, you will not be able to anticipate a correct answer choice. Therefore, you should proceed directly to eliminating answer choices. Refer back to your initial analysis of the passage to determine where the topic of each answer choice is discussed in the passage. Then, read the relevant content to determine whether or not the answer choice is a logical inference based on the information in the passage.

Let's look at Example Question 4 (page 167):

Information in the passage most strongly supports which one of the following statements?

(A) Strawberry crops can support populations of both cyclamen mites and *Typhlodromus* mites without significant damage to those crops.
(B) For control of cyclamen mites by another mite species to be effective, it is crucial that the two species have the same mode of reproduction.
(C) Factors that make *Typhlodromus* effective against cyclamen mites also make it effective

against certain other pests of strawberry plants.
- (D) When *Typhlodromus* is relied on to control cyclamen mites in strawberry crops, pesticides may be necessary to prevent significant damage during the first year.
- (E) Strawberry growers have unintentionally caused cyclamen mites to become a serious crop pest by the indiscriminate use of parathion.

The prompt does not reference a topic from a specific part of the passage. Therefore, we cannot anticipate a correct answer choice and must proceed directly to eliminating answer choices.

(A) Strawberry crops can support populations of both cyclamen mites and *Typhlodromus* mites without significant damage to those crops.

This seems like a logical inference based on the information in the passage. The first paragraph says that *Typhlodromus* invade strawberry fields and keep the cyclamen mite population from reaching significantly damaging levels. The third and fourth paragraphs describe how cyclamen mite populations do not reach damaging levels when *Typhlodromus* are present. This is a candidate.

(B) For control of cyclamen mites by another mite species to be effective, it is crucial that the two species have the same mode of reproduction.

This answer choice makes too strong of a claim. The second paragraph states that cyclamen mites and *Typhlodromus* both reproduce by parthenogenesis. However, there is no indication that having the same mode of reproduction is a requirement for one mite species to be an effective predator of another. This is a loser.

(C) Factors that make *Typhlodromus* effective against cyclamen mites also make it effective against certain other pests of strawberry plants.

This answer choice includes irrelevant information. There is no mention in the passage of other pests of strawberry plants. This is also a loser.

(D) When *Typhlodromus* is relied on to control cyclamen mites in strawberry crops, pesticides may be necessary to prevent significant damage during the first year.

This answer choice includes contradictory information. The first paragraph states that *Typhlodromus* usually invade strawberry fields in the second year. They then reduce the cyclamen mite population and keep it from reaching significantly damaging levels. This implies that cyclamen mites do not cause significant damage in the first year. This is another loser.

(E) Strawberry growers have unintentionally caused cyclamen mites to become a serious crop pest by the indiscriminate use of parathion.

This answer choice includes irrelevant information. The passage does not discuss the indiscriminate use of parathion by strawberry growers in the past. This is a loser.

As (A) is the only candidate, it is the correct answer choice.

If the Prompt References a Specific Part of the Passage

When a question prompt references a topic from a specific part of the passage, you should attempt to anticipate a correct answer choice. Refer back to your initial analysis of the passage to determine where the topic is discussed in the passage. Then, read through the relevant content to determine if there are any logical inferences that can be drawn. If you are able to identify such an inference, you should anticipate a correct answer choice that fully and accurately expresses it. Occasionally, it may be difficult to identify an inference, or it may be possible to make many inferences. In these cases, simply proceed to eliminating answer choices.

Let's look at Example Question 1 (page 165):

> Based on the passage, which one of the following can most reasonably be inferred about abstract expressionism?
>
> (A) Over time, it moved from abstraction to realism.
> (B) Over time, it moved from intensity to lyricism.
> (C) Over time, it moved from intellectualism to emotionalism.
> (D) Over time, it moved from obscurity to clarity.
> (E) Over time, it moved from density to sparseness.

The topic of the prompt is abstract expressionism. Looking back at our analysis of the passage, we can see that abstract expressionism is discussed in the second paragraph of the passage. That paragraph states that pop art painters were not quarreling with the powerful early abstract expressionist works of the late 1940s but with the airy, high-minded, and overly lyrical abstract expressionism of the early 1960s. It also states that Lichtenstein's work was part of a general rebellion against the fading emotional power of abstract expressionism. One inference that stands out is that abstract expressionism initially had emotional power, but this power diminished as the art movement became overly lyrical. We should anticipate a correct answer choice that expresses this inference or another one that can be logically drawn from this section of the passage.

(A) Over time, it moved from abstraction to realism.

This answer choice includes information from the wrong part of the passage. Realism is discussed in the third paragraph in terms of describing Lichtenstein's work. This is a loser.

(B) Over time, it moved from intensity to lyricism.

This matches our anticipated answer choice. The passage states that abstract expressionism in the 1940s was powerful and that it had become overly lyrical in the 1960s. It also indicates that during this transitional period, abstract expressionism's emotional power (intensity) faded. This is a candidate.

(C) Over time, it moved from intellectualism to emotionalism.

This answer choice includes irrelevant and contradictory information. Intellectualism is not discussed in the passage. In addition, the second paragraph mentions that the emotional power of abstract expressionism faded over time. This is another loser.

(D) Over time, it moved from obscurity to clarity.

This answer choice includes irrelevant information. Neither *obscurity* nor *clarity* is mentioned in the passage. This is also a loser.

(E) Over time, it moved from density to sparseness.

Again, this answer choice includes irrelevant information. Neither *density* nor *sparseness* is mentioned in the passage. This is another loser.

As (B) is the only candidate, it is the correct answer choice.

Let's look at another example, Example Question 5 (page 167):

Suppose that pesticide X drastically slows the reproductive rate of cyclamen mites and has no other direct effect on cyclamen mites or *Typhlodromus*. Based on the information in the passage, which one of the following would most likely have occurred if, in the experiments mentioned in the passage, pesticide X had been used instead of parathion, with all other conditions affecting the experiments remaining the same?

(A) In both treated and untreated plots inhabited by both *Typhlodromus* and cyclamen mites, the latter would have been effectively controlled.
(B) Cyclamen mite populations in all treated plots from which *Typhlodromus* was absent would have been substantially lower than in untreated plots inhabited by both kinds of mites.
(C) In the treated plots, slowed reproduction in cyclamen mites would have led to a loss of reproductive synchrony between *Typhlodromus* and cyclamen mites.
(D) In the treated plots, *Typhlodromus* populations would have decreased temporarily and would have eventually increased.
(E) In the treated plots, cyclamen mite populations would have reached significantly damaging levels more slowly, but would have remained at those levels longer, than in untreated plots.

This is an example of an IMP question that provides a hypothetical scenario for consideration and then asks for an inference based on this scenario and the information in the passage. Although this question is more complex than the previous one, the process to solve it is the same. The question prompt includes a topic from specific parts of the passage; namely, the reproductive rate of cyclamen mites, which is discussed in the second paragraph, and the experiments involving the use of parathion, which are discussed in the third and fourth paragraphs.

The question prompt describes a scenario in which pesticide X drastically slows the reproduction rate of cyclamen mites and has no other direct effect on cyclamen mites or *Typhlodromus*. It then asks what would have occurred if pesticide X had been used in the experiments rather than parathion. The second paragraph states that if the reproduction rate of cyclamen mites decreases, then the reproduction rate of *Typhlodromus* decreases as well. It also indicates that *Typhlodromus* can survive periods with a low cyclamen mite population by utilizing other food sources. This means that the slower reproduction rate of cyclamen mites would not have had a detrimental effect on *Typhlodromus*. The third and fourth paragraphs state that in plots treated with parathion, the population of cyclamen mites increased because *Typhlodromus* was eliminated. In untreated plots, the population of cyclamen mites declined due to predation by *Typhlodromus*.

Based on this information, we can infer that if pesticide X had been used instead of parathion, the population of cyclamen mites would have declined in all plots. In the untreated plots, the cyclamen mite population would be reduced by *Typhlodromus*. In the treated plots, the cyclamen mite population would be reduced by both *Typhlodromus* and pesticide X. We should anticipate a correct answer choice that expresses this inference or another one that can be logically drawn from this section of the passage.

(A) In both treated and untreated plots inhabited by both *Typhlodromus* and cyclamen mites, the latter would have been effectively controlled.

This matches our anticipated answer choice. The population of cyclamen mites in both plots would be controlled. This is a candidate.

(B) Cyclamen mite populations in all treated plots from which *Typhlodromus* was absent would have been substantially lower than in untreated plots inhabited by both kinds of mites.

This answer choice includes irrelevant and contradictory information. The passage does not provide any information about plots that did not include *Typhlodromus*. In addition, based on the passage, it seems more likely that these plots would have higher cyclamen mite populations because *Typhlodromus* is an effective predator of this pest. This is a loser.

(C) In the treated plots, slowed reproduction in cyclamen mites would have led to a loss of reproductive synchrony between *Typhlodromus* and cyclamen mites.

This answer choice also includes irrelevant information. There is nothing to indicate that a slower reproduction rate for cyclamen mites would result in a loss of reproductive synchrony. This is another loser.

(D) In the treated plots, *Typhlodromus* populations would have decreased temporarily and would have eventually increased.

Again, this answer choice includes irrelevant information. The *Typhlodromus* population in the treated plots would likely decrease due to the slowed reproduction rate of cyclamen mites. However, there is no information to support the claim that the *Typhlodromus* population would eventually increase. This is also a loser.

(E) In the treated plots, cyclamen mite populations would have reached significantly damaging levels more slowly, but would have remained at those levels longer, than in untreated plots.

This answer choice includes contradictory information. In the treated plots, the cyclamen mite population would be kept low and remain low due to the *Typhlodromus* population. This is another loser.

As (A) is the only candidate, it is the correct answer choice.

Looking at the Answer Choices

The correct answer choice is a statement that is a clear and logical inference based on specific information in the passage.

Incorrect answer choices often include irrelevant information. These may seem somewhat plausible based on the content of the passage, but there is no direct evidence to support them. It is also common for incorrect answer choices to include statements that make too strong of a claim. These can be tricky because the claim may be closely related to specific information in the passage. As weak claims are much easier to support than strong ones, you should always be suspicious of answer choices that make strong claims. Incorrect answer choices that include information from the wrong part of the passage or contradictory information appear frequently as well.

Viewpoint

INFERENCE FAMILY

Implication
Viewpoint
Attitude
Principle

Viewpoint
≈ 3.38 questions per test

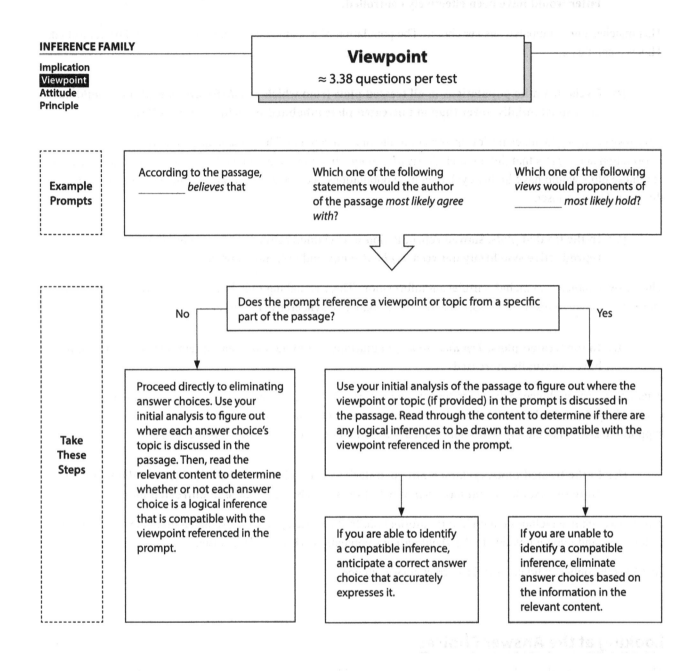

Example Prompts

According to the passage, _____ *believes* that

Which one of the following statements would the author of the passage *most likely agree with*?

Which one of the following *views* would proponents of _____ *most likely hold*?

Does the prompt reference a viewpoint or topic from a specific part of the passage?

No → **Take These Steps**

Proceed directly to eliminating answer choices. Use your initial analysis to figure out where each answer choice's topic is discussed in the passage. Then, read the relevant content to determine whether or not each answer choice is a logical inference that is compatible with the viewpoint referenced in the prompt.

Yes →

Use your initial analysis of the passage to figure out where the viewpoint or topic (if provided) in the prompt is discussed in the passage. Read through the content to determine if there are any logical inferences to be drawn that are compatible with the viewpoint referenced in the prompt.

If you are able to identify a compatible inference, anticipate a correct answer choice that accurately expresses it.

If you are unable to identify a compatible inference, eliminate answer choices based on the information in the relevant content.

Answer Choices

Correct Answer Choices	Incorrect Answer Choices
Clear and logical inferences that are supported by specific information in the passage and that is compatible with the viewpoint referenced in the prompt	Wrong viewpoint
	Wrong part of passage
	Too strong
	Contradictory information
	Irrelevant information

Viewpoint (V) questions ask you to identify an inference that is compatible with the viewpoint of a specific person (including the author) or group in the passage.

V question prompts usually include terms such as *view*, *believe*, *most likely agree with*, or *most likely hold*. In addition, they may include the term *inferred*. However, when this appears in a V question prompt, it is always accompanied by one of the other terms. V questions can appear in any passage type, but they are most common in Argumentative and Debate passages.

How to Solve V Questions

The first step in solving a V question is to determine whether or not the prompt references a viewpoint or topic from a specific part of the passage. The prompt will always mention a viewpoint. In some cases, this will be a viewpoint that is presented throughout the passage (most commonly, the author's). In others, it will be a viewpoint that is presented in a one- or two-paragraph section of the passage. The prompt may also specify a topic that is discussed throughout the passage or in one section.

For example, consider a passage about market structures that presents the author's viewpoint throughout and that includes a discussion of monopolies in the third paragraph. Within this paragraph, the viewpoint of a researcher named Sutherland is presented. A V question for this passage might include one of the following prompts:

Which one of the following would the author most likely agree with?
Which one of the following would the author most likely agree with about market structures?

Which one of the following would the author most likely agree with about monopolies?
Which one of the following would Sutherland most likely agree with about monopolies?
Which one of the following would Sutherland most likely agree with?

The first two prompts provide no indication about where the required information is located in the passage. The viewpoint referenced in the first prompt is the author's (which is presented throughout the passage), and it does not include a topic. The second prompt also references the author's viewpoint, and the topic it includes is the main topic of the passage. In contrast, the last three prompts clearly indicate the information needed to answer the question is in the third paragraph. Both the viewpoint (Sutherland's) and the topic (monopolies) are discussed only in this paragraph.

The process for solving a V question varies depending on whether or not the prompt references a viewpoint or topic from a specific part of the passage.

If the Prompt Does Not Reference a Specific Part of the Passage

When the prompt does not reference a viewpoint or topic from a specific part of the passage, you will not be able to anticipate a correct answer choice. In this case, the prompt will most likely be asking about the author's viewpoint, although in rare cases it may ask about another viewpoint that is presented throughout the passage. Regardless, you should proceed directly to eliminating answer choices. Refer back to your initial analysis of the passage to determine where the topic of each answer choice is discussed in the passage. Then, read the relevant content to determine whether or not the answer choice is a logical inference based on the information in the passage. This inference must be compatible with the viewpoint referenced in the prompt.

Let's look at Example Question 6 (page 167):

It can be inferred from the passage that the author would be most likely to agree with which one of the following statements about the use of predators to control pest populations?

(A) If the use of predators to control cyclamen mite populations fails, then parathion should be used to control these populations.
(B) Until the effects of the predators on beneficial insects that live in strawberry fields are assessed, such predators should be used with caution to control cyclamen mite populations.
(C) Insecticides should be used to control certain pest populations in fields of crops only if the use of natural predators has proven inadequate.
(D) If an insecticide can effectively control pest populations as well as predator populations, then it should be used instead of predators to control pest populations.
(E) Predators generally control pest populations more effectively than pesticides because they do not harm the crops that their prey feed on.

The prompt does not include a topic or viewpoint from a specific part of the passage. The author's viewpoint is presented throughout the passage, and the use of predators to control pest populations is the main topic of the passage. Therefore, we cannot anticipate a correct answer choice and must proceed directly to eliminating answer choices.

(A) If the use of predators to control cyclamen mite populations fails, then parathion should be used to control these populations.

This answer choice includes contradictory information. The third paragraph of the passage states that parathion does not affect cyclamen mites. Therefore, it would be ineffective in controlling the cyclamen mite population. This is a loser.

(B) Until the effects of the predators on beneficial insects that live in strawberry fields are assessed, such predators should be used with caution to control cyclamen mite populations.

This answer choice includes irrelevant information. The effects of predators on beneficial insects are not discussed in the passage. This is also a loser.

(C) Insecticides should be used to control certain pest populations in fields of crops only if the use of natural predators have proven inadequate.

This seems like a statement the author would agree with based on the information in the passage. The first paragraph states that the use of natural predators is sometimes the most effective way to eliminate agricultural pests. This suggests that natural predators should be used before insecticides. Although we cannot say for sure that the author would agree with the use of insecticides, it is apparent that the author would agree that natural predators should be tried before insecticides. This is a candidate.

(D) If an insecticide can effectively control pest populations as well as predator populations, then it should be used instead of predators to control pest populations.

This answer choice includes irrelevant information. The first paragraph shows that the author believes that, in some cases, natural predators are more effective than insecticides. However, there is nothing in the passage to indicate that the author would choose the use of insecticides over natural predators if both methods were equally effective. This is another loser.

> **(E) Predators generally control pest populations more effectively than pesticides because they do not harm the crops that their prey feed on.**

This is another answer choice with irrelevant information. Although the author provides reasons for the effectiveness of natural predators in the second paragraph, there is no information about predators or pesticides harming crops. This is also a loser.

As (C) is the only candidate, it is the correct answer choice.

If the Prompt References a Specific Part of the Passage

When a question prompt references a viewpoint or a topic from a specific part of the passage, you should try to anticipate a correct answer choice. Use your initial analysis to locate the relevant information in the passage. Then, read through this content to determine whether you can identify an inference that is compatible with the specified viewpoint. If the prompt includes a specific topic, it may be easier to anticipate a correct answer choice because you will have a clearer sense of which information is most relevant. However, if a specific topic is not included, it may still be possible to anticipate a correct answer choice. This is because a viewpoint from one specific part of the passage often focuses on a specific topic. If you are unable to anticipate an inference or are able to anticipate many, proceed directly to eliminating answer choices.

Let's look at Example Question 2 (page 165):

> Based on the passage, which one of the following does the author appear to believe about the rebellious aspect of Lichtenstein's work?
>
> (A) It was directed less against abstract expressionism exclusively than against overly sophisticated art.
> (B) It was directed less against later abstract expressionism than against commercial art.
> (C) It was directed less against later abstract expressionism exclusively than against abstract expressionism in general.
> (D) It was an objection to the consumerism of the culture.
> (E) It was an objection to the simplicity of line and color used by pop artists.

The prompt asks about the author's viewpoint regarding the rebellious aspect of Lichtenstein's work. Although the author's viewpoint is presented throughout the passage, we can use our analysis to locate the content relevant to the topic in the prompt. The second paragraph states that Lichtenstein's work was part of a general rebellion against the fading emotional power of abstract expressionism. It also states that pop art painters weren't quarreling with the powerful early abstract expressionist work of the late 1940s but with a second generation of abstract expressionists whose work seemed airy, high-minded, and overly lyrical. This suggests that Lichtenstein's rebellion against abstract expressionism was an aspect of his broader opposition to art that was airy, high-minded, and overly lyrical. We should anticipate a correct answer choice that expresses this inference or another one related to the rebellious aspect of Lichtenstein's work that the author would agree with.

(A) It was directed less against abstract expressionism exclusively than against overly sophisticated art.

This matches our anticipated answer choice. Lichtenstein's rebellion against abstract expressionism was part of his larger rebellion against airy, high-minded, and overly lyrical art. This is a candidate.

(B) It was directed less against later abstract expressionism than against commercial art.

This answer choice includes irrelevant information. It is similar to the previous one but introduces the concept of commercial art, which is not discussed in the passage. This is a loser.

(C) It was directed less against later abstract expressionism exclusively than against abstract expressionism in general.

This answer choice includes contradictory information. The second paragraph explicitly states that pop art painters (a group that includes Lichtenstein) did not have an issue with the early abstract expressionists but with the later ones (second generation). This is another loser.

(D) It was an objection to the consumerism of the culture.

This answer choice includes contradictory information. Consumer culture is discussed in the middle of the last paragraph. However, the author claims that Lichtenstein's work was not cynical about consumer culture but had a kind of deliberate naivete. There is no indication of rebellion against consumerism or consumer culture. This is another loser.

(E) It was an objection to the simplicity of line and color used by pop artists.

This answer choice also includes contradictory information. The first paragraph states that Lichtenstein helped to define pop art, and the second paragraph describes pop art as being full of simple black lines and large areas of primary color. While Lichtenstein was not a typical pop artist, there is no indication that he was rebelling against the simplicity of pop art. This is another loser.

As (A) is the only candidate, it is the correct answer choice.

Looking at the Answer Choices

The correct answer choice is an inference that is strongly supported by specific information in the passage and that is compatible with the viewpoint specified in the prompt.

Incorrect answer choices are often based on the wrong viewpoint. These are statements that are accurate according to the information in the passage but that relate to a person or group other than the one specified in the prompt. Answer choices that include irrelevant or contradictory information are common as well. You will also encounter incorrect answer choices that make too strong of a claim or include details from the wrong part of the passage.

Attitude

INFERENCE FAMILY

Implication
Viewpoint
Attitude
Principle

Attitude
≈ 1.13 questions per test

Example Prompts

According to the passage, *the author's attitude* toward _____ can most accurately be described as

It can be most reasonably inferred that *the author views* _____ as

Which one of the following most accurately characterizes *the author's stance* toward _____?

Take These Steps

Does the prompt reference a viewpoint or topic from a specific part of the passage?

No →

Determine whether the passage includes keywords that indicate the author's attitude toward the viewpoint or topic.

Yes →

Use your initial analysis of the passage to figure out where the viewpoint or topic in the prompt is discussed in the passage. Examine the content and any keywords present to determine the author's attitude toward the viewpoint or topic.

If there are keywords, anticipate a correct answer choice that accurately expresses the author's attitude.

If there are no keywords, proceed directly to eliminating answer choices. Use your initial analysis to figure out where each answer choice's topic is discussed in the passage. Then, read the relevant content to determine whether or not each answer choice is an accurate expression of the author's attitude.

If you are able to identify the author's attitude, anticipate a correct answer choice that accurately expresses it.

If you are unable to identify the author's attitude, eliminate answer choices based on the information in the relevant content.

Answer Choices

Correct Answer Choices	**Incorrect Answer Choices**
Statements that accurately express the author's attitude toward the viewpoint or topic referenced in the prompt	Wrong viewpoint
	Wrong part of passage
	Too strong
	Contradictory information
	Irrelevant information

Chapter 5

Attitude (ATT) questions ask you to determine the author's attitude toward a topic or the viewpoint of a specific person or group in the passage.

ATT question prompts usually include terms such as *the author's attitude, the author's stance,* or *the author views.* Like V question prompts, they occasionally include the term *inferred* as well. ATT questions can appear in any passage type but are most common in Argumentative and Debate passages. If they appear in a passage that does not include the author's viewpoint, the correct answer choice will almost always include the term *neutral* or a synonym (this is rare).

How to Solve ATT Questions

The first step in solving an ATT question is to determine whether or not the prompt references a viewpoint or topic from a specific part of the passage. The prompt always asks about the author's attitude toward another viewpoint or a topic in the passage.

For example, consider a passage about genetically modified crops that discusses government regulations in the third paragraph. The third paragraph includes the viewpoint of proponents of government regulation. An ATT question for this passage might include one of the following prompts:

> **Which one of the following most accurately describes the author's attitude toward genetically modified crops?**
>
> **Which one of the following most accurately describes the author's attitude toward government regulation of the use of genetically modified crops?**
> **Which one of the following most accurately describes the author's attitude toward proponents of government regulation?**

The first prompt does not include any information about where in the passage the required information is located. In effect, it is asking for the author's attitude toward the main topic of the passage. However, the second and third prompts clearly indicate that you need to consider only the information in the third paragraph. The second prompt includes a topic (government regulation) that is discussed only in this paragraph, and the third prompt includes a viewpoint (proponents of government regulation).

The process for solving an ATT question varies depending on whether or not the prompt references a viewpoint or topic from a specific part of the passage.

If the Prompt Does Not Reference a Specific Part of the Passage

When the viewpoint or topic referenced in the prompt is found throughout the passage, it is still possible to anticipate a correct answer choice. This is because the passage may include keywords that indicate the author's attitude. Examples of these were included in Chapter 1 and are provided here for your reference:

- correct – incorrect
- appropriate – inappropriate
- supported – unsupported
- likely – unlikely
- probable – improbable
- reasonable – unreasonable

Obviously, there are many other terms that can be used for this purpose. Assuming you have marked these during the initial analysis of the passage, you should review them when you encounter an ATT question prompt that mentions a viewpoint or topic discussed throughout the passage. If these keywords give you a sense of the author's attitude toward the viewpoint or topic in the prompt, anticipate a correct answer choice that accurately expresses this.

If you are unable to identify any such keywords, proceed directly to eliminating answer choices. Use the analysis to determine where each answer choice's topic is discussed in the passage. Read the relevant information to determine if the answer choice expresses the author's attitude.

Let's look at Example Question 3 (page 165):

Which one of the following best captures the author's attitude toward Lichtenstein's work?

(A) enthusiasm for its more rebellious aspects
(B) respect for its successful parody of youth and innocence
(C) pleasure in its blatant rejection of abstract expressionism
(D) admiration for its subtle critique of contemporary culture
(E) appreciation for its ability to incorporate both realism and naivete

The prompt does not reference a viewpoint or topic from a specific part of the passage. Lichtenstein's work is the main topic of the passage and is discussed throughout. In addition, the passage does not include any obvious keywords that indicate the author's attitude toward Lichtenstein's work. Therefore, we must proceed directly to eliminating answer choices.

(A) enthusiasm for its more rebellious aspects

This answer choice seems to capture the author's attitude toward Lichtenstein's work. The second paragraph states that Lichtenstein's work was part of a general rebellion against the fading emotional power of abstract expressionism, rather than an aloof attempt to ignore it. The use of the term *aloof* suggests that the author approves of Lichtenstein's decision to rebel against abstract expressionism instead of simply ignoring it. In addition, the first paragraph states that while poking fun at the pretensions of the art world, Lichtenstein's work also managed to convey a seriousness of theme that enabled it to transcend mere parody. Again, this suggests the author's approval of the rebellious aspects of Lichtenstein's work. This is a candidate.

(B) respect for its successful parody of youth and innocence

This answer choice includes irrelevant information. The third paragraph states that comics are typically the domain of youth and innocence. However, there is no mention of Lichtenstein attempting to parody these characteristics. This is a loser.

(C) pleasure in its blatant rejection of abstract expressionism

This answer choice makes too strong of a claim. Although the second paragraph indicates that Lichtenstein's work was part of a general rebellion against abstract expressionism, it also makes it clear that this general rebellion was against the later abstract expressionists rather than the early ones. Based on this, we cannot say for certain that Lichtenstein rejected abstract expressionism outright. This is a loser.

(D) admiration for its subtle critique of contemporary culture

This answer choice includes contradictory information. *Contemporary culture* seems to mean *consumer culture*, as the last paragraph describes aspects of consumerism and claims these were reflections of the culture Lichtenstein inhabited. However, the author claims that Lichtenstein's attitude toward consumer culture was not cynical but instead showed a kind of deliberate naivete. This is a loser.

(E) appreciation for its ability to incorporate both realism and naivete

This answer choice also seems to reflect the author's attitude toward Lichtenstein's work. In the last paragraph, the author presents Lichtenstein's impulse toward realism as a positive characteristic because it provides his work with something more than the reflective power that parodies generally have. The author also makes it clear that Lichtenstein's deliberate naivete was preferable to cynicism and was a response to the excess of sophistication displayed by other artists. Therefore, it seems that the author appreciates both the realism and naivete in Lichtenstein's work. This is another candidate.

We have two candidates, (A) and (E), so we need to eliminate one. Looking back at (A), we can see that it makes too strong of a claim. The term *enthusiasm* is not supported by the passage. While the author seems generally supportive of the rebellious aspects of Lichtenstein's work, there is nothing that indicates enthusiasm. In addition, the first sentence of the third paragraph states that Lichtenstein's work was important for more than just its rebellious aspects. The term *appreciation* in the answer choice (E) seems to match the author's attitude toward the inclusion of realism and naivete in Lichtenstein's work. Therefore, (E) is the correct answer choice.

If the Prompt References a Specific Part of the Passage

When a question prompt references a viewpoint or topic from a specific part of the passage, use your initial analysis to determine where the viewpoint or topic is discussed. Review the content in that part of the passage to determine the author's attitude, paying close attention to any keywords that indicate the opinion of the author. Then, anticipate a correct answer choice that expresses this attitude. If you are unable to get a clear sense of how the author feels about the topic or viewpoint, proceed directly to eliminating answer choices.

Looking at the Answer Choices

The correct answer choice is a statement that accurately expresses the author's attitude toward the viewpoint or topic in the prompt. This will be strongly supported by evidence in the passage but not explicitly stated.

Incorrect answer choices that make too strong of a claim are particularly tricky. They may either overstate a detail from the passage or overstate the author's opinion. Keep in mind that the passages are often based on actual academic journal articles, which strive for an objective, neutral tone even when advancing a position. Therefore, you should generally be suspicious of any answer choice that attributes too strong of an opinion to the author. You will also encounter incorrect answer choices that describe the attitude of a person or group other than the author. This is an example of why it is important to keep track of the various viewpoints in a passage when doing the initial analysis. Answer choices that include irrelevant or contradictory information are also common.

Principle

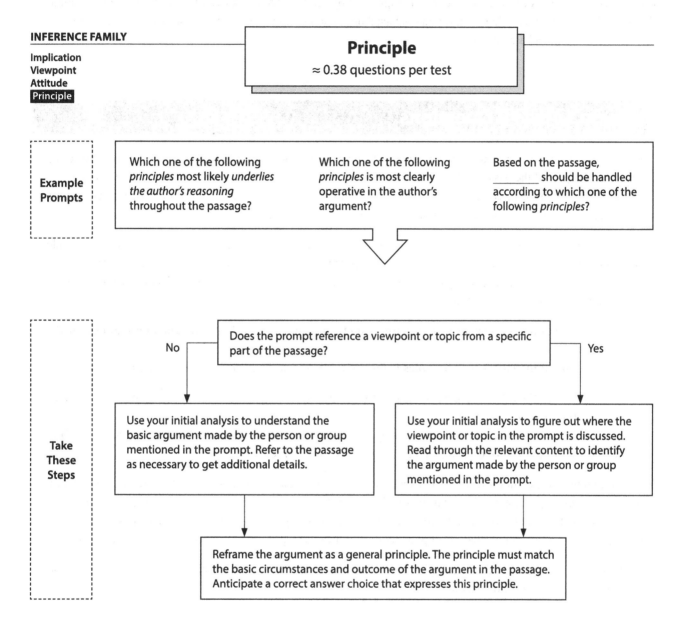

INFERENCE FAMILY

Implication
Viewpoint
Attitude
Principle

Principle
≈ 0.38 questions per test

Example Prompts

Which one of the following *principles* most likely *underlies the author's reasoning* throughout the passage?

Which one of the following *principles* is most clearly operative in the author's argument?

Based on the passage, _____ should be handled according to which one of the following *principles*?

Take These Steps

Does the prompt reference a viewpoint or topic from a specific part of the passage?

No → Use your initial analysis to understand the basic argument made by the person or group mentioned in the prompt. Refer to the passage as necessary to get additional details.

Yes → Use your initial analysis to figure out where the viewpoint or topic in the prompt is discussed. Read through the relevant content to identify the argument made by the person or group mentioned in the prompt.

Reframe the argument as a general principle. The principle must match the basic circumstances and outcome of the argument in the passage. Anticipate a correct answer choice that expresses this principle.

Answer Choices

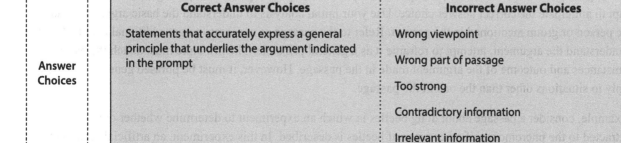

Correct Answer Choices	Incorrect Answer Choices
Statements that accurately express a general principle that underlies the argument indicated in the prompt	Wrong viewpoint
	Wrong part of passage
	Too strong
	Contradictory information
	Irrelevant information

Principle (PR) questions ask you to identify the general rule or principle that underlies an argument in the passage. This argument will be related to the viewpoint or topic in the prompt.

PR question prompts always include the term *principle*. However, on rare occasions, this term will appear in other question types. A PR question can be distinguished by the fact that it asks you to find the general principle that underlies an argument, that an argument is based on, or something similar. PR questions appear only in Argumentative and Debate Passages.

How to Solve PR Questions

The first step in solving a PR question is to determine whether or not the prompt references a viewpoint or topic from a specific part of the passage. The prompt of a PR question always references a viewpoint that is either presented throughout the passage (most commonly, the author's) or in a small section of the passage. The prompt may also specify a topic that is discussed throughout the passage or in one section.

For example, consider a passage in which the author argues against electoral reform throughout and that includes a discussion of proportional representation in the third paragraph. Within this paragraph, the viewpoint of individuals in favor of proportional representation is presented, along with the author's reasons for opposing it. A PR question for this passage might include one of the following prompts:

> **Which one of the following principles most likely underlies the author's argument about electoral reform?**
> **Which one of the following principles is most clearly operative in the author's argument?**
>
> **Which one of the following principles most likely underlies the author's reasoning in his position on proportional representation?**
> **Based on the passage, a proponent of proportional representation is most likely to claim that a fair electoral system is based on which one of the following principles?**

The first two prompts do not direct you to a specific part of the passage. The first prompt references a viewpoint (the author's) and topic (electoral reform) that is discussed throughout the passage, while the second prompt references only the author's viewpoint. However, the last two prompts include either a topic (proportional representation) or a viewpoint (that of proponents of proportional representation) from the third paragraph.

The process for solving a PR question varies depending on whether or not the prompt references a viewpoint or topic from a specific part of the passage.

If the Prompt Does Not Reference a Specific Part of the Passage

When the prompt does not reference a viewpoint or topic from a specific part of the passage, you should still attempt to anticipate the correct answer choice. Use your initial analysis to understand the basic argument made by the person or group mentioned in the prompt. Refer to the passage as necessary to get additional details. Once you understand the argument, attempt to reframe it as a general principle. The principle must match the basic circumstances and outcome of the argument made in the passage. However, it must be phrased generally enough to apply to situations other than the one in the passage.

For example, consider a passage about dung beetles in which an experiment to determine whether dung-beetles are attracted to the pheromones of other types of beetles is described. In this experiment, an artificial scent that matches the pheromone of another beetle species is applied to one section of a dung beetle enclosure. Then, a variety of other artificial scents are applied to other sections of the enclosure. When the beetle proceeds directly to the artificial pheromone, the researcher is able to say for certain that the beetle is attracted to pheromones and is not simply attracted to new, unfamiliar scents in its enclosure.

An appropriate principle would be the following:

> **A variety of substances must be presented at the same time to determine if an animal is attracted to a particular one.**

Note that the wording of this principle is general enough to apply to other situations—beetles, pheromones, and enclosures are not mentioned. In addition, the basic circumstances and outcome are the same—various substances are presented, and the animal is attracted to one.

When attempting to anticipate a correct answer choice, it is best to be as general as possible and to recognize that you are unlikely to match the correct answer choice exactly.

Let's look at Example Question 7 (page 167):

> Based on the passage, the author would probably hold that which one of the following principles is fundamental to long-term predatory control of agricultural pests?
>
> (A) The reproduction of the predator population should be synchronized with that of the prey population, so that the number of predators surges just prior to a surge in prey numbers.
> (B) The effectiveness of the predatory relationship should be experimentally demonstrable in greenhouse as well as field applications.
> (C) The prey population should be able to survive in times of low crop productivity, so that the predator population will not decrease to very low levels.
> (D) The predator population's level of consumption of the prey species should be responsive to variations in the size of the prey population.
> (E) The predator population should be vulnerable only to pesticides to which the prey population is also vulnerable.

The prompt does not reference a viewpoint or topic from a specific part of the passage. The long-term predatory control of agricultural pests is central to the author's argument, which is developed throughout the passage. However, looking at the second paragraph of the passage, we can identify several factors that the author claims are fundamental to long-term predatory control of agricultural pests. These include rapid reproduction of the prey species, the use of the same reproduction method by both species, reproductive synchrony, and the ability of prey species to survive periods with low prey density. A general principle to describe this may be that the predator should be able to adapt to changes in the prey population. We should anticipate a correct answer choice that expresses this principle or a similar one.

> **(A) The reproduction of the predator population should be synchronized with that of the prey population, so that the number of predators surges just prior to a surge in prey numbers.**

This answer choice includes contradictory information. The second paragraph states that the two species have reproductive synchrony. However, the first paragraph indicates that *Typhlodromus* invade strawberry fields in the second year of a cyclamen mite infestation, after the prey population has reached damaging levels. In addition, fourth paragraph clearly states that when the cyclamen population increased in an untreated planting, the *Typhlodromus* population responded to reduce the outbreak. This is a loser.

(B) The effectiveness of the predatory relationship should be experimentally demonstrable in greenhouse as well as field applications.

This answer choice makes too strong of a claim. It is true that both the greenhouse experiments and field applications described in the third and fourth paragraphs of the passage demonstrate the effectiveness of the predatory relationship. However, there is no indication that both experiments are necessary to demonstrate this. The field applications may have been sufficient on their own. This is another loser.

(C) The prey population should be able to survive in times of low crop productivity, so that the predator population will not decrease to very low levels.

This answer choice includes contradictory information. The second paragraph suggests that cyclamen mites are able to survive in times of low crop productivity. However, this is not necessary for the *Typhlodromus* population to avoid a significant decline. That paragraph also states that *Typhlodromus* can utilize other food sources when not feeding on cyclamen mites. This is also a loser.

(D) The predator population's level of consumption of the prey species should be responsive to variations in the size of the prey population.

This matches our anticipated answer choice. The *Typhlodromus* population expands when feeding on cyclamen mites, meaning that its level of consumption increases. However, when the size of the cyclamen mite population decreases, *Typhlodromus* can utilize other food sources, meaning that its level of consumption of cyclamen mites decreases. This is a candidate.

(E) The predator population should be vulnerable only to pesticides to which the prey population is also vulnerable.

This answer choice includes irrelevant information. The passage does not discuss pesticides that affect both species. It also does not indicate that this is necessary for long-term predatory control. This is a loser.

As (D) is the only candidate, it is the correct answer choice.

If the Prompt References a Specific Part of the Passage

When the prompt references a viewpoint or topic from a specific part of the passage, use your initial analysis to figure out where the viewpoint or topic is discussed. You should read through the relevant content and try to identify the argument made by the person or group mentioned in the prompt. Then, develop a general principle that matches the basic circumstances and outcome of this argument. Anticipate a correct answer choice that expresses this principle or a similar one.

Looking at the Answer Choices

The correct answer choice is a statement expressing a general principle that underlies the argument indicated in the prompt. It must match the circumstances and outcome described in the passage but be broad enough to apply to other scenarios.

Incorrect answer choices that include contradictory or irrelevant information are common. An incorrect answer choice includes circumstances that match the passage but an outcome that does not, or vice versa. You will also likely encounter incorrect answer choices that make too strong of a claim or present information related to the wrong viewpoint.

Practice Sets: Inference Family

Analyze the passages below. Mark the <u>keywords</u>, <u>main points</u>, and <u>viewpoints</u> other than the author's. Note the function of each paragraph. Summarize the main points, paragraph content, and viewpoints. Then answer the questions that follow each passage.

Fairy tales address themselves to two communities, each with its own interests and each in periodic conflict with the other: parents and children. Nearly every study of fairy tales has taken the perspective of the
(5) parent, constructing the meaning of the tales by using the reading strategies of an adult bent on identifying universally valid tenets of moral instruction for children.

For example, the plot of "Hansel and Gretel" is set
(10) in motion by hard-hearted parents who abandon their children in the woods, but for psychologist Bruno Bettelheim the tale is really about children who learn to give up their unhealthy dependency on their parents. According to Bettelheim, this story—in which the
(15) children ultimately overpower a witch who has taken them prisoner for the crime of attempting to eat the witch's gingerbread house—forces its young audience to recognize the dangers of unrestrained greed. As dependent children, Bettelheim argues, Hansel and
(20) Gretel had been a burden to their parents, but on their return home with the witch's jewels, they become the family's support. Thus, says Bettelheim, does the story train its young listeners to become "mature children."

There are two ways of interpreting a story: one is a
(25) "superficial" reading that focuses on the tale's manifest content, and the other is a "deeper" reading that looks for latent meanings. Many adults who read fairy tales are drawn to this second kind of interpretation in order to avoid facing the unpleasant truths that can emerge
(30) from the tales when adults—even parents—are portrayed as capable of acting out of selfish motives themselves. What makes fairy tales attractive to Bettelheim and other psychologists is that they can be used as scenarios that position the child as a
(35) transgressor whose deserved punishment provides a lesson for unruly children. Stories that run counter to such orthodoxies about child-rearing are, to a large extent, suppressed by Bettelheim or "rewritten" through reinterpretation. Once we examine his
(40) interpretations closely, we see that his readings produce meanings that are very different from those constructed by readers with different cultural assumptions and expectations, who, unlike Bettelheim, do not find inflexible tenets of moral instruction in the
(45) tales.

Bettelheim interprets all fairy tales as driven by children's fantasies of desire and revenge, and in doing so suppresses the true nature of parental behavior ranging from abuse to indulgence. Fortunately, these
(50) characterizations of selfish children and innocent adults have been discredited to some extent by recent psychoanalytic literature. The need to deny adult evil has been a pervasive feature of our society, leading us

to position children not only as the sole agents of evil
(55) but also as the objects of unending moral instruction, hence the idea that a literature targeted for them must stand in the service of pragmatic instrumentality rather than foster an unproductive form of playful pleasure.

Main Point

Paragraph 1

Paragraph 2

Paragraph 3

Paragraph 4

Identify Viewpoints

1. Which one of the following is the most accurate description of the author's attitude toward Bettelheim's view of fairy tales?

   (A) concern that the view will undermine the ability of fairy tales to provide moral instruction
   (B) scorn toward the view's supposition that moral tenets can be universally valid
   (C) disapproval of the view's depiction of children as selfish and adults as innocent
   (D) anger toward the view's claim that children often improve as a result of deserved punishment
   (E) disappointment with the view's emphasis on the manifest content of a tale

2. The author of the passage would be most likely to agree with which one of the following statements?

   (A) Children who never attempt to look for the deeper meanings in fairy tales will miss out on one of the principal pleasures of reading such tales.
   (B) It is better if children discover fairy tales on their own than for an adult to suggest that they read the tales.
   (C) A child who is unruly will behave better after reading a fairy tale if the tale is suggested to them by another child.
   (D) Most children are too young to comprehend the deeper meanings contained in fairy tales.
   (E) Children should be allowed to enjoy literature that has no instructive purpose.

3. Which one of the following principles most likely underlies the author's characterization of literary interpretation?

   (A) Only those trained in literary interpretation can detect the latent meanings in stories.
   (B) Only adults are psychologically mature enough to find the latent meanings in stories.
   (C) Only one of the various meanings readers may find in a story is truly correct.
   (D) The meanings we see in stories are influenced by the assumptions and expectations we bring to the story.
   (E) The latent meanings a story contains are deliberately placed there by the author.

4. It can be inferred from the passage that Bettelheim believes that children are

   (A) uninterested in inflexible tenets of moral instruction
   (B) unfairly subjected to the moral beliefs of their parents
   (C) often aware of inappropriate parental behavior
   (D) capable of shedding undesirable personal qualities
   (E) basically playful and carefree

5. Which one of the following statements is least compatible with Bettelheim's views, as those views are described in the passage?

   (A) The imaginations of children do not draw clear distinctions between inanimate objects and living things.
   (B) Children must learn that their own needs and feelings are to be valued, even when these differ from those of their parents.
   (C) As their minds mature, children tend to experience the world in terms of the dynamics of the family into which they were born.
   (D) The more secure that children feel within the world, the less they need to hold onto infantile notions.
   (E) Children's ability to distinguish between stories and reality is not fully developed until puberty.

In spite of a shared language, Latin American
poetry written in Spanish differs from Spanish poetry
in many respects. The Spanish of Latin American poets
is more open than that of Spanish poets, more exposed

(5) to outside influences—indigenous, English, French,
and other languages. While some literary critics
maintain that there is as much linguistic unity in Latin
American poetry as there is in Spanish poetry, they
base this claim on the fact that Castilian Spanish, the

(10) official and literary version of the Spanish language
based largely on the dialect originally spoken in the
Castile region of Spain, was transplanted to the
Americas when it was already a relatively standardized
idiom. Although such unity may have characterized the

(15) earliest Latin American poetry, after centuries in the
Americas the language of Latin American poetry
cannot help but reveal the influences of its unique
cultural history.

Latin American poetry is critical or irreverent in its

(20) attitude toward language, where that of Spanish poets
is more accepting. For example, the Spanish-language
incarnations of modernism and the avant-garde, two
literary movements that used language in innovative
and challenging ways, originated with Latin American

(25) poets. By contrast, when these movements later
reached Spain, Spanish poets greeted them with
reluctance. Spanish poets, even those of the modern
era, seem to take their language for granted, rarely
using it in radical or experimental ways.

(30) The most distinctive note in Latin American poetry
is its enthusiastic response to the modern world, while
Spanish poetry displays a kind of cultural
conservatism—the desire to return to an ideal culture
of the distant past. Because no Spanish-language

(35) culture lies in the equally distant (i.e., pre-Columbian)
past of the Americas, but has instead been invented by
Latin Americans day by day, Latin American poetry
has no such long-standing past to romanticize. Instead,
Latin American poetry often displays a curiosity about

(40) the literature of other cultures, an interest in exploring
poetic structures beyond those typical of Spanish
poetry. For example, the first Spanish-language
haiku—a Japanese poetic form—were written by José
Juan Tablada, a Mexican. Another of the Latin

(45) American poets' responses to this absence is the search
for a world before recorded history—not only that of
Spain or the Americas, but in some cases of the planet;
the Chilean poet Pablo Neruda's work, for example, is
noteworthy for its development of an ahistorical

(50) mythology for the creation of the earth. For Latin
American poets there is no such thing as the pristine
cultural past affirmed in the poetry of Spain: there is
only the fluid interaction of all world cultures, or else
the extensive time before cultures began.

Main Point

Paragraph 1

Paragraph 2

Paragraph 3

Identify Viewpoints

6. Which one of the following can most reasonably be inferred from the passage about Latin American poetry's use of poetic structures from other world cultures?

(A) The use of poetic structures from other world cultures is an attempt by Latin American poets to create a cultural past.

(B) The use of poetic structures from other world cultures by Latin American poets is a response to their lack of a long-standing Spanish-language cultural past in the Americas.

(C) The use of poetic structures from other world cultures has led Latin American poets to reconsider their lack of a long-standing Spanish-language cultural past in the Americas.

(D) Latin American poets who write about a world before recorded history do not use poetic structures from other world cultures.

(E) Latin American poetry does not borrow poetic structures from other world cultures whose literature exhibits cultural conservatism.

7. Based on the passage, the author most likely holds which one of the following views toward Spanish poetry's relationship to the Spanish cultural past?

(A) This relationship has inspired Spanish poets to examine their cultural past with a critical eye.

(B) This relationship forces Spanish poets to write about subjects with which they feel little natural affinity.

(C) This relationship is itself the central theme of much Spanish poetry.

(D) This relationship infuses Spanish poetry with a romanticism that is reluctant to embrace the modern era.

(E) This relationship results in poems that are of little interest to contemporary Spanish readers.

8. Which one of the following inferences is most supported by the passage?

(A) A tradition of cultural conservatism has allowed the Spanish language to evolve into a stable, reliable form of expression.

(B) It was only recently that Latin American poetry began to incorporate elements of other languages.

(C) The cultural conservatism of Spanish poetry is exemplified by the uncritical attitude of Spanish poets toward the Spanish language.

(D) Latin American poets' interest in other world cultures is illustrated by their use of Japanese words and phrases.

(E) Spanish poetry is receptive to the influence of some Spanish-language poets outside of Spain.

The proponents of the Modern Movement in architecture considered that, compared with the historical styles that it replaced, Modernist architecture more accurately reflected the functional
(5) spirit of twentieth-century technology and was better suited to the newest building methods. It is ironic, then, that the Movement fostered an ideology of design that proved to be at odds with the way buildings were really built.

(10) The tenacious adherence of Modernist architects and critics to this ideology was in part responsible for the Movement's decline. Originating in the 1920s as a marginal, almost bohemian art movement, the Modern Movement was never very popular with the public,
(15) but this very lack of popular support produced in Modernist architects a high-minded sense of mission—not content merely to interpret the needs of the client, these architects now sought to persuade, to educate, and, if necessary, to dictate. By 1945 the
(20) tenets of the Movement had come to dominate mainstream architecture, and by the early 1950s, to dominate architectural criticism—architects whose work seemed not to advance the evolution of the Modern Movement tended to be dismissed by
(25) proponents of Modernism. On the other hand, when architects were identified as innovators—as was the case with Otto Wagner, or the young Frank Lloyd Wright—attention was drawn to only those features of their work that were "Modern"; other aspects were
(30) conveniently ignored.

The decline of the Modern Movement later in the twentieth century occurred partly as a result of Modernist architects' ignorance of building methods, and partly because Modernist architects were
(35) reluctant to admit that their concerns were chiefly aesthetic. Moreover, the building industry was evolving in a direction Modernists had not anticipated: it was more specialized and the process of construction was much more fragmented than in
(40) the past. Up until the twentieth century, construction had been carried out by a relatively small number of tradespeople, but as the building industry evolved, buildings came to be built by many specialized subcontractors working independently. The architect's
(45) design not only had to accommodate a sequence of independent operations, but now had to reflect the allowable degree of inaccuracy of the different trades. However, one of the chief construction ideals of the Modern Movement was to "honestly" expose
(50) structural materials such as steel and concrete. To do this and still produce a visually acceptable interior called for an unrealistically high level of craftsmanship. Exposure of a building's internal structural elements, if it could be achieved at all,
(55) could only be accomplished at considerable cost— hence the well-founded reputation of Modern architecture as prohibitively expensive.

As Postmodern architects recognized, the need to expose structural elements imposed unnecessary
(60) limitations on building design. The unwillingness of architects of the Modern Movement to abandon their ideals contributed to the decline of interest in the Modern Movement.

Main Point

Paragraph 1

Paragraph 2

Paragraph 3

Paragraph 4

Identify Viewpoints

9. With respect to the proponents of the Modern Movement, the author of the passage can best be described as

    (A) forbearing
    (B) defensive
    (C) unimpressed
    (D) exasperated
    (E) indifferent

10. It can be inferred that the author of the passage believes which one of the following about Modern Movement architects' ideal of exposing structural materials?

    (A) The repudiation of the ideal by some of these architects undermined its validity.
    (B) The ideal was rarely achieved because of its lack of popular appeal.
    (C) The ideal was unrealistic because most builders were unwilling to attempt it.
    (D) The ideal originated in the work of Otto Wagner and Frank Lloyd Wright.
    (E) The ideal arose from aesthetic rather than practical concerns.

The Japanese American sculptor Isamu Noguchi (1904–1988) was an artist who intuitively asked—and responded to—deeply original questions. He might well have become a scientist within a standard
(5) scientific discipline, but he instead became an artist who repeatedly veered off at wide angles from the well-known courses followed by conventionally talented artists of both the traditional and modern schools. The story behind one particular sculpture
(10) typifies this aspect of his creativeness.

By his early twenties, Noguchi's sculptures showed such exquisite comprehension of human anatomy and deft conceptual realization that he won a Guggenheim Fellowship for travel in Europe. After
(15) arriving in Paris in 1927, Noguchi asked the Romanian-born sculptor Constantin Brancusi if he might become his student. When Brancusi said no, that he never took students, Noguchi asked if he needed a stonecutter. Brancusi did. Noguchi cut and
(20) polished stone for Brancusi in his studio, frequently also polishing Brancusi's brass and bronze sculptures. Noguchi, with his scientist's mind, pondered the fact that sculptors through the ages had relied exclusively upon negative light—that is, shadows—for their
(25) conceptual communication, precisely because no metals, other than the expensive, nonoxidizing gold, could be relied upon to give off positive-light reflections.

Noguchi wanted to create a sculpture that was purely reflective. In 1929, after returning to the
(30) United States, he met the architect and philosopher R. Buckminster Fuller, offering to sculpt a portrait of him. When Fuller heard of Noguchi's ideas regarding positive-light sculpture, he suggested using chrome-nickel steel, which Henry Ford, through automotive
(35) research and development, had just made commercially available for the first time in history. Here, finally, was a permanently reflective surface, economically available in massive quantities.

In sculpting his portrait of Fuller, Noguchi did not
(40) think of it as merely a shiny alternate model of traditional, negative-light sculptures. What he saw was that completely reflective surfaces provided a fundamental invisibility of surface like that of utterly still waters, whose presence can be apprehended only
(45) when objects—a ship's mast, a tree, or sky—are reflected in them. Seaplane pilots making offshore landings in dead calm cannot tell where the water is and must glide in, waiting for the unpredictable touchdown. Noguchi conceived a similarly invisible sculpture,
(50) hidden in and communicating through the reflections of images surrounding it. Then only the distortion of familiar shapes in the surrounding environment could be seen by the viewer. The viewer's awareness of the "invisible" sculpture's presence and dimensional
(55) relationships would be derived only secondarily.

Even after this stunning discovery, Noguchi remained faithful to his inquisitive nature. At the moment when his explorations had won critical recognition of the genius of his original and
(60) fundamental conception, Noguchi proceeded to the next phase of his evolution.

Main Point

Paragraph 1

Paragraph 2

Paragraph 3

Paragraph 4

Paragraph 5

Identify Viewpoints

11. The passage offers the strongest evidence that the author would agree with which one of the following statements?

(A) Noguchi's work in Paris contributed significantly to the art of sculpture in that it embodied solutions to problems that other sculptors, including Brancusi, had sought unsuccessfully to overcome.

(B) Noguchi's scientific approach to designing sculptures and to selecting materials for sculptures is especially remarkable in that he had no formal scientific training.

(C) Despite the fact that Brancusi was a sculptor and Fuller was not, Fuller played a more pivotal role than did Brancusi in Noguchi's realization of the importance of negative light to the work of previous sculptors.

(D) Noguchi was more interested in addressing fundamental aesthetic questions than in maintaining a consistent artistic style.

(E) Noguchi's work is of special interest for what it reveals not only about the value of scientific thinking in the arts but also about the value of aesthetic approaches to scientific inquiry.

12. The passage most strongly supports which one of the following inferences?

(A) Prior to suggesting the sculptural use of chrome-nickel steel to Noguchi, Fuller himself has made architectural designs that called for the use of this material.

(B) Noguchi believed that the use of industrial materials to create sculptures would make the sculptures more commercially viable.

(C) Noguchi's "invisible" sculpture appears to have no shape or dimensions of its own, but rather those of surrounding objects.

(D) If a positive-light sculpture depicting a person in a realistic manner were coated with a metal subject to oxidation, it would eventually cease to be recognizable as a realistic likeness.

(E) The perception of the shape and dimensions of a negative-light sculpture does not depend on its reflection of objects from the environment around it.

13. Which one of the following inferences about the portrait of Fuller does the passage most strongly support?

(A) The material that Noguchi used in it had been tentatively investigated by other sculptors but not in direct connection with its reflective properties.

(B) It was similar to at least some of the sculptures that Noguchi produced prior to 1927 in that it represented a human form.

(C) Noguchi did not initially think of it as especially innovative or revolutionary and thus was surprised by Fuller's reaction to it.

(D) It was produced as a personal favor to Fuller and thus was not initially intended to be noticed and commented on by art critics.

(E) It was unlike the sculptures that Noguchi had helped Brancusi to produce in that the latter's aesthetic effects did not depend on contrasts of light and shadow.

A vigorous debate in astronomy centers on an epoch in planetary history that was first identified by analysis of rock samples obtained in lunar missions. Scientists discovered that the major craters on the
(5) Moon were created by a vigorous bombardment of debris approximately four billion years ago—the so-called late heavy bombardment (LHB). Projectiles from this bombardment that affected the Moon should also have struck Earth, a likelihood with profound
(10) consequences for the history of Earth since, until the LHB ended, life could not have survived here.

Various theoretical approaches have been developed to account for both the evidence gleaned from samples of Moon rock collected during lunar
(15) explorations and the size and distribution of craters on the Moon. Since the sizes of LHB craters suggest they were formed by large bodies, some astronomers believe that the LHB was linked to the disintegration of an asteroid or comet orbiting the Sun. In this view,
(20) a large body broke apart and peppered the inner solar system with debris. Other scientists disagree and believe that the label "LHB" is in itself a misnomer. These researchers claim that a cataclysm is not necessary to explain the LHB evidence. They claim
(25) that the Moon's evidence merely provides a view of the period concluding billions of years of a continuous, declining heavy bombardment throughout the inner solar system. According to them, the impacts from the latter part of the bombardment were
(30) so intense that they obliterated evidence of earlier impacts. A third group contends that the Moon's evidence supports the view that the LHB was a sharply defined cataclysmic cratering period, but these scientists believe that because of its relatively brief
(35) duration, this cataclysm did not extend throughout the inner solar system. They hold that the LHB involved only the disintegration of a body within the Earth-Moon system, because the debris from such an event would have been swept up relatively quickly.
(40) New support for the hypothesis that a late bombardment extended throughout the inner solar system has been found in evidence from the textural features and chemical makeup of a meteorite that has been found on Earth. It seems to be a rare example of
(45) a Mars rock that made its way to Earth after being knocked from the surface of Mars. The rock has recently been experimentally dated at about four billion years old, which means that, if the rock is indeed from Mars, it was knocked from the planet at
(50) about the same time that the Moon was experiencing the LHB. This tiny piece of evidence suggests that at least two planetary systems in the inner solar system experienced bombardment at the same time. However, to determine the pervasiveness of the LHB, scientists
(55) will need to locate many more such rocks and perhaps obtain surface samples from other planets in the inner solar system.

Main Point

Paragraph 1

Paragraph 2

Paragraph 3

Identify Viewpoints

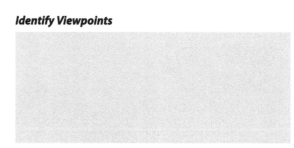

14. The author's attitude toward arguments that might be based on the evidence of the rock mentioned in the passage as being from Mars (lines 44–46) can most accurately be described as

(A) ambivalence because the theory of the rock's migration to Earth is at once both appealing and difficult to believe

(B) caution because even if the claims concerning the rock's origins can be proven, it is unwise to draw general conclusions without copious evidence

(C) skepticism because it seems unlikely that a rock could somehow make its way from Mars to Earth after being dislodged

(D) curiosity because many details of the rock's interplanetary travel, its chemical analysis, and its dating analysis have not yet been published

(E) outright acceptance because the origins of the rock have been sufficiently corroborated

15. The author implies that all theoretical approaches to the LHB would agree on which one of the following?

(A) the approximate duration of the LHB

(B) the origin of the debris involved in the LHB

(C) the idea that cratering decreased significantly after the LHB

(D) the idea that the LHB destroyed the life that existed on Earth four billion years ago

(E) the approximate amount of debris involved in the LHB

16. According to the passage, the third group of scientists (line 31) believes that the LHB

(A) affected only the moon

(B) was so brief that its extent had to be fairly localized

(C) consisted of so little debris that it was absorbed quickly by the planets in the inner solar system

(D) occurred more recently than four billion years ago

(E) may have lasted a long time, but all its debris remained within the Earth-Moon system

For Questions 1–5

Fairy tales address themselves to two communities, each with its own interests and each in periodic conflict with the other: A)parents and B)children. Nearly every study of fairy tales has taken the perspective of the

(5) parent, constructing the meaning of the tales by using the reading strategies of an adult bent on identifying universally valid tenets of moral instruction for children.

For example, the plot of "Hansel and Gretel" is set

(10) in motion by hard-hearted parents who abandon their children in the woods, but for psychologist A)Bruno Bettelheim the tale is really about children who learn to give up their unhealthy dependency on their parents. According to Bettelheim, this story—in which the

(15) children ultimately overpower a witch who has taken them prisoner for the crime of attempting to eat the witch's gingerbread house—forces its young audience to recognize the dangers of unrestrained greed. As dependent children, Bettelheim argues, Hansel and

(20) Gretel had been a burden to their parents, but on their return home with the witch's jewels, they become the family's support. Thus, says Bettelheim, does the story train its young listeners to become "mature children."

There are two ways of interpreting a story: one is a

(25) B)"superficial" reading that focuses on the tale's manifest content, and the other is a A)"deeper" reading that looks for latent meanings. A)Many adults who read fairy tales are drawn to this second kind of interpretation in order to avoid facing the unpleasant truths that can emerge

(30) from the tales when adults—even parents—are portrayed as capable of acting out of selfish motives themselves. What makes fairy tales attractive to A)Bettelheim and other psychologists is that they can be used as scenarios that position the child as a

(35) transgressor whose deserved punishment provides a lesson for unruly children. Stories that run counter to such orthodoxies about child-rearing are, to a large extent, suppressed by Bettelheim or "rewritten" through reinterpretation. Once we examine his

(40) interpretations closely, we see that his readings produce meanings that are very different from those constructed by B)readers with different cultural assumptions and expectations, who, unlike Bettelheim, do not find inflexible tenets of moral instruction in the

(45) tales.

Bettelheim interprets all fairy tales as driven by children's fantasies of desire and revenge, and in doing so suppresses the true nature of parental behavior ranging from abuse to indulgence. Fortunately, these

(50) characterizations of selfish children and innocent adults have been discredited to some extent by B)recent psychoanalytic literature. The need to deny adult evil has been a pervasive feature of our society, leading us to position children not only as the sole agents of evil

(55) but also as the objects of unending moral instruction, hence the idea that a literature targeted for them must stand in the service of pragmatic instrumentality rather than foster an unproductive form of playful pleasure.

Main Point

The main point is stated in the first and third sentences of the last paragraph. It is that the need to deny adult evil has led psychologists and others to wrongly view fairy tales as instruments of moral instruction for children, denying the superficial reading of parental wrongdoing. This is the author's conclusion.

Paragraph 1

This paragraph introduces the two opposing viewpoints: the parents' viewpoint (supported by Bettelheim and others) and the children's viewpoint (supported by the author). It also provides background information about the first viewpoint.

Paragraph 2

This paragraph provides an example ("Hansel and Gretel") to illustrate the first viewpoint. It explores Bettelheim's argument that the story is about children learning to give up their unhealthy dependence on their parents.

Paragraph 3

This paragraph provides supporting details for the viewpoint of children. It states that stories that do not feature the child as the transgressor are suppressed or rewritten. It also states that people with other cultural assumptions do not see moral instruction in fairy tales. This paragraph also introduces the author's viewpoint.

Paragraph 4

This paragraph presents the author's viewpoint in greater detail. It also specifies that the author's and children's viewpoint is supported by recent psychoanalytic literature.

Identify Viewpoints

The two main viewpoints in this passage are the parents' and children's readings of fairy tales. The author's viewpoint is present and supports the children's viewpoint.

1. **Correct Answer (C).** *Prep Test 39, Section 3, Passage 2, Question 11.*

> **Which one of the following is the most accurate description of the author's attitude toward Bettelheim's view of fairy tales?**

This is an ATT question. The prompt does not reference a viewpoint or topic from a specific part of the passage. Bettelheim's viewpoint, which corresponds with the parents' viewpoint, is discussed throughout the passage. In addition, *fairy tales* is the main topic of the passage. However, there are a number of keywords that indicate the author's attitude. The term *bent* in the first paragraph suggests that the author thinks that the parents' viewpoint unnecessarily and excessively looks for moral instruction in fairy tales. The term *fortunately* in the fourth paragraph suggests that the author is pleased that the parents' viewpoint has been discredited. Therefore, the author seems to be critical of Bettelheim's viewpoint that children are selfish and in need of moral instruction while adults are innocent. We should anticipate a correct answer choice that expresses this attitude.

> **(A) concern that the view will undermine the ability of fairy tales to provide moral instruction**

This answer choice includes contradictory information. The author is critical of the viewpoint that fairy tales are intended to provide moral instruction; therefore, the author would not be concerned that this ability is undermined. This is a loser.

> **(B) scorn toward the view's supposition that moral tenets can be universally valid**

This answer choice includes irrelevant information. Whether or not moral tenets can be universally valid is never discussed in the passage. This is a loser.

> **(C) disapproval of the view's depiction of children as selfish and adults as innocent**

This matches our anticipated answer choice. The fourth paragraph states that it is fortunate that the viewpoint of selfish children and innocent adults has been discredited. This is a candidate.

> **(D) anger toward the view's claim that children often improve as a result of deserved punishment**

This answer choice includes irrelevant information. Bettelheim never claims that children will improve as a result of punishment. This is a loser.

> **(E) disappointment with the view's emphasis on the manifest content of a tale**

This answer choice addresses the wrong viewpoint. An emphasis on the manifest content of a tale is a feature of the children's viewpoint, not Bettelheim's. This is another loser.

As (C) is the only candidate, it is the correct answer choice.

2. **Correct Answer (E).** *Prep Test 39, Section 3, Passage 2, Question 12.*

> **The author of the passage would be most likely to agree with which one of the following statements?**

This is a V question. The prompt does not reference a viewpoint or topic from a specific part of the passage. Therefore, we cannot anticipate a correct answer choice and must proceed directly to eliminating answer choices.

> **(A) Children who never attempt to look for the deeper meanings in fairy tales will miss out on one of the principal pleasures of reading such tales.**

This answer choice addresses the wrong viewpoint and includes irrelevant information. The idea that fairy tales include deeper meanings is part of the parents' viewpoint, which the author opposes. In addition, the passage does not discuss the principlal pleasures of reading fairy tales. This is a loser.

(B) It is better if children discover fairy tales on their own than for an adult to suggest that they read the tales.

This answer choice includes irrelevant information. The passage does not discuss how fairy tales should be discovered by children. This is another loser.

(C) A child who is unruly will behave better after reading a fairy tale if the tale is suggested to them by another child.

This answer choice also includes irrelevant information. There is no mention of children suggesting fairy tales to other children. This is also a loser.

(D) Most children are too young to comprehend the deeper meanings contained in fairy tales.

This seems like a statement the author would agree with based on the information in the passage. The third paragraph states that adults are drawn to a deeper reading, suggesting that children are not. This is a candidate.

(E) Children should be allowed to enjoy literature that has no instructive purpose.

This also seems like a statement the author would agree with. The last sentence of the fourth paragraph makes it clear that the author opposes the viewpoint that fairy tales must be instructive rather than foster an unproductive form of playful pleasure. This is also a candidate.

We have two candidates, (D) and (E), so we need to eliminate one. Looking back at (D), we can see that it makes too strong of a claim. The fact that adults are drawn to deeper meanings does not necessarily mean that children are unable to comprehend them. In contrast, (E) is directly supported by the content of the fourth paragraph. Therefore, (E) is the correct answer choice.

---

3. **Correct Answer (D).** *Prep Test 39, Section 3, Passage 2, Question 13.*

Which one of the following principles most likely underlies the author's characterization of literary interpretation?

This is a PR question. The prompt does not reference a viewpoint or topic from a specific part of the passage. Literary interpretation is the main topic of the passage. The author focuses on discrediting Bettelheim's (who represents the parents' viewpoint) interpretation of fairy tales. In the third paragraph, the author claims that Bettelheim suppresses or misconstrues fairy tales that do not support his interpretation. The author also points out that individuals with other cultural assumptions do not agree with Bettelheim's interpretation. The author seems to be stressing the need for objectivity. A general principle to describe this may be that personal biases should not affect the process of literary interpretation. We should anticipate a correct answer choice that expresses this principle or a similar one.

(A) Only those trained in literary interpretation can detect the latent meanings in stories.

This answer choice includes irrelevant information. The author does not discuss training in literary interpretation anywhere in the passage. This is a loser.

(B) Only adults are psychologically mature enough to find the latent meanings in stories.

This answer choice makes too strong of a claim. The author claims that adults are drawn to hidden meanings, but this does not mean that children are not capable of finding latent meanings. This is another loser.

(C) Only one of the various meanings readers may find in a story is truly correct.

Again, this answer choice makes too strong of a claim. The author is critical of the parents' viewpoint and supportive of the children's, but this does not mean that there is only one correct meaning in a story. This is also a loser.

(D) The meanings we see in stories are influenced by the assumptions and expectations we bring to the story.

This matches our anticipated answer choice. In the third paragraph, the author states that stories can be misconstrued due to cultural assumptions and a reader's expectations of meaning. This is a candidate.

(E) The latent meanings a story contains are deliberately placed there by the author.

This answer choice includes irrelevant information. The authors of stories are never discussed in the passage. This is a loser.

As (D) is the only candidate, it is the correct answer choice.

4. **Correct Answer (D).** *Prep Test 39, Section 3, Passage 2, Question 15.*

It can be inferred from the passage that Bettelheim believes that children are

This is a V question. The prompt does not reference a viewpoint or topic from a specific part of the passage. Therefore, we cannot anticipate a correct answer choice and must proceed directly to eliminating answer choices.

(A) uninterested in inflexible tenets of moral instruction

This answer choice includes irrelevant information. The passage does not discuss children's interests in moral instruction. This is a loser.

(B) unfairly subjected to the moral beliefs of their parents

This answer choice is related to the wrong viewpoint. Bettelheim wants children to be morally instructed by fairy tales, which are interpreted through the lens of parents. This is also a loser.

(C) often aware of inappropriate parental behavior

This answer choice includes irrelevant information. The passage never states what children are or are not aware of with regard to parental behavior. This is another loser.

(D) capable of shedding undesirable personal qualities

This seems like a statement the Bettelheim would agree with based on the information in the passage. The last sentence of the second paragraph states that Bettelheim believes that fairy tales can train young listeners to become mature students. The third paragraph states that he feels that fairy tales can provide a lesson for unruly children. This is a candidate.

(E) basically playful and carefree

This answer choice is related to the wrong viewpoint. It clearly aligns with the author's viewpoint, which favors fairy tales as forms of playful pleasure. This is a loser.

As (D) is the only candidate, it is the correct answer choice.

5. Correct Answer (B). *Prep Test 39, Section 3, Passage 2, Question 16.*

Which one of the following statements is least compatible with Bettelheim's views, as those views are described in the passage?

This is a V EXCEPT question. Therefore, the correct answer will be incompatible with Bettelheim's viewpoint. The incorrect answer choices will either be compatible with his viewpoint or include information that makes it impossible to determine whether or not they are compatible. The prompt does not reference a viewpoint or topic from a specific part of the passage. Therefore, we should proceed directly to eliminating answer choices.

(A) The imaginations of children do not draw clear distinctions between inanimate objects and living things.

This answer choice includes irrelevant information. Distinctions between inanimate objects and living things are not discussed in the passage. Therefore, we cannot determine whether this statement is compatible with Bettelheim's viewpoint. This is a loser.

(B) Children must learn that their own needs and feelings are to be valued, even when these differ from those of their parents.

This seems like a statement that Bettelheim would disagree with based on the information in the passage. Bettelheim believes that children should be morally instructed by fairy tales as interpreted by parents. Therefore, it does not seem likely that Bettelheim believes that children must learn their own needs and feelings are to be valued over those of their parents. This is a candidate for now.

(C) As their minds mature, children tend to experience the world in terms of the dynamics of the family into which they were born.

This answer choice includes irrelevant information. There is no discussion of family dynamics in the passage. This is a loser.

(D) The more secure that children feel within the world, the less they need to hold onto infantile notions.

This answer choice also includes irrelevant information. Children's feelings of security are not discussed in the passage. This is another loser.

(E) Children's ability to distinguish between stories and reality is not fully developed until puberty.

This answer choice includes irrelevant information as well. Puberty and the ability to distinguish between stories and reality are not discussed. This is also a loser.

As (B) is the only candidate, it is the correct answer choice.

For Questions 6–8

In spite of a shared language, Latin American poetry written in Spanish differs from Spanish poetry in many respects. The Spanish of Latin American poets is more open than that of Spanish poets, more exposed

(5) to outside influences—indigenous, English, French, and other languages. While ᴬ⁾ some literary critics maintain that there is as much linguistic unity in Latin American poetry as there is in Spanish poetry, they base this claim on the fact that Castilian Spanish, the

(10) official and literary version of the Spanish language based largely on the dialect originally spoken in the Castile region of Spain, was transplanted to the Americas when it was already a relatively standardized idiom. Although such unity may have characterized the

(15) earliest Latin American poetry, after centuries in the Americas the language of Latin American poetry cannot help but reveal the influences of its unique cultural history.

Latin American poetry is critical or irreverent in its

(20) attitude toward language, where that of Spanish poets is more accepting. For example, the Spanish-language incarnations of modernism and the avant-garde, two literary movements that used language in innovative and challenging ways, originated with Latin American

(25) poets. By contrast, when these movements later reached Spain, Spanish poets greeted them with reluctance. Spanish poets, even those of the modern era, seem to take their language for granted, rarely using it in radical or experimental ways.

(30) The most distinctive note in Latin American poetry is its enthusiastic response to the modern world, while Spanish poetry displays a kind of cultural conservatism—the desire to return to an ideal culture of the distant past. Because no Spanish-language

(35) culture lies in the equally distant (i.e., pre-Columbian) past of the Americas, but has instead been invented by Latin Americans day by day, Latin American poetry has no such long-standing past to romanticize. Instead, Latin American poetry often displays a curiosity about

(40) the literature of other cultures, an interest in exploring poetic structures beyond those typical of Spanish poetry. For example, the first Spanish-language haiku—a Japanese poetic form—were written by José Juan Tablada, a Mexican. Another of the Latin

(45) American poets' responses to this absence is the search for a world before recorded history—not only that of Spain or the Americas, but in some cases of the planet; the Chilean poet Pablo Neruda's work, for example, is noteworthy for its development of an ahistorical

(50) mythology for the creation of the earth. For Latin American poets there is no such thing as the pristine cultural past affirmed in the poetry of Spain: there is only the fluid interaction of all world cultures, or else the extensive time before cultures began.

Main Point

The main point is stated in the first sentence of the first paragraph. It is that Latin American poetry is distinct from Spanish poetry.

Paragraph 1

This paragraph states the main point and mentions the viewpoint of literary critics who believe that Latin American poetry has linguistic unity in passing. It also provides background information, stating that Latin American poetry is more open to outside influences and has less linguistic unity than Spanish poetry.

Paragraph 2

This paragraph provides support for the main point by stating a key difference between the two types of poetry: Latin American poetry is more critical or irreverent with regards to language. It then provides the example of Spanish-Language modernism and the avant-garde, two literary movements that originated in Latin America and that were greeted with reluctance in Spain.

Paragraph 3

This paragraph points out another key difference. It states that Latin American poetry is more enthusiastic in its response to the modern world. It explains that Spanish poetry is conservative and focused on an ideal Spanish culture of the past, whereas Latin American poetry has no such long-standing past to romanticize. Therefore, Latin American poetry is curious about the literature of other cultures. It then provides an example to illustrate this (Tablada's use of the Japanese haiku). It also discusses Latin American poets' interest in the world before recorded history, and provides an example (Neruda's creation myth).

Identify Viewpoints

The author's viewpoint is present and is the focus of the passage. The viewpoint of literary critics who maintain that Latin American poetry has linguistic unity is mentioned in passing.

6. **Correct Answer (B).** *Prep Test 40, Section 4, Passage 2, Question 10.*

> **Which one of the following can most reasonably be inferred from the passage about Latin American poetry's use of poetic structures from other world cultures?**

This is an IMP question. The topic of the prompt is poetic structures from other world cultures. Looking back at our analysis of the passage, we can see that the literature of other cultures is discussed in the third paragraph. That paragraph states that Latin American poets do not have a long-standing past to romanticize and, instead, are curious about the poetry of other cultures. It seems logical to infer that this curiosity was a result of not having a long-standing past to romanticize. We should anticipate a correct answer choice that expresses this inference or another one that can be logically drawn from this section of the passage.

> **(A) The use of poetic structures from other world cultures is an attempt by Latin American poets to create a cultural past.**

This seems like a logical inference based on the information in the passage. The third paragraph states that Latin American poets did not have a long-standing cultural past, so they were forced to invent it day by day. This process may have involved the use of poetic structures from other cultures. This is a candidate.

> **(B) The use of poetic structures from other world cultures by Latin American poets is a response to their lack of a long-standing Spanish-language cultural past in the Americas.**

This matches our anticipated answer. The use of poetic structures from other cultures was a result of not having a long-standing cultural past. This is a candidate as well.

> **(C) The use of poetic structures from other world cultures has led Latin American poets to reconsider their lack of a long-standing Spanish-language cultural past in the Americas.**

This answer choice includes contradictory information. The third paragraph clearly states that the use of poetic structures from other cultures was a response to the lack of a long-standing cultural past. This answer choice states the opposite. This is a loser.

> **(D) Latin American poets who write about a world before recorded history do not use poetic structures from other world cultures.**

This answer choice includes irrelevant information. Neruda is provided as an example of a Latin American poet who wrote about a world before recorded history, but there is no mention of whether or not he borrowed poetic structures from other cultures. This is another loser.

> **(E) Latin American poetry does not borrow poetic structures from other world cultures whose literature exhibits cultural conservatism.**

This answer choice includes irrelevant information as well. The passage does not indicate whether or not Latin American poets borrow poetic structures from conservative cultures. This is also a loser.

We have two candidates, (A) and (B), so we need to eliminate one. Looking back at (A), we can see that it makes too strong of a claim. The passage indicates that the borrowing of poetic structures from other cultures was a response to the lack of a long-standing cultural past, but it does not provide clear evidence that this was an attempt to recreate a cultural past. In contrast, there is direct support for (B). Therefore, (B) is the correct answer choice.

7. **Correct Answer (D).** *Prep Test 40, Section 4, Passage 2, Question 11.*

> **Based on the passage, the author most likely holds which one of the following views toward**

Spanish poetry's relationship to the Spanish cultural past?

This is a V question. The prompt does not reference a viewpoint or topic from a specific part of the passage. Therefore, we cannot anticipate a correct answer choice and must proceed directly to eliminating answer choices.

(A) This relationship has inspired Spanish poets to examine their cultural past with a critical eye.

This answer choice includes contradictory information. The third paragraph clearly states that Spanish poets romanticized their cultural past and wished to return to it. This is a loser.

(B) This relationship forces Spanish poets to write about subjects with which they feel little natural affinity.

This answer choice includes irrelevant information. The topic of Spanish poets writing about subjects with which they have little natural affinity does not appear in the passage. This is another loser.

(C) This relationship is itself the central theme of much Spanish poetry.

This answer choice also includes irrelevant information. Themes of Spanish poetry are not discussed in the passage. This is another loser.

(D) This relationship infuses Spanish poetry with a romanticism that is reluctant to embrace the modern era.

This seems like a statement the author would agree with based on the information in the passage. The third paragraph states that Spanish poetry does not have an enthusiastic response to the modern world because of its desire to return to an ideal culture of the distant past. This is a candidate.

(E) This relationship results in poems that are of little interest to contemporary Spanish readers.

This answer choice also includes irrelevant information. The interest of contemporary Spanish readers is a topic that does not appear in the passage. This is a loser.

As (D) is the only candidate, it is the correct answer choice.

8. **Correct Answer (C).** *Prep Test 40, Section 4, Passage 2, Question 12.*

Which one of the following inferences is most supported by the passage?

This is an IMP question. The prompt does not include a topic from a specific part of the passage. Therefore, we cannot anticipate a correct answer choice and must proceed directly to eliminating answer choices.

(A) A tradition of cultural conservatism has allowed the Spanish language to evolve into a stable, reliable form of expression.

This answer choice makes too strong of a claim. The passage states that cultural conservatism has restricted Spanish poets' ability to explore the poetic structures of other cultures and use the Spanish language creatively, but this does not mean that Spanish poetry is a stable and reliable form of expression. This is a loser.

(B) It was only recently that Latin American poetry began to incorporate elements of other languages.

This answer choice includes irrelevant information. The passage does not indicate when Latin American poets began to incorporate elements of other languages. This is another loser.

(C) The cultural conservatism of Spanish poetry is exemplified by the uncritical attitude of Spanish poets toward the Spanish language.

This seems like a logical inference based on the information in the passage. It connects two ideas from the passage—the uncritical attitude of Spanish poets toward the Spanish language discussed in the second paragraph and the cultural conservatism of Spanish poetry discussed in the third paragraph. While the passage does not directly state that this uncritical attitude is an example of cultural conservatism, it seems like a logical inference. Cultural conservatism is the desire to return to an ideal distant past, which would explain why Spanish poets are less experimental with the Spanish language. This is a candidate.

(D) Latin American poets' interest in other world cultures is illustrated by their use of Japanese words and phrases.

This answer choice includes irrelevant information. Although an example of a use of Japanese poetic structures by a Latin American poet is given in the third paragraph, there is no reference to the use of Japanese words and phrases. This is a loser.

(E) Spanish poetry is receptive to the influence of some Spanish-language poets outside of Spain.

This answer choice also includes irrelevant information. The influence of Spanish-language poets outside of Spain on Spanish poetry is not discussed in the passage. This is another loser.

As (C) is the only candidate, it is the correct answer choice.

For Questions 9–10

The A)proponents of the Modern Movement in architecture considered that, compared with the historical styles that it replaced, Modernist architecture more accurately reflected the functional
(5) spirit of twentieth-century technology and was better suited to the newest building methods. It is ironic, then, that the Movement fostered an ideology of design that proved to be at odds with the way buildings were really built.
(10) The tenacious adherence of A)Modernist architects and critics to this ideology was in part responsible for the Movement's decline. Originating in the 1920s as a marginal, almost bohemian art movement, the Modern Movement was never very popular with the public,
(15) but this very lack of popular support produced in Modernist architects a high-minded sense of mission—not content merely to interpret the needs of the client, these architects now sought to persuade, to educate, and, if necessary, to dictate. By 1945 the
(20) tenets of the Movement had come to dominate mainstream architecture, and by the early 1950s, to dominate architectural criticism—architects whose work seemed not to advance the evolution of the Modern Movement tended to be dismissed by
(25) A)proponents of Modernism. On the other hand, when architects were identified as innovators—as was the case with Otto Wagner, or the young Frank Lloyd Wright—attention was drawn to only those features of their work that were "Modern"; other aspects were
(30) conveniently ignored.
The decline of the Modern Movement later in the twentieth century occurred partly as a result of Modernist architects' ignorance of building methods, and partly because A)Modernist architects were
(35) reluctant to admit that their concerns were chiefly aesthetic. Moreover, the building industry was evolving in a direction Modernists had not anticipated: it was more specialized and the process of construction was much more fragmented than in
(40) the past. Up until the twentieth century, construction had been carried out by a relatively small number of tradespeople, but as the building industry evolved, buildings came to be built by many specialized subcontractors working independently. The architect's
(45) design not only had to accommodate a sequence of independent operations, but now had to reflect the allowable degree of inaccuracy of the different trades. However, one of the chief construction A)ideals of the Modern Movement was to "honestly" expose
(50) structural materials such as steel and concrete. To do this and still produce a visually acceptable interior called for an unrealistically high level of craftmanship. Exposure of a building's internal structural elements, if it could be achieved at all,
(55) could only be accomplished at considerable cost— hence the well-founded reputation of Modern architecture as prohibitively expensive.
As B)Postmodern architects recognized, the need to expose structural elements imposed unnecessary
(60) limitations on building design. The unwillingness of architects of the Modern Movement to abandon their ideals contributed to the decline of interest in the Modern Movement.

Main Point

The main point is stated in the last sentences of the first and fourth paragraphs. It is that the Modern Movement promoted a design ideology that was incompatible with how buildings were really built, and the unwillingness to abandon these ideals led to the decline of this movement.

Paragraph 1

This paragraph introduces the viewpoint of proponents of the Modern Movement, and then states part of the main point.

Paragraph 2

This paragraph provides background information. It discusses the origins of the Modern Movement and its influence on mainstream architecture and architectural criticism.

Paragraph 3

This paragraph provides supporting details for the main point. Modernist architects were ignorant of building methods and concerned chiefly with aesthetics. Their designs were incompatible with changes in the building industry. In addition, their designs required an unrealistic level of craftsmanship because of the inclusion of exposed building materials. As a result, the buildings they designed were prohibitively expensive to build.

Paragraph 4

This paragraph briefly mentions another viewpoint (Postmodern architects) and then states part of the main point.

Identify Viewpoints

The author's viewpoint is present and is the focus of the passage. The viewpoint of proponents of the Modern Movement is also discussed throughout the passage. The viewpoint of Postmodern architects is mentioned in passing.

9. **Correct Answer (C).** *Prep Test 44, Section 1, Passage 4, Question 23.*

> **With respect to the proponents of the Modern Movement, the author of the passage can best be described as**

This is an ATT question. The prompt does not reference a viewpoint or topic from a specific part of the passage. The viewpoints of the author and proponents of the Modern Movement are discussed throughout. However, the bulk of the passage is focused on describing the failings of the movement that led to its decline. In addition, there are a number of keywords that indicate the author's attitude. The use of the terms *ironic* in the first paragraph, *conveniently* in the second paragraph, and *well-founded* in the third paragraph suggests that the author is somewhat dismissive of the movement. We should anticipate a correct answer choice that expresses this attitude.

(A) forbearing

This answer choice includes contradictory information. *Forbearing* means to be patient or restrained. Nothing in the passage indicates that this is how the author feels toward the movement. This is a loser.

(B) defensive

This answer choice also includes contradictory information. It is the opposite of our anticipated answer choice, as the author does not defend the movement. This is another loser.

(C) unimpressed

This matches our anticipated answer choice. The author believes that the decline of the movement was due to its own failings and the reluctance of proponents to abandon their ideals. This is a candidate.

(D) exasperated

This answer choice makes too strong of a claim. Although the author has a negative opinion of the movement, he does not seem to be angry or annoyed with it. This is a loser.

(E) indifferent

This answer choice includes contradictory information. The author clearly has a negative opinion of the movement. This is another loser.

As (C) is the only candidate, it is the correct answer choice.

10. **Correct Answer (E).** *Prep Test 44, Section 1, Passage 4, Question 24.*

> **It can be inferred that the author of the passage believes which one of the following about Modern Movement architects' ideal of exposing structural materials?**

This is a V question. The prompt references a topic from a specific part of the passage. The discussion of exposed structural materials is limited to the third paragraph. The author describes the use of exposed structural materials as an ideal of the Modern Movement and then specifies that it required unrealistic levels of craftmanship and resulted in prohibitively expensive buildings. Earlier in that paragraph, the author states that Modernist architects were reluctant to admit their concern was chiefly aesthetic. This suggests that the decision to use exposed structural materials was based primarily on aesthetics rather than other factors like costs. We should anticipate a correct answer choice that expresses this inference or another one related to the ideal of exposing structural materials that the author would agree with.

(A) The repudiation of the ideal by some of these architects undermined its validity.

This answer choice includes irrelevant information. The repudiation of the ideal by Modernist architects is not discussed in the passage. This is a loser.

(B) The ideal was rarely achieved because of its lack of popular appeal.

This answer choice includes irrelevant information. The passage does not discuss the popular appeal of using exposed structural materials. In addition, the passage implies that cost was the main factor preventing this ideal from being achieved. This is another loser.

(C) The ideal was unrealistic because most builders were unwilling to attempt it.

This answer choice also includes irrelevant information. The willingness of builders is not discussed in the passage. While the passage suggests that many builders did not have the craftmanship to use exposed structure materials, this does not mean most were unwilling to attempt it. This is a loser.

(D) The ideal originated in the work of Otto Wagner and Frank Lloyd Wright.

This answer choice includes irrelevant information as well. These two architects are mentioned in the passage, but there is no connection between them and the ideal of exposing structural materials. This is also a loser.

(E) The ideal arose from aesthetic rather than practical concerns.

This matches our anticipated answer choice. The use of exposed structural materials was the result of a focus on aesthetics rather than on practical concerns like cost. This is the correct answer choice.

For Questions 11–13

The Japanese American sculptor Isamu Noguchi (1904–1988) was an artist who intuitively asked—and responded to—deeply original questions. He might well have become a scientist within a standard
(5) scientific discipline, but he instead became an artist who repeatedly veered off at wide angles from the well-known courses followed by conventionally talented artists of both the traditional and modern schools. The story behind one particular sculpture
(10) typifies this aspect of his creativeness.

By his early twenties, Noguchi's sculptures showed such exquisite comprehension of human anatomy and deft conceptual realization that he won a Guggenheim Fellowship for travel in Europe. After
(15) arriving in Paris in 1927, Noguchi asked the Romanian-born sculptor Constantin Brancusi if he might become his student. When Brancusi said no, that he never took students, Noguchi asked if he needed a stonecutter. Brancusi did. Noguchi cut and
(20) polished stone for Brancusi in his studio, frequently also polishing Brancusi's brass and bronze sculptures. Noguchi, with his scientist's mind, pondered the fact that sculptors through the ages had relied exclusively upon negative light—that is, shadows—for their
(25) conceptual communication, precisely because no metals, other than the expensive, nonoxidizing gold, could be relied upon to give off positive-light reflections.

Noguchi wanted to create a sculpture that was purely reflective. In 1929, after returning to the
(30) United States, he met the architect and philosopher R. Buckminster Fuller, offering to sculpt a portrait of him. When Fuller heard of Noguchi's ideas regarding positive-light sculpture, he suggested using chrome-nickel steel, which Henry Ford, through automotive
(35) research and development, had just made commercially available for the first time in history. Here, finally, was a permanently reflective surface, economically available in massive quantities.

In sculpting his portrait of Fuller, Noguchi did not
(40) think of it as merely a shiny alternate model of traditional, negative-light sculptures. What he saw was that completely reflective surfaces provided a fundamental invisibility of surface like that of utterly still waters, whose presence can be apprehended only
(45) when objects—a ship's mast, a tree, or sky—are reflected in them. Seaplane pilots making offshore landings in dead calm cannot tell where the water is and must glide in, waiting for the unpredictable touchdown. Noguchi conceived a similarly invisible sculpture,
(50) hidden in and communicating through the reflections of images surrounding it. Then only the distortion of familiar shapes in the surrounding environment could be seen by the viewer. The viewer's awareness of the "invisible" sculpture's presence and dimensional
(55) relationships would be derived only secondarily.

Even after this stunning discovery, Noguchi remained faithful to his inquisitive nature. At the moment when his explorations had won critical recognition of the genius of his original and
(60) fundamental conception, Noguchi proceeded to the next phase of his evolution.

Main Point

The main point is stated in the last sentences of the first paragraph. It is that Noguchi's sculpture of Fuller typifies his unconventional approach to art.

Paragraph 1

The first paragraph provides background information about Noguchi and states the main point.

Paragraph 2

This paragraph provides background information. It describes how Noguchi won a Guggenheim Fellowship due to his representation of human anatomy and conceptual realization, and how the work he did for the sculptor Brancusi led to his interest in creating a positive-light sculpture.

Paragraph 3

This paragraph provides background information. It states that Noguchi wanted to create a purely reflective sculpture. When he offered to sculpt a portrait of Fuller, Fuller suggested the use of the chrome-nickel steel developed by Ford.

Paragraph 4

This paragraph provides background information. It explains how Noguchi envisioned his sculpture of Fuller. He wanted it to be invisible and to only communicate through reflections of the images surrounding it. A viewer's awareness of the sculpture would be indirect.

Paragraph 5

This paragraph provides background information. It stresses that Noguchi remained inquisitive after winning recognition for his original conception (the positive-light sculpture) because he went on the next phase of his evolution.

Identify Viewpoints

The author's viewpoint is present and is the focus of the passage. There are no other viewpoints in this passage.

11. **Correct Answer (D).** *Prep Test 59, Section 4, Passage 3, Question 18.*

> **The passage offers the strongest evidence that the author would agree with which one of the following statements?**

This is a V question. The prompt does not reference a viewpoint or topic from a specific part of the passage. Therefore, we cannot anticipate a correct answer choice and must proceed directly to eliminating answer choices.

> **(A) Noguchi's work in Paris contributed significantly to the art of sculpture in that it embodied solutions to problems that other sculptors, including Brancusi, had sought unsuccessfully to overcome.**

The answer choice includes irrelevant information. The second paragraph states that Noguchi's interest in creating a positive-light sculpture stemmed from the realization that other sculptors, including Brancusi, relied exclusively on negative light. However, the passage does not suggest that this was a problem that other sculptors had tried to overcome. This is a loser.

> **(B) Noguchi's scientific approach to designing sculptures and to selecting materials for sculptures is especially remarkable in that he had no formal scientific training.**

This answer choice also includes irrelevant information. The passage does not state that Noguchi had no formal scientific training. This is another loser.

> **(C) Despite the fact that Brancusi was a sculptor and Fuller was not, Fuller played a more pivotal role than did Brancusi in Noguchi's realization of the importance of negative light to the work of previous sculptors.**

This is answer choice includes contradictory information. The passage clearly states that Noguchi realized the importance of negative light to other sculptors while working with Brancusi. Fuller suggested a material to use to create a reflective sculpture. This is also a loser.

> **(D) Noguchi was more interested in addressing fundamental aesthetic questions than in maintaining a consistent artistic style.**

This seems like a statement the author would agree with. The first paragraph states that Noguchi was an artist who asked and responded to deeply original questions. The last paragraph describes how he remained true to his inquisitive nature and proceeded to the next phase of his evolution after completing the positive-light sculpture. This is a candidate.

> **(E) Noguchi's work is of special interest for what it reveals not only about the value of scientific thinking in the arts but also about the value of aesthetic approaches to scientific inquiry.**

This answer choice includes contradictory information. The passage suggests that Noguchi's work shows the value of scientific thinking in the arts. However, there is no discussion of the value of aesthetic approaches to scientific inquiry. This is a loser.

As (D) is the only candidate, it is the correct answer choice.

12. **Correct Answer (E).** *Prep Test 59, Section 4, Passage 3, Question 20.*

> **The passage most strongly supports which one of the following inferences?**

This is an IMP question. The prompt does not reference a topic from a specific part of the passage. Therefore, we cannot anticipate a correct answer choice and must proceed directly to eliminating answer choices.

(A) Prior to suggesting the sculptural use of chrome-nickel steel to Noguchi, Fuller himself has made architectural designs that called for the use of this material.

This answer choice includes irrelevant information. The passage makes no reference to Fuller's architectural designs. This is a loser.

(B) Noguchi believed that the use of industrial materials to create sculptures would make the sculptures more commercially viable.

This answer choice includes irrelevant information as well. This concept of commercial viability never appears in the passage. This is also a loser.

(C) Noguchi's "invisible" sculpture appears to have no shape or dimensions of its own, but rather those of surrounding objects.

This answer choice includes contradictory information. The fourth paragraph states that Noguchi's positive-light sculpture would only be detectable by the reflection of other images. However, it also states that a viewer would be aware of the sculpture's dimensions through secondary means. This is another loser.

(D) If a positive-light sculpture depicting a person in a realistic manner were coated with a metal subject to oxidation, it would eventually cease to be recognizable as a realistic likeness.

This answer choice makes too strong of a claim. The fourth paragraph states that the dimensions of the positive-light sculpture would be apparent through secondary means. Therefore, a positive-light sculpture may continue to be recognizable as a realistic likeness. In addition, it is not clear from the passage how oxidization would affect the sculpture. This is a loser.

(E) The perception of the shape and dimensions of a negative-light sculpture does not depend on its reflection of objects from the environment around it.

This seems like a logical inference based on the information in the passage. The second paragraph makes it clear that negative-light sculptures are not purely reflective like Noguchi's positive-light sculpture is. Therefore, perception of a negative-light sculpture would likely not be dependent on the reflection of other objects. This is the correct answer choice.

---

13. **Correct Answer (B).** *Prep Test 59, Section 4, Passage 3, Question 21.*

Which one of the following inferences about the portrait of Fuller does the passage most strongly support?

This is an IMP question. The prompt does not reference a topic from a specific part of the passage. The portrait of Fuller is the positive-light sculpture that is the main topic of the passage. Therefore, we cannot anticipate a correct answer choice and must proceed directly to eliminating answer choices.

(A) The material that Noguchi used in it had been tentatively investigated by other sculptors but not in direct connection with its reflective properties.

This answer choice includes irrelevant information. There is no discussion in the passage of other sculptors investigating the chrome-nickel steel used by Noguchi. This is a loser.

(B) It was similar to at least some of the sculptures that Noguchi produced prior to 1927 in that it represented a human form.

This seems like a logical inference based on the information in the passage. The second paragraph states that Noguchi's early sculptures (prior to 1927) showed an exquisite comprehension of human anatomy, so it is safe to assume that Noguchi was sculpting the human form. Therefore, they were similar in this regard to the portrait of Fuller. This is a candidate.

(C) Noguchi did not initially think of it as especially innovative or revolutionary and thus was surprised by Fuller's reaction to it.

This answer choice includes irrelevant and contradictory information. Fuller's reaction to the sculpture was never mentioned in the passage. In addition, the second and third paragraphs makes it clear that Noguchi was attempting to create a type of sculpture that had never been made before. Therefore, he likely thought of the work as innovative. This is a loser.

(D) It was produced as a personal favor to Fuller and thus was not initially intended to be noticed and commented on by art critics.

This answer choice also includes irrelevant information. The passage does not suggest that the positive-light sculpture was produced as a personal favor to Fuller. This is another loser.

(E) It was unlike the sculptures that Noguchi had helped Brancusi to produce in that the latter's aesthetic effects did not depend on contrasts of light and shadow.

This answer choice includes contradictory information. The second paragraph clearly states that Brancusi's sculptures were dependent on negative light, which means light and shadow were important for their aesthetic effects. This is also a loser.

As (B) is the only candidate, it is the correct answer choice.

For Questions 14–16

A vigorous debate in astronomy centers on an epoch in planetary history that was first identified by analysis of rock samples obtained in lunar missions. Scientists discovered that the major craters on the
(5) Moon were created by a vigorous bombardment of debris approximately four billion years ago—the so-called late heavy bombardment (LHB). Projectiles from this bombardment that affected the Moon should also have struck Earth, a likelihood with profound
(10) consequences for the history of Earth since, until the LHB ended, life could not have survived here.

Various theoretical approaches have been developed to account for both the evidence gleaned from samples of Moon rock collected during lunar
(15) explorations and the size and distribution of craters on the Moon. Since the sizes of LHB craters suggest they were formed by large bodies, A)some astronomers believe that the LHB was linked to the disintegration of an asteroid or comet orbiting the Sun. In this view,
(20) a large body broke apart and peppered the inner solar system with debris. B)Other scientists disagree and believe that the label "LHB" is in itself a misnomer. These researchers claim that a cataclysm is not necessary to explain the LHB evidence. They claim
(25) that the Moon's evidence merely provides a view of the period concluding billions of years of a continuous, declining heavy bombardment throughout the inner solar system. According to them, the impacts from the latter part of the bombardment were
(30) so intense that they obliterated evidence of earlier impacts. C)A third group contends that the Moon's evidence supports the view that the LHB was a sharply defined cataclysmic cratering period, but these scientists believe that because of its relatively brief
(35) duration, this cataclysm did not extend throughout the inner solar system. They hold that the LHB involved only the disintegration of a body within the Earth-Moon system, because the debris from such an event would have been swept up relatively quickly.
(40)   New support for the hypothesis that a late bombardment extended throughout the inner solar system has been found in evidence from the textural features and chemical makeup of a meteorite that has been found on Earth. It seems to be a rare example of
(45) a Mars rock that made its way to Earth after being knocked from the surface of Mars. The rock has recently been experimentally dated at about four billion years old, which means that, if the rock is indeed from Mars, it was knocked from the planet at
(50) about the same time that the Moon was experiencing the LHB. This tiny piece of evidence suggests that at least two planetary systems in the inner solar system experienced bombardment at the same time. However, to determine the pervasiveness of the LHB, scientists
(55) will need to locate many more such rocks and perhaps obtain surface samples from other planets in the inner solar system.

Main Point

The main point is stated in the first and last sentences of the third paragraph. It is that new evidence suggests that the late heavy bombardment (LHB) extended through the inner solar system, but we must gather more evidence before we can determine its pervasiveness. This is the author's conclusion.

Paragraph 1

The first paragraph provides background information. It states that the Moon's major craters were created during the LHB and that the LHB would have affected Earth as well. It also adds that life could not have survived on Earth until the LHB ended.

Paragraph 2

This paragraph presents theories related to three competing viewpoints regarding the LHB—1) that the LHB affected the whole inner solar system, 2) that there was no LHB and that the bombardment occurred continuously over billions of years, and 3) that the LHB only affected the Earth-Moon system.

Paragraph 3

This paragraph states the main point of the paragraph. It discusses how the discovery that a meteorite on Earth is composed of material from Mars is evidence for the first theory.

Identify Viewpoints

The three viewpoints explored in this passage are those of the three groups of scientists that present the competing theories about the LHB. The author's viewpoint is also present, and it tentatively supports the theory that the LHB extended throughout the inner solar system.

14. **Correct Answer (B).** *Prep Test 51, Section 2, Passage 2, Question 9.*

> **The author's attitude toward arguments that might be based on the evidence of the rock mentioned in the passage as being from Mars (lines 44–46) can most accurately be described as**

This is an ATT question. The prompt asks about the author's attitude toward arguments based on the rock from Mars. We know from our analysis that this topic is discussed in the third paragraph. In addition, the question includes a specific line reference, making the process of finding the relevant information easier. Although we did not identify any keywords that express the opinion of the author, looking back we can see the phrases *it seems to be a rare example* in the second sentence, *if the rock is indeed from Mars* in the third sentence, and *tiny piece of evidence suggests* in the fourth sentence. In addition, in the final sentence of the paragraph, the author clearly states that additional rocks must be located. Therefore, the author seems to cautiously support the claim that the rock is from Mars and agree that this would support the theory that LHB occurred throughout the inner solar system, but feels more evidence is required. We should anticipate a correct answer choice that expresses this attitude.

> **(A) ambivalence because the theory of the rock's migration to Earth is at once both appealing and difficult to believe**

This answer choice includes irrelevant information. There is no indication that the author finds the rock's migration to Earth difficult to believe. This is a loser.

> **(B) caution because even if the claims concerning the rock's origins can be proven, it is unwise to draw general conclusions without copious evidence**

This matches our anticipated answer choice. The author cautiously supports the claim that the rock is from Mars and that this supports the first theory about LHB, but feels more evidence must be gathered. This is a candidate.

> **(C) skepticism because it seems unlikely that a rock could somehow make its way from Mars to Earth after being dislodged**

This answer choice includes contradictory information. The author does not seem skeptical of the fact that a rock from Mars could make it to Earth. In fact, the author is cautiously supportive of this claim. This is a loser.

> **(D) curiosity because many details of the rock's interplanetary travel, its chemical analysis, and its dating analysis have not yet been published**

The answer choice includes irrelevant information. There is no discussion about whether or not this information has been published. This is another loser.

> **(E) outright acceptance because the origins of the rock have been sufficiently corroborated**

This answer choice makes too strong of a claim. The author cautiously supports the arguments but feels that more evidence needs to be gathered. This is also a loser.

As (B) is the only candidate, it is the correct answer choice.

15. **Correct Answer (C).** *Prep Test 51, Section 2, Passage 2, Question 11.*

> **The author implies that all theoretical approaches to the LHB would agree on which one of the following?**

This is a V question, but the prompt does not reference a viewpoint or topic from a specific part of the passage. The author's viewpoint is presented throughout the passage, and the three theories are discussed in the second and third paragraph, which make up most of the passage. Therefore, we cannot anticipate a correct answer choice and must proceed directly to eliminating answer choices.

(A) the approximate duration of the LHB

This answer choice includes contradictory information. The second paragraph states that the second theory is that the LHB was not a cataclysmic event but rather an ongoing process that lasted billions of years, putting it at odds with the other two theories. This is a loser.

(B) the origin of the debris involved in the LHB

This answer choice also includes contradictory information. The first theory suggests that the debris was formed by an asteroid or comet orbiting the Sun, while the third theory holds that the debris originated with the disintegration of a body within the Earth-Moon system. This is another loser.

(C) the idea that cratering decreased significantly after the LHB

This seems like a statement that is compatible with all three theories. The first and third theories specify that the cratering was caused by a cataclysmic event, which implies that cratering decreased after the event finished. The second theory claims that the cratering was caused by years of continuous, declining heavy bombardment, which suggests that cratering decreased after an extended period. Therefore, this is a candidate.

(D) the idea that the LHB destroyed the life that existed on Earth four billion years ago

This answer choice includes irrelevant information. The passage does not state that life existed on Earth before four billion years ago, only that life could not survive during the LHB. This is also a loser.

(E) the approximate amount of debris involved in the LHB

This answer choice includes irrelevant information. The author does not address the amount of debris involved in the LHB according to each theory. However, the fact that the second theory states that the bombardment occurred over a significantly longer period of time than is proposed by the other two suggests that there would be disagreement regarding the amount of debris. This is also a loser.

As (C) is the only candidate, it is the correct answer choice.

---

16. **Correct Answer (B).** *Prep Test 51, Section 2, Passage 2, Question 12.*

According to the passage, the third group of scientists (line 31) believes that the LHB

This is a V question. The prompt asks about the viewpoint of the third group of scientists regarding the LHB. Although the LHB is discussed throughout the passage, the viewpoint of the third group of scientists is discussed in the second paragraph. This states that the third group of scientists believes the LHB was a sharply defined cataclysmic cratering period and that it involved the disintegration of a body within the Earth-Moon system. We should anticipate a correct answer choice that expresses one or both of these assertions.

(A) affected only the moon

The answer includes contradictory information. The third group believes the LHB affected both Earth and the Moon. This is a loser.

(B) was so brief that its extent had to be fairly localized

This matches our anticipated answer choice. The second paragraph states that the third group of scientists believes that the LHB involved only the disintegration of a body within the Earth-Moon system because the debris would have been swept up relatively quickly. This is a candidate.

(C) consisted of so little debris that it was absorbed quickly by the planets in the inner solar system

This answer choice includes irrelevant information. The passage does not mention the debris being absorbed quickly by other planets. This is a loser.

(D) occurred more recently than four billion years ago

This answer choice includes contradictory information. The author states in the first paragraph that the LHB ended approximately four billion years ago, and nothing in the passage suggests that the third group of scientists disagrees. This is also a loser.

(E) may have lasted a long time, but all its debris remained within the Earth-Moon system

This answer choice also includes contradictory information. The last sentence of the second paragraph indicates that the third group of scientists believed that the LHB ended relatively quickly. This is another loser.

As (B) is the only candidate, it is the correct answer choice.

Key Takeaways

29.8% of RC Questions

Implication (IMP) – 11.7% of RC Questions
Viewpoint (V) – 12.5% of RC Questions
Attitude (ATT) – 4.2% of RC Questions
Principle (PR) – 1.4% of RC Questions

Synthesize information to reach a conclusion that is strongly supported by the passage but not explicitly stated.

Question Tasks

IMP: Identify an inference based on information presented in the passage

V: Identify an inference that is compatible with a viewpoint in the passage

ATT: Determine the author's attitude toward a topic or viewpoint in the passage

PR: Identify a general rule or principle that underlies an argument in the passage

Example Prompts

IMP: The passage suggests which one of the following about _____?
IMP: Which one of the following can be most reasonably inferred from the information in the passage?
IMP: The information in the passage provides the most support for which one of the following statements?

V: According to the passage, _____ believes that
V: Which one of the following statements would the author of the passage most likely agree with?
V: Which one of the following views would proponents of _____ most likely hold?

ATT: According to the passage, the author's attitude toward _____ can most accurately be described as
ATT: It can be most reasonably inferred that the author views _____ as
ATT: Which one of the following most accurately characterizes the author's stance toward _____?

PR: Which of the following principles most likely underlies the author's reasoning throughout the passage?
PR: Which one of the following principles is most clearly operative in the author's argument?
PR: Based on the passage, _____ should be handled according to which one of the following principles?

Correct Answer Choices

IMP: Clear and logical inferences that are supported by specific information in the passage

V: Clear and logical inferences that are supported by specific information in the passage and that is compatible with the viewpoint referenced in the prompt

ATT: Statements that accurately express the author's attitude toward the viewpoint or topic referenced in the prompt

PR: Statements that accurately express a general principle that underlies the argument indicated in the prompt

Incorrect Answer Choices

Statemets that describe the attitude of a person or group other than the author (ATT)

Wrong Viewpoint: Accurate statements about a viewpoint other than the one specified in the prompt (V, ATT, PR)

Wrong Part of Passage: Accurate statements about a part of the passage not specified by the prompt (IMP)

Too Strong: Claims that are too strong to be supported (IMP, V, ATT, PR)

Contradictory Information: Statements that contradict information in the passage (IMP, V, ATT, PR)

Irrelevant Information: Statements that present new information that is not relevant to the task specified in the prompt (IMP, V, ATT, PR)

HACKERS
LSAT *Reading Comprehension*

Chapter 6

Process Family

Chapter 6: Process Family

Overview

Example Passages and Questions

In this chapter, you will learn how to identify and solve Process Family questions.

Process Family questions ask you to apply a process to information in the passage. Many of these questions types are similar to the ones that appear in the Logical Reasoning section of the LSAT. The initial analysis of the passage makes it possible to quickly locate the relevant information when answering Process Family questions.

The five question types in this family—Application (APP), Strengthen (S), Weaken (W), Evaluation (E), and Extension (EXT)—are examined in detail in separate sections. Each section includes step-by-step instructions on how to solve the question type and detailed analyses of example questions. In addition, you will get to tackle practice questions taken from previous administrations of the LSAT. The methods for solving these practice questions are explained thoroughly in the answer keys.

Chapter 6

Example Passages and Questions

The example questions analyzed in the How-to-Solve subsections reference the following passages, and you should refer back to them as necessary. The analysis of each passage has already been done for you.

For Example Questions 1

With his first published works in the 1950s, Amos Tutuola became the first Nigerian writer to receive wide international recognition. Written in a mix of standard English, idiomatic Nigerian English, and
(5) literal translation of his native language, Yoruba, Tutuola's works were quick to be praised by A)many literary critics as fresh, inventive approaches to the form of the novel. B)Others, however, dismissed his works as simple retellings of local tales, full of
(10) unwelcome liberties taken with the details of the well-known story lines. However, to estimate properly Tutuola's rightful position in world literature, it is essential to be clear about the genre in which he wrote; literary critics have assumed too facilely that
(15) he wrote novels.

No matter how flexible a definition of the novel one uses, establishing a set of criteria that enable Tutuola's works to be described as such applies to his works a body of assumptions the works are not
(20) designed to satisfy. Tutuola is not a novelist but a teller of folktales. B)Many of his critics are right to suggest that Tutuola's subjects are not strikingly original, but it is important to bear in mind that whereas realism and originality are expected of the
(25) novel, the teller of folktales is expected to derive subjects and frameworks from the corpus of traditional lore. The most useful approach to Tutuola's works, then, is one that regards him as working within the African oral tradition.
(30) Within this tradition, a folktale is common property, an expression of a people's culture and social circumstances. The teller of folktales knows that the basic story is already known to most listeners and, equally, that the teller's reputation depends on
(35) the inventiveness with which the tale is modified and embellished, for what the audience anticipates is not an accurate retelling of the story but effective improvisation and delivery. Thus, within the framework of the basic story, the teller is allowed
(40) considerable room to maneuver—in fact, the most brilliant tellers of folktales transform them into unique works.

Tutuola's adherence to this tradition is clear: specific episodes, for example, are often repeated for
(45) emphasis, and he embellishes familiar tales with personal interpretations or by transferring them to modern settings. The blend of English with local idiom and Yoruba grammatical constructs, in which adjectives and verbs are often interchangeable,
(50) re-creates the folktales in singular ways. And, perhaps most revealingly, in the majority of Tutuola's works, the traditional accents and techniques of the teller of folktales are clearly discernible, for example in the adoption of an omniscient, summarizing voice at the
(55) end of his narratives, a device that is generally

recognized as being employed to conclude most folktales.

Main Point

The main point is stated in the last sentence of the first paragraph and the last sentence of the second paragraph. It is that critics have inaccurately assumed that Tutuola wrote novels, but he actually belonged to the African oral tradition. This is the author's conclusion.

Paragraph 1

This paragraph provides background information about Tutuola. It states that he was the first Nigerian writer to gain international recognition, and that his works include a mix of languages. This paragraph also introduces two opposing viewpoints. Supporters of Tutuola feel his works are fresh approaches to the novel, while critics dismiss his works as simple retellings of local tales. This paragraph also states the first part of the main point.

Paragraph 2

This paragraph provides details to support the author's claim that Tutuola is not a novelist but instead belonged to the African oral tradition. The second part of the main point is stated in this paragraph as well.

Paragraph 3

This paragraph provides background information about the folktale, which is an important part of the African oral tradition.

Paragraph 4

The last paragraph supports the claim that Tutuola's works are part of the African oral tradition. It describes the elements of his works that demonstrate his adherence to this tradition.

Identify Viewpoints

The viewpoints of those who praise Tutuola's works are mentioned briefly, while the viewpoint of those who criticize Tutuola's works is explored in more detail. The author's viewpoint is also present. It rebuts both of the other viewpoints.

1. Tutuola's approach to writing folktales would be most clearly exemplified by a modern-day Irish author who

    (A) applied conventions of the modern novel to the retelling of Irish folktales
    (B) re-created important elements of the Irish literary style within a purely oral art form
    (C) combined characters from English and Irish folktales to tell a story of modern life
    (D) transplanted traditional Irish folktales from their original setting to contemporary Irish life
    (E) utilized an omniscient narrator in telling original stories about contemporary Irish life

For Example Question 2–4

The Japanese American sculptor Isamu Noguchi (1904–1988) was an artist who intuitively asked—and responded to—deeply original questions. He might well have become a scientist within a standard

(5) scientific discipline, but he instead became an artist who repeatedly veered off at wide angles from the well-known courses followed by conventionally talented artists of both the traditional and modern schools. The story behind one particular sculpture

(10) typifies this aspect of his creativeness.

By his early twenties, Noguchi's sculptures showed such exquisite comprehension of human anatomy and deft conceptual realization that he won a Guggenheim Fellowship for travel in Europe. After

(15) arriving in Paris in 1927, Noguchi asked the Romanian-born sculptor Constantin Brancusi if he might become his student. When Brancusi said no, that he never took students, Noguchi asked if he needed a stonecutter. Brancusi did. Noguchi cut and

(20) polished stone for Brancusi in his studio, frequently also polishing Brancusi's brass and bronze sculptures. Noguchi, with his scientist's mind, pondered the fact that sculptors through the ages had relied exclusively upon negative light—that is, shadows—for their

(25) conceptual communication, precisely because no metals, other than the expensive, nonoxidizing gold, could be relied upon to give off positive-light reflections.

Noguchi wanted to create a sculpture that was purely reflective. In 1929, after returning to the

(30) United States, he met the architect and philosopher R. Buckminster Fuller, offering to sculpt a portrait of him. When Fuller heard of Noguchi's ideas regarding positive-light sculpture, he suggested using chrome-nickel steel, which Henry Ford, through automotive

(35) research and development, had just made commercially available for the first time in history. Here, finally, was a permanently reflective surface, economically available in massive quantities.

In sculpting his portrait of Fuller, Noguchi did not

(40) think of it as merely a shiny alternate model of traditional, negative-light sculptures. What he saw was that completely reflective surfaces provided a fundamental invisibility of surface like that of utterly still waters, whose presence can be apprehended only

(45) when objects—a ship's mast, a tree, or sky—are reflected in them. Seaplane pilots making offshore landings in dead calm cannot tell where the water is and must glide in, waiting for the unpredictable touchdown. Noguchi conceived a similarly invisible sculpture,

(50) hidden in and communicating through the reflections of images surrounding it. Then only the distortion of familiar shapes in the surrounding environment could be seen by the viewer. The viewer's awareness of the "invisible" sculpture's presence and dimensional

(55) relationships would be derived only secondarily.

Even after this stunning discovery, Noguchi remained faithful to his inquisitive nature. At the moment when his explorations had won critical recognition of the genius of his original and

(60) fundamental conception, Noguchi proceeded to the next phase of his evolution.

Main Point

The main point is stated in the last sentence of the first paragraph. It is that Noguchi's sculpture of Fuller typifies his unconventional approach to art.

Paragraph 1

The first paragraph provides background information about Noguchi and states the main point.

Paragraph 2

This paragraph provides background information. It describes how Noguchi won a Guggenheim Fellowship due to his representation of human anatomy and conceptual realization, and how the work he did for the sculptor Brancusi led to his interest in creating a positive-light sculpture.

Paragraph 3

This paragraph provides background information. It states that Noguchi wanted to create a purely reflective sculpture. When he offered to sculpt a portrait of Fuller, Fuller suggested the use of the chrome-nickel steel developed by Ford.

Paragraph 4

This paragraph provides background information. It explains how Noguchi envisioned his sculpture of Fuller. He wanted it to be invisible and to only communicate through reflections of the images surrounding it. A viewer's awareness of the sculpture would be indirect.

Paragraph 5

This paragraph provides background information. It stresses that Noguchi remained inquisitive after winning recognition for his original conception (the positive-light sculpture) because he went on the next phase of his evolution.

Identify Viewpoints

The author's viewpoint is present and is the focus of the passage. There are no other viewpoints in this passage.

2. In which one of the following is the relation between the two people most analogous to the relation between Ford and Noguchi as indicated by the passage?

(A) A building-materials dealer decides to market a new type of especially durable simulated-wood flooring material after learning that a famous architect has praised the material.

(B) An expert skier begins experimenting with the use of a new type of material in the soles of ski boots after a shoe manufacturer suggests that that material might be appropriate for that use.

(C) A producer of shipping containers begins using a new type of strapping material, which a rock-climbing expert soon finds useful as an especially strong and reliable component of safety ropes for climbing.

(D) A consultant to a book editor suggests the use of a new type of software for typesetting, and after researching the software the editor decides not to adopt it but finds a better alternative as a result of the research.

(E) A friend of a landscaping expert advises the use of a certain material for the creation of retaining walls and, as a result, the landscape explores the use of several similar materials.

3. Which one of the following would, if true, most weaken the author's position in the passage?

(A) Between 1927 and 1929, Brancusi experimented with the use of highly reflective material for the creation of positive-light sculptures.

(B) After completing the portrait of Fuller, Noguchi produced only a few positive-light sculptures and in fact changed his style of sculpture repeatedly throughout his career.

(C) When Noguchi arrived in Paris, he was already well aware of the international acclaim that Brancusi's sculptures were receiving at the time.

(D) Many of Noguchi's sculptures were, unlike the portrait of Fuller, entirely abstract.

(E) Despite his inquisitive and scientific approach to the art of sculpture, Noguchi neither thought of himself as a scientist nor had extensive scientific training.

4. The passage provides information sufficient to answer which one of the following questions?

(A) In what way did Noguchi first begin to acquire experience in the cutting and polishing of stone for use in sculpture?

(B) In the course of his career, did Noguchi ever work in any art form other than sculpture?

(C) What are some materials other than metal that Noguchi used in his sculptures after ending his association with Brancusi?

(D) During Noguchi's lifetime, was there any favorable critical response to his creation of a positive-light sculpture?

(E) Did Noguchi at any time in his career consider creating a transparent or translucent sculpture lighted from within?

For Example Questions 5–6

     In an experiment, two strangers are given the opportunity to share $100, subject to the following constraints: One person—the "proposer"—is to suggest how to divide the money and can make only
(5) one such proposal. The other person—the "responder"— must either accept or reject the offer without qualification. Both parties know that if the offer is accepted, the money will be split as agreed, but if the offer is rejected, neither will receive
(10) anything.

     This scenario is called the Ultimatum Game. Researchers have conducted it numerous times with a wide variety of volunteers. Many participants in the role of the proposer seem instinctively to feel that
(15) they should offer 50 percent to the responder, because such a division is "fair" and therefore likely to be accepted. Two-thirds of proposers offer responders between 40 and 50 percent. Only 4 in 100 offer less than 20 percent. Offering such a small amount is
(20) quite risky; most responders reject such offers. This is a puzzle: Why would anyone reject an offer as too small? Responders who reject an offer receive nothing, so if one assumes—as A) theoretical economics traditionally has—that people make economic
(25) decisions primarily out of rational self-interest, one would expect that an individual would accept any offer.

     B) Some theorists explain the insistence on fair divisions in the Ultimatum Game by citing our
(30) prehistoric ancestors' need for the support of a strong group. Small groups of hunter-gatherers depended for survival on their members' strengths. It is counterproductive to outcompete rivals within one's group to the point where one can no longer depend
(35) on them in contests with other groups. But this hypothesis at best explains why proposers offer large amounts, not why responders reject low offers.

     A more compelling explanation is that our emotional apparatus has been shaped by millions of
(40) years of living in small groups, where it is hard to keep secrets. Our emotions are therefore not finely tuned to one-time, strictly anonymous interactions. In real life we expect our friends and neighbors to notice our decisions. If people know that someone is
(45) content with a small share, they are likely to make that person low offers. But if someone is known to angrily reject low offers, others have an incentive to make that person high offers. Consequently, evolution should have favored angry responses to low offers; if
(50) one regularly receives fair offers when food is divided, one is more likely to survive. Because one-shot interactions were rare during human evolution, our emotions do not discriminate between one-shot and repeated interactions. Therefore, we respond
(55) emotionally to low offers in the Ultimatum Game because we instinctively feel the need to reject dismal offers in order to keep our self-esteem. This self-esteem helps us to acquire a reputation that is beneficial in future encounters.

Main Point

The main point is stated in the last two sentences of the fourth paragraph. It is that the rejection of low offers in the Ultimatum Game is most likely explained by the evolutionary need to maintain a reputation that is beneficial for future interactions. This is the author's conclusion.

Paragraph 1

This paragraph presents background information that explains how the Ultimatum Game is played.

Paragraph 2

This paragraph provides additional background information, describing how most people reject an unfair offer even though this results in them receiving nothing. This contradicts the viewpoint of traditional theoretical economics, which holds that people would accept any offer.

Paragraph 3

This paragraph introduces the viewpoint of other theorists. It explains that the insistence on fair divisions is a result of prehistoric hunter-gatherers' need for support in a group. It then introduces the author's viewpoint, which is that this explanation is inadequate.

Paragraph 4

This paragraph presents the author's viewpoint in detail, which is that the rejection of unfair offers is a result of humans living for millions of years in small groups. In this context, evolution favored angry responses to low offers because these provide incentives for others to make high offers. Our emotions do not discriminate between one-shot and repeated interactions.

Identify Viewpoints

The viewpoint of traditional theoretical economists is mentioned briefly. The viewpoint of theorists making the argument regarding hunter-gatherer is explained in more detail. The author's viewpoint is also present. The author rebuts both of the other viewpoints.

5. In the context of the passage, the author would be most likely to consider the explanation in the third paragraph more favorably if it were shown that

   (A) our prehistoric ancestors often belonged to large groups of more than a hundred people
   (B) in many prehistoric cultures, there were hierarchies within groups that dictated which allocations of goods were to be considered fair and which were not
   (C) it is just as difficult to keep secrets in relatively large social groups as it is in small social groups
   (D) it is just as counterproductive to a small social group to allow oneself to be outcompeted by one's rivals within the group as it is to outcompete those rivals
   (E) in many social groups, there is a mutual understanding among the group's members that allocations of goods will be based on individual needs as opposed to equal shares

6. Which one of the following sentences would most logically conclude the final paragraph of the passage?

   (A) Contrary to the assumptions of theoretical economics, human beings do not act primarily out of self-interest.
   (B) Unfortunately, one-time, anonymous interactions are becoming increasingly common in contemporary society.
   (C) The instinctive urge to acquire a favorable reputation may also help to explain the desire of many proposers in the Ultimatum Game to make "fair" offers.
   (D) High self-esteem and a positive reputation offer individuals living in small groups many other benefits as well.
   (E) The behavior of participants in the Ultimatum Game sheds light on the question of what constitutes a "fair" division.

Application

Application
Strengthen
Weaken
Evaluation
Extension

Application

≈ 1.13 questions per test

Example Prompts

Which one of the following *best exemplifies* _____ discussed in the passage?

Based on the passage, which one of the following *relationships is most analogous to* _____?

Which one of the following is *most similar* to that discussed in the last paragraph?

Take These Steps

Does the prompt ask for an analogous situation or an analogous argument or approach?

Situation

Use the analysis you performed during the initial read-through of the passage to locate the relevant content. Reframe the situation in general terms to compare it with situations unrelated to the specific content of the passage. Anticipate a correct answer choice that presents a situation that includes and is compatible with the key characteristics of the situation specified in the prompt.

Argument/Approach

Use the analysis you performed during the initial read-through of the passage to locate the relevant content. Identify the rules of the argument or approach. Anticipate a correct answer choice that conforms to at least one of these rules and does not violate any of the others.

Answer Choices

Correct Answer Choices

Statements that present a situation that includes and is compatible with the key characteristics of the situation specified in the prompt

Statements that present an argument or approach that conforms to at least one of the rules of the argument or approach referenced in the prompt and does not violate any of these rules

Incorrect Answer Choices

Contradictory information

Irrelevant information

Incomplete information

Application (APP) questions ask you to identify a situation, argument, or approach that is analogous to the one specified in the prompt.

APP question prompts usually include terms such as *analogous*, *relationship*, *most similar*, *exemplify*, *best illustrate*, or *best explain*. Other terms with similar meanings may be used as well. Regardless, APP questions can be identified by the fact that they ask you to determine which answer choice presents a situation, argument, or approach that is analogous to a specific one in the passage. APP questions can appear in any passage type.

How to Solve APP Questions

The first step in solving an APP question is to determine whether the prompt asks about a situation, argument, or approach. APP questions will most commonly ask you to find a situation that is analogous to the one referenced in the prompt. However, they may also ask you to identify an argument or approach. In the context of an APP question, an approach can be a theory, a set of criteria, a method, a process, or anything similar.

If the Prompt Asks for an Analogous Situation

When the prompt references a situation in the passage and asks you to find an analogous one, use the analysis you performed during the initial read-through of the passage to locate the relevant content in the passage. In most cases, the situation will be presented in a specific part of the passage. However, you may be required to look at information from a larger section or even the passage as a whole. Once you understand the situation, attempt to reframe it in general terms so that it is easy to compare with descriptions of situations unrelated to the specific content of the passage.

For example, consider a passage about attempts to treat Disease X in which several different medicines were tested as possible treatments but proved to be ineffective. Later research determined that Disease X could be treated by a combination of all of these medicines.

A description of this situation in general terms would be the following:

Several options were unsuccessful when applied individually but successful when applied together.

Note that the wording is general enough to apply to other situations, in that there is no reference to medicines or disease. This description only includes the key elements of the situation.

Once you have created a general description, anticipate a correct answer choice that presents a situation that includes and is compatible with the key characteristics of the situation specified in the prompt.

Let's look at Example Question 2 (page 225):

> In which one of the following is the relation between the two people most analogous to the relation between Ford and Noguchi as indicated by the passage?
>
> (A) A building-materials dealer decides to market a new type of especially durable simulated-wood flooring material after learning that a famous architect has praised the material.
> (B) An expert skier begins experimenting with the use of a new type of material in the soles of ski boots after a shoe manufacturer suggests that that material might be appropriate

for that use.

(C) A producer of shipping containers begins using a new type of strapping material, which a rock-climbing expert soon finds useful as an especially strong and reliable component of safety ropes for climbing.

(D) A consultant to a book editor suggests the use of a new type of software for typesetting, and after researching the software the editor decides not to adopt it but finds a better alternative as a result of the research.

(E) A friend of a landscaping expert advises the use of a certain material for the creation of retaining walls and, as a result the landscape explores the use of several similar materials.

The prompt asks for a relationship between two people that is most analogous to the relationship between Ford and Noguchi. Looking back at our analysis, we can see that Ford is discussed in the third paragraph of the passage. It states that Ford developed chrome-nickel steel through automotive research, making it commercially available for the first time. Following Fuller's suggestion, Noguchi used this material for his positive-light sculpture. We can reframe this in general terms as Person A creates a product for one purpose, and Person B uses the product for a different purpose. We should anticipate a correct answer choice that describes a comparable situation.

(A) A building-materials dealer decides to market a new type of especially durable simulated-wood flooring material after learning that that a famous architect has praised the material.

This answer choice includes contradictory information. Both parties are using the product in the way that it was developed to be used. This is a loser.

(B) An expert skier begins experimenting with the use of a new type of material in the soles of ski boots after a shoe manufacturer suggests that material might be appropriate for that use.

This answer choice also includes contradictory information. The material in this situation is being used the same way by both parties (in footwear). In addition, there is no indication of whether or not this was the purpose for which the material was developed. This is another loser.

(C) A producer of shipping containers begins using a new type of strapping material, which a rock-climbing expert soon finds useful as an especially strong and reliable component of safety ropes for climbing.

This matches our anticipated answer choice. A material designed for strapping is used by a producer of shipping containers (original purpose), and the same material is then used by a rock climber to make safety ropes (different purpose). Although this answer choice does not explicitly state that the producer developed the strapping material, it is very close to the situation in the passage. This is a candidate.

(D) A consultant to a book editor suggests the use of a new type of software for typesetting, and after researching the software the editor decides not to adopt it but finds a better alternative as a result of the research.

This answer choice includes contradictory and irrelevant information. First, the software would have been used for the same purpose by both parties. In addition, the situation in the passage does not involve one party looking for alternatives. This is a loser.

(E) A friend of a landscaping expert advises the use of a certain material for the creation of retaining walls and, as a result, the landscaper explores the use of several similar materials.

This answer choice includes irrelevant information. The situation in the passage does not involve using several similar products. This is also a loser.

As (C) is the only candidate, it is the correct answer choice.

If the Prompt Asks for an Analogous Argument or Approach

When the prompt asks you to identify an answer choice that describes an analogous argument or approach, use the analysis you performed during the initial read-through of the passage to locate the relevant content in the passage. You will rarely have to look at the entire passage. Then, identify the rules of the argument or approach. For an argument, these will be the conclusion and supporting ideas. The rules of an approach may be more difficult to identify because this is a broader category. They will be explicit directives that govern conduct, behavior, classification, or something similar. Once you have identified the rules of the argument or approach, anticipate a correct answer choice that conforms to at least one of these rules and does not violate any of the others.

Let's look at Example Question 1 (page 223):

Tutuola's approach to writing folktales would be most clearly exemplified by a modern-day Irish author who

(A) applied conventions of the modern novel to the retelling of Irish folktales
(B) re-created important elements of the Irish literary style within a purely oral art form
(C) combined characters from English and Irish folktales to tell a story of modern life
(D) transplanted traditional Irish folktales from their original setting to contemporary Irish life
(E) utilized an omniscient narrator in telling original stories about contemporary Irish life

The prompt asks for an approach to writing folk tales that is analogous to Tutuola's approach. The analysis shows that the elements of Tutuola's work that correspond to the African oral tradition are discussed in the last paragraph. These can be interpreted at the rules that govern Tutuola's approach to writing folktales. We are told that he 1) often repeats episodes for emphasis, 2) embellishes familiar tales with personal interpretation or transfers them to modern settings, 3) blends English with local language and grammar, and 4) uses an omniscient voice at the end of his narratives. We should anticipate a correct answer choice that describes an approach that adheres to at least one of these rules and does not violate any of the others.

(A) applied conventions of the modern novel to the retelling of Irish folktales

This answer choice includes irrelevant information. Applying the conventions of the modern novel to folktales is not discussed in the passage. This is a loser.

(B) re-created important elements of the Irish literary style within a purely oral art form

This answer choice includes contradictory information. Tutuola did not work within a purely oral art form. This is another loser.

(C) combined characters from English and Irish folktales to tell a story of modern life

This answer choice includes irrelevant information. The passage does not discuss combining characters from different groups of folktales. This is also a loser.

(D) transplanted traditional Irish folktales from their original setting to contemporary Irish life

This matches our anticipated answer choice. The second rule we identified involves transferring familiar tales to a modern setting. This example adheres to that rule and does not violate the others. This is a candidate.

(E) utilized an omniscient narrator in telling original stories about contemporary Irish life

This answer choice includes contradictory information. Tutuola does not tell original stories about contemporary life. Instead, he tells folktales with modern settings. This is a loser.

As (D) is the only candidate, it is the correct answer choice.

Looking at the Answer Choices

The correct answer choice is a statement that presents a situation, argument, or approach that is analogous to the one referenced in the prompt. If the prompt specifies a situation, the correct answer choice includes and is compatible with its key characteristics. If the prompt specifies an argument or approach, the correct answer choice conforms to at least one of its rules and does not violate any.

Incorrect answer choices often include irrelevant information in the form of new characteristics of a situation or new rules for an argument or approach. In addition, you will often encounter incorrect answer choices with contradictory information. Frequently, there will be multiple elements that are compatible with the situation, argument, or approach in the prompt along with one or two elements that are incompatible because they include irrelevant or contradictory information. Finally, incorrect answer choices that present incomplete information are common for questions asking about analogous situations. A key characteristic that is necessary to create an analogous situation is omitted.

Strengthen

Chapter 6

PROCESS FAMILY

Application
Strengthen
Weaken
Evaluation
Extension

Strengthen
≈ 0.63 questions per test

Example Prompts

Which one of the following, if true, would *most strengthen* the author's primary conclusion?

Which one of the following, if true, *most supports* the author's claim about _____?

Which one of the following, if true, *lends the most credence to* _____?

Take These Steps

Use the initial analysis to determine where the argument referenced in the prompt is presented in the passage. It may be developed in a small section of the passage or throughout.

Reread the relevant content and summarize the core elements of the argument. Identify the claim and how it is supported. Does the argument include an obvious weakness?

Yes

No

Anticipate a correct answer choice that eliminates or diminishes this weakness.

Proceed to eliminating answer choices. Look for one that addresses a weakness you failed to identify or that provides additional support for the conclusion of the argument.

Answer Choices

Correct Answer Choices	Incorrect Answer Choices
Statements that strengthen the argument referenced in the prompt	Statements that weaken the argument referenced in the prompt
	Irrelevant Information
	Incomplete Information

Strengthen (S) questions ask you to identify a statement that strengthens the argument referenced in the prompt. S question prompts usually include terms such as *strengthen*, *support*, or *lend credence*. Other terms with similar meanings may be used as well. They also include terms such as *if true*, *if established*, or *if shown* to indicate that you must accept that the answer choices are true. S questions can appear in any passage type.

How to Solve S Questions

The first step in solving an S question is to use your initial analysis to determine where the argument referenced in the prompt is developed in the passage. In some cases, the argument is presented in a small section of the passage. In others, the argument is developed throughout the passage, increasing the difficulty level of the question. Once you have located the argument, reread the relevant content in the text and summarize the core elements of the argument. Make sure you understand the conclusion of the argument and how it is supported. Then, attempt to identify any weaknesses in the reasoning. If you are able to do this, anticipate a correct answer choice that eliminates or diminishes this weakness. If not, proceed to eliminating answer choices. Look for one that addresses a weakness you failed to identify or that provides additional support for the conclusion of the argument.

Let's look at Example Question 5 (page 227):

In the context of the passage, the author would be most likely to consider the explanation in the third paragraph more favorably if it were shown that

(A) our prehistoric ancestors often belonged to large groups of more than a hundred people
(B) in many prehistoric cultures, there were hierarchies within groups that dictated which allocations of goods were to be considered fair and which were not
(C) it is just as difficult to keep secrets in relatively large social groups as it is in small social groups
(D) it is just as counterproductive to a small social group to allow oneself to be outcompeted by one's rivals within the group as it is to outcompete those rivals
(E) in many social groups, there is a mutual understanding among the group's members that allocations of goods will be based on individual needs as opposed to equal shares

This is an uncommonly worded S question prompt that specifies the exact location of the argument in the passage. The third paragraph presents the theorists' argument regarding the rejection of low offers in the Ultimatum Game. Their claim is that this is because our ancestors needed the support of a strong group. The support for this claim is that small groups depended on their members' strengths for survival. Therefore, it is counterproductive to outcompete rivals within one's group to the point where one cannot depend on them in contests with other groups. The weakness in this argument is readily apparent, and, in fact, the author specifies this weakness in the last sentence of the paragraph. It is that this theory explains why proposers offer large amounts but not why low offers are rejected. Therefore, we should anticipate a correct answer choice that eliminates or diminishes this weakness.

(A) our prehistoric ancestors often belonged to large groups of more than a hundred people

This answer choice weakens the argument. If our ancestors belonged to large groups, there would be more people to depend on. Therefore, outcompeting rivals to the extent that they could not be depended on in contests with other groups would not be as harmful. This is a loser.

(B) in many prehistoric cultures, there were hierarchies within groups that dictated which allocations of goods were to be considered fair and which were not

This answer choice includes irrelevant information. The discussion of many prehistoric cultures with hierarchies that dictated the distribution of goods has no connection to the argument and, therefore, does not strengthen it. This is another loser.

(C) it is just as difficult to keep secrets in relatively large social groups as it is in small social groups

This answer choice also includes irrelevant information. Secret keeping has no connection to the argument. This is a loser.

(D) it is just as counterproductive to a small social group to allow oneself to be outcompeted by one's rivals within the group as it is to outcompete those rivals

This matches our anticipated answer choice. It eliminates the weakness we identified in the argument. If it is just as counterproductive in a small group to be outcompeted by rivals as it is to outcompete rivals, then members would likely reject low offers. This is a candidate.

(E) in many social groups, there is a mutual understanding among the group's members that allocations of goods will be based on individual needs as opposed to equal shares

This answer choice includes irrelevant information. Allocating goods based on need rather than on providing equal shares has no connection to the argument. This is a loser.

As (D) is the only candidate, it is the correct answer choice.

Looking at the Answer Choices

The correct answer choice is a statement that strengthens the argument referenced in the prompt. It will either eliminate or diminish a weakness in the reasoning or provide additional support for the argument's conclusion.

Incorrect answer choices that include irrelevant information are very common. These will neither strengthen nor weaken the argument. It is also common for incorrect answer choices to weaken the argument. These can be tricky to eliminate because they often address a specific line of reasoning. In many cases, they focus on a weakness in the reasoning, magnifying it instead of eliminating or diminishing it. You may also encounter answer choices that include incomplete information, in that they do not address an important element of the argument referenced in the prompt.

Weaken

PROCESS FAMILY

Application
Strengthen
Weaken
Evaluation
Extension

Weaken
≈ 0.38 questions per test

Example Prompts

Which one of the following, if true, *most weakens* the author's primary conclusion?

Which one of the following, if true, would *most seriously challenge* _____?

Which one of the following, if true, would *undermine* the claim that _____?

Take These Steps

Use the initial analysis to determine where the argument referenced in the prompt is presented in the passage. It may be developed in a small section of the passage or throughout.

Reread the relevant content and summarize the core elements of the argument. Identify the claim and how it is supported. Does the argument include an obvious weakness?

Yes

No

Anticipate a correct answer choice that emphasizes this weakness.

Proceed to eliminating answer choices. Look for one that addresses a weakness you failed to identify or that attacks the support for the conclusion of the argument.

Answer Choices

Correct Answer Choices	**Incorrect Answer Choices**
Statements that weaken the argument referenced in the prompt	Statements that strengthen the argument referenced in the prompt
	Irrelevant information
	Incomplete information

Weaken (W) questions ask you to identify a statement that weakens the argument referenced in the prompt. W question prompts usually include terms such as *weaken, challenge,* or *undermine.* Other terms with similar meanings may be used as well. As with S questions, W question prompts will also include terms such as *if true, if established,* or *if shown* to indicate that you must accept that the answer choices are true. W questions can appear in any passage type.

How to Solve W Questions

The process for solving W questions is very similar to that for S questions, except that you are looking for an answer choice that weakens the argument referenced in the prompt rather than one that strengthens it. Use the analysis performed during the initial read-through to locate the argument in the passage. Then, summarize it, taking note of the conclusion and the evidence that supports it. Try to determine if the argument has an obvious weakness. If so, anticipate a correct answer choice that emphasizes this weakness. For example, if the conclusion is dependent on an assumption—information assumed to be true but not explicitly stated—the correct answer choice to W question may state that this assumption is not valid. If you are not able to identify a weakness, proceed to eliminating answer choices. Look for one that emphasizes a weakness you failed to identify or that attacks the support for the conclusion of the argument.

Let's look at Example Question 3 (page 225):

Which one of the following would, if true, most weaken the author's position in the passage?

(A) Between 1927 and 1929, Brancusi experimented with the use of highly reflective material for the creation of positive-light sculptures.
(B) After completing the portrait of Fuller, Noguchi produced only a few positive-light sculptures and in fact changed his style of sculpture repeatedly throughout his career.
(C) When Noguchi arrived in Paris, he was already well aware of the international acclaim that Brancusi's sculptures were receiving at the time.
(D) Many of Noguchi's sculptures were, unlike the portrait of Fuller, entirely abstract.
(E) Despite his inquisitive and scientific approach to the art of sculpture, Noguchi neither thought of himself as a scientist nor had extensive scientific training.

Looking back at our analysis, we can see that the author's position is stated in the last sentence of the first paragraph. It is that Noguchi's sculpture of Fuller typifies his unconventional approach to art. The previous sentence states that Noguchi veered off from the courses followed by conventional artists. The second sentence of that paragraph also implies that Noguchi had a scientific approach to art. Looking through the rest of the passage, it is hard to identify a specific weakness in the reasoning related to the authors' claim. Therefore, we should probably focus on the first paragraph. As the author claims that the positive-light sculpture typifies Noguchi's approach to art and suggests that Noguchi's approach to art was both unconventional and scientific, any answer choice that shows that this particular sculpture is not unconventional or scientific would weaken the argument.

(A) Between 1927 and 1929, Brancusi experimented with the use of highly reflective material for the creation of positive-light sculptures.

This matches our anticipated answer choice. Noguchi began working on his positive-light sculpture after 1929, and he spent time working in Brancusi's workshop during the period from 1927 to 1929. If Brancusi experimented with creating positive-light sculptures during this period, then Noguchi's sculpture is not as unconventional, which weakens the author's argument that it typifies Noguchi's unconventional approach to art. This is a candidate.

(B) After completing the portrait of Fuller, Noguchi produced only a few positive-light sculptures and in fact changed his style of sculpture repeatedly throughout his career.

This answer choice includes irrelevant information. The fact that Noguchi made only a few positive-light sculptures does not weaken the author's argument. The author is not claiming that the sculpture represents Noguchi's style, only that it is an example of his unconventional and scientific approach to art. This is a loser.

(C) When Noguchi arrived in Paris, he was already well aware of the international acclaim that Brancusi's sculptures were receiving at the time.

This answer choice also includes irrelevant information. Whether or not Noguchi was aware of the acclaim that Brancusi's sculptures were receiving has no effect on the author's argument. This is another loser.

(D) Many of Noguchi's sculptures were, unlike the portrait of Fuller, entirely abstract.

This answer choice includes irrelevant information as well. If many of Noguchi's sculptures were abstract, that does not mean they, or Fuller's sculpture, were not unconventional and scientific. This is a loser.

(E) Despite his inquisitive and scientific approach to the art of sculpture, Noguchi neither thought of himself as a scientist nor had extensive scientific training.

This matches our anticipated answer choice as well. If Brancusi did not view himself as a scientist and did not have extensive scientific training, then the author's claim that he had a scientific approach to art is weakened. This is also a candidate.

As we have two candidates, we need to eliminate one. Answer choice (E) is a less-likely candidate. That Noguchi did not receive formal scientific training and did not view himself as a scientist does not mean he did not have a scientific approach to art. In fact, this answer choice clearly states that he did have a scientific approach. Therefore, it does not weaken the author's argument, and we can select (A) as the correct answer choice.

Looking at the Answer Choices

The correct answer choice is a statement that weakens the argument referenced in the prompt. It will either emphasize a weakness in the argument or it will attack the evidence that supports the argument.

Incorrect answer choices that include irrelevant information are very common. These will neither strengthen nor weaken the argument. It is also common for incorrect answer choices to strengthen the argument by eliminating or diminishing a weakness in the argument. Some answer choices may include incomplete information, as they do not address an important element of the argument referenced in the prompt.

Evaluation

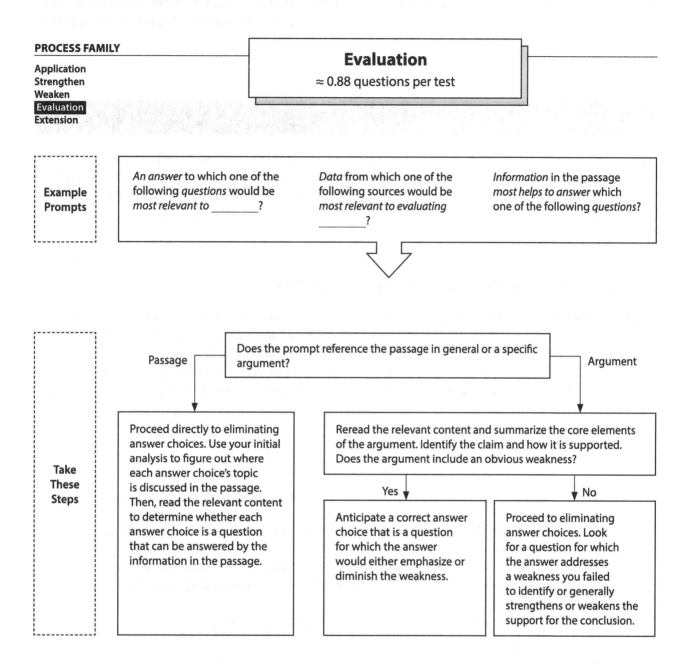

Application
Strengthen
Weaken
Evaluation
Extension

Evaluation
≈ 0.88 questions per test

Example Prompts

An answer to which one of the following *questions* would be *most relevant to* _____?

Data from which one of the following sources would be *most relevant to evaluating* _____?

Information in the passage *most helps to answer* which one of the following *questions*?

Take These Steps

Does the prompt reference the passage in general or a specific argument?

Passage

Argument

Proceed directly to eliminating answer choices. Use your initial analysis to figure out where each answer choice's topic is discussed in the passage. Then, read the relevant content to determine whether each answer choice is a question that can be answered by the information in the passage.

Reread the relevant content and summarize the core elements of the argument. Identify the claim and how it is supported. Does the argument include an obvious weakness?

Yes

No

Anticipate a correct answer choice that is a question for which the answer would either emphasize or diminish the weakness.

Proceed to eliminating answer choices. Look for a question for which the answer addresses a weakness you failed to identify or generally strengthens or weakens the support for the conclusion.

Answer Choices

Correct Answer Choices

Questions that can be answered by information in the passage

Questions for which the answer would strengthen or weaken an argument in the passage

Incorrect Answer Choices

Questions for which the answer does not strengthen or weaken the argument in the prompt

Irrelevant information

Chapter 6

Evaluation (E) questions ask you to identify a question that can be answered by information in the passage or one for which the answer would strengthen or weaken an argument in the passage. E question prompts usually include terms such as *question, information most help to answer*, or *most relevant to evaluating*. Other terms with similar meanings may be used as well. Regardless of the wording of the prompt, an E question is easy to identify because it is asking for a question and all of the answer choices will be in the form of a question. E questions can appear in any passage type.

How to Solve E Questions

The first step in solving an E question is to determine whether or not the prompt references the passage in general or a specific argument. The majority of E questions ask you to identify a question that can be answered by the passage in general. However, you may occasionally be asked to identify a question related to a particular argument. These questions will almost always be related to content from a specific part of the passage.

If the Prompt References the Passage in General

When the prompt references the passage in general, you will not be able to anticipate a correct answer choice. Therefore, you should proceed directly to eliminating answer choices. Refer back to your initial analysis of the passage to determine where the topic of each answer choice is discussed in the passage. Then, read the relevant content to determine whether or not the answer choice is a question that can be answered by the information in the passage. If the answer choice includes subject matter that is not discussed anywhere in the passage, it can be quickly eliminated.

Let's look at Example Question 4 (page 225):

The passage provides information sufficient to answer which one of the following questions?

(A) In what way did Noguchi first begin to acquire experience in the cutting and polishing of stone for use in sculpture?

(B) In the course of his career, did Noguchi ever work in any art form other than sculpture?

(C) What are some materials other than metal that Noguchi used in his sculptures after ending his association with Brancusi?

(D) During Noguchi's lifetime, was there any favorable critical response to his creation of a positive-light sculpture?

(E) Did Noguchi at any time in his career consider creating a transparent or translucent sculpture lighted from within?

The prompt references the passage in general. Therefore, we cannot anticipate a correct answer choice and must proceed directly to eliminating answer choices.

(A) In what way did Noguchi first begin to acquire experience in the cutting and polishing of stone for use in sculpture?

This answer choice includes irrelevant information. The second paragraph states that the work Noguchi did for

Brancusi involved cutting and polishing stone, but there is no indication that this was Noguchi's first experience with these activities. This is a loser.

(B) In the course of his career, did Noguchi ever work in any art form other than sculpture?

This answer choice also includes irrelevant information. The passage only discusses Noguchi's work in sculpture. This is another loser.

(C) What are some materials other than metal that Noguchi used in his sculptures after ending his association with Brancusi?

This answer choice includes irrelevant information as well. The only reference to materials other than metal is the stone Noguchi worked with during his association with Brancusi. This is also a loser.

(D) During Noguchi's lifetime, was there any favorable critical response to his creation of a positive-light sculpture?

This seems to be a question that is answered by the passage. The last sentence of the fifth paragraph states that Noguchi's explorations won critical recognition. In the context, the term *explorations* refers to his work creating the positive-light sculpture. This is a candidate.

(E) Did Noguchi at any time in his career consider creating a transparent or translucent sculpture lighted from within?

This answer choice includes irrelevant information. The passage does not discuss the creation of a transparent or translucent sculpture lighted from within. This is a loser.

As (D) is the only candidate, it is the correct answer choice.

If the Prompt References a Specific Argument

When the prompt references a specific argument, you will usually have to look only at a small section of the passage. Use the initial analysis to determine where in the passage the argument is presented. Then, reread the relevant content and summarize the core elements of the argument. Identify the claim and how it is supported. At this point, you should proceed as if you were answering a hybrid S and W question. When the prompt references a specific argument in the passage, it will always ask you to identify a question that can be used to evaluate the argument. Therefore, you need to identify factors that will strengthen or weaken the argument. As with S and W questions, focus initially on any obvious weaknesses. Then, anticipate a correct answer choice that is a question for which the answer would either emphasize or diminish the weakness. If you cannot identify a weakness, proceed to eliminating answer choices. Look for a question for which the answer addresses a weakness you failed to identify or strengthens or weakens the support for the conclusion.

For example, consider a passage about the solar system that includes an argument in favor of reclassifying Pluto as a planet in the third paragraph. A question for this passage might include the following prompt:

An answer to which one of the following questions is most relevant in evaluating the claim that Pluto should be reclassified as a planet?

The argument favor of the reclassification of Pluto referenced in the prompt above might be based on the assertion that the requirements to be considered a planet are being applied more strictly to Pluto than to other planets. If that was true, then a possible correct answer choice would be as follows.

Are there any celestial bodies that do not meet the requirements applied to Pluto that are classified as planets?

If the answer is yes, then the argument is strengthened. If the answer is no, then the argument is weakened. Therefore, this question is relevant to evaluating the argument referenced in the prompt, and it is the correct answer choice.

Looking at the Answer Choices

The correct answer choice is either a question that can be answered by information in the passage (when the prompt references the passage in general) or a question for which the answer would strengthen or weaken an argument in the passage (when the prompt references a specific argument).

For the first type of prompt, the incorrect answer choices will always include irrelevant information, meaning that they cannot be answered by the information in the passage. For the second type of prompt, the incorrect answer choices will be questions for which the answer would not strengthen or weaken the referenced argument.

Extension

PROCESS FAMILY

Application
Strengthen
Weaken
Evaluation
Extension

Extension
≈ 0.25 questions per test

Example Prompts

Based on the information in the passage, which one of the following sentences could *most logically be added to the end of the passage*?

Given the information in the passage, which one of the following *most logically completes the last paragraph*?

Which one of the following sentences could *most logically be appended to* the passage as *a concluding sentence*?

Take These Steps

Does the prompt include a conclusion, supporting details without a conclusion, or neither a conclusion nor supporting details?

Conclusion

Supporting Details

Neither

Take note of the conclusion and make sure that you understand the immediate context and other relevant information in the passage. Anticipate a correct answer choice that is a logical implication of the conclusion.

Anticipate a correct answer choice that can serve as a conclusion. An appropriate conclusion would be a conclusive judgment on the subject matter in the passage that is supported explicitly by evidence in the last paragraph.

Proceed directly to eliminating answer choices. Use your initial analysis to figure out where each answer choice's topic is discussed in the passage. Eliminate any that do not have a logical connection to the information in the last paragraph.

Answer Choices

Correct Answer Choices

Statements that can be logically added after the last sentence of the last paragraph in the passage

Incorrect Answer Choices

Wrong part of passage

Contradictory information

Irrelevant information

Chapter 6

Extension (EXT) questions ask you to identify a statement that can be added after the last sentence of the last paragraph in the passage. EXT question prompts usually include terms such as *most logically be added*, *complete*, or *appended*. Other terms with similar meanings may be used as well. EXT questions can appear in any passage type, but they are most common in Argumentative and Debate passages.

How to Solve EXT Questions

The first step in solving an EXT question is to reread the last paragraph to identify its basic structural elements. You must determine whether or not it includes the author's conclusion, supporting details without a conclusion, or neither a conclusion nor supporting details.

If the Last Paragraph Includes the Author's Conclusion

When the last paragraph includes the author's conclusion, you should take note of it and make sure you understand the immediate context and any relevant information in other parts of the passage. Then, anticipate a correct answer choice that is a logical implication of the conclusion.

Let's look at Example Question 6 (page 227):

> Which one of the following sentences would most logically conclude the final paragraph of the passage?
>
> (A) Contrary to the assumptions of theoretical economics, human beings do not act primarily out of self-interest.
> (B) Unfortunately, one-time, anonymous interactions are becoming increasingly common in contemporary society.
> (C) The instinctive urge to acquire a favorable reputation may also help to explain the desire of many proposers in the Ultimatum Game to make "fair" offers.
> (D) High self-esteem and a positive reputation offer individuals living in small groups many other benefits as well.
> (E) The behavior of participants in the Ultimatum Game sheds light on the question of what constitutes a "fair" division.

The last paragraph of the passage includes the author's conclusion. This is that the rejection of low offers in the Ultimatum Game can be explained by the evolutionary need to maintain a reputation that is beneficial in future encounters. Reviewing the author's argument, one thing that stands out is that the tendency of people to make fair offers is never really addressed. This is odd because the viewpoint presented in the third paragraph was explicitly rejected by the author because it only explained why proposers offer large amounts, not why responders reject low offers. In other words, the author rejected this argument because it explained A but not B, and then presented an argument that explained B but not A. Looking more closely at the author's conclusion, we can see that an implication may be that the evolutionary need to maintain a reputation also explains the actions of people who offer large amounts initially. We should anticipate this or another logical implication of the author's conclusion as the correct answer choice.

(A) Contrary to the assumptions of theoretical economics, human beings do not act primarily out of self-interest.

This answer choice includes contradictory information. The author's conclusion suggests that people are acting out of self interest (maintaining beneficial reputations) when rejecting low offers. This is a loser.

(B) Unfortunately, one-time, anonymous interactions are becoming increasingly common in contemporary society.

This answer choice includes irrelevant information. There is nothing in the passage to make this statement a logical implication of the conclusion. This is also a loser.

(C) The instinctive urge to acquire a favorable reputation may also help to explain the desire of many proposers in the Ultimatum Game to make "fair" offers.

This matches our anticipated answer choice. This is a logical implication because the author's conclusion does not address the issue of people making fair offers. This is a candidate.

(D) High self-esteem and a positive reputation offer individuals living in small groups many other benefits as well.

This answer choice includes irrelevant information. The passage does not address other benefits that can come from a positive reputation. Therefore, this cannot be a logical implication of the author's conclusion. This is a loser.

(E) The behavior of participants in the Ultimatum Game sheds light on the question of what constitutes a "fair" division.

This answer choice addresses the wrong part of the passage. What constitutes a fair division is discussed in the first paragraph, but this does not have any connection to the author's conclusion. This is also a loser.

As (C) is the only candidate, it is the correct answer choice.

Chapter 6

If the Last Paragraph Contains Supporting Details without a Conclusion

When the last paragraph includes supporting details but no conclusion, you should anticipate a correct answer choice that can serve as a conclusion. An appropriate conclusion would be a conclusive judgment on the subject matter in the passage that is supported explicitly by evidence in the last paragraph.

If the Last Paragraph Contains Neither a Conclusion nor Supporting Details

When the last paragraph includes neither a conclusion nor supporting details, it is very difficult to anticipate a correct answer choice. You are simply looking for a statement that has a strong logical connection to the content. Therefore, you should proceed directly to eliminating answer choices. Use your initial analysis to figure out where each answer choice's topic is discussed in the passage. Then, eliminate any answer choices that are not logically connected to information in the last paragraph.

Looking at the Answer Choices

The correct answer choice is a statement that has a strong logical connection to the information in the last paragraph. It may be a conclusion, a logical implication of a conclusion, or simply a statement with a strong logical connection to the information in the last paragraph.

Incorrect answer choices will commonly include irrelevant or contradictory information. They may also focus on details from the wrong part of the passage.

Practice Sets: Process Family

Analyze the passages below. Mark the <u>keywords</u>, <u>main points</u>, and ~~viewpoints~~ other than the author's. Note the function of each paragraph. Summarize the main points, paragraph content, and viewpoints. Then answer the questions that follow each passage.

Leading questions—questions worded in such a way as to suggest a particular answer—can yield unreliable testimony either by design, as when a lawyer tries to trick a witness into affirming a particular
(5) version of the evidence of a case, or by accident, when a questioner unintentionally prejudices the witness's response. For this reason, a judge can disallow such questions in the courtroom interrogation of witnesses. But their exclusion from the courtroom by no means
(10) eliminates the remote effects of earlier leading questions on eyewitness testimony. Alarmingly, the beliefs about an event that a witness brings to the courtroom may often be adulterated by the effects of leading questions that were introduced intentionally or
(15) unintentionally by lawyers, police investigators, reporters, or others with whom the witness has already interacted.

Recent studies have confirmed the ability of leading questions to alter the details of our memories
(20) and have led to a better understanding of how this process occurs and, perhaps, of the conditions that make for greater risks that an eyewitness's memories have been tainted by leading questions. These studies suggest that not all details of our experiences become
(25) clearly or stably stored in memory—only those to which we give adequate attention. Moreover, experimental evidence indicates that if subtly introduced new data involving remembered events do not actively conflict with our stored memory data, we
(30) tend to process such new data similarly whether they correspond to details as we remember them, or to gaps in those details. In the former case, we often retain the new data as a reinforcement of the corresponding aspect of the memory, and in the latter case, we often
(35) retain them as a construction to fill the corresponding gap. An eyewitness who is asked, prior to courtroom testimony, "How fast was the car going when it passed the stop sign?" may respond to the query about speed without addressing the question of the stop sign. But
(40) the "stop sign" datum has now been introduced, and when later recalled, perhaps during courtroom testimony, it may be processed as belonging to the original memory even if the witness actually saw no stop sign.
(45) The farther removed from the event, the greater the chance of a vague or incomplete recollection and the greater the likelihood of newly suggested information blending with original memories. Since we can be more easily misled with respect to fainter and more
(50) uncertain memories, tangential details are more apt to become constructed out of subsequently introduced information than are more central details. But what is tangential to a witness's original experience of an event

may nevertheless be crucial to the courtroom issues
(55) that the witness's memories are supposed to resolve. For example, a perpetrator's shirt color or hairstyle might be tangential to one's shocked observance of an armed robbery, but later those factors might be crucial to establishing the identity of the perpetrator.

Main Point

Paragraph 1

Paragraph 2

Paragraph 3

Identify Viewpoints

1. In discussing the tangential details of events, the passage contrasts their original significance to witnesses with their possible significance in the courtroom (lines 52–59). That contrast is most closely analogous to which one of the following?

   (A) For purposes of flavor and preservation, salt and vinegar are important additions to cucumbers during the process of pickling, but these purposes could be attained by adding other ingredients instead.

   (B) For the purpose of adding a mild stimulant effect, caffeine is included in some types of carbonated drinks, but for the purposes of appealing to health-conscious consumers, some types of carbonated drinks are advertised as being caffeine-free.

   (C) For purposes of flavor and tenderness, the skins of apples and some other fruits are removed during preparation for drying, but grape skins are an essential part of raisins, and thus grape skins are not removed.

   (D) For purposes of flavor and appearance, wheat germ is not needed in flour and is usually removed during milling, but for purposes of nutrition, the germ is an important part of the grain.

   (E) For purposes of texture and appearance, some fat may be removed from meat when it is ground into sausage, but the removal of fat is also important for purposes of health.

2. Which one of the following questions is most directly answered by information in the passage?

   (A) In witnessing what types of crimes are people especially likely to pay close attention to circumstantial details?

   (B) Which aspects of courtroom interrogation cause witnesses to be especially reluctant to testify in extensive detail?

   (C) Can the stress of having to testify in a courtroom situation affect the accuracy of memory storage and retrieval?

   (D) Do different people tend to possess different capacities for remembering details accurately?

   (E) When is it more likely that a detail of an observed event will be accurately remembered?

In many Western societies, modern bankruptcy laws have undergone a shift away from a focus on punishment and toward a focus on bankruptcy as a remedy for individuals and corporations in financial
(5) trouble—and, perhaps unexpectedly, for their creditors. This shift has coincided with an ever-increasing reliance on declarations of bankruptcy by individuals and corporations with excessive debt, a trend that has drawn widespread criticism. However,
(10) any measure seeking to make bankruptcy protection less available would run the risk of preventing continued economic activity of financially troubled individuals and institutions. It is for this reason that the temptation to return to a focus on punishment of
(15) individuals or corporations that become insolvent must be resisted. Modern bankruptcy laws, in serving the needs of an interdependent society, serve the varied interests of the greatest number of citizens.

The harsh punishment for insolvency in centuries
(20) past included imprisonment of individuals and dissolution of enterprises, and reflected societies' beliefs that the accumulation of excessive debt resulted either from debtors' unwillingness to meet obligations or from their negligence. Insolvent debtors
(25) were thought to be breaking sacrosanct social contracts; placing debtors in prison was considered necessary in order to remove from society those who would violate such contracts and thereby defraud creditors. But creditors derive little benefit from
(30) imprisoned debtors unable to repay even a portion of their debt. And if the entity to be punished is a large enterprise, for example, an auto manufacturer, its dissolution would cause significant unemployment and the disruption of much-needed services.

(35) Modern bankruptcy law has attempted to address the shortcomings of the punitive approach. Two beliefs underlie this shift: that the public good ought to be paramount in considering the financial insolvency of individuals and corporations; and that
(40) the public good is better served by allowing debt-heavy corporations to continue to operate, and indebted individuals to continue to earn wages, than by disabling insolvent economic entities. The mechanism for executing these goals is usually a
(45) court-directed reorganization of debtors' obligations to creditors. Such reorganizations typically comprise debt relief and plans for court-directed transfers of certain assets from debtor to creditor. Certain strictures connected to bankruptcy—such as the fact
(50) that bankruptcies become matters of public record and are reported to credit bureaus for a number of years—may still serve a punitive function, but not by denying absolution of debts or financial reorganization. Through these mechanisms, today's
(55) bankruptcy laws are designed primarily to assure continued engagement in productive economic activity, with the ultimate goal of restoring businesses and individuals to a degree of economic health and providing creditors with the best hope of collecting.

Main Point

Paragraph 1

Paragraph 2

Paragraph 3

Identify Viewpoints

3. Which one of the following sentences could most logically be appended to the end of the last paragraph of the passage?

(A) Only when today's bankruptcy laws are ultimately seen as inadequate on a large scale will bankruptcy legislation return to its original intent.

(B) Punishment is no longer the primary goal of bankruptcy law, even if some of its side effects still function punitively.

(C) Since leniency serves the public interest in bankruptcy law, it is likely to do so in criminal law as well.

(D) Future bankruptcy legislation could include punitive measures, but only if such measures ultimately benefit creditors.

(E) Today's bankruptcy laws place the burden of insolvency squarely on the shoulders of creditors, in marked contrast to the antiquated laws that weighed heavily on debtors.

4. Which one of the following, if true, would most weaken the author's argument against harsh punishment for debtors?

(A) Extensive study of the economic and legal history of many countries has shown that most individuals who served prison time for bankruptcy subsequently exhibited greater economic responsibility.

(B) The bankruptcy of a certain large company has had a significant negative impact on the local economy even though virtually all of the affected employees were able to obtain similar jobs within the community.

(C) Once imprisonment was no longer a consequence of insolvency, bankruptcy filings increased dramatically, then leveled off before increasing again during the 1930s.

(D) The court-ordered liquidation of a large and insolvent company's assets threw hundreds of people out of work, but the local economy nevertheless demonstrated robust growth in the immediate aftermath.

(E) Countries that continue to imprison debtors enjoy greater economic health than do comparable countries that have ceased to do so.

With their recognition of Maxine Hong Kingston
as a major literary figure, some critics have suggested
that her works have been produced almost ex nihilo,
saying that they lack a large traceable body of direct
(5) literary antecedents especially within the Chinese
American heritage in which her work is embedded. But
these critics, who have examined only the development
of written texts, the most visible signs of a culture's
narrative production, have overlooked Kingston's
(10) connection to the long Chinese tradition of a highly
developed genre of song and spoken narrative known
as "talk-story" (*gong gu tsai*).

Traditionally performed in the dialects of various
ethnic enclaves, talk-story has been maintained within
(15) the confines of the family and has rarely surfaced into
print. The tradition dates back to Sung dynasty
(A.D. 970–1279) storytellers in China, and in the
United States it is continually revitalized by an
overlapping sequence of immigration from China.
(20) Thus, Chinese immigrants to the U.S. had a fully
established, sophisticated oral culture, already ancient
and capable of producing masterpieces, by the time
they began arriving in the early nineteenth century.
This transplanted oral heritage simply embraced new
(25) subject matter or new forms of Western discourse, as in
the case of Kingston's adaptations written in English.

Kingston herself believes that as a literary artist she
is one in a long line of performers shaping a
recalcitrant history into talk-story form. She
(30) distinguishes her "thematic" storytelling memory
processes, which sift and reconstruct the essential
elements of personally remembered stories, from the
memory processes of a print-oriented culture that
emphasizes the retention of precise sequences of
(35) words. Nor does the entry of print into the storytelling
process substantially change her notion of the character
of oral tradition. For Kingston, "writer" is synonymous
with "singer" or "performer" in the ancient sense of
privileged keeper, transmitter, and creator of stories
(40) whose current stage of development can be frozen in
print, but which continue to grow both around and
from that frozen text.

Kingston's participation in the tradition of
talk-story is evidenced in her book *China Men*, which
(45) utilizes forms typical of that genre and common to
most oral cultures including: a fixed "grammar" of
repetitive themes; a spectrum of stock characters;
symmetrical structures, including balanced oppositions
(verbal or physical contests, antithetical characters,
(50) dialectical discourse such as question-answer forms
and riddles); and repetition. In *China Men*, Kingston
also succeeds in investing idiomatic English with the
allusive texture and oral-aural qualities of the Chinese
language, a language rich in aural and visual puns,
(55) making her work a written form of talk-story.

Main Point

Paragraph 1

Paragraph 2

Paragraph 3

Paragraph 4

Identify Viewpoints

5. In which one of the following is the use of cotton fibers or cotton cloth most analogous to Kingston's use of the English language as described in lines 51–55?

(A) Scraps of plain cotton cloth are used to create a multicolored quilt.
(B) The surface texture of woolen cloth is simulated in a piece of cotton cloth by a special process of weaving.
(C) Because of its texture, cotton cloth is used for a certain type of clothes for which linen is inappropriate.
(D) In making a piece of cloth, cotton fiber is substituted for linen because of the roughly similar texture of the two materials.
(E) Because of their somewhat similar textures, cotton and linen fibers are woven together in a piece of cloth to achieve a savings in price over a pure linen cloth.

6. The author's argument in the passage would be most weakened if which one of the following were true?

(A) Numerous writers in the United States have been influenced by oral traditions.
(B) Most Chinese American writers' work is very different from Kingston's.
(C) Native American storytellers use narrative devices similar to those used in talk-story.
(D) *China Men* is for the most part atypical of Kingston's literary works.
(E) Literary critics generally appreciate the authenticity of Kingston's work.

A proficiency in understanding, applying, and even formulating statutes—the actual texts of laws enacted by legislative bodies—is a vital aspect of the practice of law, but statutory law is often given too little
(5) attention by law schools. Much of legal education, with its focus on judicial decisions and analysis of cases, can give a law student the impression that the practice of law consists mainly in analyzing past cases to determine their relevance to a client's situation and
(10) arriving at a speculative interpretation of the law relevant to the client's legal problem.

Lawyers discover fairly soon, however, that much of their practice does not depend on the kind of painstaking analysis of cases that is performed in law
(15) school. For example, a lawyer representing the owner of a business can often find an explicit answer as to what the client should do about a certain tax-related issue by consulting the relevant statutes. In such a case the facts are clear and the statutes' relation to them
(20) transparent, so that the client's question can be answered by direct reference to the wording of the statutes. But statutes' meanings and their applicability to relevant situations are not always so obvious, and that is one reason that the ability to interpret them
(25) accurately is an essential skill for law students to learn.

Another skill that teaching statutory law would improve is synthesis. Law professors work hard at developing their students' ability to analyze individual cases, but in so doing they favor the ability to apply the
(30) law in particular cases over the ability to understand the interrelations among laws. In contrast, the study of all the statutes of a legal system in a certain small area of the law would enable the student to see how these laws form a coherent whole. Students would then be
(35) able to apply this ability to synthesize in other areas of statutory law that they encounter in their study or practice. This is especially important because most students intend to specialize in a chosen area, or areas, of the law.
(40) One possible argument against including training in statutory law as a standard part of law school curricula is that many statutes vary from region to region within a nation, so that the mastery of a set of statutes would usually not be generally applicable. There is some truth
(45) to this objection; law schools that currently provide some training in statutes generally intend it as a preparation for practice in their particular region, but for schools that are nationally oriented, this could seem to be an inappropriate investment of time and
(50) resources. But while the knowledge of a particular region's statutory law is not generally transferable to other regions, the skills acquired in mastering a particular set of statutes are, making the study of statutory law an important undertaking even for law
(55) schools with a national orientation.

Main Point

Paragraph 1

Paragraph 2

Paragraph 3

Paragraph 4

Identify Viewpoints

7. Which one of the following would, if true, most weaken the author's argument as expressed in the passage?

(A) Many law school administrators recommend the inclusion of statutory law training in the curricula of their schools.

(B) Most lawyers easily and quickly develop proficiency in statutory law through their work experiences after law school.

(C) Most lawyers do not practice law in the same geographic area in which they attended law school.

(D) The curricula of many regionally oriented law schools rely primarily on analysis of cases.

(E) Most lawyers who have undergone training in statutory law are thoroughly familiar with only a narrow range of statutes.

8. Which one of the following questions can be most clearly and directly answered by reference to information in the passage?

(A) What are some ways in which synthetic skills are strengthened or encouraged through the analysis of cases and judicial decisions?

(B) In which areas of legal practice is a proficiency in case analysis more valuable than a proficiency in statutory law?

(C) What skills are common to the study of both statutory law and judicial decisions?

(D) What are some objections that have been raised against including the study of statutes in regionally oriented law schools?

(E) What is the primary focus of the curriculum currently offered in most law schools?

For Questions 1–2

Leading questions—questions worded in such a way as to suggest a particular answer—can yield unreliable testimony either by design, as when a lawyer tries to trick a witness into affirming a particular

(5) version of the evidence of a case, or by accident, when a questioner unintentionally prejudices the witness's response. For this reason, a judge can disallow such questions in the courtroom interrogation of witnesses. But their exclusion from the courtroom by no means

(10) eliminates the remote effects of earlier leading questions on eyewitness testimony. Alarmingly, the beliefs about an event that a witness brings to the courtroom may often be adulterated by the effects of leading questions that were introduced intentionally or

(15) unintentionally by lawyers, police investigators, reporters, or others with whom the witness has already interacted.

Recent studies have confirmed the ability of leading questions to alter the details of our memories

(20) and have led to a better understanding of how this process occurs and, perhaps, of the conditions that make for greater risks that an eyewitness's memories have been tainted by leading questions. These studies suggest that not all details of our experiences become

(25) clearly or stably stored in memory—only those to which we give adequate attention. Moreover, experimental evidence indicates that if subtly introduced new data involving remembered events do not actively conflict with our stored memory data, we

(30) tend to process such new data similarly whether they correspond to details as we remember them, or to gaps in those details. In the former case, we often retain the new data as a reinforcement of the corresponding aspect of the memory, and in the latter case, we often

(35) retain them as a construction to fill the corresponding gap. An eyewitness who is asked, prior to courtroom testimony, "How fast was the car going when it passed the stop sign?" may respond to the query about speed without addressing the question of the stop sign. But

(40) the "stop sign" datum has now been introduced, and when later recalled, perhaps during courtroom testimony, it may be processed as belonging to the original memory even if the witness actually saw no stop sign.

(45) The farther removed from the event, the greater the chance of a vague or incomplete recollection and the greater the likelihood of newly suggested information blending with original memories. Since we can be more easily misled with respect to fainter and more

(50) uncertain memories, tangential details are more apt to become constructed out of subsequently introduced information than are more central details. But what is tangential to a witness's original experience of an event may nevertheless be crucial to the courtroom issues

(55) that the witness's memories are supposed to resolve. For example, a perpetrator's shirt color or hairstyle might be tangential to one's shocked observance of an armed robbery, but later those factors might be crucial to establishing the identity of the perpetrator.

Main Point

The main point is stated in the first and third sentences of the first paragraph. It is that early leading questions may make later courtroom testimony from witnesses unreliable.

Paragraph 1

This paragraph provides background information. It includes a definition of leading questions, explains that they can be disallowed in courtrooms, and stresses that early leading questions have an impact on witness testimony. It also states the main point.

Paragraph 2

This paragraph provides support for the main point by explaining how earlier leading questions can affect memory. It discusses studies that show that not all details of an experience become stably stored in memory and that we process new data about remembered events in the same way as the actual memory.

Paragraph 3

This paragraph describes an implication of the main point, which is how seemingly insignificant lapses in memory can change courtroom testimony dramatically. It explains that in the case of fainter memories, witnesses are more likely to construct tangential details from subsequently introduced information.

Identify Viewpoints

The author's viewpoint is present and is the focus of the passage. There are no other viewpoints.

Chapter 6

1. **Correct Answer (D).** *Prep Test 40, Section 4, Passage 4, Question 23.*

> **In discussing the tangential details of events, the passage contrasts their original significance to witnesses with their possible significance in the courtroom (lines 52–59). That contrast is most closely analogous to which one of the following?**

This is an APP question. The prompt asks for the contrast that is most analogous to the contrast between the significance of tangential details to witnesses and their possible significance in the courtroom. Therefore, we are looking for an analogous situation. Looking back at our analysis, tangential details are discussed in the third paragraph. Rereading the relevant content, we can see the author presents this contrast with a hypothetical example. Although shirt color or hairstyle may have felt unimportant when a person was witnessing an armed robbery, both may be very important when identifying the perpetrator of a crime. We can reframe this in general terms as something can be unimportant in one context and very important in another context. We should anticipate a correct answer choice that describes a comparable situation.

> **(A) For purposes of flavor and preservation, salt and vinegar are important additions to cucumbers during the process of pickling, but these purposes could be attained by adding other ingredients instead.**

This answer choice includes irrelevant information. It states that something can fulfill the function of another thing. This is a loser.

> **(B) For the purpose of adding a mild stimulant effect, caffeine is included in some types of carbonated drinks, but for the purposes of appealing to health-conscious consumers, some types of carbonated drinks are advertised as being caffeine-free.**

This answer choice also includes irrelevant information. It describes a situation in which something is present in one context but absent in another. This is another loser.

> **(C) For purposes of flavor and tenderness, the skins of apples and some other fruits are removed during preparation for drying, but grape skins are an essential part of raisins, and thus grape skins are not removed.**

This answer choice includes contradictory information. It discusses two different things, instead of the same thing in different contexts. This is a loser as well.

> **(D) For purposes of flavor and appearance, wheat germ is not needed in flour and is usually removed during milling, but for purposes of nutrition, the germ is an important part of the grain.**

This matches our anticipated answer choice. It presents a situation in which something (wheat germ) is unimportant in one context (flavor and appearance) but important in another (nutrition). This is a candidate.

> **(E) For purposes of texture and appearance, some fat may be removed from meat when it is ground into sausage, but the removal of fat is also important for purposes of health.**

This answer choice includes contradictory information. It discusses a situation in which something is important in both contexts. This is a loser.

As (D) is the only candidate, it is the correct answer choice.

2. **Correct Answer (E).** *Prep Test 40, Section 4, Passage 4, Question 24.*

> **Which one of the following questions is most directly answered by information in the passage?**

This is an E question. The prompt references the passage in general. Therefore, we cannot anticipate a correct answer choice and must proceed directly to eliminating answer choices.

> **(A) In witnessing what types of crimes are people especially likely to pay close attention to circumstantial details?**

This answer choice includes irrelevant information. The passage does not discuss the relationship between types of crime and the likelihood of people paying attention to circumstantial details. This is a loser.

> **(B) Which aspects of courtroom interrogation cause witnesses to be especially reluctant to testify in extensive detail?**

This answer choice also includes irrelevant information. The passage does not discuss the causes of witnesses being reluctant to testify. This is a loser.

> **(C) Can the stress of having to testify in a courtroom situation affect the accuracy of memory storage and retrieval?**

This answer choice includes irrelevant information as well. The passage does not discuss stress and its effect on memory storage and retrieval. This is another loser.

> **(D) Do different people tend to possess different capacities for remembering details accurately?**

This answer choice also includes irrelevant information. There is no mention of different people's capacities for remembering details. This is a loser.

> **(E) When is it more likely that a detail of an observed event will be accurately remembered?**

This seems like a question that can be answered by the information in the passage. The last paragraph states that fainter memories are more likely to include constructed details. The first sentence of this paragraph explicitly states that the further removed from the event, the greater the chance of vague or incomplete recollection. This is the only candidate and is, therefore, the correct answer choice.

For Questions 3–4

In many Western societies, modern bankruptcy laws have undergone a shift away from ^A)^a focus on punishment and toward ^B)^a focus on bankruptcy as a remedy for individuals and corporations in financial
(5) trouble—and, perhaps unexpectedly, for their creditors. This shift has coincided with an ever-increasing reliance on declarations of bankruptcy by individuals and corporations with excessive debt, a trend that has drawn widespread criticism. However,
(10) any measure seeking to make bankruptcy protection less available would run the risk of preventing continued economic activity of financially troubled individuals and institutions. It is for this reason that the temptation to return to a focus on punishment of
(15) individuals or corporations that become insolvent must be resisted. Modern bankruptcy laws, in serving the needs of an interdependent society, serve the varied interests of the greatest number of citizens.
        ^A)^The harsh punishment for insolvency in centuries
(20) past included imprisonment of individuals and dissolution of enterprises, and reflected societies' beliefs that the accumulation of excessive debt resulted either from debtors' unwillingness to meet obligations or from their negligence. Insolvent debtors
(25) were thought to be breaking sacrosanct social contracts; placing debtors in prison was considered necessary in order to remove from society those who would violate such contracts and thereby defraud creditors. But creditors derive little benefit from
(30) imprisoned debtors unable to repay even a portion of their debt. And if the entity to be punished is a large enterprise, for example, an auto manufacturer, its dissolution would cause significant unemployment and the disruption of much-needed services.
(35)   ^B)^Modern bankruptcy law has attempted to address the shortcomings of the punitive approach. Two beliefs underlie this shift: that the public good ought to be paramount in considering the financial insolvency of individuals and corporations; and that
(40) the public good is better served by allowing debt-heavy corporations to continue to operate, and indebted individuals to continue to earn wages, than by disabling insolvent economic entities. The mechanism for executing these goals is usually a
(45) court-directed reorganization of debtors' obligations to creditors. Such reorganizations typically comprise debt relief and plans for court-directed transfers of certain assets from debtor to creditor. Certain strictures connected to bankruptcy—such as the fact
(50) that bankruptcies become matters of public record and are reported to credit bureaus for a number of years—may still serve a punitive function, but not by denying absolution of debts or financial reorganization. Through these mechanisms, today's
(55) bankruptcy laws are designed primarily to assure continued engagement in productive economic activity, with the ultimate goal of restoring businesses and individuals to a degree of economic health and providing creditors with the best hope of collecting.

Main Point

The main point is stated in the last two sentences of the first paragraph. It is also restated in the first sentence of the last paragraph. It is that the punitive approach to bankruptcy should be resisted in favor of the modern approach. This is the author's conclusion.

Paragraph 1

The first paragraph provides background information to introduce the topic and two opposing viewpoints. It describes the shift from the punitive approach to the modern system. It also states the main point of the passage.

Paragraph 2

This paragraph presents the viewpoint of the punitive approach and describes how it worked in the past. It also presents some drawbacks of this approach.

Paragraph 3

This paragraph presents the viewpoint of modern bankruptcy law (which the author supports) and describes how it addresses the drawbacks of the punitive approach and serves the public good. It also restates the main point.

Identify Viewpoints

The two main viewpoints presented in this passage are those of the punitive approach to insolvency and modern bankruptcy law. The author's viewpoint is also present, and it supports modern bankruptcy laws.

3. **Correct Answer (B).** *Prep Test 50, Section 1, Passage 2, Question 11.*

> **Which one of the following sentences could most logically be appended to the end of the last paragraph of the passage?**

This is an EXT question. The last paragraph of the passage includes a restatement of the author's conclusion. This is that the punitive approach to bankruptcy should be resisted in favor of the modern approach. The rest of this paragraph provides support for this claim. The last sentence talks about the ultimate goal of modern bankruptcy law being the restoration of businesses and individuals to the economic health and providing creditors with the best hope of collecting debts. We should anticipate a logical implication of the author's conclusion. It may be somehow related to the fact that the modern approach to bankruptcy has a goal other than punishment.

> **(A) Only when today's bankruptcy laws are ultimately seen as inadequate on a large scale will bankruptcy legislation return to its original intent.**

This answer choice includes contradictory information. The author is clearly in favor of modern bankruptcy laws and feels that the earlier laws had shortcomings. Therefore, the suggestion that modern bankruptcy legislation is inadequate and should return to its original intent is not a logical implication of the author's conclusion. This is a loser.

> **(B) Punishment is no longer the primary goal of bankruptcy law, even if some of its side effects still function punitively.**

This matches our anticipated answer choice. Modern bankruptcy laws have a goal other than simple punishment. This is a logical implication of the conclusion, and it is logically connected to the content of the last paragraph. This is a candidate.

> **(C) Since leniency serves the public interest in bankruptcy law, it is likely to do so in criminal law as well.**

This answer choice includes irrelevant information. The topic of criminal law is not discussed in the passage and does not have a strong logical connection to the final paragraph. This is also a loser.

> **(D) Future bankruptcy legislation could include punitive measures, but only if such measures ultimately benefit creditors.**

This does not match our anticipated answer choice, but it seems like a possible implication of the conclusion. A shortcoming of the punitive approach mentioned in the second paragraph is that creditors derive little benefit from debtors who have been punished. If this shortcoming was overcome, then punitive measures could be included. In addition, the third paragraph states that modern bankruptcy laws may still serve a punitive function. This is also a candidate.

> **(E) Today's bankruptcy laws place the burden of insolvency squarely on the shoulders of creditors, in marked contrast to the antiquated laws that weighed heavily on debtors.**

This answer choice includes contradictory information. The third paragraph clearly states that modern bankruptcy laws recognize the obligations of debtors to creditors and direct the transfer of assets from debtors to creditors. This is a loser.

As we have two candidates, we must eliminate one. Looking back at answer choice (D), we can see it is the weaker candidate. First, the sentence does not logically flow from the last sentence of the paragraph, which is focused on the non-punitive goal of modern bankruptcy laws. Second, the punitive measures related to modern bankruptcy laws discussed in the third paragraph do not directly benefit creditors. For these reasons, we can eliminate (D) and select (B) as the correct answer choice.

4. Correct Answer (E). *Prep Test 50, Section 1, Passage 2, Question 13.*

> **Which one of the following, if true, would most weaken the author's argument against harsh punishment for debtors?**

This is a W question. Looking back at our analysis, we can see that the argument against harsh punishment is presented in the second paragraph. The argument is two-fold: 1) creditors are hurt because debtors cannot pay debts in prison, and 2) punishment of large enterprises may cause significant economic disruption. This argument does not have a clear weakness, so we will proceed to eliminating answer choices. The correct answer choice will be a statement that either exposes a weakness in the argument or attacks the support for it.

> **(A) Extensive study of the economic and legal history of many countries has shown that most individuals who served prison time for bankruptcy subsequently exhibited greater economic responsibility.**

This seems to weaken the argument. If individuals who have been punished for bankruptcy subsequently exhibit greater economic responsibility, then the harsh penalties may be beneficial. This is a candidate.

> **(B) The bankruptcy of a certain large company has had a significant negative impact on the local economy even though virtually all of the affected employees were able to obtain similar jobs within the community.**

This answer choice includes incomplete information. It makes no reference to punishment, which is a key element of the argument referenced in the prompt. This is a loser.

> **(C) Once imprisonment was no longer a consequence of insolvency, bankruptcy filings increased dramatically, then leveled off before increasing again during the 1930s.**

This answer choice includes irrelevant information. There is no apparent connection between an increase in bankruptcy filings and the author's argument against harsh punishment. This is also a loser.

> **(D) The court-ordered liquidation of a large and insolvent company's assets threw hundreds of people out of work, but the local economy nevertheless demonstrated robust growth in the immediate aftermath.**

The first part of this answer choice actually strengthens the author's argument. It matches the claim in the third paragraph that the dissolution of a company results in unemployment. Although the second part of the answer choice seems like it may weaken the author's argument, there is no indication the economic growth was the result of the court order. And it may be the case that the economy would have grown even more if the company had not been forced to liquidate its assets and put hundreds of people out of work. This is also a loser.

> **(E) Countries that continue to imprison debtors enjoy greater economic health than do comparable countries that have ceased to do so.**

This seems to weaken the argument as well. If countries that imprison debtors enjoy greater economic health than comparable countries that do not, then the negative effects of the punitive approach identified by the author may not actually cause economic disruption. This is a candidate.

As we have two candidates, we must eliminate one. Looking back at answer choice (A), we can see that it is the weaker candidate. The author's argument is that creditors are hurt because imprisoned debtors are unable to repay their debts. The fact that these debtors become more responsible after being released does not benefit the creditors. If this answer choice suggested that other debtors were somehow deterred by the threat of harsh punishment and become more responsible, it would be a stronger candidate. Therefore, (E) is the correct answer choice.

For Questions 5–6

With their recognition of Maxine Hong Kingston as a major literary figure, A)some critics have suggested that her works have been produced almost ex nihilo, saying that they lack a large traceable body of direct
(5) literary antecedents especially within the Chinese American heritage in which her work is embedded. But these critics, who have examined only the development of written texts, the most visible signs of a culture's narrative production, have overlooked Kingston's
(10) connection to the long Chinese tradition of a highly developed genre of song and spoken narrative known as "talk-story" (*gong gu tsai*).

Traditionally performed in the dialects of various ethnic enclaves, talk-story has been maintained within
(15) the confines of the family and has rarely surfaced into print. The tradition dates back to Sung dynasty (A.D. 970–1279) storytellers in China, and in the United States it is continually revitalized by an overlapping sequence of immigration from China.
(20) Thus, Chinese immigrants to the U.S. had a fully established, sophisticated oral culture, already ancient and capable of producing masterpieces, by the time they began arriving in the early nineteenth century. This transplanted oral heritage simply embraced new
(25) subject matter or new forms of Western discourse, as in the case of Kingston's adaptations written in English.

B)Kingston herself believes that as a literary artist she is one in a long line of performers shaping a recalcitrant history into talk-story form. She
(30) distinguishes her "thematic" storytelling memory processes, which sift and reconstruct the essential elements of personally remembered stories, from the memory processes of a print-oriented culture that emphasizes the retention of precise sequences of
(35) words. Nor does the entry of print into the storytelling process substantially change her notion of the character of oral tradition. For Kingston, "writer" is synonymous with "singer" or "performer" in the ancient sense of privileged keeper, transmitter, and creator of stories
(40) whose current stage of development can be frozen in print, but which continue to grow both around and from that frozen text.

Kingston's participation in the tradition of talk-story is evidenced in her book *China Men*, which
(45) utilizes forms typical of that genre and common to most oral cultures including: a fixed "grammar" of repetitive themes; a spectrum of stock characters; symmetrical structures, including balanced oppositions (verbal or physical contests, antithetical characters,
(50) dialectical discourse such as question-answer forms and riddles); and repetition. In *China Men*, Kingston also succeeds in investing idiomatic English with the allusive texture and oral-aural qualities of the Chinese language, a language rich in aural and visual puns,
(55) making her work a written form of talk-story.

Main Point

The main point is stated in the second and last sentences of the first paragraph. It is that Maxine Hong Kingston's works have Chinese American antecedents because she is connected to a Chinese form of oral narrative known as talk-story.

Paragraph 1

This paragraph briefly introduces the viewpoint of critics who hold that Kingston does not have Chinese-American antecedents. It also presents the main point.

Paragraph 2

This paragraph provides background information. It explains the historical background of talk-story. It discusses how talk-story dates back to the Sung dynasty, and how immigrants constantly revitalize it in the US. It also specifies that Kingston's works are an example of how this form has been adapted.

Paragraph 3

This paragraph presents the viewpoint of Kingston regarding her writing and how it is connected to talk-story. It discusses how she differentiates between thematic memory and the memory process of print-oriented culture. It also states that her storytelling process does not change with the entry of print into the storytelling process.

Paragraph 4

This paragraph provides an example to support the main point. It presents Kingston's book *China Men* as an example of how she participates in the tradition of talk-story. It also includes a list of elements typical of the talk-story genre.

Identify Viewpoints

The critics' viewpoint is mentioned briefly, while the viewpoint of Kingston is explored in more detail. The author's viewpoint is the focus of the passage.

5. **Correct Answer (B).** *Prep Test 55, Section 2, Passage 3, Question 17.*

> **In which one of the following is the use of cotton fibers or cotton cloth most analogous to Kingston's use of the English language as described in lines 51–55?**

This is an APP question. The prompt asks for a use of cotton fibers or cloths that is most analogous to Kingston's use of the English language. Therefore, it is asking for an analogous situation. The prompt also directs us to the specific part of the passage where Kingston's use of the English language is discussed. Rereading that section and the immediate context, we can see that Kingston invests the English language with qualities of the Chinese language. In effect, she is using a process to make one element have the characteristics of another element. We should anticipate a correct answer choice that describes a comparable situation.

> **(A) Scraps of plain cotton cloth are used to create a multicolored quilt.**

This answer choice includes irrelevant information. It presents a situation in which an item is made from pieces of another element. This is a loser.

> **(B) The surface texture of woolen cloth is simulated in a piece of cotton cloth by a special process of weaving.**

This matches our anticipated answer choice. A process (weaving) is used to make one element (cotton) appear like another (wool). This is a candidate.

> **(C) Because of its texture, cotton cloth is used for a certain type of clothes for which linen is inappropriate.**

This answer choice includes irrelevant information. It discusses a situation in which one element is more suitable than another. This is a loser.

> **(D) In making a piece of cloth, cotton fiber is substituted for linen because of the roughly similar texture of the two materials.**

This answer choice also includes irrelevant information. It discusses the substitution of one item for another. This is another loser.

> **(E) Because of their somewhat similar textures, cotton and linen fibers are woven together in a piece of cloth to achieve a savings in price over a pure linen cloth.**

This answer choice includes irrelevant information as well. It describes a situation in which two elements are combined for price savings. This is also a loser.

As (B) is the only candidate, it is the correct answer choice.

6. **Correct Answer (D).** *Prep Test 55, Section 2, Passage 3, Question 19.*

> **The author's argument in the passage would be most weakened if which one of the following were true?**

This is a W question. Looking back at our analysis, we can see that the author's position is stated in the last sentence of the first paragraph. It is that Maxine Hong Kingston's works have Chinese American antecedents because she is connected to a Chinese form of oral narrative known as talk-story. The third paragraph explains in detail how her writings are connected to talk-story, and the fourth paragraph provides an example to support this claim. We now need to identify any potential weaknesses in the argument. One is that there may be other key elements of talk-story that are not discussed in the passage that Kingston's works do not include. Another is that the example of Kingston's work provided to support the author's claim may not be typical. We should anticipate a correct answer choice that eliminates or diminishes one of these weaknesses.

(A) Numerous writers in the United States have been influenced by oral traditions.

This answer choice includes irrelevant information. Whether or not other US writers have been influenced by oral traditions has no connection to the author's argument. This is a loser.

(B) Most Chinese American writers' work is very different from Kingston's.

This answer choice also includes irrelevant information. Whether Kingston's work is similar to other Chinese American writers or other Chinese American writers' work is connected to talk-story does not affect the author's argument. This is another loser.

(C) Native American storytellers use narrative devices similar to those used in talk-story.

This answer choice includes irrelevant information as well. The narrative devices used by Native American storytellers have no relevance to the argument. This is also a loser.

(D) *China Men* is for the most part atypical of Kingston's literary works.

This matches one of our anticipated answer choices. If Kingston's other works are significantly different from *China Men*, then the author's argument is weakened because *China Men* is provided as an example of her connection to talk-story. This is a candidate.

(E) Literary critics generally appreciate the authenticity of Kingston's work.

This answer choice includes irrelevant information. The fact that literary critics appreciate the authenticity of Kingston's work does not affect the validity of the argument. This is a loser.

As (D) is the only candidate, it is the correct answer choice.

For Questions 7–8

A proficiency in understanding, applying, and even formulating statutes—the actual texts of laws enacted by legislative bodies—is a vital aspect of the practice of law, but statutory law is often given too little
(5) attention by law schools. Much of legal education, with its focus on judicial decisions and analysis of cases, can give a law student the impression that the practice of law consists mainly in analyzing past cases to determine their relevance to a client's situation and
(10) arriving at a speculative interpretation of the law relevant to the client's legal problem.

Lawyers discover fairly soon, however, that much of their practice does not depend on the kind of painstaking analysis of cases that is performed in law
(15) school. For example, a lawyer representing the owner of a business can often find an explicit answer as to what the client should do about a certain tax-related issue by consulting the relevant statutes. In such a case the facts are clear and the statutes' relation to them
(20) transparent, so that the client's question can be answered by direct reference to the wording of the statutes. But statutes' meanings and their applicability to relevant situations are not always so obvious, and that is one reason that the ability to interpret them
(25) accurately is an essential skill for law students to learn.

Another skill that teaching statutory law would improve is synthesis. Law professors work hard at developing their students' ability to analyze individual cases, but in so doing they favor the ability to apply the
(30) law in particular cases over the ability to understand the interrelations among laws. In contrast, the study of all the statutes of a legal system in a certain small area of the law would enable the student to see how these laws form a coherent whole. Students would then be
(35) able to apply this ability to synthesize in other areas of statutory law that they encounter in their study or practice. This is especially important because most students intend to specialize in a chosen area, or areas, of the law.
(40)   A)One possible argument against including training in statutory law as a standard part of law school curricula is that many statutes vary from region to region within a nation, so that the mastery of a set of statutes would usually not be generally applicable. There is some truth
(45) to this objection; law schools that currently provide some training in statutes generally intend it as a preparation for practice in their particular region, but for schools that are nationally oriented, this could seem to be an inappropriate investment of time and
(50) resources. But while the knowledge of a particular region's statutory law is not generally transferable to other regions, the skills acquired in mastering a particular set of statutes are, making the study of statutory law an important undertaking even for law
(55) schools with a national orientation.

Main Point

The main point is stated in the first sentence of the first paragraph and the last sentence of the last paragraph. It is that law schools should focus more on statutory law.

Paragraph 1

This paragraph states the main point of the passage. It then provides background information about the current focus of law education—judicial decisions and analysis of cases.

Paragraph 2

This paragraph provides support for the main point by establishing that a lawyer's practice does not depend on the kind of case analysis performed in law school. It then presents the example of a lawyer finding an explicit answer to a question about a tax-related issue by consulting relevant statutes. It also explains the necessity of being able to interpret the meanings and applicability of statutes.

Paragraph 3

This paragraph provides additional support for the main point by explaining that teaching statutory law would improve a student's synthesis skills. It states that studying all statutes in a certain area of law allows students to see how they form a coherent whole. This ability to synthesize can then be applied to other areas of law.

Paragraph 4

This paragraph presents an argument against providing training in statutory law; namely, that statutory law is region-specific. It then states that while this counterargument may be valid, statutory law should still be studied because doing so provides valuable skills (main point).

Identify Viewpoints

The author's viewpoint is present and is the focus of the passage. The viewpoint of those who feel that training in statutory law is not necessary because statutory law varies from region to region is mentioned in passing.

7. **Correct Answer (B).** *Prep Test 59, Section 4, Passage 2, Question 11.*

> **Which one of the following would, if true, most weaken the author's argument as expressed in the passage?**

This is a W question. Looking back at our analysis, we can see that the author's position is stated in the first sentence of the first paragraph and the last sentence of the last paragraph. It is that law school students should study statutory law. The support for this claim is in the second paragraph—which states that a lawyer's practice does not depend on the type of case analysis performed in law school—and in the third paragraph—which states that studying statutory law improves synthesis skills. In the fourth paragraph, the author identifies a weakness in his claim (statutory law is region-specific). The author does not dispute this claim but asserts that the skills students develop are transferable to other regions, which justifies the study of statutory law even though it is region-specific. It is difficult to identify a clear weakness in this argument (other than the one the author rebuts), so we should proceed to eliminating answer choices. The correct answer choice will be a statement that either exposes a weakness in the argument or attacks the support for the argument.

> **(A) Many law school administrators recommend the inclusion of statutory law training in the curricula of their schools.**

This answer choice strengthens the argument. The author's claim that statutory law should be studied in law schools would be more compelling if many laws school administrators agreed with it. This is a loser.

> **(B) Most lawyers easily and quickly develop proficiency in statutory law through their work experiences after law school.**

This seems to weaken the argument. If lawyers were able to easily and quickly develop proficiency in statutory law after they complete law school, then there would be no need for them to study statutory law in law school. This is a candidate.

> **(C) Most lawyers do not practice law in the same geographic area in which they attended law school.**

This answer choice includes irrelevant information. It is related to the weakness that the author addresses in the final paragraph—that statutory law varies from region to region. In that paragraph, the author acknowledges that the statutory law a student studies may not be directly applicable to other regions. However, the author claims that the study of statutory results in the development of vital skills that are transferable. In effect, this answer choice simply restates a weakness that the author has already acknowledged and rebutted. This is a loser.

> **(D) The curricula of many regionally oriented law schools rely primarily on analysis of cases.**

This answer choice also includes irrelevant information. The fact that the curricula of law schools rely on case analysis does not weaken the argument. In the first paragraph, the author presents this as a shortcoming of legal education that can be addressed by including the study of statutory law. This is also a loser.

> **(E) Most lawyers who have undergone training in statutory law are thoroughly familiar with only a narrow range of statutes.**

This answer choice includes irrelevant information as well. Whether lawyers who have studied statutory law are familiar with a narrow or broad range of statutes has no bearing on the argument. In the third paragraph, the author states that becoming familiar with all statutes in a small area of law is beneficial because students develop synthesis skills. This is a loser as well.

As (B) is the only candidate, it is the correct answer choice.

8. **Correct Answer (E).** *Prep Test 59, Section 4, Passage 2, Question 13.*

> **Which one of the following questions can be most clearly and directly answered by reference to information in the passage?**

This is an E question. The prompt references the passage in general. Therefore, we cannot anticipate a correct answer choice and must proceed directly to eliminating answer choices.

> **(A) What are some ways in which synthetic skills are strengthened or encouraged through the analysis of cases and judicial decisions?**

This answer choice includes irrelevant information. The passage does not mention how synthetic skills are strengthened through the analysis of cases and judicial decisions. Instead, it discusses how these skills can be improved by studying statutory law. This is a loser.

> **(B) In which areas of legal practice is a proficiency in case analysis more valuable than a proficiency in statutory law?**

This answer choice also includes irrelevant information. The passage does not discuss the specific areas in which a proficiency in case analysis is more valuable than a proficiency in statutory law. This is also a loser.

> **(C) What skills are common to the study of both statutory law and judicial decisions?**

Again, this answer choice includes irrelevant information. The passage does not discuss skills common to the study of both statutory law and judicial decisions. This is another loser.

> **(D) What are some objections that have been raised against including the study of statutes in regionally oriented law schools?**

This answer choice includes irrelevant information as well. In the fourth paragraph, the author discusses an objection to the study of statutes in nationally oriented law schools. However, there is no mention of regionally oriented law schools. This is a loser.

> **(E) What is the primary focus of the curriculum currently offered in most law schools?**

This seems to be a question that is answered by the passage. The first sentence of the first paragraph clearly states that judicial decisions and analysis of cases is the focus of much of legal education. As this is the only candidate, it is the correct answer choice.

Key Takeaways

Correct Answer Choices

12.1% of RC Questions

Application (APP) – 4.2% of RC Questions
Strengthen (S) – 2.3% of RC Questions
Weaken (W) – 1.4% of RC Questions
Evaluation (E) – 3.3% of RC Questions
Extension (EXT) – 0.9% of RC Questions

Apply a process to a detail, argument, or viewpoint in the passage.

Question Tasks

APP: Identify a situation, argument, or approach that is analogous to the one specified in the prompt

S: Identify a statement that strengthens the argument referenced in the prompt

W: Identify a statement that weakens the argument referenced in the prompt

E: Identify a question that can be answered by information in the passage or one for which the answer would strengthen or weaken an argument in the passage

EXT: Identify a statement that can be added after the last sentence of the last paragraph in the passage

Example Prompts

APP: Which one of the following best exemplifies _____ discussed in the passage?
APP: Based on the passage, which one of the following relationships is most analogous to _____?
APP: Which one of the following is most similar to that discussed in the last paragraph?

S: Which one of the following, if true, would most strengthen the author's primary conclusion?
S: Which one of the following, if true, most supports the author's claim that _____?
S: Which one of the following, if true, lends the most credence to _____?

W: Which one of the following, if true, most weakens the author's primary conclusion?
W: Which one of the following, if true, would most seriously challenge _____?
W: Which one of the following, if true, would undermine the claim that _____?

E: An answer to which one of the following questions would be most relevant to _____?
E: Data from which one of the following sources would be most relevant to evaluating _____?
E: Information in the passage most helps to answer which one of the following questions?

EXT: Based on the information in the passage, which one of the following sentences could most logically be added to the end of the passage?
EXT: Given the information in the passage, which one of the following sentences most logically completes the last paragraph?
EXT: Which one of the following sentences could most logically be appended to the passage as a concluding sentence?

Chapter 6

Correct Answer Choices

APP: Statements that present a situation that includes and is compatible with the key characteristics of the situation specified in the prompt

APP: Statements that present an argument or approach that conforms to at least one of the rules of the argument or approach referenced in the prompt and does not violate any of these rules

S: Statements that strengthen the argument referenced in the prompt

W: Statements that weaken the argument referenced in the prompt

E: Questions that can be answered by information in the passage

E: Questions for which the answer would strengthen or weaken an argument in the passage

EXT: Statements that can be logically added after the last sentence of the last paragraph in the passage

Incorrect Answer Choices

Statements that weaken the argument referenced in the prompt (S)

Statements that strengthen the argument referenced in the prompt (W)

Questions for which the answer does not strengthen or weaken the argument in the prompt (E)

Wrong Part of Passage: Accurate statements about a part of the passage not specified by the prompt (EXT)

Contradictory Information: Statements that contradict information in the passage (APP, EXT)

Irrelevant Information: Statements that present new information that is not relevant to the task specified in the prompt (APP, S, W, E, EXT)

Incomplete Information: An accurate statement that omits details necessary to address the task specified in the prompt (APP, S, W)

Chapter 7

Comparative Reading Family

Chapter 7: Comparative Reading Family

Overview

Example Passages and Questions

In this chapter, you will learn how to identify and solve Comparative Reading Family questions.

Comparative Reading Family questions generally ask you to identify a relationship between the two short passages that comprise a Comparative Reading passage. However, some ask about only one of the dual passages. For Relationship and Agree/Disagree questions, the initial analysis of the passage is particularly useful because it focuses on the similarities and dissimilarities between the two passages. For Comparative questions, which is a broad category that includes question types discussed previously in this book, the role of the analysis is dependent on the question subtype.

The three question types in this family—Relationship (R), Agree/Disagree (A/D), and Comparative (C)—are examined in detail in separate sections. Each section includes step-by-step instructions on how to solve the question type and detailed analyses of example questions. In addition, you will get to tackle practice questions taken from previous administrations of the LSAT. The methods for solving these practice questions are explained thoroughly in the answer keys.

Example Passages and Questions

The example questions analyzed in the How-to-Solve subsections reference the following passages, and you should refer back to them as necessary. The analysis of each passage has already been done for you.

For Example Questions 1–5

Passage A

Recent studies have shown that sophisticated computer models of the oceans and atmosphere are capable of simulating large-scale climate trends with remarkable accuracy. But these models make use of
(5) large numbers of variables, many of which have wide ranges of possible values. Because even small differences in those values can have a significant impact on what the simulations predict, it is important to determine the impact when values differ even
(10) slightly.

Since the interactions between the many variables in climate simulations are highly complex, there is no alternative to a "brute force" exploration of all possible combinations of their values if predictions
(15) are to be reliable. This method requires very large numbers of calculations and simulation runs. For example, exhaustive examination of five values for each of only nine variables would require 2 million calculation-intensive simulation runs. Currently
(20) available individual computers are completely inadequate for such a task.

However, the continuing increase in computing capacity of the average desktop computer means that climate simulations can now be run on privately
(25) owned desktop machines connected to one another via the Internet. The calculations are divided among the individual desktop computers, which work simultaneously on their share of the overall problem. Some public resource computing projects of this kind
(30) have already been successful, although only when they captured the public's interest sufficiently to secure widespread participation.

Passage B

Researchers are now learning that many problems in nature, human society, science, and engineering are
(35) naturally "parallel"; that is, that they can be effectively solved by using methods that work simultaneously in parallel. These problems share the common characteristic of involving a large number of similar elements such as molecules, animals, even
(40) people, whose individual actions are governed by simple rules but, taken collectively, function as a highly complex system.

An example is the method used by ants to forage for food. As Lewis Thomas observed, a solitary ant is
(45) little more than a few neurons strung together by fibers. Its behavior follows a few simple rules. But when one sees a dense mass of thousands of ants, crowded together around their anthill retrieving food or repelling an intruder, a more complex picture
(50) emerges; it is as if the whole is thinking, planning, calculating. It is an intelligence, a kind of live

computer, with crawling bits for wits.

We are now living through a great paradigm shift in the field of computing, a shift from sequential
(55) computing (performing one calculation at a time) to massive parallel computing, which employs thousands of computers working simultaneously to solve one computation-intensive problem. Since many computation-intensive problems are inherently
(60) parallel, it only makes sense to use a computing model that exploits that parallelism. A computing model that resembles the inherently parallel problem it is trying to solve will perform best. The old paradigm, in contrast, is subject to the speed limits
(65) imposed by purely sequential computing.

Main Point of Passage A

The main point is stated in the second and third paragraphs. It is that climate simulations require brute force explorations of possible values, which may be done on privately owned computers that are connected via the Internet (parallel computing).

Main Point of Passage B

The main point is stated in the third paragraph. It is that there is a paradigm shift to parallel computing because it is the best way to solve computation-intensive problems that arise in many fields.

Similarities Between Passages

Both passages suggest that parallel computing is increasing in use and has the ability to solve computation-intensive problems.

Dissimilarities Between Passages

Passage A focuses on one computation-intensive problem (climate modeling) that can be solved using parallel computing, while Passage B discusses the characteristics of certain problems that make parallel computing the best way to solve them. Passage A discusses climate simulations as an example of a computation-intensive problem, while Passage B presents ant foraging as an example of a complex parallel system in nature.

1. Passage B relates to Passage A in which one of the following ways?

   (A) The argument in passage B has little bearing on the issues discussed in passage A.
   (B) The explanation offered in passage B shows why the plan proposed in passage A is unlikely to be implemented.
   (C) The ideas advanced in passage B provide a rationale for the solution proposed in passage A.
   (D) The example given in passage B illustrates the need for the "brute force" exploration mentioned in passage A.
   (E) The discussion in passage B conflicts with the assumptions about individual computers made in passage A.

2. It can be inferred that the authors of the two passages would be most likely to agree on which one of the following statements concerning computing systems?

   (A) Massive, parallel computing systems are able to solve complex computation-intensive problems without having to resort to "brute force."
   (B) Computer models are not capable of simulating the behavior of very large biological populations such as insect colonies.
   (C) Parallel computing systems that link privately owned desktop computers via the Internet are not feasible because they rely too heavily on public participation.
   (D) Currently available computers are not well-suited to running simulations, even if the simulated problems are relatively simple.
   (E) Parallel computing systems employing multiple computers are the best means for simulating large-scale climate trends.

3. Which one of the following most accurately expresses the main point of Passage B?

   (A) Many difficult problems in computing are naturally parallel.
   (B) Sequential computing is no longer useful because of the speed limits it imposes.
   (C) There is currently a paradigm shift occurring in the field of computing toward parallel computing.
   (D) Complex biological and social systems are the next frontier in the field of computer simulation.
   (E) Inherently parallel computing problems are best solved by means of computers modeled on the human mind.

4. The passages share which one of the following as their primary purpose?

   (A) to show that the traditional paradigm in computing is ineffective for many common computing tasks
   (B) to argue that a new approach to computing is an effective way to solve a difficult type of problem
   (C) to convince skeptics of the usefulness of desktop computers for calculation-intensive problems
   (D) to demonstrate that a new computing paradigm has supplanted the traditional paradigm for most large-scale computing problems
   (E) to describe complex and as yet unsolved problems that have recently arisen in computing

5. The large-scale climate trends discussed in Passage A are most analogous to which one of the following elements in Passage B?

   (A) the thousands of computers working simultaneously to solve a calculation-intensive problem
   (B) the simple rules that shape the behavior of a single ant
   (C) the highly complex behavior of a dense mass of thousands of ants
   (D) the paradigm shift from sequential to parallel computing
   (E) the speed limits imposed by computing purely sequentially

For Example Questions 6–7

The following passages concern a plant called purple loosestrife. Passage A is excerpted from a report issued by a prairie research council; passage B from a journal of sociology.

Passage A

Purple loosestrife (Lythrum salicaria), an aggressive and invasive perennial of Eurasian origin, arrived with settlers in eastern North America in the early 1800s and has spread across the continent's
(5) midlatitude wetlands. The impact of purple loosestrife on native vegetation has been disastrous, with more than 50 percent of the biomass of some wetland communities displaced. Monospecific blocks of this weed have maintained themselves for at least 20 years.
(10) Impacts on wildlife have not been well studied, but serious reductions in waterfowl and aquatic furbearer productivity have been observed. In addition, several endangered species of vertebrates are threatened with further degradation of their
(15) breeding habitats. Although purple loosestrife can invade relatively undisturbed habitats, the spread and dominance of this weed have been greatly accelerated in disturbed habitats. While digging out the plants can temporarily halt their spread, there has been little
(20) research on long-term purple loosestrife control. Glyphosate has been used successfully, but no measure of the impact of this herbicide on native plant communities has been made.

With the spread of purple loosestrife growing
(25) exponentially, some form of integrated control is needed. At present, coping with purple loosestrife hinges on early detection of the weed's arrival in areas, which allows local eradication to be carried out with minimum damage to the native plant community.

Passage B

(30) The war on purple loosestrife is apparently conducted on behalf of nature, an attempt to liberate the biotic community from the tyrannical influence of a life-destroying invasive weed. Indeed, purple loosestrife control is portrayed by its ^A)practitioners as
(35) an environmental initiative intended to save nature rather than control it. Accordingly, ^A)the purple loosestrife literature, scientific and otherwise, dutifully discusses the impacts of the weed on endangered species—and on threatened biodiversity
(40) more generally. Purple loosestrife is a pollution, according to the ^A)scientific community, and all of nature suffers under its pervasive influence.

Regardless of the perceived and actual ecological effects of the purple invader, it is apparent that
(45) popular pollution ideologies have been extended into the wetlands of North America. Consequently, the scientific effort to liberate nature from purple loosestrife has failed to decouple itself from its philosophical origin as an instrument to control nature
(50) to the satisfaction of human desires. Birds, particularly game birds and waterfowl, provide the bulk of the justification for loosestrife management. However, no bird species other than the canvasback has been identified in the literature as endangered by
(55) purple loosestrife. The impact of purple loosestrife on

furbearing mammals is discussed at great length, though none of the species highlighted (muskrat, mink) can be considered threatened in North America. What is threatened by purple loosestrife is the
(60) economics of exploiting such preferred species and the millions of dollars that will be lost to the economies of the United States and Canada from reduced hunting, trapping, and recreation revenues due to a decline in the production of the wetland
(65) resource.

Main Point of Passage A

> The main point is stated in the first and last paragraph. It is that purple loosestrife has a disastrous impact on native vegetation and some form of integrated control is needed.

Main Point of Passage B

> The main point is stated in the last paragraph. It is that purple loosestrife has a negative economic impact rather than an environmental one.

Similarities Between Passages

> Both discuss purple loosestrife and its effect on wetlands.
> Both discuss efforts to control purple loosestrife.
> Both discuss the impact of purple loosestrife on furbearing animals.

Dissimilarities Between Passages

> Passage A claims the purple loosestrife is an environmental threat and must be controlled, while Passage B does not consider it an environmental threat and argues that efforts to control it have economic motives.
> Passage A states that waterfowl, aquatic furbearers, and endangered vertebrates are threatened by the effect of purple loosestrife on habitats, while Passage B states that only one bird species is threatened by purple loosestrife and that none of the furbearing mammals impacted by purple loosestrife are threatened.

6. It can be inferred that the authors would be most likely to disagree about which one of the following?

(A) Purple loosestrife spreads more quickly in disturbed habitats than in undisturbed habitats.
(B) The threat posed by purple loosestrife to local aquatic furbearer populations is serious.
(C) Most people who advocate that eradication measures be taken to control purple loosestrife are not genuine in their concern for the environment.
(D) The size of the biomass that has been displaced by purple loosestrife is larger than is generally thought.
(E) Measures should be taken to prevent other non-native plant species from invading North America.

7. Both passages explicitly mention which one of the following?

(A) furbearing animals
(B) glyphosate
(C) the threat purple loosestrife poses to economies
(D) popular pollution ideologies
(E) literature on purple loosestrife control

Relationship

Relationship

≈ 0.25 questions per test

Example Prompts

Which one of the following most accurately describes *the relationship between passage A and passage B*?	Which one of the following most accurately describes a way in which *the two passages are related* to one another?	*The relationship between the two passages* can best be described as

Take These Steps

Refer back to your initial analysis to identify the similarities and dissimilarities between the two passages.

Determine the structural relationship between Passage A and Passage B. This relationship is often dependent on how each passage treats the overlapping subject matter.

Anticipate a correct answer choice that expresses the structural relationship between the two passages in general terms.

Answer Choices

Correct Answer Choices	**Incorrect Answer Choices**
Statements that accurately describe the structural relationship between the two passages	Statements that misrepresent the relationship between the two passages
	Statements that reverse elements of the relationship between the two passages
	Too strong
	Contradictory information
	Irrelevant information

Relationship (R) questions ask you to find the answer choice that describes the structural relationship between the two passages. To answer this question type, you must identify their similarities and dissimilarities. This should be done during the initial analysis of the passage.

R question prompts usually include terms such as *relationship between* or *are related*. Other terms with similar meanings may be used as well. In addition, the prompt will always reference both passages. R questions only appear in Comparative Reading passages.

How to Solve R Questions

The first step in solving an R question is to identify the similarities and dissimilarities between the two passages. Refer back to your initial analysis to do this. Once you are clear on how the passages are similar and dissimilar, try to determine the broader structural relationship between them. This relationship is dependent on how each passage treats the overlapping subject matter. For example, one passage might describe a theory or principle in general terms, while the other discusses a specific application. Or, one passage might make a claim, while the other presents a counterclaim. Obviously, there are a wide variety of possible relationships. Here are some examples of R question correct answer choices that describe the structural relationship between two passages:

Passage A describes an approach that Passage B dismisses.
Passage A offers a critique of forensic accounting, while Passage B offers partial support for that practice.
Passage A describes a scientific phenomenon, while Passage B uses that phenomenon to discuss larger implications.
Passage A and Passage B advance similar arguments but arrive at somewhat different conclusions.
Passage A raises a question concerning legal precedent, while Passage B is concerned with answering that question.
The example given in Passage A illustrates a solution similar to the one arrived at in Passage B.
Passage A and Passage B have similar underlying principles but arrive at conflicting interpretations of what they mean in practice.
Passage A criticizes Passage B for not accounting for all of the available evidence in reaching its conclusion.

Once you have identified the relationship between the two passages, anticipate a correct answer choice that expresses it.

Let's look at Example Question 1 (page 273):

Passage B relates to passage A in which one of the following ways?

(A) The argument in passage B has little bearing on the issues discussed in passage A.
(B) The explanation offered in passage B shows why the plan proposed in passage A is unlikely to be implemented.
(C) The ideas advanced in passage B provide a rationale for the solution proposed in passage A.
(D) The example given in passage B illustrates the need for the "brute force" exploration mentioned in passage A.
(E) The discussion in passage B conflicts with the assumptions about individual computers made in passage A.

Looking back at our initial analysis, we can see that both passages suggest that parallel computing is increasingly being used and has the ability to solve computation-intensive problems. The main dissimilarity seems to be that Passage A focuses on one specific problem and explains why parallel computing is the best way to solve it, while Passage B discusses the characteristics of problems that are best solved using parallel computing. The structural relationship between these two passages seems to be that Passage B provides a reason or additional support for the solution suggested in Passage A. We should anticipate a correct answer choice that expresses this relationship.

(A) **The argument in Passage B has little bearing on the issues discussed in Passage A.**

This answer choice misrepresents the relationship. Passage B and Passage A discuss almost identical issues. This is a loser.

(B) **The explanation offered in Passage B shows why the plan proposed in Passage A is unlikely to be implemented.**

This answer choice also misrepresents the relationship. Passage B provides support for the solution (parallel computing) in Passage A. In addition, both passages indicate that the use of parallel computing is increasing. This is another loser.

(C) **The ideas advanced in Passage B provide a rationale for the solution proposed in Passage A.**

This matches our anticipated answer choice. Passage A proposes the use of parallel computing to solve a problem, and Passage B provides a rationale for this; namely, that many computation-intensive problems are inherently parallel, making parallel computing the best way to solve them. This is a candidate.

(D) **The example given in Passage B illustrates the need for the "brute force" exploration mentioned in Passage A.**

This answer choice includes contradictory information. The example given in Passage B is ant foraging. This is used to show the parallel nature of complex systems. In doing so, it shows an example of a "brute force" approach, but does nothing to establish or demonstrate the need for one. This is a loser.

(E) **The discussion in Passage B conflicts with the assumptions about individual computers made in Passage A.**

This answer choice misrepresents the relationship. Passage A states that individual computers are incapable of creating climate simulations. The discussion in Passage B does not conflict (or even really address) this assumption. This is also a loser.

As (C) is the only candidate, this is the correct answer choice.

Looking at the Answer Choices

The correct answer choice is a statement that accurately describes the structural relationship between the two passages.

Incorrect answer choices may simply misrepresent the relationship between the two passages. In some cases, they will actually reverse elements of the relationship. For example, if Passage A describes a specific situation in which a method is effective and Passage B provides a detailed explanation of the method, then an incorrect answer choice might state that Passage B provides an example to demonstrate how a method described in Passage A is used. You will also encounter incorrect answer choices that make too strong of a claim or include contradictory or irrelevant information.

Agree/Disagree

Relationship
Agree/Disagree
Comparative

Agree/Disagree
≈ 0.63 questions per test

Example Prompts

It is most likely that *the authors of the passages* would *disagree* with each other about the truth of which one of the following statements?

Which one of the following is a statement central to *the argument made by* the author of *passage A* that would *most likely be rejected by* the author of *passage B*?

The authors of the two passages would *most likely agree* with which one of the following statements?

Does the prompt direct you to a point of agreement or disagreement?

Agreement

Disagreement

Take These Steps

Review the initial analysis to determine the similarities between the two passages. Focus on the major points that both authors agree on.

Review the initial analysis to determine the dissimilarities between the two passages. Focus on the major points that both authors disagree about.

Anticipate a correct answer choice that expresses one of these points. If either author would not agree with a statement or if either author's position is unclear, it cannot be the correct answer choice.

Anticipate a correct answer choice that expresses one of these points. If both authors would agree or disagree with the statement or if either author's position is unclear, it cannot be the correct answer choice.

Answer Choices

Correct Answer Choices

Statements that both authors would agree with (point of agreement)

Statements that one author would agree with and one would disagree with (point of disagreement)

Incorrect Answer Choices

Statements for which either author's position is unclear

Statements that one author would disagree with (point of agreement)

Statements that both authors would agree or disagree with (point of disagreement)

Too strong

Contradictory information

Irrelevant information

Agree/Disagree (A/D) questions ask you to find the answer choice that includes a statement that the authors of both passages would agree with (point of agreement) or that one author would agree with and the other would disagree with (point of disagreement). As is the case with R questions, you must understand the similarities and dissimilarities between the two passages to answer this question type. This information should be included in your initial analysis.

A/D question prompts always include terms such as *agree* or *disagree*. Other terms with similar meanings may be used as well. Furthermore, they will always ask about the authors of both passages. A/D questions only appear in Comparative Reading passages.

How to Solve A/D Questions

The first step in solving an A/D question is to determine whether the prompt asks about a point of agreement or disagreement. A/D prompts that ask about what the authors agree on are more common than ones that ask about what the authors disagree about.

If the Prompt Asks about a Point of Agreement

When the prompt asks about a point of agreement, you should review your initial analysis to determine the similarities between the two passages. Focus on the major points that both authors agree on. If the prompt contains details that allow you to narrow down the specific topic, focus on similarities related to this topic. Then, anticipate a correct answer choice that expresses one of the points of agreement. When going through the answer choices, keep in mind that if either author would disagree with a statement or if you cannot clearly identify an author's position regarding the statement, it cannot be the correct answer choice.

Let's look at Example Question 2 (page 273):

It can be inferred that the authors of the two passages would be most likely to agree on which one of the following statements concerning computing systems?

(A) Massive, parallel computing systems are able to solve complex computation-intensive problems without having to resort to "brute force."

(B) Computer models are not capable of simulating the behavior of very large biological populations such as insect colonies.

(C) Parallel computing systems that link privately owned desktop computers via the Internet are not feasible because they rely too heavily on public participation.

(D) Currently available computers are not well-suited to running simulations, even if the simulated problems are relatively simple.

(E) Parallel computing systems employing multiple computers are the best means for simulating large-scale climate trends.

The prompt asks us to locate a statement that both authors would agree with about parallel computing. Looking back at our analysis, we can see that both authors feel that the use of parallel computing is increasing and that parallel computing has the ability to solve computation-intensive problems. Therefore, we should anticipate a correct answer choice that expresses one of these points.

(A) **Massive, parallel computing systems are able to solve complex computation-intensive problems without having to resort to "brute force."**

This answer choice includes contradictory information. The author of Passage A would disagree with this statement. Passage A clearly states that brute force is necessary to create reliable climate simulations. The creation of a climate simulation is the computation-intensive problem addressed in the first passage. Therefore, this is a loser.

(B) **Computer models are not capable of simulating the behavior of very large biological populations such as insect colonies.**

This answer choice includes contradictory information. The author of Passage A would disagree with this statement. Passage A implies that this is possible because it claims that parallel computing can be used to solve computation-intensive problems such as creating climate simulations. This is a loser.

(C) **Parallel computing systems that link privately owned desktop computers via the Internet are not feasible because they rely too heavily on public participation.**

This answer choice includes irrelevant information. It is unclear whether both authors would agree with this statement. Passage A states that these computing projects can be successful only when they involve public participation. However, Passage A does not address the feasibility of receiving public participation. In addition, public participation is never discussed in Passage B. This is also a loser.

(D) **Currently available computers are not well-suited to running simulations, even if the simulated problems are relatively simple.**

This answer choice includes irrelevant information. It is unclear whether both authors would agree with this statement. Neither passage discusses currently available computers simulating relatively simple problems. This is a loser as well.

(E) **Parallel computing systems employing multiple computers are the best means for simulating large-scale climate trends.**

This matches our anticipated answer choice. Both authors would agree with this statement. Passage A presents climate simulations as an example of a problem that requires the use of parallel computing to solve. Passage B states that many computation-intensive problems are inherently parallel, so parallel computing is the best way to solve them. Even though Passage B does not discuss climate simulations specifically, these are clearly examples of computation-intensive problems. As this is the only candidate, it is the correct answer choice.

If the Prompt Asks about a Point of Disagreement

When the prompt asks about a point of disagreement, you should go back to the initial analysis to look for dissimilarities between the passages. Again, pay close attention to the main points that the authors disagree about and look for any information in the prompt that will help you determine which points to focus on. Then, anticipate a correct answer choice that expresses one of the points of disagreement. Remember, an answer choice is correct if one author would agree with the statement and one would disagree with it. If both authors would agree or disagree with the statement, or if you cannot clearly identify an author's position regarding the statement, the answer choice is incorrect.

Let's look at Example Question 6 (page 275):

It can be inferred that the authors would be most likely to disagree about which one of the following?

(A) Purple loosestrife spreads more quickly in disturbed habitats than in undisturbed habitats.
(B) The threat posed by purple loosestrife to local aquatic furbearer populations is serious.
(C) Most people who advocate that eradication measures be taken to control purple loosestrife are not genuine in their concern for the environment.
(D) The size of the biomass that has been displaced by purple loosestrife is larger than is generally thought.
(E) Measures should be taken to prevent other non-native plant species from invading North America.

The prompt asks us to locate a statement that both authors would disagree about. Looking back at our analysis, we can see that the most significant point of disagreement is that the author of Passage A feels that purple loosestrife is an environmental threat that must be controlled while the author of Passage B does not consider it an environmental threat and instead argues that efforts to control it are economically motivated. In addition, the author of Passage A feels that waterfowl and aquatic furbearers are threatened by purple loosestrife whereas the author of Passage B claims that only one species of waterfowl has been negatively affected and that no species of furbearing mammals are threatened. We should anticipate a correct answer choice that expresses one of these points.

(A) Purple loosestrife spreads more quickly in disturbed habitats than in undisturbed habitats.

This answer choice includes irrelevant information. It is unclear whether the author of Passage B would agree or disagree with this statement. Passage B makes no reference to the spread of purple loosestrife in disturbed or undisturbed habitats. This is a loser.

(B) The threat posed by purple loosestrife to local aquatic furbearer populations is serious.

This matches our anticipated answer choice. Passage A clearly indicates that purple loosestrife is a threat to aquatic furbearer species. In contrast, Passage B states that no species of furbearing mammal is threatened. This is a candidate.

(C) Most people who advocate that eradication measures be taken to control purple loosestrife are not genuine in their concern for the environment.

This also matches our anticipated answer choice. Passage A states that purple loosestrife is an environmental threat and must be controlled. Passage B claims that those who advocate for eradication measures are primarily motivated by economic concerns. This is a candidate as well.

(D) The size of the biomass that has been displaced by purple loosestrife is larger than is generally thought.

This answer choice includes irrelevant information. It is unclear whether each author would agree or disagree with this statement. Passage A does not include information about whether or not the biomass lost is larger than generally thought. Passage B does not discuss the loss of biomass at all. This is a loser.

(E) Measures should be taken to prevent other non-native plant species from invading North America.

This answer choice includes irrelevant information. It is unclear whether each author would agree or disagree with this statement. Neither passage discusses other non-native plant species. This is a loser.

We have two candidates, (B) and (C), so we need to eliminate one. Looking back at (C), we can see that it is the weaker candidate. First, it is not clear whether or not the author of Passage A would agree or disagree with this statement. The author of Passage A clearly advocates for control due to environmental concerns. However, the author is just speaking from his or her own point of view. There is no discussion about the motivations of others who advocate for eradication. In addition, there is also uncertainty about whether or not the author of Passage B would agree or disagree. The problem is that this answer choice makes too strong of a claim because of the inclusion of the term *most*. The author of Passage B obviously feels that economic concerns are a significant factor in efforts to control purple loosestrife. However, there is no indication that the author believes that the majority (*most*) of the people advocating for control are not genuine in their concerns for the environment. So, it is uncertain whether or not the author of Passage B would disagree with the statement. Therefore, (B) is the correct answer choice.

Looking at the Answer Choices

The correct answer choice is either a statement that both authors would agree with (point of agreement) or a statement that one author would agree with and one would disagree with (point of disagreement).

When the prompt references a point of agreement, incorrect answer choices will be statements that one or both authors would disagree with. When the prompt references a point of disagreement, incorrect answer choices will be statements that both authors would agree or disagree with. You will also encounter answer choices that are incorrect because it is impossible to say with certainty whether one or both authors would agree or disagree with them. Answer choices that make too strong of a claim or that include contradictory or irrelevant information are common as well.

Comparative

comparative (C.) questions are variants of the standard question types presented in earlier chapters; C. question
rompts are generally quite similar to those of the other question types. Consider the

COMPARATIVE READING FAMILY

Relationship
Agree/Disagree
Comparative

Comparative

≈ 4.38 questions per test

Example Prompts

Which one of the following most accurately describes *the stance* expressed by the author of *passage A* toward _____?

Which one of the following is *addressed by* the author of *passage A but not by* the author of *passage B*?

Which one of the following *conforms to* _____ advocated *by* the authors of *both passages*?

Take These Steps

Identify the question subtype. Does the prompt refer to one passage or to both passages?

One Passage

Both Passages

Apply the strategy for the corresponding standard question type discussed earlier in this book. Consider only the information from the passage referenced in the prompt and ignore the information in the other passage.

Apply a variation of the strategy for the corresponding standard question type discussed earlier in this book. Consider the information in both passages. Understanding the relationship between the main point of each passage, the viewpoint of each author, and the similarities and dissimilarities in content is critical.

Answer Choices

Correct Answer Choices

Statements that match the criteria to be a correct answer choice for the corresponding standard question type

Incorrect Answer Choices

Statements that include information from the wrong passage or both passages (prompt references one passage)

Statements that include information from only one passage (prompt references both passages)

Statements that meet the criteria to be an incorrect answer choice for the corresponding standard question type

Comparative (C) questions are variants of the standard question types presented in earlier chapters. C question prompts are generally quite similar to those of the other question types. Consider the following examples:

Which one of the following most accurately expresses the main point of the passage?
Which one of the following most accurately expresses the main point of Passage B?
Which one of the following most accurately expresses the main point of each passage?

The first is the prompt of a standard MP question for a single passage. The second is a C question prompt asking about the main point of one of the passages. The third is a C question prompt asking about the main point of both passages. Note that prompts that refer to both passages show much greater variety in terms of wording. Examples of these types of prompts are provided later in this section.

How to Solve C Questions

The first step in solving a C question is to identify the question subtype. C Main Point and C Implication are the most common subtypes, but all of the standard question types discussed previously can be adapted for use in Comparative Reading passages. Once you have identified the subtype, determine whether the prompt is asking about one of the passages or both.

If the Prompt References One Passage

When a prompt references only one passage, you should use the strategy for the corresponding question type discussed earlier in this book. For example, if the C question asks about the main point of Passage B, you would apply the steps outlined in the MP question section of Chapter 3. Note that although the analysis of a Comparative Reading passage does not include the function of each paragraph and a summary of its content, this should not be an issue for answering questions. The reason is that the dual passages in a Comparative Reading passage are usually less complex in terms of structure and content than the long single reading passages.

When answering C questions that ask about one passage, it is important to consider only the content of the passage that the prompt references. A common trick used to increase the difficulty level of these questions is to include related details from the other passage in the incorrect answer choices. Therefore, you should focus on the passage referenced in the prompt and ignore the other passage when answering these questions.

Let's look at Example Question 3 (page 273):

Which one of the following most accurately expresses the main point of Passage B?

(A) Many difficult problems in computing are naturally parallel.
(B) Sequential computing is no longer useful because of the speed limits it imposes.
(C) There is currently a paradigm shift occurring in the field of computing toward parallel computing.
(D) Complex biological and social systems are the next frontier in the field of computer simulation.
(E) Inherently parallel computing problems are best solved by means of computers modeled on the human mind.

This C question asks about the main point of Passage B. Therefore, we should ignore Passage A altogether. The main point of Passage B is that there is a paradigm shift to parallel computing because it is the best way to solve computation-intensive problems that arise in many fields. We should anticipate a correct answer choice that expresses this.

(A) Many difficult problems in computing are naturally parallel.

This answer choice addresses the wrong task. It presents a supporting idea rather than the main point of the passage. This is a loser.

(B) Sequential computing is no longer useful because of the speed limits it imposes.

This answer choice makes too strong of a claim. The third paragraph states that sequential computing faces speed limits, but this does not necessarily mean that sequential computing is no longer useful. In addition, this statement is not related to the main point of the passage. This is another loser.

(C) There is currently a paradigm shift occurring in the field of computing toward parallel computing.

This answer choice almost matches our anticipated answer choice. It expresses the first part of the main point we identified but not the second part. However, as it accurately restates the most important part of the main point, we will keep it as a candidate for now.

(D) Complex biological and social systems are the next frontier in the field of computer simulation.

This answer choice includes irrelevant information. The passage does not make any reference to complex biological and social systems being the next frontier in the field of computer simulation. This is a loser.

(E) Inherently parallel computing problems are best solved by means of computers modeled on the human mind.

This answer choice includes irrelevant information. The passage never mentions computers modeled on the human mind. This is also a loser.

As answer choice (C) is our only candidate, it is the correct answer choice. While this answer choice is not perfect, it captures the most important part of the main point—that there is a paradigm shift towards parallel computing.

If the Prompt References Both Passages

When a prompt references both passages, you should use a variation of the strategy for the corresponding question type that was presented earlier in this book. It is crucial that you focus on the information in both passages. Understanding the relationship between the main point of each passage, the viewpoint of each author, and how the content is similar and dissimilar is important when answering these types of questions. Fortunately, the two passages that make up a Comparative Reading passage are much simpler than the regular reading passages. Therefore, it is usually not that difficult to find the information required to answer these questions.

Answering C questions that refer to both passages requires that you deviate from the steps outlined in the earlier chapters of this book. The most common C question subtypes that include prompts that reference both passages are as follows:

C Main Point Questions

C Main Point questions that reference both passages are the most common C question subtype. They ask you to identify a main topic that is common to both passages. Apply the methods described in the MP question subsection of Chapter 3 to each passage. Once you have determined the main point of each passage, identify the elements of each main point that overlap. Anticipate a correct answer choice that expresses these overlapping elements.

The following are examples of C Main Point question prompts that reference both passages:

> **A discussion of which one of the following is central to both passages?**
> **Both of the passages are concerned with answering which one of the following questions?**

C Purpose Questions

C Purpose questions that reference both passages ask you to identify the shared purpose of the two passages. Apply the methods described in the P question subsection of Chapter 3 to each passage. Once you have determined the purpose of each passage, identify the elements that overlap. Anticipate a correct answer choice that expresses these overlapping elements. Keep in mind that the dual passages in a Comparative Reading passage are usually Argumentative. Therefore, the correct answer choice will almost always include an action verb related to making a claim.

The following are examples of C Purpose question prompts that reference both passages:

> **The primary purpose of each of the passages is to**
> **Which one of the following is a shared central purpose of each passage?**

Let's look at Example Question 4 (page 273):

The passages share which one of the following as their primary purpose?

(A) to show that the traditional paradigm in computing is ineffective for many common computing tasks
(B) to argue that a new approach to computing is an effective way to solve a difficult type of problem
(C) to convince skeptics of the usefulness of desktop computers for calculation-intensive problems
(D) to demonstrate that a new computing paradigm has supplanted the traditional paradigm for most large-scale computing problems
(E) to describe complex and as yet unsolved problems that have recently arisen in computing

This is a C Purpose question. Therefore, we need to identify the purpose of each passage and identify the elements that overlap. The main point of Passage A is that climate simulations require brute force explorations of possible values, which may be done on privately owned computers that are connected via the Internet (parallel computing). The main point of Passage B is that there is a paradigm shift to parallel computing because it is the best way to solve computation-intensive problems that arise in many fields. Both authors seem to be arguing that parallel computing can be used to solve computation-intensive problems. We should anticipate a correct answer choice that combines an appropriate action verb with a description of this shared element of each passage's main point. It would likely be something like "to argue in favor of a new computing system's ability to solve computation-intensive problems."

(A) to show that the traditional paradigm in computing is ineffective for many common computing tasks

This answer choice includes irrelevant information. Neither passage suggests that traditional sequential computing is ineffective for many common computing tasks. This is a loser.

(B) to argue that a new approach to computing is an effective way to solve a difficult type of problem

This matches our anticipated answer choice. Both passages are arguing that parallel computing is effective at solving computation-intensive (difficult) problems. This is a candidate.

(C) to convince skeptics of the usefulness of desktop computers for calculation-intensive problems

This answer choice includes irrelevant information. The viewpoint of skeptics is not mentioned in either passage. This is also a loser.

(D) to demonstrate that a new computing paradigm has supplanted the traditional paradigm for most large-scale computing problems

This answer choice makes too strong of a claim. Both passages argue that parallel computing can be used to solve computation-intensive problems. However, this does not necessarily mean that parallel computing has supplanted traditional computing for the majority of large-scale problems. This is a loser as well.

(E) to describe complex and as yet unsolved problems that have recently arisen in computing

This answer choice includes an inappropriate action verb. Since the dual passages of a Comparative Reading passage are always Argumentative, we require an action verb related to making a claim. This is also a loser.

As (B) is the only candidate, it is the correct answer choice.

C Detail Questions

C Detail questions that reference both passages ask you to retrieve a specific piece of information that is explicitly stated in each of the passages. As the initial analysis does not include a summary of the content of each paragraph, you will not be able to use it to locate the content related to the topic in the prompt. However, it may be the case that one of the similarities between the two passages that you included in your analysis is related to the topic. In this case, you can anticipate a restatement of this detail as the correct answer choice. If the topic is not related to one of the similarities in the analysis, you will need to proceed to eliminating answer choices. Scan Paragraph A for the detail stated in each answer choice. If a detail appears in Passage A, scan Passage B. If the detail appears in both passages, it is the correct answer choice.

The following are examples of C Detail question prompts that reference both passages:

> **Which one of the following is a feature of X mentioned in both of the passage?**
> **Both passages place in opposition the members of which one of the following pairs?**

C Existence Questions

C Existence questions that reference both passages ask you to determine whether or not a specific detail appears in both passages. You should first quickly scan the answer choices to determine if any express one of the similarities between both passages that you identified during your initial analysis. If so, that answer choice is likely the correct answer choice. If not, proceed to eliminating answer choices. As with C Detail questions, focus on Passage A first.

If a detail appears in Passage A, check if it appears in Passage B.

The following are examples of C Existence question prompts that reference both passages:

> **Both passages mention which one of the following?**
> **Each of the two passages mentions the relation of X to**

Let's look at Example Question 7 (page 275):

> Both passages explicitly mention which one of the following?
>
> (A) furbearing animals
> (B) glyphosate
> (C) the threat purple loosestrife poses to economies
> (D) popular pollution ideologies
> (E) literature on purple loosestrife control

This is a C Existence question. Scanning the answer choices quickly, we can see that answer choice (A) matches one of the similarities we identified—both passages discuss the impact of purple loosestrife on furbearing animals. This is almost certainly the correct answer choice. However, we will go through the answer choices one-by-one to be certain.

(A) furbearing animals

This detail is mentioned in both passages. Passage A refers to furbearing animals in the first paragraph, and Passage B refers to them in the last paragraph. This is a candidate.

(B) glyphosate

This detail is mentioned in Passage A but not in Passage B. This is a loser.

(C) the threat purple loosestrife poses to economies

This detail is mentioned in Passage B but not in Passage A. This is also a loser.

(D) popular pollution ideologies

This detail is mentioned in Passage B but not in Passage A. This is a loser as well.

(E) literature on purple loosestrife control

This detail is also mentioned in Passage B but not in Passage A. This is a loser.

As (A) is the only candidate, it is the correct answer choice.

C Meaning Questions

C Meaning questions that reference both passages ask you to determine the meaning of the referenced term. They may ask you directly how a term is used in both passages, or they may ask you to identify a term in one passage that has a meaning that is similar to a term in the other passage. In either case, you should apply the methods described in the M question subsection of Chapter 4 to both passages.

The following are examples of C Meaning question prompts that reference both passages:

> **The term "X" has which one of the following meanings in both Passage A (line #) and Passage B (line #)?**
>
> **The meaning of the word "X" (line #) as it is used in Passage A is most closely related to which one of the following concepts in Passage B?**

C Implication Questions

C Implication questions that reference both passages are the second most common C question subtype. They ask you to identify an inference based on the information presented in both passages. If the prompt includes a specific topic that is related to a similarity you identified during the initial analysis, check if there are any inferences you can anticipate based on this information. Otherwise, attempt to locate the relevant content in the passages to determine if there are any obvious inferences. If you cannot identify an inference or if the prompt does not include a topic, proceed to eliminating answer choices. Focus on Passage A initially. If you find support for an answer choice in Passage A, check for support in Passage B.

The following are examples of C Implication question prompts that reference both passages:

> **Both passages most strongly support which one of the following inferences regarding the authors' relationships to X?**
>
> **Which one of the following can be most reasonably inferred from the two passages taken together, but not from either one individually?**

C Viewpoint Questions

C Viewpoint questions that reference both passages ask you to identify an inference that is compatible with the viewpoint of both authors or the viewpoint of one author toward a topic discussed in the other passage. They will not ask about other viewpoints in the passages. Regardless, the method for solving these questions is similar to that for a C Implication question. If the specific topic in the prompt is related to similarity or dissimilarity you identified during your initial analysis, check if there are any inferences you can anticipate based on this information that are compatible with both authors' viewpoints or with the viewpoint of the author specified in the prompt. If the prompt does not include a topic from a specific part of the passage, proceed to eliminating answer choices.

The following are examples of C Viewpoint question prompts that reference both passages:

> **It can be inferred that the author of Passage B has which one of the following opinions about X discussed in Passage A?**
>
> **The authors' views regarding X can most accurately be described in which one of the following ways?**

C Attitude Questions

C Attitude questions that reference both passages ask you to identify the attitude of both authors toward a topic or, more commonly, the attitude of one author toward the other author's viewpoint. In the first case, you should apply the methods described in the ATT subsection of Chapter 5 to both passages. In the second case, you need to identify the viewpoint of the author being asked about and then apply the methods described in the ATT subsection to the passage written by the author whose attitude you are being asked to determine.

The following are examples of C Attitude question prompts that reference both passages:

The attitudes of the author of Passage A and the author of Passage B, respectively, toward X, may be most accurately described as
Which one of the following most accurately characterizes the attitude of the author of Passage A toward the argument put forth in Passage B?

C Application Questions

C Application questions that reference both passages ask you to identify analogous situations, arguments, or approaches. These include 1) a relationship that is analogous to the relationship between the two passages, 2) a situation, argument, or approach in one passage that is analogous to one in the other, 3) a situation, argument, or approach that both authors would feel is analogous one in the passages, or 4) a situation, argument, or approach that an author would feel is analogous to one in the other passage. In the first case, you need to review the similarities and dissimilarities you identified during the initial analysis to determine the underlying relationship between both passages and then reframe this relationship in general terms. This process is similar to how you would answer an R question. Therefore, you should anticipate a correct answer choice that describes an analogous relationship. In the other cases, apply the methods in the APP subsection of Chapter 6.

The following are examples of C Application question prompts that reference both passages:

> **The relationship between which one of the following pairs is most analogous to the relationship between X in Passage A and Passage B?**
> **X in Passage A is most analogous to which one of the following concepts in Passage B?**
> **It can be inferred that the author of Passage A would be most likely to regard which one of the following X in Passage B as exemplifying Y?**

Let's look at Example Question 5 (page 273):

> The large-scale climate trends discussed in Passage A are most analogous to which one of the following elements in Passage B?
>
> (A) the thousands of computers working simultaneously to solve a calculation-intensive problem
> (B) the simple rules that shape the behavior of a single ant
> (C) the highly complex behavior of a dense mass of thousands of ants
> (D) the paradigm shift from sequential to parallel computing
> (E) the speed limits imposed by computing purely sequentially

This is a C Application question. The prompt is asking us to find a situation in Passage B that is analogous to the large-scale climate trends discussed in Passage A. Looking at the first paragraph of Passage A, we can see that large-scale climate trends can be modeled using a large number of variables with a wide range of values. We should anticipate a correct answer choice that describes a comparable situation.

(A) the thousands of computers working simultaneously to solve a calculation-intensive problem

This answer choice includes irrelevant information. This is not a complex system that can be modeled but rather a method of creating models. This is a loser.

(B) the simple rules that shape the behavior of a single ant

This answer choice includes irrelevant information. The situation in Passage A describes a complex system made up of many individual variables. It does not discuss the behavior of a single individual. This is also a loser.

(C) the highly complex behavior of a dense mass of thousands of ants

This matches our anticipated answer choice. The mass of ants is a complex system made up of a large number of individual variables. It can also be modeled. This is a candidate.

(D) the paradigm shift from sequential to parallel computing

This answer choice includes irrelevant information. It describes the transition from one method of modeling to another. It does not describe a complex system that can be modeled. This is a loser.

(E) the speed limits imposed by computing purely sequentially

This answer choice includes irrelevant information. The speed limits on sequential computing are not complex systems that can be modeled. This is also a loser.

As (C) is the only candidate, it is the correct answer choice.

Looking at the Answer Choices

The correct answer choice is a statement that meets the criteria to be a correct answer choice for the corresponding standard question type. Note, however, that there may be some variation when the prompt references both passages. For example, the correct answer choice of an MP question for a passage that includes the author's viewpoint is an accurate restatement of the author's conclusion. The correct answer choice of a C Main Point question that references one passage is the same. However, the correct answer choice of a C Main Point question that references both passages is an accurate restatement of the overlapping elements of both author's conclusions.

For questions with prompts that reference only one passage, incorrect answer choices are often statements with information from the wrong passage or both passages. For ones with prompts that reference both passages, incorrect answer choices often include information from only one passage. For all C question subtypes, incorrect answer choices include statements that meet the criteria to be an incorrect answer choice for the corresponding standard question type.

Practice Sets: Comparative Reading Family

Analyze the passages below. Mark the <u>keywords</u>, <u>main point</u>, and <u>viewpoints</u> other than the author's.
Summarize the main points and take note of the similarities and dissimilarities between the two passages.
Then answer the questions that follow each passage.

The two passages discuss recent scientific research on music. They are adapted from two different papers presented at a scholarly conference.

Passage A

Did music and human language originate separately or together? Both systems use intonation and rhythm to communicate emotions. Both can be produced vocally or with tools, and people can produce
(5) both music and language silently to themselves.

Brain imaging studies suggest that music and language are part of one large, vastly complicated, neurological system for processing sound. In fact, fewer differences than similarities exist between the
(10) neurological processing of the two. One could think of the two activities as different radio programs that can be broadcast over the same hardware. One noteworthy difference, though, is that, generally speaking, people are better at language than music. In music, anyone
(15) can listen easily enough, but most people do not perform well, and in many cultures composition is left to specialists. In language, by contrast, nearly everyone actively performs and composes.

Given their shared neurological basis, it appears
(20) that music and language evolved together as brain size increased over the course of hominid evolution. But the primacy of language over music that we can observe today suggests that language, not music, was the primary function natural selection operated on.
(25) Music, it would seem, had little adaptive value of its own, and most likely developed on the coattails of language.

Passage B

Darwin claimed that since "neither the enjoyment nor the capacity of producing musical notes are
(30) faculties of the least [practical] use to man . . . they must be ranked amongst the most mysterious with which he is endowed." I suggest that the enjoyment of and the capacity to produce musical notes are faculties of indispensable use to mothers and their infants and
(35) that it is in the emotional bonds created by the interaction of mother and child that we can discover the evolutionary origins of human music.

Even excluding lullabies, which parents sing to infants, human mothers and infants under six months
(40) of age engage in ritualized, sequential behaviors, involving vocal, facial, and bodily interactions. Using face-to-face mother-infant interactions filmed at 24 frames per second, researchers have shown that mothers and infants jointly construct mutually
(45) improvised interactions in which each partner tracks the actions of the other. Such episodes last from one-half second to three seconds and are composed of

musical elements—variations in pitch, rhythm, timbre, volume, and tempo.
(50) What evolutionary advantage would such behavior have? In the course of hominid evolution, brain size increased rapidly. Contemporaneously, the increase in bipedality caused the birth canal to narrow. This resulted in hominid infants being born ever-more
(55) prematurely, leaving them much more helpless at birth. This helplessness necessitated longer, better maternal care. Under such conditions, the emotional bonds created in the premusical mother-infant interactions we observe in Homo sapiens today—behavior whose
(60) neurological basis essentially constitutes the capacity to make and enjoy music—would have conferred considerable evolutionary advantage.

Main Point of Passage A

Main Point of Passage B

Similarities Between Passages

Dissimilarities Between Passages

1. Both passages were written primarily in order to answer which one of the following questions?

   (A) What evolutionary advantage did larger brain size confer on early hominids?
   (B) Why do human mothers and infants engage in bonding behavior that is composed of musical elements?
   (C) What are the evolutionary origins of the human ability to make music?
   (D) Do the human abilities to make music and to use language depend on the same neurological systems?
   (E) Why are most people more adept at using language than they are at making music?

2. Each of the two passages mentions the relation of music to

   (A) bonding between humans
   (B) human emotion
   (C) neurological research
   (D) the increasing helplessness of hominid infants
   (E) the use of tools to produce sounds

3. It can be inferred that the authors of the two passages would be most likely to disagree over whether

   (A) the increase in hominid brain size necessitated earlier births
   (B) fewer differences than similarities exist between the neurological processing of music and human language
   (C) brain size increased rapidly over the course of human evolution
   (D) the capacity to produce music has great adaptive value to humans
   (E) mother-infant bonding involves temporally patterned vocal interactions

4. The authors would be most likely to agree on the answer to which one of the following questions regarding musical capacity in humans?

   (A) Does it manifest itself in some form in early infancy?
   (B) Does it affect the strength of mother-infant bonds?
   (C) Is it at least partly a result of evolutionary increases in brain size?
   (D) Did its evolution spur the development of new neurological systems?
   (E) Why does it vary so greatly among different individuals?

5. Which one of the following principles underlies the arguments in both passages?

   (A) Investigations of the evolutionary origins of human behaviors must take into account the behavior of nonhuman animals.
   (B) All human capacities can be explained in terms of the evolutionary advantages they offer.
   (C) The fact that a single neurological system underlies two different capacities is evidence that those capacities evolved concurrently.
   (D) The discovery of the neurological basis of a human behavior constitutes the discovery of the essence of that behavior.
   (E) The behavior of modern-day humans can provide legitimate evidence concerning the evolutionary origins of human abilities.

6. Which one of the following most accurately characterizes a relationship between the two passages?

   (A) Passage A and Passage B use different evidence to draw divergent conclusions.
   (B) Passage A poses the question that Passage B attempts to answer.
   (C) Passage A proposes a hypothesis that Passage B attempts to substantiate with new evidence.
   (D) Passage A expresses a stronger commitment to its hypothesis than does Passage B.
   (E) Passage A and Passage B use different evidence to support the same conclusion.

The passages discuss relationships between business interests and university research.

Passage A

As university researchers working in a "gift economy" dedicated to collegial sharing of ideas, we have long been insulated from market pressures. The recent tendency to treat research findings as
(5) commodities, tradable for cash, threatens this tradition and the role of research as a public good.

The nurseries for new ideas are traditionally universities, which provide an environment uniquely suited to the painstaking testing and revision of
(10) theories. Unfortunately, the market process and values governing commodity exchange are ill suited to the cultivation and management of new ideas. With their shareholders impatient for quick returns, businesses are averse to wide-ranging experimentation. And, what
(15) is even more important, few commercial enterprises contain the range of expertise needed to handle the replacement of shattered theoretical frameworks.

Further, since entrepreneurs usually have little affinity for adventure of the intellectual sort, they can
(20) buy research and bury its products, hiding knowledge useful to society or to their competitors. The growth of industrial biotechnology, for example, has been accompanied by a reduction in the free sharing of research methods and results—a high price to pay for
(25) the undoubted benefits of new drugs and therapies.

Important new experimental results once led university scientists to rush down the hall and share their excitement with colleagues. When instead the rush is to patent lawyers and venture capitalists, I
(30) worry about the long-term future of scientific discovery.

Passage B

The fruits of pure science were once considered primarily a public good, available for society as a whole. The argument for this view was that most of
(35) these benefits were produced through government support of universities, and thus no individual was entitled to restrict access to them.

Today, however, the critical role of science in the modern "information economy" means that what was
(40) previously seen as a public good is being transformed into a market commodity. For example, by exploiting the information that basic research has accumulated about the detailed structures of cells and genes, the biotechnology industry can derive profitable
(45) pharmaceuticals or medical screening technologies. In this context, assertion of legal claims to "intellectual property"—not just in commercial products but in the underlying scientific knowledge—becomes crucial.

Previously, the distinction between a scientific
(50) "discovery" (which could not be patented) and a technical "invention" (which could) defined the limits of industry's ability to patent something. Today, however, the speed with which scientific discoveries can be turned into products and the large profits
(55) resulting from this transformation have led to a blurring of both the legal distinction between discovery and invention and the moral distinction between what should and should not be patented.

Industry argues that if it has supported—either in
(60) its own laboratories or in a university—the makers of a scientific discovery, then it is entitled to seek a return on its investment, either by charging others for using the discovery or by keeping it for its own exclusive use.

Main Point of Passage A

Main Point of Passage B

Similarities Between Passages

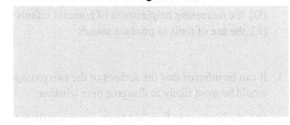

Dissimilarities Between Passages

7. Which one of the following is discussed in Passage B but not in Passage A?

(A) the blurring of the legal distinction between discovery and invention
(B) the general effects of the market on the exchange of scientific knowledge
(C) the role of scientific research in supplying public goods
(D) new pharmaceuticals that result from industrial research
(E) industry's practice of restricting access to research findings

8. Both passages place in opposition the members of which one of the following pairs?

(A) commercially successful research and commercially unsuccessful research
(B) research methods and research results
(C) a marketable commodity and a public good
(D) a discovery and an invention
(E) scientific research and other types of inquiry

9. Both passages refer to which one of the following?

(A) theoretical frameworks
(B) venture capitalists
(C) physics and chemistry
(D) industrial biotechnology
(E) shareholders

10. It can be inferred from the passages that the authors believe that the increased constraint on access to scientific information and ideas arises from

(A) the enormous increase in the volume of scientific knowledge that is being generated
(B) the desire of individual researchers to receive credit for their discoveries
(C) the striving of commercial enterprises to gain a competitive advantage in the market
(D) moral reservations about the social impact of some scientific research
(E) a drastic reduction in government funding for university research

11. Which one of the following statements is most strongly supported by both passages?

(A) Many scientific researchers who previously worked in universities have begun to work in the biotechnology industry.
(B) Private biotechnology companies have invalidly patented the basic research findings of university researchers.
(C) Because of the nature of current scientific research, patent authorities no longer consider the distinction between discoveries and inventions to be clear-cut.
(D) In the past, scientists working in industry had free access to the results of basic research conducted in universities.
(E) Government-funded research in universities has traditionally been motivated by the goals of private industry.

Passage A

Drilling fluids, including the various mixtures known as drilling muds, play essential roles in oil-well drilling. As they are circulated down through the drill pipe and back up the well itself, they lubricate the
(5) drill bit, bearings, and drill pipe; clean and cool the drill bit as it cuts into the rock; lift rock chips (cuttings) to the surface; provide information about what is happening downhole, allowing the drillers to monitor the behavior, flow rate, pressure, and
(10) composition of the drilling fluid; and maintain well pressure to control cave-ins.

Drilling muds are made of bentonite and other clays and polymers, mixed with a fluid to the desired viscosity. By far the largest ingredient of drilling
(15) muds, by weight, is barite, a very heavy mineral of density 4.3 to 4.6. It is also used as an inert filler in some foods and is more familiar in its medical use as the "barium meal" administered before X-raying the digestive tract.
(20) Over the years individual drilling companies and their expert drillers have devised proprietary formulations, or mud "recipes," to deal with specific types of drilling jobs. One problem in studying the effects of drilling waste discharges is that the drilling
(25) fluids are made from a range of over 1,000, sometimes toxic, ingredients—many of them known, confusingly, by different trade names, generic descriptions, chemical formulae, and regional or industry slang words, and many of them kept secret by companies or individual
(30) formulators.

Passage B

Drilling mud, cuttings, and associated chemicals are normally released only during the drilling phase of a well's existence. These discharges are the main environmental concern in offshore oil production, and
(35) their use is tightly regulated. The discharges are closely monitored by the offshore operator, and releases are controlled as a condition of the operating permit.

One type of mud—water-based mud (WBM)—is a mixture of water, bentonite clay, and chemical
(40) additives, and is used to drill shallow parts of wells. It is not particularly toxic to marine organisms and disperses readily. Under current regulations, it can be dumped directly overboard. Companies typically recycle WBMs until their properties are no longer
(45) suitable and then, over a period of hours, dump the entire batch into the sea.

For drilling deeper wells, oil-based mud (OBM) is normally used. The typical difference from WBM is the high content of mineral oil (typically 30 percent).
(50) OBMs also contain greater concentrations of barite, a powdered heavy mineral, and a number of additives. OBMs have a greater potential for negative environmental impact, partly because they do not disperse as readily. Barite may impact some
(55) organisms, particularly scallops, and the mineral oil may have toxic effects. Currently only the residues of OBMs adhering to cuttings that remain after the cuttings are sieved from the drilling fluids may be discharged overboard, and then only mixtures up to a
(60) specified maximum oil content.

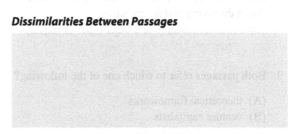

Main Point of Passage A

Main Point of Passage B

Similarities Between Passages

Dissimilarities Between Passages

12. A primary purpose of each of the passages is to

(A) provide causal explanations for a type of environmental pollution
(B) describe the general composition and properties of drilling muds
(C) point out possible environmental impacts associated with oil drilling
(D) explain why oil-well drilling requires the use of drilling muds
(E) identify difficulties inherent in the regulation of oil-well drilling operations

13. Which one of the following is a characteristic of barite that is mentioned in both of the passages?

(A) It does not disperse readily in seawater.
(B) It is not found in drilling muds containing bentonite.
(C) Its use in drilling muds is tightly regulated.
(D) It is the most commonly used ingredient in drilling muds.
(E) It is a heavy mineral.

14. Each of the following is supported by one or both of the passages EXCEPT:

(A) Clay is an important constituent of many, if not all, drilling muds.
(B) At least one type of drilling mud is not significantly toxic to marine life.
(C) There has been some study of the environmental effects of drilling-mud discharges.
(D) Government regulations allow drilling muds to contain 30 percent mineral oil.
(E) During the drilling of an oil well, drilling mud is continuously discharged into the sea.

15. Which one of the following can be most reasonably inferred from the two passages taken together, but not from either one individually?

(A) Barite is the largest ingredient of drilling muds, by weight, and also the most environmentally damaging.
(B) Although barite can be harmful to marine organisms, it can be consumed safely by humans.
(C) Offshore drilling is more damaging to the environment than is land-based drilling.
(D) The use of drilling muds needs to be more tightly controlled by government.
(E) If offshore drilling did not generate cuttings, it would be less harmful to the environment.

16. Each of the following is supported by one or both of the passages EXCEPT:

(A) Drillers monitor the suitability of the mud they are using.
(B) The government requires drilling companies to disclose all ingredients used in their drilling muds.
(C) In certain quantities, barite is not toxic to humans.
(D) Oil reserves can be found within or beneath layers of rock.
(E) Drilling deep oil wells requires the use of different mud recipes than does drilling shallow oil wells.

17. According to passage B, one reason OBMs are potentially more environmentally damaging than WBMs is that OBMs

(A) are slower to disperse
(B) contain greater concentrations of bentonite
(C) contain a greater number of additives
(D) are used for drilling deeper wells
(E) cannot be recycled

For Questions 1–6

The two passages discuss recent scientific research on music. They are adapted from two different papers presented at a scholarly conference.

Passage A

Did music and human language originate separately or together? Both systems use intonation and rhythm to communicate emotions. Both can be produced vocally or with tools, and people can produce
(5) both music and language silently to themselves.

Brain imaging studies suggest that music and language are part of one large, vastly complicated, neurological system for processing sound. In fact, fewer differences than similarities exist between the
(10) neurological processing of the two. One could think of the two activities as different radio programs that can be broadcast over the same hardware. One noteworthy difference, though, is that, generally speaking, people are better at language than music. In music, anyone
(15) can listen easily enough, but most people do not perform well, and in many cultures composition is left to specialists. In language, by contrast, nearly everyone actively performs and composes.

Given their shared neurological basis, it appears
(20) that music and language evolved together as brain size increased over the course of hominid evolution. But the primacy of language over music that we can observe today suggests that language, not music, was the primary function natural selection operated on.
(25) Music, it would seem, had little adaptive value of its own, and most likely developed on the coattails of language.

Passage B

A) Darwin claimed that since "neither the enjoyment nor the capacity of producing musical notes are
(30) faculties of the least [practical] use to man . . . they must be ranked amongst the most mysterious with which he is endowed." B) I suggest that the enjoyment of and the capacity to produce musical notes are faculties of indispensable use to mothers and their infants and
(35) that it is in the emotional bonds created by the interaction of mother and child that we can discover the evolutionary origins of human music.

Even excluding lullabies, which parents sing to infants, human mothers and infants under six months
(40) of age engage in ritualized, sequential behaviors, involving vocal, facial, and bodily interactions. Using face-to-face mother-infant interactions filmed at 24 frames per second, researchers have shown that mothers and infants jointly construct mutually
(45) improvised interactions in which each partner tracks the actions of the other. Such episodes last from one-half second to three seconds and are composed of musical elements—variations in pitch, rhythm, timbre, volume, and tempo.
(50) What evolutionary advantage would such behavior have? In the course of hominid evolution, brain size increased rapidly. Contemporaneously, the increase in bipedality caused the birth canal to narrow. This resulted in hominid infants being born ever-more
(55) prematurely, leaving them much more helpless at birth. This helplessness necessitated longer, better maternal care. Under such conditions, the emotional bonds created in the premusical mother-infant interactions we observe in Homo sapiens today—behavior whose
(60) neurological basis essentially constitutes the capacity to make and enjoy music—would have conferred considerable evolutionary advantage.

Main Point of Passage A

The main point is stated in all three sentences of the final paragraph. Music and language share a neurological basis and evolved together, but language was the driving evolutionary factor, with music having little adaptive value of its own.

Main Point of Passage B

The main point is stated in the last sentence of the final paragraph. The neurological basis for emotional bonding between mother and infant constitutes the capacity to create and enjoy music, making this an evolutionary advantage.

Similarities Between Passages

Both discuss the relationship between music and human evolution.
Both connect music to another human trait (language in Passage A, emotional bonding between mother and child in Passage B).
Both mention the use of music to express emotions.
Both mention the increase in human brain size that accompanied the development of music.
Both mention musical elements like intonation, rhythm, pitch, etc.

Dissimilarities Between Passages

Passage A examines the relationship between music and language, while Passage B examines the relationship between music and emotional bonding between mothers and infants.
Passage A concludes that music did not have evolutionary adaptive value for early humans while Passage B concludes that it did.

1. **Correct Answer (C).** *Prep Test 51.5, Section 4, Passage 2, Question 9.*

   Both passages were written primarily in order to answer which one of the following questions?

   This is a C Main Point question. The main point of Passage A is stated in all three sentences of the final paragraph. It is that music and language share a neurological basis and evolved together, but language was the driving evolutionary factor, with music having little adaptive value of its own. The main point of Passage B is stated in the last sentence of the final paragraph. It is that the neurological basis for emotional bonding between mother and infant constitutes the capacity to create and enjoy music, making this an evolutionary advantage. This is a variant C Main Point question that asks you to determine the question that each passage was written to answer. Looking at the main points, we can see that, although each author has a different conclusion and addresses other details, both address the evolutionary development of music. We should anticipate a correct answer choice that expresses this overlapping content in the main points.

   (A) What evolutionary advantage did larger brain size confer on early hominids?

   This answer choice addresses the wrong task. Brain size is presented in each passage as a supporting detail. This is a loser.

   (B) Why do human mothers and infants engage in bonding behavior that is composed of musical elements?

   This detail is mentioned in Passage B but not in Passage A. This is also a loser.

   (C) What are the evolutionary origins of the human ability to make music?

   This matches our anticipated answer choice. Both passages focus in part on how and why humans developed the ability to make music. This is a candidate.

   (D) Do the human abilities to make music and to use language depend on the same neurological systems?

   This detail is mentioned in Passage A but not in Passage B. This is also a loser.

   (E) Why are most people more adept at using language than they are at making music?

   This detail is mentioned in Passage A but not in Passage B. This is a loser as well.

   As (C) is the only candidate, it is the correct answer choice.

2. **Correct Answer (B).** *Prep Test 51.5, Section 4, Passage 2, Question 10.*

   Each of the two passages mentions the relation of music to

   This is a C Existence question. Scanning the answer choices quickly, we can see that answer choice (B) matches one of the similarities we identified—both passages mention the use of music to express emotions. This is almost certainly the correct answer choice. However, we will go through the answer choices one-by-one to be certain.

   (A) bonding between humans

   This detail is mentioned in Passage B but not in Passage A. This is a loser.

   (B) human emotion

This detail is mentioned in both passages. Passage A mentions that music can be used to express emotion in the first paragraph, and Passage B states that music is indispensable to the emotional bond between mothers and children in the first paragraph. This is a candidate.

(C) neurological research

This detail is mentioned in Passage A but not in Passage B. This is another loser.

(D) the increasing helplessness of hominid infants

This detail is mentioned in Passage B but not in Passage A. This is also a loser.

(E) the use of tools to produce sounds

This detail is mentioned in Passage A but not in Passage B. This is another loser.

As (B) is the only candidate, it is the correct answer choice.

---

3. **Correct Answer (D).** *Prep Test 51.5, Section 4, Passage 2, Question 11.*

> It can be inferred that the authors of the two passages would be most likely to disagree over whether

This is an A/D question. The prompt asks us to identify a point that both authors would disagree about. Looking back at our analysis, we can see that the most significant point of disagreement is whether or not music had evolutionary adaptive value. The author of Passage A believes it had little value, while the author of Passage B believes it had significant value. We should anticipate a correct answer choice that expresses this point of disagreement.

(A) the increase in hominid brain size necessitated earlier births

This answer choice includes irrelevant information. It is unclear whether the author of Passage A would agree or disagree with this statement. Although earlier births are discussed in Passage B, they are not addressed in Passage A at all. This is a loser.

(B) fewer differences than similarities exist between the neurological processing of music and human language

This answer choice includes irrelevant information. It is unclear whether the author of Passage B would agree or disagree with this statement. Human language is discussed in Passage A but not in Passage B. This is also a loser.

(C) brain size increased rapidly over the course of human evolution

This answer choice includes irrelevant information. It is unclear whether the author of Passage A would agree or disagree with this statement. Although both authors agree that brain size increased over the course of human evolution, Passage A makes no reference to how quickly it increased. This is a loser as well.

(D) the capacity to produce music has great adaptive value to humans

This matches our anticipated answer choice. The third paragraph of Passage A clearly states that music had little adaptive value, while the third paragraph of Passage B states that it had significant adaptive value. This is a candidate.

(E) mother-infant bonding involves temporally patterned vocal interactions

This answer choice includes irrelevant information. It is unclear whether the author of Passage A would agree or disagree with this statement. Mother-infant bonding is not discussed in Passage A. This is a loser.

As (D) is the only candidate, it is the correct answer choice.

4. **Correct Answer (C).** *Prep Test 51.5, Section 4, Passage 2, Question 12.*

The authors would be most likely to agree on the answer to which one of the following questions regarding musical capacity in humans?

This is an A/D question. The prompt asks us to locate a statement that both authors would agree with regarding musical capacity in humans. Looking back at our analysis, we can see that there are a number of points of agreement. Both authors believe that musical capacity is connected to the expression of human emotion, corresponds to increased brain size, and involves elements such as intonation, rhythm, and pitch. We should anticipate a correct answer choice that expresses one of these points of agreement.

(A) Does it manifest itself in some form in early infancy?

This answer choice includes irrelevant information. It is unclear whether the author of Passage A would agree with this statement. Passage A does not discuss human infancy. This is a loser.

(B) Does it affect the strength of mother-infant bonds?

This answer choice also includes irrelevant information. It is unclear whether the author of Passage A would agree with this statement. Mother-infant bonds are not mentioned in Passage A. This is a loser.

(C) Is it at least partly a result of evolutionary increases in brain size?

This matches one of our anticipated answers. Both authors would agree with this statement. The third paragraph of Passage A implies a connection between the increase in brain size and the evolution of music, and the third paragraph of Passage B states that the increase in brain size was one cause for mothers beginning to give birth prematurely, which caused musical ability to develop as a way of strengthening the necessary bond between mother and infant. This is a candidate.

(D) Did its evolution spur the development of new neurological systems?

This answer choice also includes irrelevant information. It is unclear whether the author of Passage B would agree with this statement. New neurological systems are not discussed in Passage B. This is a loser.

(E) Why does it vary so greatly among different individuals?

This answer choice also includes irrelevant information. It is unclear whether the author of Passage B would agree with this statement. Passage B does not discuss differences in musical capacity among individuals. This is a loser as well.

As (C) is the only candidate, it is the correct answer choice.

5. **Correct Answer (E).** *Prep Test 51.5, Section 4, Passage 2, Question 13.*

Which one of the following principles underlies the arguments in both passages?

This is a C Principle question. As the prompt does not reference a viewpoint or topic from a specific part of either passage, it would be very difficult and time-consuming to come up with a general principle that underlies the arguments of two passages. Therefore, we should proceed to eliminating answer choices. We should look for a general principle that is compatible with the circumstances and outcome of both authors' arguments.

(A) Investigations of the evolutionary origins of human behaviors must take into account the behavior of nonhuman animals.

This answer choice includes irrelevant information. Neither passage discusses non-human animals. This is a loser.

(B) All human capacities can be explained in terms of the evolutionary advantages they offer.

This answer choice makes too strong of a claim. Both passages make it clear that musical capacity can be explained in terms of evolutionary advantage, but neither passage argues that all human capacities can be explained in these terms. This is also a loser.

(C) The fact that a single neurological system underlies two different capacities is evidence that those capacities evolved concurrently.

This answer choice includes irrelevant information. Although Passage A discusses two different capacities (music and language), Passage B only discusses one capacity (music). This is a loser as well.

(D) The discovery of the neurological basis of a human behavior constitutes the discovery of the essence of that behavior.

This answer choice includes irrelevant information. Neither passage discusses the relationship between the neurological basis of a behavior and the essence of a behavior. This is a loser.

(E) The behavior of modern-day humans can provide legitimate evidence concerning the evolutionary origins of human abilities.

This seems like a principle that underlies the arguments in both passages. The third paragraph of Passage A states that the primacy of language today suggests that language rather than music was the primary function natural selection operated on. The first paragraph of Paragraph B states that it is in the interaction of mother and child that the evolutionary origins of music can be discovered. Both point to the behavior of modern humans (language use / mother-child interactions) as evidence of the evolutionary origin of a human ability (music). As this is the only candidate, it is the correct answer choice.

6. **Correct Answer (A).** *Prep Test 51.5, Section 4, Passage 2, Question 14.*

Which one of the following most accurately characterizes a relationship between the two passages?

This is an R question. Looking back at our initial analysis, we can see that both passages focus on the evolutionary origins of music. However, they make significantly different claims. Passage A argues that music had little adaptive value for humans. In contrast, Passage B maintains that music was an evolutionary advantage. Each passage presents different evidence to support its claim. The structural relationship between these two passages seems to be that Passage A and Passage B make different claims about the same subject matter based on different evidence. We should anticipate a correct answer choice that expresses this relationship.

(A) Passage A and Passage B use different evidence to draw divergent conclusions.

This matches our anticipated answer choice. Both passages draw divergent conclusions using different evidence. Passage A states that music had little adaptive value and uses neurological research to support this claim. Passage B argues that it was an evolutionary advantage and uses an analysis of mother-child interactions to support this claim.

This is a candidate.

(B) Passage A poses the question that Passage B attempts to answer.

This answer choice misrepresents the relationship. Passage A poses a question, but Passage B does not attempt to answer it. This is a loser.

(C) Passage A proposes a hypothesis that Passage B attempts to substantiate with new evidence.

This answer choice also misrepresents the relationship. Passage B disagrees with the conclusion of Passage A. This is another loser.

(D) Passage A expresses a stronger commitment to its hypothesis than does Passage B.

This answer choice includes irrelevant information. There is no indication that Passage A has a stronger commitment to its hypothesis than Passage B. This is a loser.

(E) Passage A and Passage B use different evidence to support the same conclusion.

This answer choice also misrepresents the relationship. Passage A and Passage B reach different conclusions. This is also a loser.

As (A) is the only candidate, it is the correct answer choice.

For Questions 7–11

The passages discuss relationships between business interests and university research.

Passage A

As university researchers working in a "gift economy" dedicated to collegial sharing of ideas, we have long been insulated from market pressures. The recent tendency to treat research findings as
(5) commodities, tradable for cash, threatens this tradition and the role of research as a public good.

The nurseries for new ideas are traditionally universities, which provide an environment uniquely suited to the painstaking testing and revision of
(10) theories. Unfortunately, the market process and values governing commodity exchange are ill suited to the cultivation and management of new ideas. With their shareholders impatient for quick returns, businesses are averse to wide-ranging experimentation. And, what
(15) is even more important, few commercial enterprises contain the range of expertise needed to handle the replacement of shattered theoretical frameworks.

Further, since entrepreneurs usually have little affinity for adventure of the intellectual sort, they can
(20) buy research and bury its products, hiding knowledge useful to society or to their competitors. The growth of industrial biotechnology, for example, has been accompanied by a reduction in the free sharing of research methods and results—a high price to pay for
(25) the undoubted benefits of new drugs and therapies.

Important new experimental results once led university scientists to rush down the hall and share their excitement with colleagues. When instead the rush is to patent lawyers and venture capitalists, I
(30) worry about the long-term future of scientific discovery.

Passage B

The fruits of pure science were once considered primarily a public good, available for society as a whole. The argument for this view was that most of
(35) these benefits were produced through government support of universities, and thus no individual was entitled to restrict access to them.

Today, however, the critical role of science in the modern "information economy" means that what was
(40) previously seen as a public good is being transformed into a market commodity. For example, by exploiting the information that basic research has accumulated about the detailed structures of cells and genes, the biotechnology industry can derive profitable
(45) pharmaceuticals or medical screening technologies. In this context, assertion of legal claims to "intellectual property"—not just in commercial products but in the underlying scientific knowledge—becomes crucial.

Previously, the distinction between a scientific
(50) "discovery" (which could not be patented) and a technical "invention" (which could) defined the limits of industry's ability to patent something. Today, however, the speed with which scientific discoveries can be turned into products and the large profits
(55) resulting from this transformation have led to a blurring of both the legal distinction between discovery and invention and the moral distinction

between what should and should not be patented.

Industry argues that if it has supported—either in
(60) its own laboratories or in a university—the makers of a scientific discovery, then it is entitled to seek a return on its investment, either by charging others for using the discovery or by keeping it for its own exclusive use.

Main Point of Passage A

The main point is stated in the last sentence of the first paragraph. It is that the tendency to treat research findings as commodities threatens the role of research as a public good.

Main Point of Passage B

The main point is stated in the first sentence of the second paragraph. It is that scientific research is being transformed from a public good into a market commodity.

Similarities Between Passages

Both passages discuss the transformation of research from a public good into a market commodity.
Both use biotechnology as an example.
Both passages discuss profit motives and the restriction of access to information.

Dissimilarities Between Passages

Passage A claims that the transformation will have a negative effect, while Passage B is neutral regarding its effect.
Passage B explores the difference between discovery and invention, but Passage A does not address this issue.

7. **Correct Answer (A).** *Prep Test 53, Section 4, Passage 3, Question 15.*

Which one of the following is discussed in passage B but not in passage A?

This is an unusual C Existence question in that the prompt asks for a detail that appears in Passage B but not in Passage A. Any answer choice that includes a detail that appears in Passage A, appears in both passages, or does not appear in either passage will be incorrect. Therefore, the correct answer choice will possibly be related to one of the dissimilarities we identified during the initial analysis. Scanning the answer choices quickly, we can see that answer choice (A) matches one of the dissimilarities—Passage B explores the difference between *discovery* and *invention*, but Passage A does not. This is almost certainly the correct answer choice. However, we will go through the answer choices one-by-one to be certain.

(A) the blurring of the legal distinction between discovery and invention

This detail appears in the third paragraph of Passage B but does not appear in Passage A. This is a candidate.

(B) the general effects of the market on the exchange of scientific knowledge

This detail appears in Passage A but does not appear in Passage B. This is a loser.

(C) the role of scientific research in supplying public goods

This detail appears in Passage A but does not appear in Passage B. This is also loser.

(D) new pharmaceuticals that result from industrial research

This detail is mentioned in both passages. This is a loser.

(E) industry's practice of restricting access to research findings

This detail is mentioned in both passages. This is a loser as well.

As (A) is the only candidate, it is the correct answer choice.

8. **Correct Answer (C).** *Prep Test 53, Section 4, Passage 3, Question 16.*

Both passages place in opposition the members of which one of the following pairs?

This is a C Detail question. The prompt asks for a pair that is placed in opposition in both passages. Looking at the similarities we noted, we can see that both passages present the public good as being opposed to tradable or marketable commodities. We should anticipate a correct answer choice that expresses this.

(A) commercially successful research and commercially unsuccessful research

This answer choice includes irrelevant information. Neither passage refers to commercially unsuccessful research. This is a loser.

(B) research methods and research results

This answer choice includes contradictory and irrelevant information. Passage A does not place research methods and results in opposition. Instead, it claims that the sharing of both has been reduced. Passage B does not discuss research methods. This is also a loser.

(C) a marketable commodity and a public good

This seems like a pair that is placed in opposition in both passages. The first paragraph of Passage A states that research as a public good is being threatened by the recent tendency to treat it as commodity tradable for cash. The second paragraph of Passage B states that research is being transformed from a public good into a market commodity. This is a candidate.

(D) a discovery and an invention

This answer choice includes irrelevant information. Passage A does not discuss these concepts. This is a loser.

(E) scientific research and other types of inquiry

This answer choice also includes irrelevant information. Neither passage mentions other types of inquiry. This is also a loser.

As (C) is the only candidate, it is the correct answer choice.

9. Correct Answer (D). *Prep Test 53, Section 4, Passage 3, Question 17.*

Both passages refer to which one of the following?

This is a C Existence question. Scanning the answer choices quickly, we can see that answer choice (D) matches one of the similarities we identified—both passages use biotechnology as an example. This is almost certainly the correct answer choice. However, we will go through the answer choices one-by-one to be certain.

(A) theoretical frameworks

This detail is mentioned in Passage A but not in Passage B. This is a loser.

(B) venture capitalists

This detail is also mentioned in Passage A but not in Passage B. This is a loser.

(C) physics and chemistry

This detail is not mentioned in either passage. This is another loser.

(D) industrial biotechnology

This detail is mentioned in both passages. Passage A mentions biotechnology in the third paragraph. Passage B mentions it in the second paragraph. This is a candidate.

(E) shareholders

This detail is also mentioned in Passage A but not in Passage B. This is a loser.

As (D) is the only candidate, it is the correct answer choice.

10. Correct Answer (C). *Prep Test 53, Section 4, Passage 3, Question 18.*

It can be inferred from the passages that the authors believe that the increased constraint on access to scientific information and ideas arises from

This is a C Viewpoint question. Looking back at our analysis, we can see that both passages mention profit motives and the restriction of access to information. The second paragraph of Passage A states that market processes and values governing commodity exchanges are ill-suited to the cultivation and management of new ideas. The third paragraph states that entrepreneurs hide knowledge from competitors. The last paragraph of Passage B states that industry argues that if it has supported the makers of scientific discovery, then it is entitled to charge others to use the discovery or to keep it for its own use. We can infer from this that both authors believe that market forces constrain access to scientific information and new ideas. We should anticipate a correct answer choice that expresses this or another compatible inference.

(A) the enormous increase in the volume of scientific knowledge that is being generated

This answer choice includes irrelevant information. Neither passage mentions an enormous increase in the volume of scientific knowledge. This is a loser.

(B) the desire of individual researchers to receive credit for their discoveries

This answer choice includes irrelevant information. Passage B does not discuss the desire of individual researchers for credit. This is also a loser.

(C) the striving of commercial enterprises to gain a competitive advantage in the market

This matches our anticipated answer choice. Commercial enterprises (market forces) are limiting access for their own advantage. This is a candidate.

(D) moral reservations about the social impact of some scientific research

This answer choice includes irrelevant information. Neither passage discusses moral reservations about the social impact of research. This is a loser.

(E) a drastic reduction in government funding for university research

This answer choice includes irrelevant information. Neither passage mentions a drastic reduction in government funding. This is also a loser.

As (C) is the only candidate, it is the correct answer choice.

---

11. **Correct Answer (D).** *Prep Test 53, Section 4, Passage 3, Question 19.*

Which one of the following statements is most strongly supported by both passages?

This is a C Implication question. Scanning the answer choices quickly, none of them seem to be clearly related to the similarities we identified. In addition, the prompt does not reference a specific topic. Therefore, we should proceed to eliminating answer choices.

(A) Many scientific researchers who previously worked in universities have begun to work in the biotechnology industry.

This answer choice includes irrelevant information. Neither passage suggests that university researchers have begun to work for the biotechnology industry. This is a loser.

(B) Private biotechnology companies have invalidly patented the basic research findings of university researchers.

Chapter 7

This answer choice includes irrelevant information as well. Neither passage suggests that private companies are invalidly patenting the findings of university researchers. This is also a loser.

(C) **Because of the nature of current scientific research, patent authorities no longer consider the distinction between discoveries and inventions to be clear-cut.**

This answer choice also includes irrelevant information. Passage A does not discuss the distinction between discoveries and inventions. This is another loser.

(D) **In the past, scientists working in industry had free access to the results of basic research conducted in universities.**

This seems to be an inference that is compatible with the viewpoint of both authors. The first paragraph of Passage A mentions the reduction in the free sharing of research methods and results. The first paragraph of Passage B states that the fruits of science were once available to society as a whole. The second paragraph mentions that the biotechnology industry was able to exploit the information that basic research accumulated. Therefore, both passages suggest that scientists working in industry had free access to basic university research in the past. This is a candidate.

(E) **Government-funded research in universities has traditionally been motivated by the goals of private industry.**

This answer choice includes contradictory information. Both passages claim that university research has traditionally been for the public good. This is a loser.

As (D) is the only candidate, it is the correct answer choice.

For Questions 12–17

Passage A

Drilling fluids, including the various mixtures known as drilling muds, play essential roles in oil-well drilling. As they are circulated down through the drill pipe and back up the well itself, they lubricate the

(5) drill bit, bearings, and drill pipe; clean and cool the drill bit as it cuts into the rock; lift rock chips (cuttings) to the surface; provide information about what is happening downhole, allowing the drillers to monitor the behavior, flow rate, pressure, and

(10) composition of the drilling fluid; and maintain well pressure to control cave-ins.

Drilling muds are made of bentonite and other clays and polymers, mixed with a fluid to the desired viscosity. By far the largest ingredient of drilling

(15) muds, by weight, is barite, a very heavy mineral of density 4.3 to 4.6. It is also used as an inert filler in some foods and is more familiar in its medical use as the "barium meal" administered before X-raying the digestive tract.

(20) Over the years individual drilling companies and their expert drillers have devised proprietary formulations, or mud "recipes," to deal with specific types of drilling jobs. One problem in studying the effects of drilling waste discharges is that the drilling

(25) fluids are made from a range of over 1,000, sometimes toxic, ingredients—many of them known, confusingly, by different trade names, generic descriptions, chemical formulae, and regional or industry slang words, and many of them kept secret by companies or individual

(30) formulators.

Passage B

Drilling mud, cuttings, and associated chemicals are normally released only during the drilling phase of a well's existence. These discharges are the main environmental concern in offshore oil production, and

(35) their use is tightly regulated. The discharges are closely monitored by the offshore operator, and releases are controlled as a condition of the operating permit.

One type of mud—water-based mud (WBM)—is a mixture of water, bentonite clay, and chemical

(40) additives, and is used to drill shallow parts of wells. It is not particularly toxic to marine organisms and disperses readily. Under current regulations, it can be dumped directly overboard. Companies typically recycle WBMs until their properties are no longer

(45) suitable and then, over a period of hours, dump the entire batch into the sea.

For drilling deeper wells, oil-based mud (OBM) is normally used. The typical difference from WBM is the high content of mineral oil (typically 30 percent).

(50) OBMs also contain greater concentrations of barite, a powdered heavy mineral, and a number of additives. OBMs have a greater potential for negative environmental impact, partly because they do not disperse as readily. Barite may impact some

(55) organisms, particularly scallops, and the mineral oil may have toxic effects. Currently only the residues of OBMs adhering to cuttings that remain after the cuttings are sieved from the drilling fluids may be discharged overboard, and then only mixtures up to a

(60) specified maximum oil content.

Main Point of Passage A

The main point is stated in the first sentence of the first paragraph. It is that drilling fluids play essential roles in oil-well drilling.

Main Point of Passage B

The main point is stated in the second sentence of the first paragraph. It is that drilling mud discharges are the main environmental concern in offshore oil production and their use is tightly regulated.

Similarities Between Passages

Both passages describe what drilling fluids (muds) are composed of.
Both passages state that drilling fluids are used in oil drilling.

Dissimilarities Between Passages

Passage A describes how drilling fluids are used in oil drilling and discusses the problem with studying them, while Passage B gives examples of drilling fluids and discusses their specific environmental impact.

12. **Correct Answer (B).** *Prep Test 54, Section 1, Passage 2, Question 6.*

A primary purpose of each of the passages is to

This is a C Purpose question. The main point of Passage A is that drilling fluids play essential roles in oil-well drilling. The main point of Passage B is that drilling mud discharges are the main environmental concern in offshore oil production and their use is tightly regulated. There does not seem to be any overlap between these main points other than the general subject matter of drilling fluids. Therefore, we should look at the similarities we identified to see if there are any major points that could function as the purpose. One thing that stands out is that both passages describe in detail what drilling fluids are composed of. Although this is not the main point of either passage, it may serve as a joint purpose of both passages. If so, we should probably expect an action verb related to presenting information (as this is not the conclusion of either passage).

(A) provide causal explanations for a type of environmental pollution

This answer choice includes irrelevant information. Passage A does not provide causal explanations for a type of environmental pollution. This is a loser.

(B) describe the general composition and properties of drilling muds

This matches our anticipated answer choice. The general composition and properties are discussed throughout both passages. This is a candidate.

(C) point out possible environmental impacts associated with oil drilling

This answer choice includes irrelevant information. Passage A does not discuss the environmental impact of drilling muds. This is a loser.

(D) explain why oil-well drilling requires the use of drilling muds

This answer choice also includes irrelevant information. Passage B does not explain the use of drilling muds. This is a loser.

(E) identify difficulties inherent in the regulation of oil-well drilling operations

This answer choice includes irrelevant information. Neither passage identifies these types of difficulties. This is a loser as well.

As (B) is the only candidate, it is the correct answer choice.

13. **Correct Answer (E).** *Prep Test 54, Section 1, Passage 2, Question 7.*

Which one of the following is a characteristic of barite that is mentioned in both of the passages?

This is a C Detail question. Barite is discussed in the second paragraph of Passage A and the third paragraph of Passage B. The only characteristic of barite mentioned by both passages is that it is a heavy mineral. We should anticipate a correct answer choice that states this detail.

(A) It does not disperse readily in seawater.

This answer choice includes information from the wrong part of the passage. Passage A identifies this as a characteristic of OBMs. This is a loser.

(B) It is not found in drilling muds containing bentonite.

This answer choice includes irrelevant information. Passage B does not mention bentonite. This is a loser.

(C) Its use in drilling muds is tightly regulated.

This answer choice includes information from the wrong part of the passage. Passage B identifies this as a characteristic of drilling mud discharges. This is also a loser.

(D) It is the most commonly used ingredient in drilling muds.

This answer choice includes irrelevant information. Neither passage states that barite is the most commonly used ingredient in drilling muds. This is a loser.

(E) It is a heavy mineral.

This matches our anticipated answer choice. This is the correct answer choice.

14. **Correct Answer (E).** *Prep Test 54, Section 1, Passage 2, Question 8.*

Each of the following is supported by one or both of the passages EXCEPT:

This is a C Implication EXCEPT question. The prompt asks us to identify a statement that cannot be inferred from either of the passages. This means that if an answer choice is supported by one or both of the passages, it is incorrect. As the prompt does not include a specific topic, we should proceed to eliminating answer choices.

(A) Clay is an important constituent of many, if not all, drilling muds.

The second paragraph of Passage A states that drilling muds are made of bentonite and other clays. This is a loser.

(B) At least one type of drilling mud is not significantly toxic to marine life.

The second paragraph of Passage B states that WBMs are not particularly toxic to marine organisms. This is another loser.

(C) There has been some study of the environmental effects of drilling-mud discharges.

The third paragraph of Passage A mentions a problem with studying the effects of drilling waste discharges. In addition, the first paragraph mentions the regulation of discharge of drilling muds due to environmental concerns, which implies that the environmental effects have been studied. This is a loser.

(D) Government regulations allow drilling muds to contain 30 percent mineral oil.

Passage B states that drilling muds are regulated. It also specifies that they contain 30 percent mineral oil. This implies the regulations allow them to contain 30 percent mineral oil. This is also a loser.

(E) During the drilling of an oil well, drilling mud is continuously discharged into the sea.

This answer choice includes irrelevant and contradictory information. Passage A does not discuss this topic. The second paragraph of Passage B states that drilling muds are recycled until they are not usable and then discharged into the sea all at once, contradicting this statement. This is the correct answer choice.

15. **Correct Answer (B).** *Prep Test 54, Section 1, Passage 2, Question 9.*

> **Which one of the following can be most reasonably inferred from the two passages taken together, but not from either one individually?**

This is a C Implication question. The prompt asks us to identify a statement that can be inferred from both passages together but not from one individually. This means that if an answer choice is supported by only one passage or is not supported by either passage, it is incorrect. As the prompt docs not include a specific topic, we should proceed to eliminating answer choices.

> **(A) Barite is the largest ingredient of drilling muds, by weight, and also the most environmentally damaging.**

This answer choice includes irrelevant information. Neither passage states that barite is the most environmentally damaging ingredient. This is a loser.

> **(B) Although barite can be harmful to marine organisms, it can be consumed safely by humans.**

This statement seems to be supported by both passages. The second paragraph of Passage A states that barite can be used as an inert filler in some foods but makes no reference to it being harmful to marine organisms. The third paragraph of Passage B states that barite can be harmful to marine organisms but makes no reference to it being consumed safely by humans. Therefore, this statement can be inferred from both passages but not from either passage individually. This is a candidate.

> **(C) Offshore drilling is more damaging to the environment than is land-based drilling.**

This answer choice includes irrelevant information. Neither passage talks about land-based drilling. This is a loser.

> **(D) The use of drilling muds needs to be more tightly controlled by government.**

This answer choice includes irrelevant information. Neither passage claims that the government needs to control the use of drilling muds more tightly. This is another loser.

> **(E) If offshore drilling did not generate cuttings, it would be less harmful to the environment.**

This answer choice includes irrelevant information. Neither passage makes a connection between cuttings and harm to the environment. This is also a loser.

As (B) is the only candidate, it is the correct answer choice.

16. **Correct Answer (B).** *Prep Test 54, Section 1, Passage 2, Question 10.*

> **Each of the following is supported by one or both of the passages EXCEPT:**

This is a C Implication EXCEPT question. The prompt asks us to identify a statement that cannot be inferred from either of the passages. This means that if an answer choice is supported by one or both of the passages, it is incorrect. As the prompt does not include a specific topic, we should proceed to eliminating answer choices.

> **(A) Drillers monitor the suitability of the mud they are using.**

The first paragraph of Passage A states that drillers monitor the behavior, flow rate, pressure, and composition of the drilling fluid they use. This is a loser.

(B) The government requires drilling companies to disclose all ingredients used in their drilling muds.

This answer choice includes irrelevant and contradictory information. This statement does not seem to be supported by either passage. The third paragraph of Passage A states that many companies keep the ingredients of their drilling muds secret. Passage B does not discuss this disclosure of ingredients at all. This is a candidate.

(C) In certain quantities, barite is not toxic to humans.

The second paragraph of Passage A states that barite is not toxic to humans. This is a loser.

(D) Oil reserves can be found within or beneath layers of rock.

The first paragraph of Passage A mentions that rock is drilled into in order to extract oil. This is also a loser.

(E) Drilling deep oil wells requires the use of different mud recipes than does drilling shallow oil wells.

The second and third paragraphs of Passage B discuss different types of drilling mud used for shallow and deep oil wells. This is a loser.

As (B) is the only candidate, it is the correct answer choice.

---

17. **Correct Answer (A).** *Prep Test 54, Section 1, Passage 2, Question 12.*

According to passage B, one reason OBMs are potentially more environmentally damaging than WBMs is that OBMs

This is a C Detail question. The prompt asks us to find a detail in Passage B only. Therefore, we should approach it like a standard D question. The topic of the prompt is a reason that OBMs are potentially more environmentally damaging than WBMs. Looking back at Passage B, we can see that the third paragraph states that a reason that OBMs have more potential for environmental damage is that they do not disperse as readily. We should anticipate a correct answer choice that restates this detail.

(A) are slower to disperse

This matches our anticipated answer. OBMs are more harmful because they do not disperse as readily. This is a candidate.

(B) contain greater concentrations of bentonite

This answer choice includes irrelevant information. Passage B does not connect bentonite to environmental damage. Additionally, Passage B does not claim that OBMs contain a greater concentration of bentonite. This is a loser.

(C) contain a greater number of additives

This answer choice includes irrelevant information. Passage B does not connect the number of additives to environmental damage. This is also a loser.

(D) are used for drilling deeper wells

This answer choice also includes irrelevant information. Passage B does not connect deeper wells with greater environmental damage. This is another loser.

(E) cannot be recycled

This answer choice includes irrelevant information as well. Passage B does not state that OBMs cannot be recycled, nor does it connect recycling to environmental damage. This is another loser.

As (A) is the only candidate, it is the correct answer choice.

Key Takeaways

19.5% of RC Questions

Example Prompts

R: Which one of the following most accurately describes the relationship between passage A and passage B?

R: Which one of the following most accurately describes a way in which the two passages are related to one another?

R: The relationship between the two passages can best be described as

A/D: It is most likely that the authors of the passages would disagree with each other about the truth of which one of the following statements?

A/D: Which one of the following is a statement central to the argument made by the author of passage A that would most likely be rejected by the author of passage B?

A/D: The authors of the two passages would most likely agree with which one of the following statements?

C: Which one of the following most accurately describes the stance expressed by the author of passage A toward _____?

C: Which one of the following is addressed by the author of passage A but not by the author of passage B?

C: Which one of the following conforms to _____ advocated by the authors of both passages?

Correct Answer Choices

R: Statements that accurately describe the structural relationship between the two passages

A/D: Statements that both authors would agree with (point of agreement)

A/D: Statements that one author would agree with and one would disagree with (point of disagreement)

C: Statements that match the criteria to be a correct answer choice for the corresponding standard question type

---

Relationship (R) – 0.9% of RC Questions
Agree/Disagree (A/D) – 2.3% of RC Questions
Comparative (C) – 16.3% of RC Questions

Identify the relationships between the dual passages that comprise a Comparative Reading Passage.

Question Tasks

R: Find the statement that accurately describes the relationship between the two passages

A/D: Identify a statement that both authors would agree with or that one author would agree with and one passage author would disagree with

C: Perform the task for the corresponding question type (C questions are variants of the question types for standard passages)

Incorrect Answer Choices

Statements that misrepresent the relationship between the two passages (R)

Statements that reverse elements of the relationship between the two passages (R)

Statements for which either author's position is unclear (A/D)

Statements that one author would disagree with (point of agreement) (A/D)

Statements that both authors would agree or disagree with (point of disagreement) (A/D)

Statements that include information from the wrong passage or both passages (prompt references one passage) (C)

Statements that include information from only one passage (prompt references both passages) (C)

Statement that meet the criteria to be an incorrect answer choice for the corresponding standard question type (C)

Too Strong: Claims that are too strong to be supported (R, A/D)

Contradictory Information: Statements that contradict information in the passage (R, A/D)

Irrelevant Information: Statements that present new information that is not relevant to the task specified in the prompt (R, A/D)

HACKERS
LSAT *Reading Comprehension*

Chapter 8

Putting It All Together

Chapter 8: Putting It All Together

HACKERS
LSAT *Reading Comprehension*

Putting It All Together

Practice Sets

The previous chapters include passages with varying levels of difficulty—from easy and straightforward to difficult and complex. Now that you are familiar with the passage and question types, you will have the opportunity to put your newly acquired knowledge to use. This chapter includes six very challenging passages and question sets from previous administrations of the LSAT. Go through them carefully, applying the strategies learned earlier in this book.

Practice Sets

Putting It All Together

Analyze the passages below. Mark the <u>keywords</u>, <u>main points</u>, and viewpoints other than the author's. If it is a single passage, note the function of each paragraph, and summarize the main points, paragraph content, and viewpoints. If it is a Comparative Reading passage, summarize the main points and take note of the similarities and dissimilarities between the two passages. Then answer the questions that follow each passage.

Every culture that has adopted the cultivation of maize—also known as corn—has been radically changed by it. This crop reshaped the cultures of the Native Americans who first cultivated it, leading to
(5) such developments as the adoption of agrarian and in some cases urban lifestyles, and much of the explosion of European populations after the fifteenth century was driven by the introduction of maize together with another crop from the Americas,
(10) potatoes. The primary reason for this plant's profound influence is its sheer productivity. With maize, ancient agriculturalists could produce far more food per acre than with any other crop, and early Central Americans recognized and valued this characteristic
(15) of the plant. But why are maize and a few similar crops so much more bountiful than others? Modern biochemistry has revealed the physical mechanism underlying maize's impressive productivity.

To obtain the hydrogen they use in the production
(20) of carbohydrates through photosynthesis, all plants split water into its constituent elements, hydrogen and oxygen. They use the resultant hydrogen to form one of the molecules they need for energy, but the oxygen is released into the atmosphere. During
(25) photosynthesis, carbon dioxide that the plant takes in from the atmosphere is used to build sugars within the plant. An enzyme, rubisco, assists in the sugar-forming chemical reaction. Because of its importance in photosynthesis, rubisco is arguably the most
(30) significant enzyme in the world. Unfortunately, though, when the concentration of oxygen relative to carbon dioxide in a leaf rises to a certain level, as can happen in the presence of many common atmospheric conditions, oxygen begins to bind competitively to the enzyme,
(35) thus interfering with the photosynthetic reaction.

Some plants, however, have evolved a photosynthetic mechanism that prevents oxygen from impairing photosynthesis. These plants separate the places where they split water atoms into hydrogen
(40) and oxygen from the places where they build sugars from carbon dioxide. Water molecules are split, as in all plants, in specialized chlorophyll-containing structures in the green leaf cells, but the rubisco is sequestered within airtight tissues in the center of the
(45) leaf. The key to the process is that in these plants, oxygen and all other atmospheric gases are excluded from the cells containing rubisco. These cells, called the bundle sheath cells, surround the vascular structures of the leaf—structures that function
(50) analogously to human blood vessels. Carbon dioxide, which cannot enter these cells as a gas, first undergoes a series of reactions to form an

intermediary, nongas molecule named C-4 for the four carbon atoms it contains. This molecule enters
(55) the bundle sheath cells and there undergoes reactions that release the carbon dioxide that will fuel the production of carbohydrates (e.g., sugars).Taking its name from the intermediary molecule, the entire process is called C-4 photosynthesis. Such C-4 plants
(60) as sugar cane, rice, and maize are among the world's most productive crops.

Main Point

Paragraph 1

Paragraph 2

Paragraph 3

Identify Viewpoints

1. Which one of the following most accurately states the main point of the passage?

   (A) The greater productivity of maize, as compared with many other crops, is due to its C-4 photosynthetic process, in which the reactions that build sugars are protected from the effects of excess oxygen.

   (B) Because of their ability to produce greater quantities and higher qualities of nutrients, those plants, including maize, that use a C-4 photosynthetic process have helped to shape the development of many human cultures.

   (C) C-4 photosynthesis, which occurs in maize, involves a complex sequence of chemical reactions that makes more efficient use of available atmospheric hydrogen than do photosynthetic reactions in non-C-4 plants.

   (D) The presence of the enzyme rubisco is a key factor in the ability of C-4 plants, including maize, to circumvent the negative effects of gases such as oxygen on the production of sugars in photosynthesis.

   (E) Some of the world's most productive crop plants, including maize, have evolved complex, effective mechanisms to prevent atmospheric gases that could bind competitively to rubisco from entering the plants' leaves.

2. Which one of the following most accurately describes the organization of the material presented in the second and third paragraphs of the passage?

   (A) The author suggests that the widespread cultivation of a particular crop is due to its high yield, explains its high yield by describing the action of a particular enzyme in that crop, and then outlines the reasons for the evolution of that enzyme.

   (B) The author explains some aspects of a biochemical process, describes a naturally occurring hindrance to that process, and then describes an evolutionary solution to that hindrance in order to explain the productivity of a particular crop.

   (C) The author describes a problem inherent in certain biochemical processes, scientifically explains two ways in which organisms solve that problem, and then explains the evolutionary basis for one of those solutions.

   (D) The author describes a widespread cultural phenomenon involving certain uses of a type of plant, explains the biochemical basis of the phenomenon, and then points out that certain other plants may be used for similar purposes.

   (E) The author introduces a natural process, describes the biochemical reaction that is widely held to be the mechanism underlying the process, and then argues for an alternate evolutionary explanation of that process.

3. Assuming that all other relevant factors remained the same, which one of the following, if it developed in a species of plant that does not have C-4 photosynthesis, would most likely give that species an advantage similar to that which the author attributes to C-4 plants?

   (A) Water is split into its constituent elements in specialized chlorophyll-containing structures in the bundle sheath cells.

   (B) An enzyme with which oxygen cannot bind performs the role of rubisco.

   (C) The vascular structures of the leaf become impermeable to both carbon dioxide gas and oxygen gas.

   (D) The specialized chlorophyll-containing structures in which water is split surround the vascular structures of the leaf.

   (E) An enzyme that does not readily react with carbon dioxide performs the role of rubisco in the green leaf cells.

4. The author's reference to "all other atmospheric gases" in line 46 plays which one of the following roles in the passage?

(A) It indicates why certain atmospheric conditions can cause excess oxygen to build up and thus hinder photosynthesis in non-C-4 plants as described in the previous paragraph.

(B) It supports the claim advanced earlier in the paragraph that oxygen is not the only atmospheric gas whose presence in the leaf can interfere with photosynthesis.

(C) It supports the conclusion that non-C-4 photosynthesis makes use of several atmospheric gases that C-4 photosynthesis does not use.

(D) It explains why carbon dioxide molecules undergo the transformations described later in the paragraph before participating in photosynthesis in C-4 plants.

(E) It advances a broader claim that oxygen levels remain constant in C-4 plants in spite of changes in atmospheric conditions.

5. The passage contains information sufficient to justify inferring which one of the following?

(A) In rice plants, atmospheric gases are prevented from entering the structures in which water is split into its constituent elements.

(B) In rice plants, oxygen produced from split water molecules binds to another type of molecule before being released into the atmosphere.

(C) Rice is an extremely productive crop that nourishes large segments of the world's population and is cultivated by various widely separated cultures.

(D) In rice plants, rubisco is isolated in the bundle sheath cells that surround the vascular structures of the leaves.

(E) Although rice is similar to maize in productivity and nutritive value, maize is the more widely cultivated crop.

6. The author of the passage would be most likely to agree with which one of the following statements?

(A) Maize's impressive productivity cannot be understood without an understanding of its cultural influences.

(B) Maize is an example of a plant in which oxygen is not released as a by-product of photosynthesis.

(C) Maize's high yields are due not only to its use of C-4 but also to its ability to produce large quantities of rubisco.

(D) Until maize was introduced to Europeans by Native Americans, European populations lacked the agricultural techniques required for the cultivation of C-4 plants.

(E) Maize's C-4 photosynthesis is an example of an effective evolutionary adaptation that has come to benefit humans.

7. The passage provides the most support for which one of the following statements?

(A) In many plants, rubisco is not isolated in airtight tissues in the center of the leaf.

(B) A rubisco molecule contains four carbon atoms.

(C) Rubisco is needed in photosynthesis to convert carbon dioxide to a nongas molecule.

(D) In maize, rubisco helps protect against the detrimental effects of oxygen buildup in the leaves.

(E) Rubisco's role in the C-4 process is optimized when oxygen levels are high relative to carbon dioxide levels.

Aida Overton Walker (1880–1914), one of the most widely acclaimed African American performers of the early twentieth century, was known largely for popularizing a dance form known as the cakewalk

(5) through her choreographing, performance, and teaching of the dance. The cakewalk was originally developed prior to the United States Civil War by African Americans, for whom dance was a means of maintaining cultural links within a slave society. It

(10) was based on traditional West African ceremonial dances, and like many other African American dances, it retained features characteristic of African dance forms, such as gliding steps and an emphasis on improvisation.

(15) To this African-derived foundation, the cakewalk added certain elements from European dances: where African dances feature flexible body postures, large groups and separate-sex dancing, the cakewalk developed into a high-kicking walk performed by a

(20) procession of couples. Ironically, while these modifications later enabled the cakewalk to appeal to European Americans and become one of the first cultural forms to cross the racial divide in North America, they were originally introduced with satiric

(25) intent. Slaves performed the grandiloquent walks in order to parody the processional dances performed at slave owners' balls and, in general, the self-important manners of slave owners. To add a further irony, by the end of the nineteenth century, the cakewalk was

(30) itself being parodied by European American stage performers, and these parodies in turn helped shape subsequent versions of the cakewalk.

While this complex evolution meant that the cakewalk was not a simple cultural phenomenon—

(35) one scholar has characterized this layering of parody upon parody with the phrase "mimetic vertigo"—it is in fact what enabled the dance to attract its wide audience. In the cultural and socioeconomic flux of the turn-of-the-century United States, where

(40) industrialization, urbanization, mass immigration, and rapid social mobility all reshaped the cultural landscape, an art form had to be capable of being many things to many people in order to appeal to a large audience.

(45) Walker's remarkable success at popularizing the cakewalk across otherwise relatively rigid racial boundaries rested on her ability to address within her interpretation of it the varying and sometimes conflicting demands placed on the dance. Middle-

(50) class African Americans, for example, often denounced the cakewalk as disreputable, a complaint reinforced by the parodies circulating at the time. Walker won over this audience by refining the cakewalk and emphasizing its fundamental grace.

(55) Meanwhile, because middle- and upper-class European Americans often felt threatened by the tremendous cultural flux around them, they prized what they regarded as authentic art forms as bastions of stability; much of Walker's success with this

(60) audience derived from her distillation of what was widely acclaimed as the most authentic cakewalk. Finally, Walker was able to gain the admiration of many newly rich industrialists and financiers, who found in the grand flourishes of her version of the

(65) cakewalk a fitting vehicle for celebrating their newfound social rank.

Main Point

Paragraph 1

Paragraph 2

Paragraph 3

Paragraph 4

Identify Viewpoints

8. Which one of the following most accurately expresses the main point of the passage?

(A) Walker, who was especially well known for her success in choreographing, performing, and teaching the cakewalk, was one of the most widely recognized African American performers of the early twentieth century.

(B) In spite of the disparate influences that shaped the cakewalk, Walker was able to give the dance broad appeal because she distilled what was regarded as the most authentic version in an era that valued authenticity highly.

(C) Walker popularized the cakewalk by capitalizing on the complex cultural mix that had developed from the dance's original blend of satire and cultural preservation, together with the effects of later parodies.

(D) Whereas other versions of the cakewalk circulating at the beginning of the twentieth century were primarily parodic in nature, the version popularized by Walker combined both satire and cultural preservation.

(E) Because Walker was able to recognize and preserve the characteristics of the cakewalk as African Americans originally performed it, it became the first popular art form to cross the racial divide in the United States.

9. The author describes the socioeconomic flux of the turn-of-the-century United States in the third paragraph primarily in order to

(A) argue that the cakewalk could have become popular only in such complex social circumstances

(B) detail the social context that prompted performers of the cakewalk to fuse African and European dance forms

(C) identify the target of the overlapping parodic layers that characterized the cakewalk

(D) indicate why a particular cultural environment was especially favorable for the success of the cakewalk

(E) explain why European American parodies of the cakewalk were able to reach wide audiences

10. Which one of the following is most analogous to the author's account in the second paragraph of how the cakewalk came to appeal to European Americans?

(A) Satirical versions of popular music songs are frequently more popular than the songs they parody.

(B) A style of popular music grows in popularity among young listeners because it parodies the musical styles admired by older listeners.

(C) A style of music becomes admired among popular music's audience in part because of elements that were introduced in order to parody popular music.

(D) A once popular style of music wins back its audience by incorporating elements of the style of music that is currently most popular.

(E) After popular music begins to appropriate elements of a traditional style of music, interest in that traditional music increases.

11. The passage asserts which one of the following about the cakewalk?

(A) It was largely unknown outside African American culture until Walker popularized it.

(B) It was mainly a folk dance, and Walker became one of only a handful of people to perform it professionally.

(C) Its performance as parody became uncommon as a result of Walker's popularization of its authentic form.

(D) Its West African origins became commonly known as a result of Walker's work.

(E) It was one of the first cultural forms to cross racial lines in the United States.

12. It can be inferred from the passage that the author would be most likely to agree with which one of the following statements?

   (A) Because of the broad appeal of humor, satiric art forms are often among the first to cross racial or cultural divisions.
   (B) The interactions between African American and European American cultural forms often result in what is appropriately characterized as "mimetic vertigo."
   (C) Middle-class European Americans who valued the cakewalk's authenticity subsequently came to admire other African American dances for the same reason.
   (D) Because of the influence of African dance forms, some popular dances that later emerged in the United States featured separate-sex dancing.
   (E) Some of Walker's admirers were attracted to her version of the cakewalk as a means for bolstering their social identities.

13. The passage most strongly suggests that the author would be likely to agree with which one of the following statements about Walker's significance in the history of the cakewalk?

   (A) Walker broadened the cakewalk's appeal by highlighting elements that were already present in the dance.
   (B) Walker's version of the cakewalk appealed to larger audiences than previous versions did because she accentuated its satiric dimension.
   (C) Walker popularized the cakewalk by choreographing various alternative interpretations of it, each tailored to the interests of a different cultural group.
   (D) Walker added a "mimetic vertigo" to the cakewalk by inserting imitations of other performers' cakewalking into her dance routines.
   (E) Walker revitalized the cakewalk by disentangling its complex admixture of African and European elements.

14. The passage provides sufficient information to answer which one of the following questions?

   (A) What were some of the attributes of African dance forms that were preserved in the cakewalk?
   (B) Who was the first performer to dance the cakewalk professionally?
   (C) What is an aspect of the cakewalk that was preserved in other North American dance forms?
   (D) What features were added to the original cakewalk by the stage parodies circulating at the end of the nineteenth century?
   (E) For about how many years into the twentieth century did the cakewalk remain widely popular?

In principle, a cohesive group—one whose members generally agree with one another and support one another's judgments—can do a much better job at decision making than it could if it were
(5) noncohesive. When cohesiveness is low or lacking entirely, compliance out of fear of recrimination is likely to be strongest. To overcome this fear, participants in the group's deliberations need to be confident that they are members in good standing and
(10) that the others will continue to value their role in the group, whether or not they agree about a particular issue under discussion. As members of a group feel more accepted by the others, they acquire greater freedom to say what they really think, becoming less
(15) likely to use deceitful arguments or to play it safe by dancing around the issues with vapid or conventional comments. Typically, then, the more cohesive a group becomes, the less its members will deliberately censor what they say out of fear of being punished socially
(20) for antagonizing their fellow members.

But group cohesiveness can have pitfalls as well: while the members of a highly cohesive group can feel much freer to deviate from the majority, their desire for genuine concurrence on every important
(25) issue often inclines them not to use this freedom. In a highly cohesive group of decision makers, the danger is not that individuals will conceal objections they harbor regarding a proposal favored by the majority, but that they will think the proposal is a good one
(30) without attempting to carry out a critical scrutiny that could reveal grounds for strong objections. Members may then decide that any misgivings they feel are not worth pursuing—that the benefit of any doubt should be given to the group consensus. In this way, they
(35) may fall victim to a syndrome known as "groupthink," which one psychologist concerned with collective decision making has defined as "a deterioration of mental efficiency, reality testing, and moral judgment that results from in-group pressures."
(40) Based on analyses of major fiascoes of international diplomacy and military decision making, researchers have identified groupthink behavior as a recurring pattern that involves several factors: overestimation of the group's power and morality,
(45) manifested, for example, in an illusion of invulnerability, which creates excessive optimism; closed-mindedness to warnings of problems and to alternative viewpoints; and unwarranted pressures toward uniformity, including self-censorship with
(50) respect to doubts about the group's reasoning and a concomitant shared illusion of unanimity concerning group decisions. Cohesiveness of the decision-making group is an essential antecedent condition for this syndrome but not a sufficient one, so it is important
(55) to work toward identifying the additional factors that determine whether group cohesiveness will deteriorate into groupthink or allow for effective decision making.

Main Point

Paragraph 1

Paragraph 2

Paragraph 3

Identify Viewpoints

15. Which one of the following most accurately expresses the main point of the passage?

(A) Despite its value in encouraging frank discussion, high cohesion can lead to a debilitating type of group decision making called groupthink.
(B) Group members can guard against groupthink if they have a good understanding of the critical role played by cohesion.
(C) Groupthink is a dysfunctional collective decision-making pattern that can occur in diplomacy and military affairs.
(D) Low cohesion in groups is sometimes desirable when higher cohesion involves a risk of groupthink behavior.
(E) Future efforts to guard against groupthink will depend on the results of ongoing research into the psychology of collective decision making.

16. A group of closely associated colleagues has made a disastrous diplomatic decision after a series of meetings marked by disagreement over conflicting alternatives. It can be inferred from the passage that the author would be most likely to say that this scenario

(A) provides evidence of chronic indecision, thus indicating a weak level of cohesion in general
(B) indicates that the group's cohesiveness was coupled with some other factor to produce a groupthink fiasco
(C) provides no evidence that groupthink played a role in the group's decision
(D) provides evidence that groupthink can develop even in some groups that do not demonstrate an "illusion of unanimity"
(E) indicates that the group probably could have made its decision-making procedure more efficient by studying the information more thoroughly

17. Which one of the following, if true, would most support the author's contentions concerning the conditions under which groupthink takes place?

(A) A study of several groups, each made up of members of various professions, found that most fell victim to groupthink.
(B) There is strong evidence that respectful dissent is more likely to occur in cohesive groups than in groups in which there is little internal support.
(C) Extensive analyses of decisions made by a large number of groups found no cases of groupthink in groups whose members generally distrust one another's judgments.
(D) There is substantial evidence that groupthink is especially likely to take place when members of a group develop factions whose intransigence prolongs the group's deliberations.
(E) Ample research demonstrates that voluntary deference to group opinion is not a necessary factor for the formation of groupthink behavior.

18. The passage mentions which one of the following as a component of groupthink?

(A) unjustified suspicions among group members regarding an adversary's intentions
(B) strong belief that the group's decisions are right
(C) group members working under unusually high stress, leading to illusions of invulnerability
(D) the deliberate use of vapid, clichéd arguments
(E) careful consideration of objections to majority positions

19. It can be inferred from the passage that both the author of the passage and the researchers mentioned in the passage would be most likely to agree with which one of the following statements about groupthink?

(A) Groupthink occurs in all strongly cohesive groups, but its contribution to collective decision making is not fully understood.
(B) The causal factors that transform group cohesion into groupthink are unique to each case.
(C) The continued study of cohesiveness of groups is probably fruitless for determining what factors elicit groupthink.
(D) Outside information cannot influence group decisions once they have become determined by groupthink.
(E) On balance, groupthink cannot be expected to have a beneficial effect in a group's decision making.

20. In the passage, the author says which one of the following about conformity in decision-making groups?

(A) Enforced conformity may be appropriate in some group decision situations.
(B) A high degree of conformity is often expected of military decision-making group members.
(C) Inappropriate group conformity can result from inadequate information.
(D) Voluntary conformity occurs much less frequently than enforced conformity.
(E) Members of noncohesive groups may experience psychological pressure to conform.

21. In line 5, the author mentions low group cohesiveness primarily in order to

(A) contribute to a claim that cohesiveness can be conducive to a freer exchange of views in groups
(B) establish a comparison between groupthink symptoms and the attributes of low-cohesion groups
(C) suggest that there may be ways to make both cohesive and noncohesive groups more open to dissent
(D) indicate that both cohesive and noncohesive groups may be susceptible to groupthink dynamics
(E) lay the groundwork for a subsequent proposal for overcoming the debilitating effects of low cohesion

22. Based on the passage, it can be inferred that the author would be most likely to agree with which one of the following?

(A) Highly cohesive groups are more likely to engage in confrontational negotiating styles with adversaries than are those with low cohesion.
(B) It is difficult for a group to examine all relevant options critically in reaching decisions unless it has a fairly high degree of cohesiveness.
(C) A group with varied viewpoints on a given issue is less likely to reach a sound decision regarding that issue than is a group whose members are unified in their outlook.
(D) Intense stress and high expectations are the key factors in the formation of groupthink.
(E) Noncohesive groups can, under certain circumstances, develop all of the symptoms of groupthink.

Faculty researchers, particularly in scientific, engineering, and medical programs, often produce scientific discoveries and invent products or processes that have potential commercial value. Many
(5) institutions have invested heavily in the administrative infrastructure to develop and exploit these discoveries, and they expect to prosper both by an increased level of research support and by the royalties from licensing those discoveries having
(10) patentable commercial applications. However, although faculty themselves are unlikely to become entrepreneurs, an increasing number of highly valued researchers will be sought and sponsored by research corporations or have consulting contracts with
(15) commercial firms. One study of such entrepreneurship concluded that "if universities do not provide the flexibility needed to venture into business, faculty will be tempted to go to those institutions that are responsive to their commercialized desires." There is
(20) therefore a need to consider the different intellectual property policies that govern the commercial exploitation of faculty inventions in order to determine which would provide the appropriate level of flexibility.

(25) In a recent study of faculty rights, Patricia Chew has suggested a fourfold classification of institutional policies. A supramaximalist institution stakes out the broadest claim possible, asserting ownership not only of all intellectual property produced by faculty in the
(30) course of their employment while using university resources, but also for any inventions or patent rights from faculty activities, even those involving research sponsored by nonuniversity funders. A maximalist institution allows faculty ownership of inventions that
(35) do not arise either "in the course of the faculty's employment [or] from the faculty's use of university resources." This approach, although not as all-encompassing as that of the supramaximalist university, can affect virtually all of a faculty
(40) member's intellectual production. A resource-provider institution asserts a claim to faculty's intellectual product in those cases where "significant use" of university time and facilities is employed. Of course, what constitutes significant use of resources is a
(45) matter of institutional judgment.

As Chew notes, in these policies "faculty rights, including the sharing of royalties, are the result of university benevolence and generosity. [However, this] presumption is contrary to the common law,
(50) which provides that faculty own their inventions." Others have pointed to this anomaly and, indeed, to the uncertain legal and historical basis upon which the ownership of intellectual property rests. Although these issues remain unsettled, and though universities
(55) may be overreaching due to faculty's limited knowledge of their rights, most major institutions behave in the ways that maximize university ownership and profit participation.

But there is a fourth way, one that seems to be
(60) free from these particular issues. Faculty-oriented institutions assume that researchers own their own intellectual products and the rights to exploit them commercially, except in the development of public health inventions or if there is previously specified

(65) "substantial university involvement." At these institutions industry practice is effectively reversed, with the university benefiting in far fewer circumstances.

Main Point

Paragraph 1

Paragraph 2

Paragraph 3

Paragraph 4

Identify Viewpoints

23. Which one of the following most accurately summarizes the main point of the passage?

(A) While institutions expect to prosper from increased research support and royalties from patentable products resulting from faculty inventions, if they do not establish clear-cut policies governing ownership of these inventions, they run the risk of losing faculty to research corporations or commercial consulting contracts.

(B) The fourfold classification of institutional policies governing exploitation of faculty inventions is sufficient to categorize the variety of steps institutions are taking to ensure that faculty inventors will not be lured away by commercial firms or research corporations.

(C) To prevent the loss of faculty to commercial firms or research corporations, institutions will have to abandon their insistence on retaining maximum ownership of and profit from faculty inventions and adopt the common-law presumption that faculty alone own their inventions.

(D) While the policies of most institutions governing exploitation of faculty inventions seek to maximize university ownership of and profit from these inventions, another policy offers faculty greater flexibility to pursue their commercial interests by regarding faculty as the owners of their intellectual products.

(E) Most institutional policies governing exploitation of faculty inventions are indefensible because they run counter to common-law notions of ownership and copyright, but they usually go unchallenged because few faculty members are aware of what other options might be available to them.

24. Which one of the following most accurately characterizes the author's view regarding the institutional intellectual property policies of most universities?

(A) The policies are in keeping with the institution's financial interests.
(B) The policies are antithetical to the mission of a university.
(C) The policies do not have a significant impact on the research of faculty.
(D) The policies are invariably harmful to the motivation of faculty attempting to pursue research projects.
(E) The policies are illegal and possibly immoral.

25. Which one of the following institutions would NOT be covered by the fourfold classification proposed by Chew?

(A) an institution in which faculty own the right to some inventions they create outside the institution
(B) an institution in which faculty own all their inventions, regardless of any circumstances, but grant the institution the right to collect a portion of their royalties
(C) an institution in which all inventions developed by faculty with institutional resources become the property of the institution
(D) an institution in which all faculty inventions related to public health become the property of the institution
(E) an institution in which some faculty inventions created with institutional resources remain the property of the faculty member

26. The passage suggests that the type of institution in which employees are likely to have the most uncertainty about who owns their intellectual products is the

(A) commercial firm
(B) supramaximalist university
(C) maximalist university
(D) resource-provider university
(E) faculty-oriented university

27. According to the passage, what distinguishes a resource-provider institution from the other types of institutions identified by Chew is its

(A) vagueness on the issue of what constitutes university as opposed to nonuniversity resources
(B) insistence on reaping substantial financial benefit from faculty inventions while still providing faculty with unlimited flexibility
(C) inversion of the usual practices regarding exploitation of faculty inventions in order to give faculty greater flexibility
(D) insistence on ownership of faculty inventions developed outside the institution in order to maximize financial benefit to the university
(E) reliance on the extent of use of institutional resources as the sole criterion in determining ownership of faculty inventions

28. The author of the passage most likely quotes one study of entrepreneurship in lines 16–19 primarily in order to

(A) explain why institutions may wish to develop intellectual property policies that are responsive to certain faculty needs
(B) draw a contrast between the worlds of academia and business that will be explored in detail later in the passage
(C) defend the intellectual property rights of faculty inventors against encroachment by the institutions that employ them
(D) describe the previous research that led Chew to study institutional policies governing ownership of faculty inventions
(E) demonstrate that some faculty inventors would be better off working for commercial firms

29. The passage suggests each of the following EXCEPT:

(A) Supramaximalist institutions run the greatest risk of losing faculty to jobs in institutions more responsive to the inventor's financial interests.
(B) A faculty-oriented institution will make no claim of ownership to a faculty invention that is unrelated to public health and created without university involvement.
(C) Faculty at maximalist institutions rarely produce inventions outside the institution without using the institution's resources.
(D) There is little practical difference between the policies of supramaximalist and maximalist institutions.
(E) The degree of ownership claimed by a resource-provider institution of the work of its faculty will not vary from case to case.

Passage A

Readers, like writers, need to search for answers. Part of the joy of reading is in being surprised, but academic historians leave little to the imagination. The perniciousness of the historiographic approach became
(5) fully evident to me when I started teaching. Historians require undergraduates to read scholarly monographs that sap the vitality of history; they visit on students what was visited on them in graduate school. They assign books with formulaic arguments that transform
(10) history into an abstract debate that would have been unfathomable to those who lived in the past. Aimed so squarely at the head, such books cannot stimulate students who yearn to connect to history emotionally as well as intellectually.
(15) In an effort to address this problem, some historians have begun to rediscover stories. It has even become something of a fad within the profession. This year, the American Historical Association chose as the theme for its annual conference some putative connection to
(20) storytelling: "Practices of Historical Narrative." Predictably, historians responded by adding the word "narrative" to their titles and presenting papers at sessions on "Oral History and the Narrative of Class Identity," and "Meaning and Time: The Problem of
(25) Historical Narrative." But it was still historiography, intended only for other academics. At meetings of historians, we still encounter very few historians telling stories or moving audiences to smiles, chills, or tears.

Passage B

Writing is at the heart of the lawyer's craft, and so,
(30) like it or not, we who teach the law inevitably teach aspiring lawyers how lawyers write. We do this in a few stand-alone courses and, to a greater extent, through the constraints that we impose on their writing throughout the curriculum. Legal writing, because of the purposes
(35) it serves, is necessarily ruled by linear logic, creating a path without diversions, surprises, or reversals. Conformity is a virtue, creativity suspect, humor forbidden, and voice mute.
Lawyers write as they see other lawyers write, and,
(40) influenced by education, profession, economic constraints, and perceived self-interest, they too often write badly. Perhaps the currently fashionable call for attention to narrative in legal education could have an effect on this. It is not yet exactly clear what role
(45) narrative should play in the law, but it is nonetheless true that every case has at its heart a story—of real events and people, of concerns, misfortunes, conflicts, feelings. But because legal analysis strips the human narrative content from the abstract, canonical legal
(50) form of the case, law students learn to act as if there is no such story.
It may well turn out that some of the terminology and public rhetoric of this potentially subversive movement toward attention to narrative will find its
(55) way into the law curriculum, but without producing corresponding changes in how legal writing is actually taught or in how our future colleagues will write. Still, even mere awareness of the value of narrative could perhaps serve as an important corrective.

Main Point of Passage A

Main Point of Passage B

Similarities Between Passages

Dissimilarities Between Passages

30. Which one of the following does each of the passages display?

(A) a concern with the question of what teaching methods are most effective in developing writing skills
(B) a concern with how a particular discipline tends to represent points of view it does not typically deal with
(C) a conviction that writing in specialized professional disciplines cannot be creatively crafted
(D) a belief that the writing in a particular profession could benefit from more attention to storytelling
(E) a desire to see writing in a particular field purged of elements from other disciplines

31. The passages most strongly support which one of the following inferences regarding the authors' relationships to the professions they discuss?

(A) Neither author is an active member of the profession that he or she discusses.
(B) Each author is an active member of the profession he or she discusses.
(C) The author of passage A is a member of the profession discussed in that passage, but the author of passage B is not a member of either of the professions discussed in the passages.
(D) Both authors are active members of the profession discussed in passage B.
(E) The author of passage B, but not the author of passage A, is an active member of both of the professions discussed in the passages.

32. Which one of the following does each passage indicate is typical of writing in the respective professions discussed in the passages?

(A) abstraction
(B) hyperbole
(C) subversion
(D) narrative
(E) imagination

33. In which one of the following ways are the passages NOT parallel?

(A) Passage A presents and rejects arguments for an opposing position, whereas passage B does not.
(B) Passage A makes evaluative claims, whereas passage B does not.
(C) Passage A describes specific examples of a phenomenon it criticizes, whereas passage B does not.
(D) Passage B offers criticism, whereas passage A does not.
(E) Passage B outlines a theory, whereas passage A does not.

34. The phrase "scholarly monographs that sap the vitality of history" in passage A (lines 6–7) plays a role in that passage's overall argument that is most analogous to the role played in passage B by which one of the following phrases?

(A) "Writing is at the heart of the lawyer's craft" (line 29)
(B) "Conformity is a virtue, creativity suspect, humor forbidden, and voice mute" (lines 37–38)
(C) "Lawyers write as they see other lawyers write" (line 39)
(D) "every case has at its heart a story" (line 46)
(E) "Still, even mere awareness of the value of narrative could perhaps serve as an important corrective" (lines 57–59)

35. Suppose that a lawyer is writing a legal document describing the facts that are at issue in a case. The author of passage B would be most likely to expect which one of the following to be true of the document?

(A) It will be poorly written because the lawyer who is writing it was not given explicit advice by law professors on how lawyers should write.
(B) It will be crafted to function like a piece of fiction in its description of the characters and motivations of the people involved in the case.
(C) It will be a concise, well-crafted piece of writing that summarizes most, if not all, of the facts that are important in the case.
(D) It will not genuinely convey the human dimension of the case, regardless of how accurate the document may be in its details.
(E) It will neglect to make appropriate connections between the details of the case and relevant legal doctrines.

Passage A

There is no universally accepted definition within international law for the term "national minority." It is most commonly applied to (1) groups of persons—not necessarily citizens—under the jurisdiction of one
(5) country who have ethnic ties to another "homeland" country, or (2) groups of citizens of a country who have lasting ties to that country and have no such ties to any other country, but are distinguished from the majority of the population by ethnicity, religion, or
(10) language. The terms "people" and "nation" are also vaguely defined in international agreements. Documents that refer to a "nation" generally link the term to the concept of "nationalism," which is often associated with ties to land. It also connotes sovereignty, for
(15) which reason, perhaps, "people" is often used instead of "nation" for groups subject to a colonial power.

While the lack of definition of the terms "minority," "people," and "nation" presents difficulties to numerous minority groups, this lack is particularly problematic
(20) for the Roma (Gypsies). The Roma are not a colonized people, they do not have a homeland, and many do not bear ties to any currently existing country. Some Roma are not even citizens of any country, in part because of their nomadic way of life, which developed in response
(25) to centuries of fleeing persecution. Instead, they have ethnic and linguistic ties to other groups of Roma that reside in other countries.

Passage B

Capotorti's definition of a minority includes four empirical criteria—a group's being numerically smaller
(30) than the rest of the population of the state; their being nondominant; their having distinctive ethnic, linguistic, or religious characteristics; and their desiring to preserve their own culture—and one legal criterion, that they be citizens of the state in question. This last
(35) element can be problematic, given the previous nomadic character of the Roma, that they still cross borders between European states to avoid persecution, and that some states have denied them citizenship, and thus minority status. Because this element essentially
(40) grants the state the arbitrary right to decide if the Roma constitute a minority without reference to empirical characteristics, it seems patently unfair that it should be included in the definition.

However, the Roma easily fulfill the four
(45) objective elements of Capotorti's definition and should, therefore, be considered a minority in all major European states. Numerically, they are nowhere near a majority, though they number in the hundreds of thousands, even millions, in some states. Their
(50) nondominant position is evident—they are not even acknowledged as a minority in some states. The Roma have a number of distinctive linguistic, ethnic, and religious characteristics. For example, most speak Romani, an Indo-European language descended from
(55) Sanskrit. Roma groups also have their own distinctive legal and court systems, which are group oriented rather than individual-rights oriented. That they have preserved their language, customs, and identity through centuries of persecution is evidence enough
(60) of their desire to preserve their culture.

Main Point of Passage A

Main Point of Passage B

Similarities Between Passages

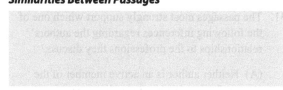

Dissimilarities Between Passages

36. Which one of the following most accurately expresses the main point of passage A?

(A) Different definitions of certain key terms in international law conflict with one another in their application to the Roma.

(B) In at least some countries in which they live, the Roma are not generally considered a minority group.

(C) The lack of agreement regarding the definitions of such terms as "minority," "people," and "nation" is partly due to the unclear application of the terms to groups such as the Roma.

(D) Any attempt to define such concepts as people, nation, or minority group will probably fail to apply to certain borderline cases such as the Roma.

(E) The absence of a clear, generally agreed-upon understanding of what constitutes a people, nation, or minority group is a problem, especially in relation to the Roma.

37. The term "problematic" has which one of the following meanings in both passage A (line 19) and passage B (line 35)?

(A) giving rise to intense debate

(B) confusing and unclear

(C) resulting in difficulties

(D) difficult to solve

(E) theoretically incoherent

38. Which one of the following claims about the Roma is NOT made in passage A?

(A) Those living in one country have ethnic ties to Roma in other countries.

(B) Some of them practice a nomadic way of life.

(C) They, as a people, have no recognizable homeland.

(D) In some countries, their population exceeds one million.

(E) The lack of a completely satisfactory definition of "minority" is a greater problem for them than for most.

39. The authors' views regarding the status of the Roma can most accurately be described in which one of the following ways?

(A) The author of passage A, but not the author of passage B, disapproves of the latitude that international law allows individual states in determining their relations to nomadic Roma populations.

(B) The author of passage B, but not the author of passage A, considers the problems of the Roma to be a noteworthy example of how international law can be ineffective.

(C) The author of passage B, but not the author of passage A, considers the Roma to be a paradigmatic example of a people who do not constitute a nation.

(D) Both authors would prefer that the political issues involving the Roma be resolved on a case-by-case basis within each individual country rather than through international law.

(E) Both authors consider the problems that the Roma face in relation to international law to be anomalous and special.

40. The relationship between which one of the following pairs of documents is most analogous to the relationship between passage A and passage B?

(A) "The Lack of Clear-Cut Criteria for Classifying Jobs as Technical Causes Problems for Welders" and "A Point-by-Point Argument That Welding Fulfills the Union's Criteria for Classification of Jobs as 'Technical'"

(B) "Why the Current Criteria for Professional Competence in Welding Have Not Been Effectively Applied" and "A Review of the Essential Elements of Any Formal Statement of Professional Standards"

(C) "The Need for a Revised Definition of the Concept of Welding in Relation to Other Technical Jobs" and "An Enumeration and Description of the Essential Job Duties Usually Carried Out by Union Welders"

(D) "The Lack of Competent Welders in Our Company Can Be Attributed to a General Disregard for Professional and Technical Staff Recruitment" and "A Discussion of the Factors That Companies Should Consider in Recruiting Employees"

(E) "The Conceptual Links Between Professionalism and Technical Expertise" and "A Refutation of the Union's Position Regarding Which Types of Jobs Should Be Classified as Neither Professional nor Technical"

41. Which one of the following is a principle that can be most reasonably considered to underlie the reasoning in both of the passages?

(A) A definition that is vaguely formulated cannot serve as the basis for the provisions contained in a document of international law.

(B) A minority group's not being officially recognized as such by the government that has jurisdiction over it can be detrimental to the group's interests.

(C) Provisions in international law that apply only to minority groups should not be considered valid.

(D) Governments should recognize the legal and court systems used by minority populations within their jurisdictions.

(E) A group that often moves back and forth across a boundary between two countries can be legitimately considered citizens of both countries.

Practice Sets – Answers

1	**A**	Main Point
2	**B**	Structure
3	**B**	Implication
4	**D**	Function of a Statement
5	**D**	Implication
6	**E**	Viewpoint
7	**A**	Implication
8	**C**	Main Point
9	**D**	Function of a Statement
10	**C**	Application
11	**E**	Existence
12	**E**	Viewpoint
13	**A**	Viewpoint
14	**A**	Evaluation
15	**A**	Main Point
16	**C**	Viewpoint
17	**C**	Strengthen
18	**B**	Existence
19	**E**	Viewpoint
20	**E**	Existence
21	**A**	Function of a Statement

22	**B**	Viewpoint
23	**D**	Main Point
24	**A**	Viewpoint
25	**B**	Application
26	**D**	Implication
27	**E**	Detail
28	**A**	Function of a Statement
29	**E**	Implication
30	**D**	Comparative (Implication)
31	**B**	Comparative (Implication)
32	**A**	Comparative (Existence)
33	**C**	Comparative (Structure)
34	**B**	Comparative (Function of a Statement)
35	**D**	Comparative (Viewpoint)
36	**E**	Comparative (Main Point)
37	**C**	Comparative (Meaning)
38	**D**	Comparative (Existence)
39	**E**	Comparative (Viewpoint)
40	**A**	Comparative (Application)
41	**B**	Comparative (Principle)

Question Families	Question Types	Number of Incorrect Questions
Synthesis	Main Point	
	Structure	
	Purpose	
	Function of a Paragraph	
	Function of a Statement	
Information	Detail	
	Existence	
	Meaning	
Inference	Implication	
	Viewpoint	
	Attitude	
	Principle	
Process	Application	
	Strengthen	
	Weaken	
	Evaluation	
	Extension	
Comparative Reading	Relationship	
	Agree/Disagree	
	Comparative	

For Questions 1–7

Every culture that has adopted the cultivation of maize—also known as corn—has been radically changed by it. This crop reshaped the cultures of the Native Americans who first cultivated it, leading to
(5) such developments as the adoption of agrarian and in some cases urban lifestyles, and much of the explosion of European populations after the fifteenth century was driven by the introduction of maize together with another crop from the Americas,
(10) potatoes. The primary reason for this plant's profound influence is its sheer productivity. With maize, ancient agriculturalists could produce far more food per acre than with any other crop, and early Central Americans recognized and valued this characteristic
(15) of the plant. But why are maize and a few similar crops so much more bountiful than others? Modern biochemistry has revealed the physical mechanism underlying maize's impressive productivity.

To obtain the hydrogen they use in the production
(20) of carbohydrates through photosynthesis, all plants split water into its constituent elements, hydrogen and oxygen. They use the resultant hydrogen to form one of the molecules they need for energy, but the oxygen is released into the atmosphere. During
(25) photosynthesis, carbon dioxide that the plant takes in from the atmosphere is used to build sugars within the plant. An enzyme, rubisco, assists in the sugar-forming chemical reaction. Because of its importance in photosynthesis, rubisco is arguably the most
(30) significant enzyme in the world. Unfortunately, though, when the concentration of oxygen relative to carbon dioxide in a leaf rises to a certain level, as can happen in the presence of many common atmospheric conditions, oxygen begins to bind competitively to the enzyme,
(35) thus interfering with the photosynthetic reaction.

Some plants, however, have evolved a photosynthetic mechanism that prevents oxygen from impairing photosynthesis. These plants separate the places where they split water atoms into hydrogen
(40) and oxygen from the places where they build sugars from carbon dioxide. Water molecules are split, as in all plants, in specialized chlorophyll-containing structures in the green leaf cells, but the rubisco is sequestered within airtight tissues in the center of the
(45) leaf. The key to the process is that in these plants, oxygen and all other atmospheric gases are excluded from the cells containing rubisco. These cells, called the bundle sheath cells, surround the vascular structures of the leaf—structures that function
(50) analogously to human blood vessels. Carbon dioxide, which cannot enter these cells as a gas, first undergoes a series of reactions to form an intermediary, nongas molecule named C-4 for the four carbon atoms it contains. This molecule enters
(55) the bundle sheath cells and there undergoes reactions that release the carbon dioxide that will fuel the production of carbohydrates (e.g., sugars). Taking its name from the intermediary molecule, the entire process is called C-4 photosynthesis. Such C-4 plants
(60) as sugar cane, rice, and maize are among the world's most productive crops.

Main Point

The main point is stated in the last two sentences of the first paragraph and throughout the third paragraph. It is that maize and similar crops are more bountiful because of an underlying physical mechanism, C-4 photosynthesis, which prevents oxygen from impairing photosynthesis.

Paragraph 1

This paragraph provides background information about the history of maize and states the first part of the main point.

Paragraph 2

This paragraph provides background information about the process of photosynthesis. It offers support for the main point by discussing how oxygen interferes with the process of photosynthesis by binding competitively with the enzyme, rubisco, which assists with the production of sugars from carbon dioxide within the plant.

Paragraph 3

This paragraph states the second part of the main point. It explains how maize and similar plants have developed a mechanism to prevent oxygen for impairing photosynthesis. Oxygen and other atmospheric gases are excluded from cells with rubisco. Carbon dioxide is converted into a molecule called C-4, and then enters the cells with rubisco to fuel the production of carbohydrates (sugars).

Identify Viewpoints

The author's viewpoint is present and is the focus of the passage. There are no other viewpoints in this passage.

1. **Correct Answer (A).** *Prep Test 49, Section 3, Passage 4, Question 21.*

Which one of the following most accurately states the main point of the passage?

This is an MP question. It is an Argumentative passage, so the author's viewpoint is present. The author's conclusion is stated in the last two sentences of the first paragraph and throughout the third paragraph. It is that maize and similar crops are more bountiful because of an underlying physical mechanism. This mechanism is C-4 photosynthesis, which prevents oxygen from impairing the process of photosynthesis. We should anticipate a correct answer choice that accurately expresses this conclusion.

(A) The greater productivity of maize, as compared with many other crops, is due to its C-4 photosynthetic process, in which the reactions that build sugars are protected from the effects of excess oxygen.

This matches our anticipated answer choice. The second paragraph makes it clear that oxygen impairs photosynthesis by interfering with the production of sugars. This is a candidate.

(B) Because of their ability to produce greater quantities and higher qualities of nutrients, those plants, including maize, that use a C-4 photosynthetic process have helped to shape the development of many human cultures.

This answer choice addresses the wrong task. It presents background information from the first paragraph about the influence of maize and similar plants on human development. This is a loser.

(C) C-4 photosynthesis, which occurs in maize, involves a complex sequence of chemical reactions that makes more efficient use of available atmospheric hydrogen than do photosynthetic reactions in non-C-4 plants.

This answer choice includes irrelevant information and addresses the wrong task. It is unclear from the passage whether or not C-4 photosynthesis makes more efficient use of hydrogen. In addition, this information is related to a supporting idea (what C-4 photosynthesis is), rather than to the main point (why maize and similar plants are more productive). This is a loser.

(D) The presence of the enzyme rubisco is a key factor in the ability of C-4 plants, including maize, to circumvent the negative effects of gases such as oxygen on the production of sugars in photosynthesis.

This answer choice includes contradictory information. Rubisco does not circumvent the negative effects of oxygen; instead, oxygen interferes with the positive effects of rubisco. C-4 plants prevent this by separating oxygen and rubisco. This is also a loser.

(E) Some of the world's most productive crop plants, including maize, have evolved complex, effective mechanisms to prevent atmospheric gases that could bind competitively to rubisco from entering the plants' leaves.

This is a descriptive statement rather than a conclusion. In addition, the language used in this statement is vague. It includes the term *effective mechanisms*, while the passage discusses one mechanism—C-4 photosynthesis. It also uses the phrase *atmospheric gases that could bind competitively*, whereas the passage only discusses oxygen in this context of binding competitively. This is a loser as well.

As (A) is the only candidate, it is the correct answer choice.

2. **Correct Answer (B).** *Prep Test 49, Section 3, Passage 4, Question 22.*

> **Which one of the following most accurately describes the organization of the material presented in the second and third paragraphs of the passage?**

This is an STR question. The prompt asks about the structure of the second and third paragraphs. Looking back at our analysis, we can see that the second paragraph provides background information about the process of photosynthesis. It also supports the main point by discussing how oxygen interferes with the process of photosynthesis. The third paragraph states the second part of the main point. It explains that maize and similar plants are productive because they have developed a mechanism to prevent oxygen for impairing photosynthesis. We should anticipate a correct answer choice that describes these functions in this order.

> **(A) The author suggests that the widespread cultivation of a particular crop is due to its high yield, explains its high yield by describing the action of a particular enzyme in that crop, and then outlines the reasons for the evolution of that enzyme.**

This answer choice addresses the wrong part of the passage and includes irrelevant information. The first part of this answer choice describes a function of the first paragraph. In addition, the evolution of the enzyme is not discussed in the passage. This is a loser.

> **(B) The author explains some aspects of a biochemical process, describes a naturally occurring hindrance to that process, and then describes an evolutionary solution to that hindrance in order to explain the productivity of a particular crop.**

This matches our anticipated answer choice. The second paragraph begins with an explanation of a biochemical process (photosynthesis) and presents a natural hindrance (oxygen) to that process. The third paragraph describes a solution (C-4 photosynthesis) to that hindrance to explain why a crop (maize) is so productive. This is a candidate.

> **(C) The author describes a problem inherent in certain biochemical processes, scientifically explains two ways in which organisms solve that problem, and then explains the evolutionary basis for one of those solutions.**

This answer contains irrelevant information. The passage only discusses one way in which organisms overcome a problem with a biochemical process. This is a loser.

> **(D) The author describes a widespread cultural phenomenon involving certain uses of a type of plant, explains the biochemical basis of the phenomenon, and then points out that certain other plants may be used for similar purposes.**

This passage includes irrelevant information. The passage does not describe a widespread cultural phenomenon involving certain uses of a plant. This is a loser.

> **(E) The author introduces a natural process, describes the biochemical reaction that is widely held to be the mechanism underlying the process, and then argues for an alternate evolutionary explanation of that process.**

This passage includes irrelevant information. The author does not describe one explanation for a process and then provide an alternative. This is a loser.

As (B) is the only candidate, it is the correct answer choice.

3. **Correct Answer (B).** *Prep Test 49, Section 3, Passage 4, Question 23.*

> **Assuming that all other relevant factors remained the same, which one of the following, if it developed in a species of plant that does not have C-4 photosynthesis, would most likely give that species an advantage similar to that which the author attributes to C-4 plants?**

This is an IMP question that provides a hypothetical scenario for consideration and then asks for an inference based on this scenario and the information in the passage. The prompt includes a topic from specific parts of the passage. C-4 photosynthesis is discussed in the third paragraph.

The question prompt describes a scenario in which a plant that does not have C-4 photosynthesis has an advantage similar to that of a plant with C-4 photosynthesis. It asks us to determine which of the answer choices would provide this advantage. Looking at the third paragraph of the passage, we can see that the primary advantage of C-4 photosynthesis is that it prevents oxygen from interfering with the process of photosynthesis by binding with rubisco. It does this by sequestering the enzyme in airtight tissues that oxygen and other atmospheric gases cannot penetrate.

Based on this information, we can infer that if a plant had another method of preventing oxygen from binding with rubisco, it would have the same advantage as a plant that has C-4 photosynthesis. Or, it may be the case that a plant may perform photosynthesis by a process that is not susceptible to interference by oxygen. We should anticipate a correct answer choice that expresses one of these inferences or another one that can be logically drawn from the passage.

(A) Water is split into its constituent elements in specialized chlorophyll-containing structures in the bundle sheath cells.

This answer choice includes irrelevant information. The third paragraph states that maize and similar plants split water into its constituent elements in chlorophyll-containing structures as all plants do. However, there is no indication that this prevents oxygen from binding with rubisco. This is a loser.

(B) An enzyme with which oxygen cannot bind performs the role of rubisco.

This matches our second anticipated answer choice. If an enzyme that does not bind with oxygen performs the role of rubisco, then the process of photosynthesis would not be impeded by oxygen. This is a candidate.

(C) The vascular structures of the leaf become impermeable to both carbon dioxide gas and oxygen gas.

This matches our first anticipated answer choice. If part of the plant is impermeable to carbon dioxide and oxygen, then rubisco within it would not bind with oxygen. This means that the process of photosynthesis would not be hindered. This is also a candidate.

(D) The specialized chlorophyll-containing structures in which water is split surround the vascular structures of the leaf.

This answer choice includes irrelevant information. The passage does not include any information indicating that having the structures in which water is split surround the vascular structures would prevent oxygen from interfering with the process of photosynthesis. This is a loser.

(E) An enzyme that does not readily react with carbon dioxide performs the role of rubisco in the green leaf cells.

This answer choice also includes irrelevant information. We are concerned with the reaction of oxygen with rubisco—not the reaction of carbon dioxide. This is a loser as well.

We have two candidates, (B) and (C), so we need to eliminate one. Looking back at (C), we can see that it is the weaker candidate. It actually includes irrelevant information. The third paragraph states that rubisco is sequestered in bundle sheath cells that surround the vascular structures of the leaf. It does not indicate that rubisco is found in the vascular structures of the leaf. Therefore, there is no way to know if having vascular structures that are impermeable to atmospheric gases would prevent oxygen from interfering with the process of photosynthesis. Therefore, (B) is the correct answer choice.

4. **Correct Answer (D).** *Prep Test 49, Section 3, Passage 4, Question 24.*

> **The author's reference to "all other atmospheric gases" in line 46 plays which one of the following roles in the passage?**

This is an FS question. Therefore, we should read the sentence that includes the referenced statement and the ones that come before and after it. The preceding sentence states that rubisco is sequestered within airtight tissues. The sentence with the referenced statement explains that this prevents oxygen and all other atmospheric gases from entering the cells containing rubisco. The sentence that follows provides a description of the cells containing rubisco. It is difficult to determine the role of the referenced statement based on this information, so we should look at the broader context. Later in the paragraph, it is explained that since carbon dioxide (an atmospheric gas) cannot enter the cells containing rubisco, it undergoes a chemical reaction to convert into a molecule called C-4, which can enter these cells (making photosynthesis possible). Therefore, it seems that the role of the referenced statement is to provide a reason for why carbon dioxide must convert to C-4 for photosynthesis to occur. We should anticipate a correct answer choice that expresses this function.

> **(A) It indicates why certain atmospheric conditions can cause excess oxygen to build up and thus hinder photosynthesis in non-C-4 plants as described in the previous paragraph.**

This answer choice addresses the wrong part of the passage. The second paragraph states that certain atmospheric conditions cause excess oxygen to build up and inhibit photosynthesis in non-C-4 plants. However, this has no connection to the referenced statement. This is a loser.

> **(B) It supports the claim advanced earlier in the paragraph that oxygen is not the only atmospheric gas whose presence in the leaf can interfere with photosynthesis.**

This answer choice includes irrelevant information. The passage does not discuss other gases interfering with photosynthesis. This is another loser.

> **(C) It supports the conclusion that non-C-4 photosynthesis makes use of several atmospheric gases that C-4 photosynthesis does not use.**

This answer choice also includes irrelevant information. The passage does not state that non-C-4 photosynthesis makes use of atmospheric gases that C-4 photosynthesis does not. This is a loser.

> **(D) It explains why carbon dioxide molecules undergo the transformations described later in the paragraph before participating in photosynthesis in C-4 plants.**

This matches our anticipated answer choice. The referenced statement provides a reason for the transformation of carbon dioxide into C-4 prior to the occurrence of photosynthesis, which is discussed later in the same paragraph. This is a candidate.

> **(E) It advances a broader claim that oxygen levels remain constant in C-4 plants in spite of changes in atmospheric conditions.**

This answer choice includes irrelevant information. The passage does not include the claim that oxygen levels remain constant in C-4 plants. This is a loser.

As (D) is the only candidate, it is the correct answer choice.

---

5. **Correct Answer (D).** *Prep Test 49, Section 3, Passage 4, Question 25.*

The passage contains information sufficient to justify inferring which one of the following?

This is an IMP question. The prompt does not reference a topic from a specific part of the passage. Therefore, we cannot anticipate a correct answer choice and must proceed directly to eliminating answer choices.

(A) In rice plants, atmospheric gases are prevented from entering the structures in which water is split into its constituent elements.

This answer choice includes contradictory information. The third paragraph states that rice is a type of C-4 plant. Earlier in that paragraph, it is explained that atmospheric gases are prevented from entering the bundle sheath cells of C-4 plants (not the chlorophyll-containing structures where water is split into its constituent elements). This is a loser.

(B) In rice plants, oxygen produced from split water molecules binds to another type of molecule before being released into the atmosphere.

This answer choice includes irrelevant information. The third paragraph states that C-4 plants prevent oxygen from binding to rubisco, but the passage does not specify what happens to the oxygen in C-4 plants. This is a loser.

(C) Rice is an extremely productive crop that nourishes large segments of the world's population and is cultivated by various widely separated cultures.

The answer choice makes too strong of a claim. The first paragraph makes this claim about maize. Although rice is also a C-4 plant, we cannot know for certain that this claim applies to rice based on the information in the passage. This is also a loser.

(D) In rice plants, rubisco is isolated in the bundle sheath cells that surround the vascular structures of the leaves.

This seems like a logical inference based on the information in the passage. The third paragraph states that rubisco is isolated in the bundle sheath cells that surround the vascular structures of the leaves of C-4 plants. This must be true of rice since it is a C-4 plant. This is a candidate.

(E) Although rice is similar to maize in productivity and nutritive value, maize is the more widely cultivated crop.

This answer choice includes irrelevant information. The passage does not compare how widely cultivated rice and maize are. This is a loser.

As (D) is the only candidate, it is the correct answer choice.

---

6. **Correct Answer (E).** *Prep Test 49, Section 3, Passage 4, Question 26.*

The author of the passage would be most likely to agree with which one of the following statements?

This is a V question. The prompt does not reference a viewpoint or topic from a specific part of the passage.

Therefore, we cannot anticipate a correct answer choice and must proceed directly to eliminating answer choices.

(A) Maize's impressive productivity cannot be understood without an understanding of its cultural influences.

This answer choice includes irrelevant information. The passage does not suggest that understanding maize's productivity is dependent on understanding its cultural influences. This is a loser.

(B) Maize is an example of a plant in which oxygen is not released as a by-product of photosynthesis.

This answer choice also includes irrelevant information. The passage states that oxygen is prevented from binding to rubisco but does not provide any other information about what happens to oxygen in maize. This is another loser.

(C) Maize's high yields are due not only to its use of C-4 but also to its ability to produce large quantities of rubisco.

This answer choice also includes irrelevant information. Maize's ability to produce large quantities of rubisco is not discussed in the passage. This is also a loser.

(D) Until maize was introduced to Europeans by Native Americans, European populations lacked the agricultural techniques required for the cultivation of C-4 plants.

This answer choice includes irrelevant information as well. The agricultural techniques of Europeans are not discussed in the passage. This is a loser.

(E) Maize's C-4 photosynthesis is an example of an effective evolutionary adaptation that has come to benefit humans.

This seems like a statement the author would agree with based on the information in the passage. The third paragraph states that C-4 photosynthesis evolved to prevent oxygen from impairing photosynthesis. The first paragraph describes how beneficial maize has been to human beings. Since maize is a C-4 plant, C-4 photosynthesis is an adaptation that benefits humans. This is the correct answer choice.

---

7. **Correct Answer (A).** *Prep Test 49, Section 3, Passage 4, Question 27.*

The passage provides the most support for which one of the following statements?

This is an IMP question. The prompt does not reference a topic from a specific part of the passage. Therefore, we cannot anticipate a correct answer choice and must proceed directly to eliminating answer choices.

(A) In many plants, rubisco is not isolated in airtight tissues in the center of the leaf.

This seems like a logical inference based on the information in the passage. The second paragraph states that in certain atmospheric conditions, the concentration of oxygen can rise to a level at which oxygen binds competitively to rubisco, interfering with photosynthesis. This does not happen in C-4 plants because rubisco is isolated in the center of the leaf. Therefore, rubisco must not be isolated in the center of the leaf in many plants. The use of the term *many* does not result in too strong of a claim because the passage makes it clear that C-4 plants are less common than non-C-4 plants. The phrase *maize and a few similar crops* is used in the first paragraph, and the term *some plants* is used in the third paragraph (both in reference to C-4 plants). This is a candidate.

(B) A rubisco molecule contains four carbon atoms.

This answer choice includes irrelevant information. The third paragraph specifies that C-4 includes four carbon atoms. However, the composition of rubisco is not discussed. This is a loser.

(C) Rubisco is needed in photosynthesis to convert carbon dioxide to a nongas molecule.

This answer choice includes contradictory information. The third paragraph states that rubisco is sequestered from gases such as carbon dioxide. Carbon dioxide can only enter the cells containing rubisco after it has converted to a nongas molecule. Therefore, rubisco does not play a role in the conversion process. This is a loser.

(D) In maize, rubisco helps protect against the detrimental effects of oxygen buildup in the leaves.

This answer choice includes contradictory information. The only detrimental effect of oxygen building up in the leaves is that it binds to rubisco, which impedes photosynthesis. Therefore, rubisco does not protect against the detrimental effects of oxygen buildup. This is a loser.

(E) Rubisco's role in the C-4 process is optimized when oxygen levels are high relative to carbon dioxide levels.

This answer choice includes irrelevant information. The passage does not discuss the effectiveness of rubisco when oxygen levels are high. This is a loser.

As (A) is the only candidate, it is the correct answer choice.

For Questions 8–14

Aida Overton Walker (1880–1914), one of the most widely acclaimed African American performers of the early twentieth century, was known largely for popularizing a dance form known as the cakewalk
(5) through her choreographing, performance, and teaching of the dance. The cakewalk was originally developed prior to the United States Civil War by African Americans, for whom dance was a means of maintaining cultural links within a slave society. It
(10) was based on traditional West African ceremonial dances, and like many other African American dances, it retained features characteristic of African dance forms, such as gliding steps and an emphasis on improvisation.
(15) To this African-derived foundation, the cakewalk added certain elements from European dances: where African dances feature flexible body postures, large groups and separate-sex dancing, the cakewalk developed into a high-kicking walk performed by a
(20) procession of couples. Ironically, while these modifications later enabled the cakewalk to appeal to European Americans and become one of the first cultural forms to cross the racial divide in North America, they were originally introduced with satiric
(25) intent. Slaves performed the grandiloquent walks in order to parody the processional dances performed at slave owners' balls and, in general, the self-important manners of slave owners. To add a further irony, by the end of the nineteenth century, the cakewalk was
(30) itself being parodied by European American stage performers, and these parodies in turn helped shape subsequent versions of the cakewalk.
While this complex evolution meant that the cakewalk was not a simple cultural phenomenon—
(35) A) one scholar has characterized this layering of parody upon parody with the phrase "mimetic vertigo"—it is in fact what enabled the dance to attract its wide audience. In the cultural and socioeconomic flux of the turn-of-the-century United States, where
(40) industrialization, urbanization, mass immigration, and rapid social mobility all reshaped the cultural landscape, an art form had to be capable of being many things to many people in order to appeal to a large audience.
(45) Walker's remarkable success at popularizing the cakewalk across otherwise relatively rigid racial boundaries rested on her ability to address within her interpretation of it the varying and sometimes conflicting demands placed on the dance. Middle-
(50) class African Americans, for example, often denounced the cakewalk as disreputable, a complaint reinforced by the parodies circulating at the time. Walker won over this audience by refining the cakewalk and emphasizing its fundamental grace.
(55) Meanwhile, because middle- and upper-class European Americans often felt threatened by the tremendous cultural flux around them, they prized what they regarded as authentic art forms as bastions of stability; much of Walker's success with this
(60) audience derived from her distillation of what was widely acclaimed as the most authentic cakewalk. Finally, Walker was able to gain the admiration of

many newly rich industrialists and financiers, who found in the grand flourishes of her version of the
(65) cakewalk a fitting vehicle for celebrating their newfound social rank.

Main Point

The main point is stated in the first sentence of the last paragraph. It is that Walker's success at popularizing the cakewalk across racial boundaries was due to her interpreting it in a way that addressed varying and conflicting demands.

Paragraph 1

The paragraph provides background information. It introduces Walker and states that she popularized the cakewalk. It then provides information about the historical origins of the cakewalk. This dance is based on traditional West African ceremonial dances and was a means of maintaining cultural links in a slave society.

Paragraph 2

This paragraph describes the evolution of the cakewalk. Elements of European dances were added to the cakewalk. These appealed to Europeans and allowed the cakewalk to cross the racial divide, but were originally introduced with satiric intent as slaves were attempting to parody slave owners. Later, European American performers parodied the cakewalk, which shaped later versions of the dance.

Paragraph 3

This paragraph posits that the complex evolution of the cakewalk allowed it to appeal to many different people because of the cultural and socioeconomic flux of the period. The paragraph also puts forth the viewpoint of a scholar with whom the author seems to agree.

Paragraph 4

This paragraph states the main point of the passage. It then explains how Walker adapted the cakewalk to win over different groups of Americans with different demands.

Identify Viewpoints

The author's viewpoint is present and is the focus of the passage. The viewpoint of a scholar whom the author appears to agree with is mentioned in passing.

8. **Correct Answer (C).** *Prep Test 54, Section 1, Passage 3, Question 13.*

Which one of the following most accurately expresses the main point of the passage?

This is an MP question. It is an Argumentative passage, so the author's viewpoint is present. The author's conclusion is stated in the first sentence of the last paragraph. It is that Walker's success at popularizing the cakewalk across racial boundaries was due to her interpreting it in a way that addressed varying and conflicting demands. We should anticipate a correct answer choice that accurately expresses this conclusion.

(A) **Walker, who was especially well known for her success in choreographing, performing, and teaching the cakewalk, was one of the most widely recognized African American performers of the early twentieth century.**

This answer choice includes incomplete information. It does not include a reference to how Walker popularized the cakewalk. This is a loser.

(B) **In spite of the disparate influences that shaped the cakewalk, Walker was able to give the dance broad appeal because she distilled what was regarded as the most authentic version in an era that valued authenticity highly.**

This answer choice also includes incomplete information. The passage states that the perceived authenticity of Walker's version of the cakewalk appealed to middle- and upper-class European Americans. This answer choice does not reference the factors that appealed to middle-class African Americans and the newly rich. This is a loser.

(C) **Walker popularized the cakewalk by capitalizing on the complex cultural mix that had developed from the dance's original blend of satire and cultural preservation, together with the effects of later parodies.**

This matches our anticipated answer choice. Walker used the complex cultural mix of the cakewalk (described in the first three paragraphs of the passage) to make it popular with different audiences. This is a candidate.

(D) **Whereas other versions of the cakewalk circulating at the beginning of the twentieth century were primarily parodic in nature, the version popularized by Walker combined both satire and cultural preservation.**

This also matches our anticipated answer choice. The passage describes how some earlier versions of the cakewalk were primarily parodic, but Walker popularized the dance by combining different elements to appeal to different audiences. This is a candidate as well.

(E) **Because Walker was able to recognize and preserve the characteristics of the cakewalk as African Americans originally performed it, it became the first popular art form to cross the racial divide in the United States.**

This answer choice includes incomplete information. The passage states that preserving the original characteristics of the cakewalk appealed to some groups of Americans but not to all. In addition, the passage does not say that the cakewalk was the first popular art form to cross the racial divide but rather one of the first. This is a loser.

We have two candidates, (C) and (D), so we need to eliminate one. Looking back at (D), we can see that it is the weaker candidate. It only addresses the cakewalk at the beginning of the 20th century and Walker's version. This means that it ignores the elements of the cakewalk that developed prior to the 20th century. In addition, it makes too strong of a claim with the use of the term *primarily*. The passage states that the cakewalk was parodied and was influenced by parodies, but it does not state that the dance was primarily parodic in nature. Therefore, (C) is the correct answer choice.

9. **Correct Answer (D).** *Prep Test 54, Section 1, Passage 3, Question 14.*

> **The author describes the socioeconomic flux of the turn-of-the-century United States in the third paragraph primarily in order to**

This is an FS question. Therefore, we should read the sentence with the referenced statement and the ones that come before and after it. The referenced statement appears in the second sentence of the third paragraph. The preceding sentence explains that the complex evolution of the cakewalk is what enabled the dance to attract a wide audience. The sentence with the referenced statement explains that the turn-of-the-century United States was in a state of cultural and socioeconomic flux, which means that an art form had to be many things to many people to have wide appeal. As this sentence is the last sentence of the paragraph, we do not need to read any further at this point. Based on the immediate context, the function of the referenced statement seems to be to present the conditions that contributed to the success of the cakewalk. We should anticipate a correct answer choice that expresses this function.

> **(A) argue that the cakewalk could have become popular only in such complex social circumstances**

This answer choice makes too strong of a claim. While these complex social circumstances helped make the cakewalk popular, we cannot say that the cakewalk only could have become popular in these circumstances. This is a loser.

> **(B) detail the social context that prompted performers of the cakewalk to fuse African and European dance forms**

This answer choice addresses the wrong part of the passage. The fusion of dance forms is discussed much earlier in the passage. The referenced statement is used to explain the popularity of the cakewalk, not what prompted performers of the cakewalk to fuse African and European dance forms. This is a loser.

> **(C) identify the target of the overlapping parodic layers that characterized the cakewalk**

This answer choice also addresses the wrong part of the passage. In the second paragraph, the author discusses a target of parody (slave owners), but this has nothing to do with the referenced statement. This is also a loser.

> **(D) indicate why a particular cultural environment was especially favorable for the success of the cakewalk**

This matches our anticipated answer choice. The turn-of-the-century United States was favorable to the success of the cakewalk because it was in a state of socioeconomic flux. This is a candidate.

> **(E) explain why European American parodies of the cakewalk were able to reach wide audiences**

The answer choice includes incomplete information. The author is trying to explain why the cakewalk itself—not just European American parodies of it—reached wide audiences. This is a loser.

As (D) is the only candidate, it is the correct answer choice.

10. **Correct Answer (C).** *Prep Test 54, Section 1, Passage 3, Question 15.*

> **Which one of the following is most analogous to the author's account in the second paragraph of how the cakewalk came to appeal to European Americans?**

This is an APP question. The prompt asks for a situation that is analogous to the author's account of how the cakewalk came to appeal to European Americans. Looking back at our analysis, as is specified in the prompt, this topic is discussed in the second paragraph. Elements of European dances were added to the cakewalk for satiric effect, and this unintentionally resulted in the cakewalk appealing to European Americans. We can reframe this in general terms as Art Form A satirizes Art Form B, and this makes Art Form A popular among fans of Art Form B. We should anticipate a correct answer choice that describes a comparable situation.

(A) Satirical versions of popular music songs are frequently more popular than the songs they parody.

This answer choice includes irrelevant information. The situation in the passage does not compare satirical works with the original works. This is a loser.

(B) A style of popular music grows in popularity among young listeners because it parodies the musical styles admired by older listeners.

This answer choice includes contradictory information. It describes a situation in which Art Form A (a style of popular music) parodies Art Form B (music admired by older listeners) and becomes popular among another group (younger listeners). This is a loser.

(C) A style of music becomes admired among popular music's audience in part because of elements that were introduced in order to parody popular music.

This matches our anticipated answer choice. Art Form A (a style of music) parodies Art Form B (popular music) and becomes popular among fans of Art Form B. This is a candidate.

(D) A once popular style of music wins back its audience by incorporating elements of the style of music that is currently most popular.

This answer choice includes irrelevant information. The passage does not discuss an art form winning back its audience by incorporating elements of a popular art form. This is a loser.

(E) After popular music begins to appropriate elements of a traditional style of music, interest in that traditional music increases.

This answer choice includes contradictory information. In this case, Art Form A (popular music) incorporates elements of Art Form B (traditional music), which makes Art Form B more popular. In addition, this answer choice makes no reference to parody. This is also a loser.

As (C) is the only candidate, it is the correct answer choice.

11. **Correct Answer (E).** *Prep Test 54, Section 1, Passage 3, Question 16.*

The passage asserts which one of the following about the cakewalk?

This is an EX question. The prompt asks for an assertion made by the passage about the cakewalk. As the entire passage is about the cakewalk, we cannot anticipate a correct answer choice and should proceed to eliminating answer choices.

(A) It was largely unknown outside African American culture until Walker popularized it.

This answer choice makes too strong of a claim. The passage makes it clear that Walker popularized the cakewalk among European Americans, but it does not state that the cakewalk was largely unknown outside African American culture previously. This is a loser.

(B) It was mainly a folk dance, and Walker became one of only a handful of people to perform it professionally.

This answer choice includes irrelevant information. The passage does not state that Walker was one of only a handful of people to perform the cakewalk. This is a loser.

(C) Its performance as parody became uncommon as a result of Walker's popularization of its authentic form.

This answer choice includes irrelevant information. The passage states that there were parodies of the cakewalk before Walker performed it and during the period she performed it. However, there is no information about parodies once she had popularized it. This is a loser.

(D) Its West African origins became commonly known as a result of Walker's work.

This answer choice also includes irrelevant information. The passage does not state that the cakewalk's West African roots became commonly known as a result of Walker's work. This is another loser.

(E) It was one of the first cultural forms to cross racial lines in the United States.

This answer choice seems compatible with the information in the passage. The second sentence of the second paragraph explicitly states that the cakewalk was one of the first cultural forms to cross the racial divide in North America. This is the correct answer choice.

12. **Correct Answer (E).** *Prep Test 54, Section 1, Passage 3, Question 17.*

    It can be inferred from the passage that the author would be most likely to agree with which one of the following statements?

This is a V question. The prompt does not reference a viewpoint or topic from a specific part of the passage. Therefore, we cannot anticipate a correct answer choice and must proceed directly to eliminating answer choices.

(A) Because of the broad appeal of humor, satiric art forms are often among the first to cross racial or cultural divisions.

This answer choice makes too strong of a claim. The only satiric art form mentioned in the passage is the cakewalk. There is no evidence to support the claim that satiric art forms, in general, are often among the first to cross racial or cultural divisions. This is a loser.

(B) The interactions between African American and European American cultural forms often result in what is appropriately characterized as "mimetic vertigo."

This answer choice also makes too strong of a claim. The third paragraph states that mimetic vertigo is the layering of parody upon parody. There is no indication that interactions between African American and European American cultural forms often result in mimetic vertigo. This is another loser.

(C) Middle-class European Americans who valued the cakewalk's authenticity subsequently came to admire other African American dances for the same reason.

This answer choice includes irrelevant information. The passage does not discuss other African American dances. This is also a loser.

(D) Because of the influence of African dance forms, some popular dances that later emerged in the United States featured separate-sex dancing.

This answer choice also includes irrelevant information. The passage does not discuss other popular dances that emerged later. This is a loser.

(E) Some of Walker's admirers were attracted to her version of the cakewalk as a means for bolstering their social identities.

This seems like a statement the author would agree with based on the information in the passage. The last sentence of the fourth paragraph states that some newly rich people were attracted to the cakewalk because it was a fitting vehicle for celebrating their newfound social rank. This is the correct answer choice.

13. **Correct Answer (A).** *Prep Test 54, Section 1, Passage 3, Question 18.*

> **The passage most strongly suggests that the author would be likely to agree with which one of the following statements about Walker's significance in the history of the cakewalk?**

This is a V question. The prompt does not reference a viewpoint or topic from a specific part of the passage. Therefore, we cannot anticipate a correct answer choice and must proceed directly to eliminating answer choices.

(A) Walker broadened the cakewalk's appeal by highlighting elements that were already present in the dance.

This seems like a statement the author would agree with based on the information in the passage. The last paragraph states that Walker appealed to middle-class African Americans by emphasizing the fundamental grace of the dance, and she appealed to middle- and upper-class European Americans by presenting the most authentic version. Both of these involve highlighting elements already present in the dance. This is a candidate.

(B) Walker's version of the cakewalk appealed to larger audiences than previous versions did because she accentuated its satiric dimension.

This answer choice includes contradictory information. The last paragraph of the passage specifies several factors that contributed to Walker's version of the cakewalk appealing to larger audiences. None of these involve accentuating its satiric dimension, and some (emphasizing its fundamental grace and presenting it as an authentic version) are not compatible with emphasizing its satiric elements. This is a loser.

(C) Walker popularized the cakewalk by choreographing various alternative interpretations of it, each tailored to the interests of a different cultural group.

This answer choice also includes contradictory information. The third paragraph clearly indicates that Walker developed her own interpretation of the cakewalk. It incorporated elements that appealed to members of different cultural groups. This is a loser as well.

(D) Walker added a "mimetic vertigo" to the cakewalk by inserting imitations of other performers' cakewalking into her dance routines.

This answer choice includes irrelevant information. There is no mention in the passage of Walker adding mimetic vertigo to the cakewalk by including imitations of other performers in her routines. This is also a loser.

(E) Walker revitalized the cakewalk by disentangling its complex admixture of African and European elements.

This answer choice includes irrelevant information. The second and third paragraphs make it clear that the cakewalk included African and European elements, and there is nothing in the passage to indicate that Walker disentangled these elements. This is a loser.

As (A) is the only candidate, it is the correct answer choice.

14. **Correct Answer (A).** *Prep Test 54, Section 1, Passage 3, Question 19.*

The passage provides sufficient information to answer which one of the following questions?

This is an E question. The prompt references the passage in general. Therefore, we cannot anticipate a correct answer choice and must proceed directly to eliminating answer choices.

(A) What were some of the attributes of African dance forms that were preserved in the cakewalk?

This seems to be a question that is answered by the passage. The last sentence of the first paragraph states that gliding steps and an emphasis on improvisation were attributes of African dance forms preserved in the cakewalk. This is a candidate.

(B) Who was the first performer to dance the cakewalk professionally?

This answer choice includes irrelevant information. There is no information in the passage about the first person to perform the cakewalk professionally. This is a loser.

(C) What is an aspect of the cakewalk that was preserved in other North American dance forms?

This answer choice also includes irrelevant information. The passage does not mention other North American dance forms that preserved an aspect of the cakewalk. This is a loser as well.

(D) What features were added to the original cakewalk by the stage parodies circulating at the end of the nineteenth century?

This answer choice also includes irrelevant information. The passage does not discuss the features added to the cakewalk by the stage parodies at the end of the nineteenth century. This is a loser.

(E) For about how many years into the twentieth century did the cakewalk remain widely popular?

This answer choice includes irrelevant information as well. The passage does not state how many years into the twentieth century the cakewalk remained popular. This is also a loser.

As (A) is the only candidate, it is the correct answer choice.

For Questions 15–22

    In principle, a cohesive group—one whose members generally agree with one another and support one another's judgments—can do a much better job at decision making than it could if it were
(5) noncohesive. When cohesiveness is low or lacking entirely, compliance out of fear of recrimination is likely to be strongest. To overcome this fear, participants in the group's deliberations need to be confident that they are members in good standing and
(10) that the others will continue to value their role in the group, whether or not they agree about a particular issue under discussion. As members of a group feel more accepted by the others, they acquire greater freedom to say what they really think, becoming less
(15) likely to use deceitful arguments or to play it safe by dancing around the issues with vapid or conventional comments. Typically, then, the more cohesive a group becomes, the less its members will deliberately censor what they say out of fear of being punished socially
(20) for antagonizing their fellow members.

    But group cohesiveness can have pitfalls as well: while the members of a highly cohesive group can feel much freer to deviate from the majority, their desire for genuine concurrence on every important
(25) issue often inclines them not to use this freedom. In a highly cohesive group of decision makers, the danger is not that individuals will conceal objections they harbor regarding a proposal favored by the majority, but that they will think the proposal is a good one
(30) without attempting to carry out a critical scrutiny that could reveal grounds for strong objections. Members may then decide that any misgivings they feel are not worth pursuing—that the benefit of any doubt should be given to the group consensus. In this way, they
(35) may fall victim to a syndrome known as "groupthink," which one [A]psychologist concerned with collective decision making has defined as "a deterioration of mental efficiency, reality testing, and moral judgment that results from in-group pressures."
(40)   Based on analyses of major fiascoes of international diplomacy and military decision making, [B]researchers have identified groupthink behavior as a recurring pattern that involves several factors: overestimation of the group's power and morality,
(45) manifested, for example, in an illusion of invulnerability, which creates excessive optimism; closed-mindedness to warnings of problems and to alternative viewpoints; and unwarranted pressures toward uniformity, including self-censorship with
(50) respect to doubts about the group's reasoning and a concomitant shared illusion of unanimity concerning group decisions. Cohesiveness of the decision-making group is an essential antecedent condition for this syndrome but not a sufficient one, so it is important
(55) to work toward identifying the additional factors that determine whether group cohesiveness will deteriorate into groupthink or allow for effective decision making.

Main Point

The main point is stated in the first sentence of the first paragraph and the last sentence of the second paragraph. It is that cohesive groups can do a better job at decision-making than noncohesive groups, but they may fall victim to a syndrome known as *groupthink*.

Paragraph 1

This paragraph states the first part of the main point—that cohesive groups are better at decision-making. It then provides evidence to support this claim. It explains that when group cohesiveness is low, members comply out of fear of recrimination. When cohesiveness is high, members are more likely to say what they really think.

Paragraph 2

This paragraph explains that in cohesive groups, members' desire for concurrence makes them less likely to deviate from the majority. They will think that a proposal favored by the majority is good without attempting critical scrutiny. It then states that this is *groupthink* (second part of the main point) and provides a definition of this term from a psychologist.

Paragraph 3

This paragraph provides additional support for the main point by listing a number of factors that may lead to groupthink. It then notes that we should identify other factors that may determine whether group cohesiveness will deteriorate into groupthink.

Identify Viewpoints

The author's viewpoint is present and is the focus of the passage. The viewpoint of a psychologist and researchers are mentioned in passing. The author seems to agree with both of these viewpoints.

15. **Correct Answer (A).** *Prep Test 54, Section 1, Passage 4, Question 20.*

Which one of the following most accurately expresses the main point of the passage?

This is an MP question. It is an Argumentative passage, so the author's viewpoint is present. The author's conclusion is stated in the first sentence of the first paragraph and the last sentence of the second paragraph. It is that cohesive groups can do a better job at decision-making than noncohesive groups, but they may fall victim to a syndrome known as *groupthink*. We should anticipate a correct answer choice that accurately expresses this conclusion.

(A) Despite its value in encouraging frank discussion, high cohesion can lead to a debilitating type of group decision making called groupthink.

This matches our anticipated answer choice. The first paragraph states that high cohesion leads to better decision making because it encourages members to say what they really think. However, it can also lead members to engage in groupthink. This is a candidate.

(B) Group members can guard against groupthink if they have a good understanding of the critical role played by cohesion.

This answer choice includes irrelevant information. The passage does not discuss how group members can guard against groupthink. This is a loser.

(C) Groupthink is a dysfunctional collective decision-making pattern that can occur in diplomacy and military affairs.

This answer choice addresses the wrong task and viewpoint. It presents background information (a definition of groupthink presented by a psychologist) rather than the main point of the passage. This is a loser.

(D) Low cohesion in groups is sometimes desirable when higher cohesion involves a risk of groupthink behavior.

This answer choice includes contradictory information. The passage presents groupthink as a possible pitfall of high group cohesion, but it does not suggest that groups with low cohesion are sometimes desirable. This is a loser.

(E) Future efforts to guard against groupthink will depend on the results of ongoing research into the psychology of collective decision making.

This answer choice includes irrelevant information. The passage does not explicitly state that efforts to guard against groupthink depend on research into collective decision-making (although this can be inferred from the last paragraph of the passage). Furthermore, this idea is not the main point of the passage. This is a loser.

As (A) is the only candidate, it is the correct answer choice.

16. **Correct Answer (C).** *Prep Test 54, Section 1, Passage 4, Question 21.*

A group of closely associated colleagues has made a disastrous diplomatic decision after a series of meetings marked by disagreement over conflicting alternatives. It can be inferred from the passage that the author would be most likely to say that this scenario

This is an unusual question. It is classified as a V question because it is asking for an inference that is compatible with the author's viewpoint. However, it is worded similarly to an IMP question that presents a hypothetical situation. In addition, the prompt does not include a topic from a specific part of the passage. Given this, it is difficult to anticipate a correct answer choice, so we should proceed to eliminating answer choices. The correct answer choice will be an inference based on evidence from the passage that is related to this scenario and compatible with the author's viewpoint.

(A) provides evidence of chronic indecision, thus indicating a weak level of cohesion in general

This answer choice makes too strong of a claim. The prompt discusses one bad decision based on disagreement over conflicting alternatives. This cannot be described as chronic indecision. This is a loser.

(B) indicates that the group's cohesiveness was coupled with some other factor to produce a groupthink fiasco

This answer choice includes contradictory information. According to the passage, groupthink occurs when members uncritically support a proposal favored by the majority of a group. The prompt specifies that the colleagues disagreed about conflicting alternatives. This is also a loser.

(C) provides no evidence that groupthink played a role in the group's decision

This seems like a statement the author would agree with based on the information in the passage. The behavior described in the prompt (disagreement over conflicting alternatives) does not match the description of groupthink in the passage. This is a candidate.

(D) provides evidence that groupthink can develop even in some groups that do not demonstrate an "illusion of unanimity"

This answer choice also includes contradictory information. As mentioned previously, the situation in the prompt is not an example of groupthink. This is a loser.

(E) indicates that the group probably could have made its decision-making procedure more efficient by studying the information more thoroughly

This answer choice includes irrelevant information. The author never states that the decision-making procedure can be made more efficient by studying information more thoroughly. This is a loser as well.

As (C) is the only candidate, it is the correct answer choice.

---

17. **Correct Answer (C).** *Prep Test 54, Section 1, Passage 4, Question 22.*

Which one of the following, if true, would most support the author's contentions concerning the conditions under which groupthink takes place?

This is an S question. The argument referenced in the prompt is the author's contentions concerning the conditions under which groupthink occurs. In the second paragraph of the passage, the author claims that a group may fall into groupthink when there is a high level of group cohesion and members fail to apply critical scrutiny to proposals favored by the majority, giving the benefit of the doubt to group consensus. It is difficult to identify a weakness in this argument. Therefore, we should proceed to eliminating answer choices.

(A) A study of several groups, each made up of members of various professions, found that most fell victim to groupthink.

This answer choice includes irrelevant information. The composition of groups in terms of profession has no connection to the referenced argument. This is a loser.

(B) There is strong evidence that respectful dissent is more likely to occur in cohesive groups than in groups in which there is little internal support.

This answer choice also includes irrelevant information. The concept of respectful dissent has no relevance to the referenced argument. This is a loser as well.

(C) Extensive analyses of decisions made by a large number of groups found no cases of groupthink in groups whose members generally distrust one another's judgments.

This answer choice seems to strengthen the argument. The author argues that groupthink occurs in groups with a high level of cohesion. The analyses described in this answer choice show that groupthink does not occur in groups with low cohesion whose members distrust one another's judgments. This is a candidate.

(D) There is substantial evidence that groupthink is especially likely to take place when members of a group develop factions whose intransigence prolongs the group's deliberations.

This answer choice weakens the argument. The author claims that groupthink occurs in groups with a high level of cohesion and members accept proposals supported by the majority. This answer choice states the opposite. This is a loser.

(E) Ample research demonstrates that voluntary deference to group opinion is not a necessary factor for the formation of groupthink behavior.

This answer choice also weakens the argument. The author claims that voluntary deference to group opinion leads to groupthink. This is a loser as well.

As (C) is the only candidate, it is the correct answer choice.

18. **Correct Answer (B).** *Prep Test 54, Section 1, Passage 4, Question 23.*

The passage mentions which one of the following as a component of groupthink?

This is an EX question. Groupthink is discussed throughout the passage. Therefore, we cannot anticipate a correct answer choice and must proceed directly to eliminating answer choices.

(A) unjustified suspicions among group members regarding an adversary's intentions

This answer choice includes irrelevant information. The passage does not discuss suspicions regarding an adversary's intentions. This is a loser.

(B) strong belief that the group's decisions are right

This answer choice seems compatible with the information in the passage. The second paragraph states that one of the elements of groupthink is that members think that a proposal favored by the majority is good and do not apply critical scrutiny to it. This is a candidate.

(C) group members working under unusually high stress, leading to illusions of invulnerability

This answer choice includes irrelevant information. Working under high stress is not mentioned as a component of groupthink in the passage. This is a loser.

(D) the deliberate use of vapid, clichéd arguments

This answer choice addresses the wrong part of the passage. It is related to the discussion in the first paragraph of how members of a low-cohesion group might behave. This is also a loser.

(E) careful consideration of objections to majority positions

This answer choice includes contradictory information. The third paragraph states that groupthink involves closed-mindedness to warnings of problems and to alternative viewpoints. A careful consideration of objections to majority positions is presented earlier in the passage as a benefit of a high level of group cohesion. This is also a loser.

As (B) is the only candidate, it is the correct answer choice.

19. **Correct Answer (E).** *Prep Test 54, Section 1, Passage 4, Question 24.*

> **It can be inferred from the passage that both the author of the passage and the researchers mentioned in the passage would be most likely to agree with which one of the following statements about groupthink?**

This is a V question. The prompt asks about the viewpoint of the author and the viewpoint of researchers. The author's viewpoint is presented throughout the passage. However, the researchers' viewpoint is presented only in the third paragraph. We can focus on this viewpoint because the author is in agreement with it. The researchers analyzed diplomatic and military fiascoes to identify groupthink as a recurring pattern that involves several factors. These include overestimation of the group's power and morality, closed-mindedness to warnings of problems and to alternative viewpoints, and unwarranted pressures toward uniformity. Given the number of possible inferences that can be made based on this, it is difficult to anticipate a correct answer choice. Therefore, we should proceed to eliminating answer choices. We are looking for an inference that the author and the researchers would agree with.

(A) Groupthink occurs in all strongly cohesive groups, but its contribution to collective decision making is not fully understood.

This answer choice makes too strong of a claim. The third paragraph states that cohesiveness is an important antecedent for groupthink but not a sufficient one. This means that although high cohesion is a requirement for groupthink to occur, it does not always lead to groupthink. This is a loser.

(B) The causal factors that transform group cohesion into groupthink are unique to each case.

This answer choice includes irrelevant information. The passage does not include any information about whether or not the causes of groupthink are unique in each case. This is a loser.

(C) The continued study of cohesiveness of groups is probably fruitless for determining what factors elicit groupthink.

This answer choice includes contradictory information. The third paragraph clearly states that it is important to work towards identifying the additional factors that determine whether group cohesiveness will deteriorate into groupthink. This is a loser.

(D) Outside information cannot influence group decisions once they have become determined by groupthink.

This answer choice makes too strong of a claim. The third paragraph states that groupthink leads to closed-mindedness. However, this does not necessarily mean that outside information cannot influence group decisions. This is a loser as well.

(E) On balance, groupthink cannot be expected to have a beneficial effect in a group's decision making.

This seems like a statement the author and researchers would agree with based on the information in the passage. The researchers relate groupthink to major fiascoes and specify several elements of groupthink that would negatively affect decision-making. The author clearly agrees with the researcher's viewpoint. In addition, the last sentence of the third paragraph states that cohesiveness can either deteriorate into groupthink or allow for effective decision-making. This is the correct answer choice.

20. **Correct Answer (E).** *Prep Test 54, Section 1, Passage 4, Question 25.*

   In the passage, the author says which one of the following about conformity in decision-making groups?

   This is an EX question. Conformity in decision-making groups is discussed throughout the passage. Therefore, we cannot anticipate a correct answer choice and must proceed directly to eliminating answer choices.

   (A) Enforced conformity may be appropriate in some group decision situations.

   This answer choice includes irrelevant information. The passage does not discuss enforced conformity being appropriate in some situations. This is a loser.

   (B) A high degree of conformity is often expected of military decision-making group members.

   This answer choice seems compatible with the information in the passage. The third paragraph states that groupthink is a recurring pattern in military decision-making and groupthink requires a high degree of conformity. This is a candidate.

   (C) Inappropriate group conformity can result from inadequate information.

   This answer choice includes irrelevant information. There is no information about the effect of inadequate information on group conformity in the passage. This is a loser.

   (D) Voluntary conformity occurs much less frequently than enforced conformity.

   This answer choice also includes irrelevant information. The relative frequency of voluntary and enforced conformity is never mentioned in the passage. This is a loser as well.

   (E) Members of noncohesive groups may experience psychological pressure to conform.

   This answer choice also seems compatible with the information in the passage. The first paragraph states that in groups with low cohesion, members comply out of fear of recrimination. This is a candidate as well.

   We have two candidates, (B) and (E), so we need to eliminate one. Looking back at (B), we can see that it actually makes too strong of a claim. In the third paragraph, the author describes how researchers looked at groupthink in military decision-making and indicates that this is a recurring pattern. However, the author does not explicitly state that conformity is expected of military group members. Therefore, (E) is the correct answer choice.

21. **Correct Answer (A).** *Prep Test 54, Section 1, Passage 4, Question 26.*

   In line 5, the author mentions low group cohesiveness primarily in order to

   This is an FS question. Therefore, we should read the sentence with the referenced statement and the ones that come before and after it. The preceding sentence includes the first part of the main point of the passage, which is that a cohesive group in which members generally agree and support each other's judgments is better at decision-making than a noncohesive group. The sentence with the referenced statement states that low cohesiveness results in compliance out of fear of recrimination. The following sentence explains that members must be confident that they are in good standing and valued whether they agree or disagree about an issue to overcome this fear. The immediate context is focused on showing an advantage of high group cohesion. The referenced statement seems to support this by showing a corresponding disadvantage of groups with low cohesion. We should anticipate a correct answer choice that expresses this function.

> **(A) contribute to a claim that cohesiveness can be conducive to a freer exchange of views in groups**

This matches our anticipated answer choice. The author mentions low-cohesion groups in order to bolster the claim that cohesiveness has an advantage—it is conducive to a freer exchange of views. This is a candidate.

> **(B) establish a comparison between groupthink symptoms and the attributes of low-cohesion groups**

This answer choice addresses the wrong part of the passage. Groupthink is not discussed until much later in the passage, so the mention of low-cohesion groups was not made to establish this particular comparison. This is a loser.

> **(C) suggest that there may be ways to make both cohesive and noncohesive groups more open to dissent**

This answer choice includes irrelevant information. The passage does not discuss making cohesive and noncohesive groups more open to dissent. This is another loser.

> **(D) indicate that both cohesive and noncohesive groups may be susceptible to groupthink dynamics**

This answer choice addresses the wrong part of the passage. Groupthink is not talked about until later in the passage. This is also a loser.

> **(E) lay the groundwork for a subsequent proposal for overcoming the debilitating effects of low cohesion**

This answer choice includes irrelevant information. The passage doesn't include a specific proposal for how to overcome the effects of low cohesion. In addition, the section of the passage that includes the referenced statement is focused on presenting a benefit of high group cohesion, not explaining how to avoid low cohesion or its effects. This is a loser.

As (A) is the only candidate, it is the correct answer choice.

---

22. **Correct Answer (B).** *Prep Test 54, Section 1, Passage 4, Question 27.*

> **Based on the passage, it can be inferred that the author would be most likely to agree with which one of the following?**

This is a V question. The prompt does not reference a viewpoint or topic from a specific part of the passage. Therefore, we cannot anticipate a correct answer choice and must proceed directly to eliminating answer choices.

(A) Highly cohesive groups are more likely to engage in confrontational negotiating styles with adversaries than are those with low cohesion.

This answer choice includes irrelevant information. The passage does not discuss negotiating with adversaries. This is a loser.

(B) It is difficult for a group to examine all relevant options critically in reaching decisions unless it has a fairly high degree of cohesiveness.

This seems like a statement the author would agree with based on the information in the passage. The first paragraph states that if a group does not have a high degree of cohesiveness, compliance out of fear is likely to be strongest. This implies that a high degree of cohesiveness is required to examine all options critically. This is a candidate.

(C) A group with varied viewpoints on a given issue is less likely to reach a sound decision regarding that issue than is a group whose members are unified in their outlook.

This answer choice includes contradictory information. The first paragraph suggests that in groups with high cohesion, members are more willing to express divergent opinions. This leads to better decision-making. The second paragraph states that when groups engage in groupthink, members support majority opinions uncritically, which leads to worse decision-making. This answer choice is a loser.

(D) Intense stress and high expectations are the key factors in the formation of groupthink.

This answer choice includes irrelevant information. The passage does not state that intense stress and high expectations are key factors in the formation of groupthink. This is a loser.

(E) Noncohesive groups can, under certain circumstances, develop all of the symptoms of groupthink.

This answer choice also includes irrelevant information. The passage does not discuss a link between noncohesive groups and groupthink. This is another loser.

As (B) is the only candidate, it is the correct answer choice.

For Questions 23–29

Faculty researchers, particularly in scientific, engineering, and medical programs, often produce scientific discoveries and invent products or processes that have potential commercial value. Many
(5) institutions have invested heavily in the administrative infrastructure to develop and exploit these discoveries, and they expect to prosper both by an increased level of research support and by the royalties from licensing those discoveries having
(10) patentable commercial applications. However, although faculty themselves are unlikely to become entrepreneurs, an increasing number of highly valued researchers will be sought and sponsored by research corporations or have consulting contracts with
(15) commercial firms. One study of such entrepreneurship concluded that "if universities do not provide the flexibility needed to venture into business, faculty will be tempted to go to those institutions that are responsive to their commercialized desires." There is
(20) therefore a need to consider the different intellectual property policies that govern the commercial exploitation of faculty inventions in order to determine which would provide the appropriate level of flexibility.
(25) In a recent study of faculty rights, A) Patricia Chew has suggested a fourfold classification of institutional policies. A supramaximalist institution stakes out the broadest claim possible, asserting ownership not only of all intellectual property produced by faculty in the
(30) course of their employment while using university resources, but also for any inventions or patent rights from faculty activities, even those involving research sponsored by nonuniversity funders. A maximalist institution allows faculty ownership of inventions that
(35) do not arise either "in the course of the faculty's employment [or] from the faculty's use of university resources." This approach, although not as all-encompassing as that of the supramaximalist university, can affect virtually all of a faculty
(40) member's intellectual production. A resource-provider institution asserts a claim to faculty's intellectual product in those cases where "significant use" of university time and facilities is employed. Of course, what constitutes significant use of resources is a
(45) matter of institutional judgment.

As Chew notes, in these policies "faculty rights, including the sharing of royalties, are the result of university benevolence and generosity. [However, this] presumption is contrary to the common law,
(50) which provides that faculty own their inventions." B) Others have pointed to this anomaly and, indeed, to the uncertain legal and historical basis upon which the ownership of intellectual property rests. Although these issues remain unsettled, and though universities
(55) may be overreaching due to faculty's limited knowledge of their rights, most major institutions behave in the ways that maximize university ownership and profit participation.

But there is a fourth way, one that seems to be
(60) free from these particular issues. Faculty-oriented institutions assume that researchers own their own intellectual products and the rights to exploit them commercially, except in the development of public

health inventions or if there is previously specified
(65) "substantial university involvement." At these institutions industry practice is effectively reversed, with the university benefiting in far fewer circumstances.

Main Point

The main point is stated in the first and second sentences of the fourth paragraph. It is that faculty-oriented institutions avoid the pitfalls of other types of institutions with regard to intellectual property policies.

Paragraph 1

This paragraph provides background information. It explains that the discoveries of faculty researchers have commercial value, and institutions hope to exploit these. It describes the problem of researchers going to institutions that are responsive to their commercialized desires. It then states that it is necessary to consider the different intellectual property policies governing faculty inventions to determine which one provides enough flexibility.

Paragraph 2

This paragraph introduces the viewpoint of Patricia Chew, who suggests four classifications of institutional policies. Three of these (supramaximalist, maximalist, and resource-provider) are explained in detail.

Paragraph 3

This paragraph points out a weakness of the three policies—there is a legal argument in favor of faculty controlling intellectual property rights. It then states that universities maximize their own ownership and profit participation.

Paragraph 4

This paragraph states the main point, which is that the fourth classification (faculty-oriented) is free of the issues affecting the other policies. It then explains this classification.

Identify Viewpoints

The viewpoint of Patricia Chew is presented throughout the passage. The fourfold classification of institutional policies is based on her study. A viewpoint that expresses doubt about the basis of universities' claim to ownership of faculty inventions is also mentioned in passing. The author's viewpoint is presented in the third and fourth paragraphs. The author favors the faculty-oriented classification over the other three.

23. **Correct Answer (D).** *Prep Test 43, Section 1, Passage 4, Question 22.*

Which one of the following most accurately summarizes the main point of the passage?

This is an MP question. It is an Argumentative passage, so the author's viewpoint is present. The author's conclusion appears in the first sentence of the last paragraph. It is that faculty-oriented institutions avoid the pitfalls of other types of institutions with regard to intellectual property policies. We should anticipate a correct answer choice that accurately expresses this conclusion.

(A) **While institutions expect to prosper from increased research support and royalties from patentable products resulting from faculty inventions, if they do not establish clear-cut policies governing ownership of these inventions, they run the risk of losing faculty to research corporations or commercial consulting contracts.**

This answer choice addresses the wrong task. It restates background information from the first paragraph rather than the main point. This is a loser.

(B) **The fourfold classification of institutional policies governing exploitation of faculty inventions is sufficient to categorize the variety of steps institutions are taking to ensure that faculty inventors will not be lured away by commercial firms or research corporations.**

This answer choice addresses the wrong viewpoint. That the steps institutions are taking can be categorized into a fourfold classification system is a claim made by Patricia Chew rather than the author. In addition, the passage does not actually state that this system is sufficient to categorize all steps being taken. This is a loser as well.

(C) **To prevent the loss of faculty to commercial firms or research corporations, institutions will have to abandon their insistence on retaining maximum ownership of and profit from faculty inventions and adopt the common-law presumption that faculty alone own their inventions.**

This answer choice makes too strong of a claim. The passage does not explicitly state that institutions should adopt the common-law presumption that faculty own their inventions. This is a loser.

(D) **While the policies of most institutions governing exploitation of faculty inventions seek to maximize university ownership of and profit from these inventions, another policy offers faculty greater flexibility to pursue their commercial interests by regarding faculty as the owners of their intellectual products.**

This matches our anticipated answer choice. The problem with the first three policies is that they focus on university ownership of faculty inventions, and the third paragraph states that most institutions take this approach. The fourth policy avoids this issue by regarding faculty as the owners of their intellectual products. This is a candidate.

(E) **Most institutional policies governing exploitation of faculty inventions are indefensible because they run counter to common-law notions of ownership and copyright, but they usually go unchallenged because few faculty members are aware of what other options might be available to them.**

This answer choice addresses the wrong task. It presents a supporting idea from the third paragraph rather than the main point. This is a loser.

As (D) is the only candidate, it is the correct answer choice.

24. Correct Answer (A). *Prep Test 43, Section 1, Passage 4, Question 23.*

Which one of the following most accurately characterizes the author's view regarding the institutional intellectual property policies of most universities?

This is a V question. The prompt asks about the author's viewpoint regarding the institutional intellectual property policies of most universities. The intellectual property policies used by most universities (the first three categories of policies) are discussed in the second and third paragraphs. However, the author's viewpoint is presented in the third and fourth paragraphs, so we should probably focus on the third paragraph. That last sentence of this paragraph states that most universities behave in ways that maximize university ownership and profit participation. This suggests that the intellectual property policies of most universities are designed to benefit the universities. We should anticipate a correct answer choice that expresses this inference or another one related to the institutional intellectual property policies of most universities that the author would agree with.

(A) The policies are in keeping with the institution's financial interests.

This matches our anticipated answer choice. The institutional policies of most universities maximize the institution's ownership and profit participation, meaning that the policies are in keeping with the institution's financial interests. This is a candidate.

(B) The policies are antithetical to the mission of a university.

This answer choice includes irrelevant information. The mission of a university is not discussed in the passage. This is a loser.

(C) The policies do not have a significant impact on the research of faculty.

This answer choice also includes irrelevant information. The passage does not discuss the impact of the policies on the research of the faculty. This is another loser.

(D) The policies are invariably harmful to the motivation of faculty attempting to pursue research projects.

This answer choice includes irrelevant information as well. There is no mention of the effect of these policies on the motivation of faculty. This is also a loser.

(E) The policies are illegal and possibly immoral.

This answer choice makes too strong of a claim. The third paragraph suggests that the legal basis for these policies is uncertain, but that does not mean that these policies are illegal. Additionally, this claim is attributed to others. It is not necessarily the viewpoint of the author. This is a loser.

As (A) is the only candidate, it is the correct answer choice.

25. Correct Answer (B). *Prep Test 43, Section 1, Passage 4, Question 24.*

Which one of the following institutions would NOT be covered by the fourfold classification proposed by Chew?

This is an APP EXCEPT question. The prompt asks for an institution that would not be covered by the fourfold classification proposed by Chew. This means that we are looking for an analogous approach. However, since this is an EXCEPT question, we should simply proceed to eliminating answer choices. Any answer choice that describes an institution that is compatible with one or more of the categories proposed by Chew is incorrect. The correct answer choice will describe an institution that is not compatible with any of the categories.

(A) **an institution in which faculty own the right to some inventions they create outside the institution**

This answer choice describes an institution that is compatible with the maximalist category, which allows for faculty ownership of inventions developed outside of a faculty member's employment without the use of university resources. This is a loser.

(B) **an institution in which faculty own all their inventions, regardless of any circumstances, but grant the institution the right to collect a portion of their royalties**

This answer choice seems to describe an institution that is not compatible with any of the four categories. The passage does not connect royalty payments to any of these policies. This is a candidate.

(C) **an institution in which all inventions developed by faculty with institutional resources become the property of the institution**

This answer choice describes an institution that is compatible with both the supramaximalist and maximalist categories. Both require that inventions developed with institutional resources become the property of the institution. This is a loser.

(D) **an institution in which all faculty inventions related to public health become the property of the institution**

This answer choice describes an institution that is compatible with the faculty-oriented category. Under this policy, all faculty inventions related to public health belong to the institution. This is a loser.

(E) **an institution in which some faculty inventions created with institutional resources remain the property of the faculty member**

This answer choice describes an institution that is compatible with the resource-provider and faculty-oriented categories. Both specify that some inventions created with institutional resources are the property of the institution. This is a loser as well.

As (B) is the only candidate, it is the correct answer choice.

---

26. **Correct Answer (D).** *Prep Test 43, Section 1, Passage 4, Question 25.*

The passage suggests that the type of institution in which employees are likely to have the most uncertainty about who owns their intellectual products is the

This is an IMP question. The topic of the prompt is the type of institution in which employees are likely to have the most uncertainty about who owns their intellectual products. The first three types of institutions are described in the second paragraph, and the fourth type is described in the fourth paragraph. Based on this content, we can see that supramaximalist, maximalist, and faculty-oriented universities have the least amount of uncertainty. Supramaximalist institutions own all intellectual products. Maximalist institutions own all intellectual products produced in the course of the faculty member's employment or with university resources. Faculty-oriented institutions let faculty own all intellectual products unless they are related to public health or were developed with previously specified university involvement. However, there seems to be the potential for uncertainty regarding ownership with resource-provider institutions. These institutions own intellectual products produced by way of significant use of university resources. It is left to the university's judgment and discretion to determine whether there has been a significant use of resources. We should anticipate a correct answer choice that expresses this inference.

(A) commercial firm

This answer choice includes irrelevant information. There is no information about the degree of uncertainty about intellectual property rights that employees have with commercial firms. This is a loser.

(B) supramaximalist university

This answer choice includes contradictory information. A supramaximalist institution owns all intellectual products. This is a loser.

(C) maximalist university

This answer choice also includes contradictory information. A maximalist institution owns all intellectual products produced in the course of the faculty member's employment or with university resources. This is a loser.

(D) resource-provider university

This matches our anticipated answer choice. A resource-provider institution owns intellectual products produced by way of significant use of university resources and makes the determination about whether or not there has been a significant use of resources. This is a candidate.

(E) faculty-oriented university

This answer choice includes contradictory information. A faculty-oriented institution lets faculty own all intellectual products unless they are related to public health or were developed with previously specified university involvement. This is a loser.

As (D) is the only candidate, it is the correct answer choice.

---

27. **Correct Answer (E).** *Prep Test 43, Section 1, Passage 4, Question 26.*

> **According to the passage, what distinguishes a resource-provider institution from the other types of institutions identified by Chew is its**

This is a D question. The topic of the prompt is what distinguishes a resource-provider institution from the other types of institutions identified by Chew. The first three types of institutions are described in the second and third paragraphs, and the fourth type is described in the fourth paragraph. Reviewing this content, the main difference seems to be that ownership of intellectual products is dependent on the extent of the university resources used to create the products. We should anticipate a correct answer choice that expresses this detail.

(A) vagueness on the issue of what constitutes university as opposed to nonuniversity resources

This answer choice includes contradictory information. The passage does not indicate that there is uncertainty about what constitutes university resources and, in fact, defines university resources as university time and facilities. This is a loser.

(B) insistence on reaping substantial financial benefit from faculty inventions while still providing faculty with unlimited flexibility

This answer choice also includes contradictory information. Substantial financial benefit on the part of the university seems to be a feature of the first three institutions, not just resource-provider institutions. Therefore, this does not distinguish resource-provider institutions from the others. This is also a loser.

(C) inversion of the usual practices regarding exploitation of faculty inventions in order to give faculty greater flexibility

This answer choice addresses the wrong part of the passage. It describes a feature of faculty-oriented institutions. This is another loser.

(D) insistence on ownership of faculty inventions developed outside the institution in order to maximize financial benefit to the university

This answer choice includes contradictory information. At resource-provider institutions, faculty can own intellectual property developed outside the institution as long as the significant use of university time and facilities was not involved. This is a loser.

(E) reliance on the extent of use of institutional resources as the sole criterion in determining ownership of faculty inventions

This matches our anticipated answer choice. Resource-provider institutions rely solely on the extent of the use of institutional resources to determine ownership of faculty inventions. None of the other institution types have the same feature. This is the correct answer choice.

28. **Correct Answer (A).** *Prep Test 43, Section 1, Passage 4, Question 27.*

The author of the passage most likely quotes one study of entrepreneurship in lines 16–19 primarily in order to

This is an FS question. Therefore, we should read the sentence with the referenced statement and the ones that come before and after it. The preceding sentence states that an increasing number of researchers will be sponsored by research corporations or have consulting contracts with commercial firms. The one with the referenced statement presents a study that shows that faculty will go to those institutions that are responsive to their commercialized desires if universities do provide the flexibility needed. The following sentence states that there is, therefore, a need to consider different intellectual property policies for faculty inventions that would provide the appropriate level of flexibility. The function of the referenced statement in the immediate context seems to be to provide a reason to explain why there is this need to consider different approaches. We should anticipate a correct answer choice that expresses this function.

(A) explain why institutions may wish to develop intellectual property policies that are responsive to certain faculty needs

This matches our anticipated answer choice. The referenced statement is explaining the claim in the sentence that follows, which is that institutions need to develop flexible intellectual property policies with regard to faculty inventions. This is a candidate.

(B) draw a contrast between the worlds of academia and business that will be explored in detail later in the passage

This answer choice includes contradictory information. The contrast between academia and business is not explored in detail anywhere in the passage. This is a loser.

(C) defend the intellectual property rights of faculty inventors against encroachment by the institutions that employ them

This answer choice also includes contradictory information. The study does not advocate for or against any system of governing institutional property rights. This is another loser.

(D) describe the previous research that led Chew to study institutional policies governing ownership of faculty inventions

This answer choice includes irrelevant information. The passage does not indicate that Chew was motivated by this study or even aware of its existence. This is also a loser.

(E) demonstrate that some faculty inventors would be better off working for commercial firms

This answer choice includes contradictory information. The study does not provide evidence to support the claim that faculty inventors would be better off working for commercial firms. In fact, the sentence with the referenced statement and the ones before and after indicate that this is a negative outcome. This is a loser.

As (A) is the only candidate, it is the correct answer choice.

---

29. **Correct Answer (E).** *Prep Test 43, Section 1, Passage 4, Question 28.*

    The passage suggests each of the following EXCEPT:

This is an IMP EXCEPT question. Therefore, we cannot anticipate a correct answer choice and should proceed directly to eliminating answer choices. The incorrect answer choices will be valid inferences, while the correct answer choice will be a statement that is not supported by the passage.

(A) Supramaximalist institutions run the greatest risk of losing faculty to jobs in institutions more responsive to the inventor's financial interests.

This seems like a logical inference based on the information in the passage. The first paragraph states that universities that do not provide the necessary flexibility with regard to intellectual property policies risk losing faculty to institutions that are responsive to their commercialized desires. The second paragraph makes it clear that supramaximalist universities do not provide this flexibility. This is a loser.

(B) A faculty-oriented institution will make no claim of ownership to a faculty invention that is unrelated to public health and created without university involvement.

This seems like a logical inference based on the information in the passage. The fourth paragraph states that faculty-oriented institutions assume that researchers own their intellectual products unless these are related to public health or created with substantial university involvement. This is also a loser.

(C) Faculty at maximalist institutions rarely produce inventions outside the institution without using the institution's resources.

This also seems like a logical inference based on the information in the passage. The second paragraph states that a maximalist institutional policy can affect virtually all of a faculty member's intellectual property. This is a loser.

(D) There is little practical difference between the policies of supramaximalist and maximalist institutions.

This also seems like a logical inference based on the information in the passage. The second paragraph states that a supramaximalist policy covers all of a faculty member's inventions and a maximalist policy affects virtually all of a faculty member's inventions. This is a loser as well.

(E) The degree of ownership claimed by a resource-provider institution of the work of its faculty will not vary from case to case.

This answer choice includes contradictory information. The second paragraph claims that substantial use is decided according to the university's judgment and discretion. This suggests that the policy is not applied uniformly and the degree of ownership will vary from case to case. This is the correct answer choice.

For Questions 30–35

Passage A

Readers, like writers, need to search for answers. Part of the joy of reading is in being surprised, but academic historians leave little to the imagination. The perniciousness of the historiographic approach became
(5) fully evident to me when I started teaching. A) Historians require undergraduates to read scholarly monographs that sap the vitality of history; they visit on students what was visited on them in graduate school. They assign books with formulaic arguments that transform
(10) history into an abstract debate that would have been unfathomable to those who lived in the past. Aimed so squarely at the head, such books cannot stimulate students who yearn to connect to history emotionally as well as intellectually.
(15) In an effort to address this problem, B) some historians have begun to rediscover stories. It has even become something of a fad within the profession. This year, the American Historical Association chose as the theme for its annual conference some putative connection to
(20) storytelling: "Practices of Historical Narrative." Predictably, historians responded by adding the word "narrative" to their titles and presenting papers at sessions on "Oral History and the Narrative of Class Identity," and "Meaning and Time: The Problem of
(25) Historical Narrative." But it was still historiography, intended only for other academics. At meetings of historians, we still encounter very few historians telling stories or moving audiences to smiles, chills, or tears.

Passage B

Writing is at the heart of the lawyer's craft, and so,
(30) like it or not, we who teach the law inevitably teach aspiring lawyers how lawyers write. A) We do this in a few stand-alone courses and, to a greater extent, through the constraints that we impose on their writing throughout the curriculum. Legal writing, because of the purposes
(35) it serves, is necessarily ruled by linear logic, creating a path without diversions, surprises, or reversals. Conformity is a virtue, creativity suspect, humor forbidden, and voice mute.
Lawyers write as they see other lawyers write, and,
(40) influenced by education, profession, economic constraints, and perceived self-interest, they too often write badly. B) Perhaps the currently fashionable call for attention to narrative in legal education could have an effect on this. It is not yet exactly clear what role
(45) narrative should play in the law, but it is nonetheless true that every case has at its heart a story—of real events and people, of concerns, misfortunes, conflicts, feelings. But because legal analysis strips the human narrative content from the abstract, canonical legal
(50) form of the case, law students learn to act as if there is no such story.
It may well turn out that some of the terminology and public rhetoric of this potentially subversive movement towards attention to narrative will find its
(55) way into the law curriculum, but without producing corresponding changes in how legal writing is actually taught or in how our future colleagues will write. Still, even mere awareness of the value of narrative could perhaps serve as an important corrective.

Main Point of Passage A

The main point is stated in the last sentence of the first paragraph and the first sentence of the second paragraph. It is that historiographic approach to writing cannot stimulate students and the use of stories (narrative) may address this problem.

Main Point of Passage B

The main point is stated in the first two sentences of the second paragraph. It is that lawyers often write badly and the attention to narrative may have an effect on this.

Similarities Between Passages

Both present a concern about the style of writing used in a profession.
Both introduce the possibility of the use of narrative as a way to address this concern.

Dissimilarities Between Passages

Passage A discusses the field of history, while Passage B discusses the field of law.

30. Correct Answer (D). *Prep Test 52, Section 4, Passage 2, Question 7.*

Which one of the following does each of the passages display?

This is an unusually worded C Implication question. The prompt does not reference a topic from a specific part of the passage. Therefore, we cannot anticipate a correct answer choice and must proceed directly to eliminating answer choices.

(A) a concern with the question of what teaching methods are most effective in developing writing skills

This answer choice includes irrelevant information. Neither passage discusses specific teaching methods. This is a loser.

(B) a concern with how a particular discipline tends to represent points of view it does not typically deal with

This answer choice also includes irrelevant information. There is no mention in either passage of a discipline representing points of view it does not typically deal with. This is a loser as well.

(C) a conviction that writing in specialized professional disciplines cannot be creatively crafted

This answer choice includes contradictory information. Passage A indicates that historians can use narrative to create moving stories that students emotionally connect to. This is a loser.

(D) a belief that the writing in a particular profession could benefit from more attention to storytelling

This seems like a logical inference based on the information in the passage. It is closely related to the similarities noted in the initial analysis. Both authors express concern about the style of writing used in their respective fields and introduce the possibility of using narrative to address this problem. This is a candidate.

(E) a desire to see writing in a particular field purged of elements from other disciplines

This answer choice includes irrelevant information. Neither passage discusses purging elements of other disciplines from a particular field. This is a loser.

As (D) is the only candidate, it is the correct answer choice.

31. Correct Answer (B). *Prep Test 52, Section 4, Passage 2, Question 8.*

The passages most strongly support which one of the following inferences regarding the authors' relationships to the professions they discuss?

This is a C Implication question. The topic of the prompt is the authors' relationships to the professions they discuss. This information is not covered in our analysis, so we need to look for the relevant details in the passage. In Passage A, the first three sentences make it clear that the author is a history professor. Likewise, the first two sentences of Passage B indicate that the author is a law professor. Therefore, both authors belong to the profession they discuss. We should anticipate a correct answer choice that expresses this inference or another one that can be logically drawn from the passage.

(A) Neither author is an active member of the profession that he or she discusses.

This answer choice includes contradictory information. Both authors are active members of the professions they discuss. This is a loser.

(B) Each author is an active member of the profession he or she discusses.

This matches our anticipated answer choice. The author of Passage A is a history professor discussing history, while the author of Passage B is a law professor discussing law. This is a candidate.

(C) The author of Passage A is a member of the profession discussed in that passage, but the author of Passage B is not a member of either of the professions discussed in the passages.

This answer choice includes contradictory information. The author of Passage B is a law professor discussing law. This is a loser.

(D) Both authors are active members of the profession discussed in Passage B.

This answer choice includes contradictory information. The author of Passage A is a history professor, and Passage B discusses law. This is a loser.

(E) The author of Passage B, but not the author of Passage A, is an active member of both of the professions discussed in the passages.

This answer choice includes contradictory information. Passage A discusses history, and the author of Passage B is a law professor. This is also a loser.

As (B) is the only candidate, it is the correct answer choice.

---

32. **Correct Answer (A).** *Prep Test 52, Section 4, Passage 2, Question 9.*

Which one of the following does each passage indicate is typical of writing in the respective professions discussed in the passages?

This is a C Existence question. The prompt asks about what is typical of writing in the respective professions discussed in the passages. However, this topic is discussed throughout both passages. The analysis does not provide any useful information, other than the fact that both authors are concerned about the writing in their respective professions. Therefore, we cannot anticipate a correct answer choice and must proceed directly to eliminating answer choices.

(A) abstraction

This detail is mentioned in both passages. In the first paragraph of Passage A, the author states that historians assign books with formulaic arguments that transform history into an abstract debate. The second paragraph of Passage B states that legal analysis strips the human narrative content from the abstract, meaning that only the abstract remains. This is a candidate.

(B) hyperbole

This answer choice includes irrelevant and contradictory information. The term *hyperbole* means the use of exaggerated claims not meant to be taken literally. This is not mentioned in Passage A. In addition, the first paragraph of Passage B clearly states that legal writing is ruled by linear logic and does not include diversions, surprises, or reversals. This is a loser.

(C) subversion

This answer choice also includes irrelevant and contradictory information. There is no reference to subversion in Passage A, and the first paragraph of Passage B states that conformity is a virtue in legal writing. This is a loser as well.

(D) narrative

This answer choice also includes contradictory information. The second paragraphs of Passage A and Passage B clearly indicate that narrative is not typically used in the writing of either profession. This is a loser.

(E) imagination

This answer choice also includes contradictory information. The author of Passage A states that historical writing leaves little to the imagination, while the author of Passage B claims that creativity is suspect in legal writing. This is also a loser.

As (A) is the only candidate, it is the correct answer choice.

---

33. **Correct Answer (C).** *Prep Test 52, Section 4, Passage 2, Question 10.*

In which one of the following ways are the passages NOT parallel?

This is an unusually worded C Structure question. The prompt asks us to determine which answer choice describes an aspect of the relationship between the two passages that is not parallel. In effect, the prompt is asking us for the answer choice that describes how the structure of the two passages is different. To do that, we need to understand the structure of each passage.

The first paragraph of Passage A includes background information that introduces the problem with historical writing. The second paragraph presents the use of narrative as a possible solution and includes examples of attempts by historians to capitalize on the trendiness of narrative. It then concludes that narrative is not widely used.

The first paragraph of Passage B includes background information that introduces the problem with legal writing. The second paragraph presents the use of narrative as a possible solution. The third paragraph indicates that narrative is not currently widely used, and expresses hope that even the mere awareness of narrative might serve as a corrective.

The structures of these passages are very similar. The main structural difference seems to be that Passage A presents examples while Passage B does not. We should anticipate a correct answer choice that expresses this.

(A) Passage A presents and rejects arguments for an opposing position, whereas passage B does not.

This answer choice includes contradictory information. Passage A does not present and reject arguments in favor of an opposing position. Instead, it criticizes a style of writing and indicates a possible solution. This is a loser.

(B) Passage A makes evaluative claims, whereas passage B does not.

This answer choice also includes contradictory information. Passage A does not make evaluative claims about the historiographic style of writing. This is also a loser.

(C) Passage A describes specific examples of a phenomenon it criticizes, whereas passage B does not.

This matches our anticipated answer choice. The second paragraph of Passage A presents specific examples of attempts to capitalize on the trendiness of narrative. The author is critical of this phenomenon. This is a candidate.

(D) Passage B offers criticism, whereas passage A does not.

This answer choice includes contradictory information. Both passages include criticisms of the writing style used in a specific profession. This is a loser.

(E) Passage B outlines a theory, whereas passage A does not.

This answer choice also includes contradictory information. Both passages outline theories regarding the causes of bad writing in a profession. The first paragraph of Passage A states that historians visit on their students what was visited on them in graduate school. The second paragraph of Passage B explains that lawyers write as they see other lawyers write. This is a loser as well.

As (C) is the only candidate, it is the correct answer choice.

---

34. **Correct Answer (B).** *Prep Test 52, Section 4, Passage 2, Question 11.*

> The phrase "scholarly monographs that sap the vitality of history" in Passage A (lines 6–7) plays a role in that passage's overall argument that is most analogous to the role played in Passage B by which one of the following phrases?

This is a C Function of a Statement question. Although the prompt includes the term analogous, it is not a C Application question. The prompt is asking you to identify a statement in Passage B that has a function similar to that of the referenced statement in Passage A.

The first step is to locate the referenced statement in Passage A, which is easy to do because its location is specified in the prompt. Then, read the sentence it appears in and the ones before and after it. The preceding sentence identifies the style of writing (historiographic approach) that is generally used by academic historians. The sentence that includes the referenced statement describes a problem with this style of writing and then explains why it continues to be used. The following sentence provides additional details about the problem with this style of writing. Therefore, the role of the referenced phrase seems to be to describe a problem with the style of writing used in a profession. We should anticipate a correct answer choice that is a phrase that plays the same role in Passage B.

(A) "Writing is at the heart of the lawyer's craft" (line 29)

This answer choice includes irrelevant information. It describes the importance of writing within a profession. This is a loser.

(B) "Conformity is a virtue, creativity suspect, humor forbidden, and voice mute" (lines 37–38)

This matches our anticipated answer choice. The preceding sentence introduces the style of writing used in the legal profession. The sentence that includes this phrase presents some problems with this style of writing. This is a candidate.

(C) "Lawyers write as they see other lawyers write" (line 39)

This answer choice includes irrelevant information. It explains why a writing style is used in a profession. This is a loser.

(D) "every case has at its heart a story" (line 46)

This answer choice also includes irrelevant information. It presents a reason for why a different style of writing (narrative) may be suitable for a profession. This is a loser as well.

(E) "Still, even mere awareness of the value of narrative could perhaps serve as an important corrective" (lines 57–59)

This answer choice includes irrelevant information. It describes how the writing style used in a profession might be improved. This is a loser.

As (B) is the only candidate, it is the correct answer choice.

35. Correct Answer (D). *Prep Test 52, Section 4, Passage 2, Question 12.*

> **Suppose that a lawyer is writing a legal document describing the facts that are at issue in a case. The author of passage B would be most likely to expect which one of the following to be true of the document?**

This is a C Viewpoint question. It only asks about Passage B, so we can ignore Passage A entirely. The prompt does not include a topic or viewpoint from a specific part of the passage. Therefore, we cannot anticipate a correct answer choice and must proceed directly to eliminating answer choices.

(A) It will be poorly written because the lawyer who is writing it was not given explicit advice by law professors on how lawyers should write.

This answer choice includes contradictory information. The first paragraph of Passage B explicitly states that those who teach law teach aspiring lawyers how to write. This is a loser.

(B) It will be crafted to function like a piece of fiction in its description of the characters and motivations of the people involved in the case.

This answer choice also includes contradictory information. The second paragraph states that legal analysis strips the human narrative content from the abstract. This is presented in the context of discussing how it is not clear what role narrative should play. This is also a loser.

(C) It will be a concise, well-crafted piece of writing that summarizes most, if not all, of the facts that are important in the case.

This answer choice also includes contradictory information. The second paragraph claims that lawyers often write badly. This is a loser.

(D) It will not genuinely convey the human dimension of the case, regardless of how accurate the document may be in its details.

This seems like a statement the author would agree with based on the information in the passage. The second paragraph makes it clear that legal writing strips the human narrative from the abstract. This is a candidate.

(E) It will neglect to make appropriate connections between the details of the case and relevant legal doctrines.

This answer choice includes contradictory information. The second paragraph suggests that legal writing presents the abstract, canonical legal form of the case. This is a loser.

As (D) is the only candidate, it is the correct answer choice.

For Questions 36–41

Passage A

There is no universally accepted definition within international law for the term "national minority." It is most commonly applied to (1) groups of persons—not necessarily citizens—under the jurisdiction of one
(5) country who have ethnic ties to another "homeland" country, or (2) groups of citizens of a country who have lasting ties to that country and have no such ties to any other country, but are distinguished from the majority of the population by ethnicity, religion, or
(10) language. The terms "people" and "nation" are also vaguely defined in international agreements. Documents that refer to a "nation" generally link the term to the concept of "nationalism," which is often associated with ties to land. It also connotes sovereignty, for
(15) which reason, perhaps, "people" is often used instead of "nation" for groups subject to a colonial power.

While the lack of definition of the terms "minority," "people," and "nation" presents difficulties to numerous minority groups, this lack is particularly problematic
(20) for the Roma (Gypsies). The Roma are not a colonized people, they do not have a homeland, and many do not bear ties to any currently existing country. Some Roma are not even citizens of any country, in part because of their nomadic way of life, which developed in response
(25) to centuries of fleeing persecution. Instead, they have ethnic and linguistic ties to other groups of Roma that reside in other countries.

Passage B

A)Capotorti's definition of a minority includes four empirical criteria—a group's being numerically smaller
(30) than the rest of the population of the state; their being nondominant; their having distinctive ethnic, linguistic, or religious characteristics; and their desiring to preserve their own culture—and one legal criterion, that they be citizens of the state in question. This last
(35) element can be problematic, given the previous nomadic character of the Roma, that they still cross borders between European states to avoid persecution, and that some states have denied them citizenship, and thus minority status. Because this element essentially
(40) grants the state the arbitrary right to decide if the Roma constitute a minority without reference to empirical characteristics, it seems patently unfair that it should be included in the definition.

However, the Roma easily fulfill the four
(45) objective elements of Capotorti's definition and should, therefore, be considered a minority in all major European states. Numerically, they are nowhere near a majority, though they number in the hundreds of thousands, even millions, in some states. Their
(50) nondominant position is evident—they are not even acknowledged as a minority in some states. The Roma have a number of distinctive linguistic, ethnic, and religious characteristics. For example, most speak Romani, an Indo-European language descended from
(55) Sanskrit. Roma groups also have their own distinctive legal and court systems, which are group oriented rather than individual-rights oriented. That they have preserved their language, customs, and identity through centuries of persecution is evidence enough

(60) of their desire to preserve their culture.

Main Point of Passage A

The main point is stated in the first sentence of the second paragraph. It is that the lack of definition of the terms *minority, people,* and *nation* presents difficulties for minority groups, particularly the Roma.

Main Point of Passage B

The main point is stated in the first sentence of the second paragraph. It is that the Roma meet the four objective criteria of Capotorti's definition of a minority and should be considered a minority in all major European states.

Similarities Between Passages

Both passages present a definition of a minority that includes multiple criteria.

Dissimilarities Between Passages

Passage A discusses terms other than minority (people, nation), while Passage B only includes a definition of minority.

Passage A concludes that a lack of clear definitions in international law results in the Roma not being classified as a national minority, while Passage B argues that the Roma should be considered a minority because this group meets the four objective criteria for this classification.

36. **Correct Answer (E).** *Prep Test 56, Section 4, Passage 3, Question 16.*

Which one of the following most accurately expresses the main point of Passage A?

This is a C Main Point question that asks for the main point of Passage A. Therefore, we can ignore Passage B entirely. Passage A is an Argumentative passage, so the author's viewpoint is present. The author's conclusion appears in the first sentence of the second paragraph. It is that the lack of definition of the terms *minority*, *people*, and *nation* presents difficulties for minority groups, particularly the Roma. We should anticipate a correct answer choice that accurately expresses this conclusion.

(A) Different definitions of certain key terms in international law conflict with one another in their application to the Roma.

This answer choice includes irrelevant information. The first and second paragraphs of Passage A make it clear that the author believes that the terms *minority*, *people*, and *nation* are poorly defined. However, there is no indication that different definitions of these terms conflict with each other when applied to the Roma. This is a loser.

(B) In at least some countries in which they live, the Roma are not generally considered a minority group.

This answer choice also includes irrelevant information. It states a detail from Passage B. The fact that some countries do not consider Roma a minority group is not mentioned in Passage A. This is a loser.

(C) The lack of agreement regarding the definitions of such terms as "minority," "people," and "nation" is partly due to the unclear application of the terms to groups such as the Roma.

This answer choice also includes irrelevant information. Passage A claims that the lack of agreement regarding the definitions of these terms is particularly problematic for the Roma. It does not state that the unclear application of these terms to the Roma has resulted in a lack of agreement regarding the definitions. This is a loser.

(D) Any attempt to define such concepts as people, nation, or minority group will probably fail to apply to certain borderline cases such as the Roma.

This answer choice makes too strong of a claim. Passage A indicates that current definitions of these concepts do not apply to the Roma, but this does not mean that all future attempts will fail. This is a loser.

(E) The absence of a clear, generally agreed-upon understanding of what constitutes a people, nation, or minority group is a problem, especially in relation to the Roma.

This matches our anticipated answer choice. It directly paraphrases the main point we identified in the passage. This is the correct answer choice.

37. **Correct Answer (C).** *Prep Test 56, Section 4, Passage 3, Question 17.*

The term "problematic" has which one of the following meanings in both Passage A (line 19) and passage B (line 35)?

This is a C Meaning question. The prompt asks for the meaning of the term *problematic* in both passages.

In Passage A, the sentence that includes the referenced term starts a paragraph, so we will begin there. This sentence states the main point of the passage, which is that the lack of definitions for key terms presents difficulties for minority groups and is particularly problematic for gypsies. The next sentence (and the following ones) explains how the Roma fail to qualify for minority status because of these vague definitions.

In Passage B, the preceding sentence presents four objective criteria and one legal one to be considered a minority. The sentence that includes the referenced term states that the last criterion (the legal one) is problematic because many Roma fail to meet it. The following sentence explains that the legal criterion is arbitrary and unfair.

In both passages, the term *problematic* is used in reference to something that creates complications for the Roma. We should anticipate a correct answer choice that expresses this meaning.

(A) giving rise to intense debate

This answer choice includes irrelevant information. Neither passage indicates that there is intense debate about the problematic definitions or criterion. This is a loser.

(B) confusing and unclear

This answer choice also includes contradictory information. Passage A states that the definitions are problematic because they are confusing and unclear. However, the problematic legal criterion in Passage B is neither confusing nor unclear. This is a loser.

(C) resulting in difficulties

This matches our anticipated answer choice. In both passages, the term *problematic* is used in reference to something that leads to difficulties for the Roma. This is a candidate.

(D) difficult to solve

This answer choice includes irrelevant information. Neither passage addresses how difficult it would be to resolve the problematic issue. This is a loser.

(E) theoretically incoherent

This answer choice also includes irrelevant information. Passage A suggests that the problematic definitions are incoherent, but Passage B does not indicate this about the problematic criterion. This is also a loser.

As (C) is the only candidate, it is the correct answer choice.

38. **Correct Answer (D).** *Prep Test 56, Section 4, Passage 3, Question 18.*

Which one of the following claims about the Roma is NOT made in passage A?

This is a C Existence EXCEPT question that refers only to Passage A. Therefore, Passage B can be ignored. The prompt asks for a claim about the Roma that is not made in Passage A. We cannot anticipate a correct answer choice and must proceed directly to eliminating answer choices.

(A) Those living in one country have ethnic ties to Roma in other countries.

This answer choice includes a detail that is stated in the second paragraph of Passage A. This is a loser.

(B) Some of them practice a nomadic way of life.

This answer choice also includes a detail that is stated in the second paragraph of Passage A. This is a loser.

(C) They, as a people, have no recognizable homeland.

This answer choice also includes a detail that is stated in the second paragraph of Passage A. This is another loser.

(D) In some countries, their population exceeds one million.

This answer choice includes irrelevant information. The number of Roma in some countries is not mentioned in Passage A. This is discussed in Passage B. This is a candidate.

(E) The lack of a completely satisfactory definition of "minority" is a greater problem for them than for most.

This answer choice includes a detail that is stated in the second paragraph of Passage A. This is a loser.

As (D) is the only candidate, it is the correct answer choice.

39. **Correct Answer (E).** *Prep Test 56, Section 4, Passage 3, Question 19.*

The authors' views regarding the status of the Roma can most accurately be described in which one of the following ways?

This is a C Viewpoint question. The prompt does not include a topic from a specific part of the passage as the status of the Roma is discussed throughout both passages. Therefore, we cannot anticipate a correct answer choice and must proceed directly to eliminating answer choices.

(A) The author of Passage A, but not the author of Passage B, disapproves of the latitude that international law allows individual states in determining their relations to nomadic Roma populations.

This answer choice includes contradictory information. Passage B criticizes as being arbitrary the right of states to determine whether or not to classify the Roma as citizens. Passage A does not address this issue. This is a loser.

(B) The author of Passage B, but not the author of Passage A, considers the problems of the Roma to be a noteworthy example of how international law can be ineffective.

This answer choice includes contradictory information. Passage A strongly indicates that international law is ineffective because the problems the Roma face stem from the lack of a universally accepted definition of *national minority* in international law. This is a loser.

(C) The author of Passage B, but not the author of Passage A, considers the Roma to be a paradigmatic example of a people who do not constitute a nation.

This answer choice includes irrelevant information. Neither passage addresses the issue of whether or not the Roma constitute or should constitute a nation. This is a loser as well.

(D) Both authors would prefer that the political issues involving the Roma be resolved on a case-by-case basis within each individual country rather than through international law.

This answer choice also includes irrelevant information. Neither passage discusses resolving issues on a case-by-case basis within individual countries. This is a loser.

(E) Both authors consider the problems that the Roma face in relation to international law to be anomalous and special.

This seems to be an inference that is compatible with each author's viewpoint. The second paragraph of Passage A clearly states that the lack of definitions is particularly problematic for the Roma compared to other minority groups. The second paragraph of Passage B states that the Roma meet all of the objective standards for minority status and, therefore, should be considered a minority in all major European states. The author obviously considers the fact that this has not happened to be unusual. This is the correct answer choice.

40. Correct Answer (A). *Prep Test 56, Section 4, Passage 3, Question 20.*

> **The relationship between which one of the following pairs of documents is most analogous to the relationship between passage A and passage B?**

This is a C Application question. The prompt asks for a relationship between a pair of documents that is analogous to the relationship between Passage A and Passage B. Given that the question is asking about the relationship between the two passages in general and the answer choices are in the form of titles, we should probably focus on the main points. These can be reframed in general terms as follows: Passage A claims that an unclear set of criteria presents problems for a group (Roma) in terms of being included in a category (national minority). Passage B claims that a group (Roma) meets the requirements to be included in a category (minority). We should anticipate a correct answer choice that describes a comparable situation.

> **(A) "The Lack of Clear-Cut Criteria for Classifying Jobs as Technical Causes Problems for Welders" and "A Point-by-Point Argument That Welding Fulfills the Union's Criteria for Classification of Jobs as 'Technical'"**

This matches our anticipated answer choice. The first title states that the lack of clear criteria causes problems for including a group (welders) in a classification (technical), while the second states that the group (welders) meets the requirements to be included in the classification (technical). This is a candidate.

> **(B) "Why the Current Criteria for Professional Competence in Welding Have Not Been Effectively Applied" and "A Review of the Essential Elements of Any Formal Statement of Professional Standards"**

This answer choice includes irrelevant and incomplete information. Passage A does not discuss whether or not a set of criteria is applied effectively, and Passage B does more than just review a set of criteria—it argues that the criteria have been met. This is a loser.

> **(C) "The Need for a Revised Definition of the Concept of Welding in Relation to Other Technical Jobs" and "An Enumeration and Description of the Essential Job Duties Usually Carried Out by Union Welders"**

This answer choice includes irrelevant and incomplete information. Passage A does not compare one classification to another, and Passage B not only outlines a set of criteria but also argues that a group has met the criteria. This is another loser.

> **(D) "The Lack of Competent Welders in Our Company Can Be Attributed to a General Disregard for Professional and Technical Staff Recruitment" and "A Discussion of the Factors That Companies Should Consider in Recruiting Employees"**

This answer choice includes irrelevant information. Passage A does not discuss the inadequacies of a group, and Passage B does not argue in favor of a set of criteria—it states that a group has met the existing set of criteria. This is also a loser.

> **(E) "The Conceptual Links Between Professionalism and Technical Expertise" and "A Refutation of the Union's Position Regarding Which Types of Jobs Should Be Classified as Neither Professional nor Technical"**

This answer choice includes irrelevant information as well. Neither Passage A nor Passage B discusses two separate classifications. This is also a loser.

As (A) is the only candidate, it is the correct answer choice.

41. **Correct Answer (B).** *Prep Test 56, Section 4, Passage 3, Question 21.*

   Which one of the following is a principle that can be most reasonably considered to underlie the reasoning in both of the passages?

This is a C Principle question. As the prompt does not reference a viewpoint or topic from a specific part of either passage, it would be very difficult and time-consuming to come up with a general principle that underlies the arguments of two passages. Therefore, we should proceed to eliminating answer choices. We should look for a general principle that is compatible with the circumstances and outcomes of both authors' arguments.

   (A) A definition that is vaguely formulated cannot serve as the basis for the provisions contained in a document of international law.

This answer choice includes irrelevant information. The issue of vague definitions is discussed in Passage A but not in Passage B. This is a loser.

   (B) A minority group's not being officially recognized as such by the government that has jurisdiction over it can be detrimental to the group's interests.

This seems like a principle that underlies the arguments in both passages. The first paragraph of Passage A makes it clear that there is not a clear set of criteria to classify a group as a minority. The second paragraph clearly states that this is particularly problematic to the Roma. The first paragraph of Passage B claims that states have the arbitrary right to deny the Roma citizenship (and, thus, minority status) and that this is unfair. This is a candidate.

   (C) Provisions in international law that apply only to minority groups should not be considered valid.

This answer choice includes irrelevant information. Neither passage claims that provisions in international law that apply only to minority groups should be considered invalid. This is a loser.

   (D) Governments should recognize the legal and court systems used by minority populations within their jurisdictions.

This answer choice also includes irrelevant information. Passage A does not discuss the legal and court systems used by minority populations, and Passage B only mentions these in passing. This is a loser as well. This is a loser as well.

   (E) A group that often moves back and forth across a boundary between two countries can be legitimately considered citizens of both countries.

This answer choice includes irrelevant information as well. Neither passage argues that nomadic groups should be given citizenship in two countries. This is a loser.

As (B) is the only candidate, it is the correct answer choice.

HACKERS
LSAT *Reading Comprehension*

Chapter 9

Pacing and Test Day Preparedness

Chapter 9: Pacing and Test Day Preparedness

Pacing and Test Day Preparedness

Pacing Strategy

An RC section may contain between 26 and 28 questions, although 27 questions are the most common. Unlike the Logical Reasoning or Analytical Reasoning sections, the RC section does not always escalate in difficulty. For example, the first passage and question set may be the most difficult of the section or the easiest. Likewise, there is no progression in difficulty within a question set.

You will have only 35 minutes to complete the RC section, and most of the time should be used to answer questions. This means that you must read and analyze the passages very quickly. Although detailed passage analyses have been provided throughout this book for instructional purposes, extensive note-taking will not be possible during an exam session due to time constraints. To complete all four passages and question sets, you will need to take concise notes and keep track of much of the key passage information (main point, paragraph function, etc.) in your head.

Skipping Passages and Question Sets

The first step in developing a pacing strategy is to determine the number of passages and question sets you will attempt to complete. Some test-takers find it very difficult to finish all four passages and question sets in the allotted time. As a result, they sacrifice accuracy for speed in order to read each passage and answer every question. If this applies to you, a better strategy may be to use the bulk of the allotted time to carefully read two or three passages and answer the accompanying questions. Then, quickly guess the correct answer choices for the remaining questions. This approach will likely result in a higher score than if you rush through the entire section.

If you apply this strategy, you will need to determine which passages and question sets to focus on when you begin the RC section. As mentioned previously, there is no regular progression in difficulty level within an RC section. Therefore, you should not automatically choose the first two or three passages. Instead, select the passages that are accompanied by the most questions. This will ensure that you have the opportunity to get the highest number of points for the passages that you take the time to read and analyze. You should also take your own personal preferences into consideration. For example, if there is a particular topic area that you have difficulties with, you may want to avoid passages related to it.

Skipping Individual Questions

In general, you should avoid skipping individual questions unless it is absolutely necessary. This is because you will have already read and analyzed the corresponding passage, which represents a significant time investment. However, if you find yourself spending too much time on a question and are unable to pick the correct answer choice, simply guess and move on. Remember, you have a very tight time budget for each question—additional time spent on one question means less time for the others.

Selecting a Pacing Strategy

Whether you decide to focus on two, three, or four passages, time management will be a critical factor with regard to your score. This is why having a pacing strategy is important. As you work through the section, you need to have a clear idea of how much time you have for each passage and question. You should also be able to keep track of whether you are running behind or ahead of schedule as you progress. If you complete a passage and question set more quickly than anticipated, then you know that you will have some extra time if you run into a difficult passage or question. If you take longer than planned, then you will have to make up time later in the section.

The following are some pacing strategies that are effective for different types of test-takers. The strategy you choose should match your ability, and you should be flexible when applying it.

Pacing Strategy 1	
Pacing	Who should follow this strategy?
1. Complete two passages and question sets in 34 minutes, allocating 17 minutes for each. 2. Guess the correct answer choices for the remaining questions in 1 minute.	This pacing strategy is intended for test-takers who are only able to complete two passages and question sets in an RC section during a practice exam.

Pacing Strategy 2	
Pacing	Who should follow this strategy?
1. Complete three passages and question sets in 34 minutes and 30 seconds, allocating 11 minutes and 30 seconds for each. 2. Guess the correct answer choices for the remaining questions in 30 seconds.	This pacing strategy is intended for test-takers who are only able to complete three passages and question sets in an RC section during a practice exam.

Pacing Strategy 3	
Pacing	Who should follow this strategy?
Complete four passages and question sets in 35 minutes allocating 8 minutes and 45 seconds for each.	This pacing strategy is intended for students who can complete all four passages and question sets with a moderate-to-high level of accuracy during a practice exam.

The below table shows the approximate number of incorrect answers permitted for each score range. Note that this table assumes that your score on the RC section is similar to your scores on the other sections of the test.

Target Score	Number of Incorrect Answers
140	15–17 on RC section
145	13–15 on RC section
150	10–12 on RC section
155	8–9 on RC section
160	6–7 on RC section
165	4–5 on RC section
170	2–3 on RC section
175	1–2 on RC section
180	0–1 on RC section

Leading up to Test Day

A Month before the Test

By this point, you should have worked your way through most of the book and become aware of which question types you have the most difficulty with. The bulk of your remaining time before the test should be focused on improving in your weakest areas. Review the sections of this book that deal with the question types you are most likely to answer incorrectly. Keep in mind, though, that certain question types appear more frequently than others. You should pay attention to the ones you will encounter most often. For example, if you are equally weak at Main Point and Evaluation questions, the time you dedicate toward practicing these question types and skills should be prioritized in that respective order, as Main Point questions are much more common than Evaluation questions.

During this period, you should also attempt to complete at least one timed practice exam. The practice test in the next chapter is a great place to start, and the LSAC offers a free practice test on its website. Attempting a timed practice test is important because it helps you prepare mentally for the challenges of completing the LSAT in the actual test environment. It also gives you a chance to test the effectiveness of your chosen practice strategy. You should also become familiar with the user interface used in the Digital LSAT. Again, the LSAC provides free access to practice tests in the digital format on its website. The more practice exams you attempt, the better prepared you'll be for the challenges of test day.

The Day before the Test

A day before the exam, you should wake up as early as possible. This is to make it less likely that you will have trouble sleeping that night due to test anxiety.

If you take the test at a test center, print out your admission ticket and make sure you have a one-gallon (or smaller) clear plastic bag filled with the items needed during test day (see the Test Day Checklist later in this chapter). Note that you are not permitted to bring a bag that is larger or made out of non-transparent material into the testing center. You should also do everything possible to ensure that you are not stressed on the day of the exam. For example, arrange transportation to the testing center, and ensure that you are familiar with the route. Also, check your admission ticket for information about the center's policy regarding cell phones.

Try not to study the day before the exam. You are unlikely to acquire any new information that will affect your exam performance at this point, and going over the material unnecessarily will likely stress you out. Instead, try to relax as much as possible.

The Day of the Test

It is best not to add anything new to your routine that may affect your test performance. For example, drinking coffee in the morning may keep you alert throughout the exam, but if you are not used to caffeine, you may feel uncomfortably jittery.

It may be helpful to read through a passage and corresponding question set just before the exam to warm up. If you choose to do this, remember that you are not permitted to bring in prep materials into the testing space itself.

For all test-takers, it is important that your appearance on the day of the test matches the photo you submitted to the LSAC. This is especially important for test-takers who have grown facial hair (or have shaved their facial hair) and thus look different from the photo in the admission ticket.

Lastly, dress in layers. The weather may be too cold (or too warm), and you want to make sure that you will not be uncomfortable during the exam.

Test Day Checklist

If you take the LSAT remotely, make sure you have the following items:

> At the test center, you will be provided with a pen and scratch paper to use during the test.

1. Valid identification
2. 5 sheets of scratch paper and writing tools (pencil, pen, highlighter, eraser, etc.)
3. Tissues (if needed)
4. Ear plugs (if needed)
5. Medication and other medical items (if needed)

If you take the LSAT at a test center, bring the following items in a one-gallon clear plastic bag:

1. LSAT admission ticket
2. Photo identification
3. Tissues (if needed)
4. Medication or feminine hygiene products (if needed)
5. Beverage in plastic container or juice box for breaks only (if needed)
6. Snacks for breaks only (if needed)

Please check your admission ticket for a comprehensive list of allowed and prohibited items as this list is occasionally updated.

HACKERS
LSAT *Reading Comprehension*

Chapter 10

Practice Test

Practice Test

Time—35 minutes

27 Questions

Directions: Each set of questions in this section is based on a single passage or a pair of passages. The questions are to be answered on the basis of what is stated or implied in the passage or pair of passages. For some of the questions, more than one of the choices could conceivably answer the question. However, you are to choose the best answer; that is, response that most accurately and completely answers the question, and mark that response on your answer sheet.

Traditional sources of evidence about ancient history are archaeological remains and surviving texts. Those investigating the crafts practiced by women in ancient times, however, often derive little information
(5) from these sources, and the archaeological record is particularly unavailing for the study of ancient textile production, as researchers are thwarted by the perishable nature of cloth. What shreds persisted through millennia were, until recently, often discarded
(10) by excavators as useless, as were loom weights, which appeared to be nothing more than blobs of clay. Ancient texts, meanwhile, rarely mention the creation of textiles; moreover, those references that do exist use archaic, unrevealing terminology. Yet despite these
(15) obstacles, researchers have learned a great deal about ancient textiles and those who made them, and also about how to piece together a whole picture from many disparate sources of evidence.

Technological advances in the analysis of
(20) archaeological remains provide much more information than was previously available, especially about minute remains. Successful modern methods include radiocarbon dating, infrared photography for seeing through dirt without removing it, isotope
(25) "fingerprinting" for tracing sources of raw materials, and thin-layer chromatography for analyzing dyes. As if in preparation for such advances, the field of archaeology has also undergone an important philosophical revolution in the past century. Once little
(30) more than a self-serving quest for artifacts to stock museums and private collections, the field has transformed itself into a scientific pursuit of knowledge about past cultures. As part of this process, archaeologists adopted the fundamental precept of
(35) preserving all objects, even those that have no immediately discernible value. Thus in the 1970s two researchers found the oldest known complete garment, a 5,000-year-old linen shirt, among a tumbled heap of dirty linens that had been preserved as part of the well-
(40) known Petrie collection decades before anyone began to study the history of textiles.

The history of textiles and of the craftswomen who produced them has also advanced on a different front: recreating the actual production of cloth.
(45) Reconstructing and implementing ancient production methods provides a valuable way of generating and checking hypotheses. For example, these techniques made it possible to confirm that the excavated pieces of clay once considered useless in fact functioned as loom
(50) weights. Similarly, scholars have until recently been obliged to speculate as to which one of two statues of Athena, one large and one small, was adorned with a dress created by a group of Athenian women for a festival, as described in surviving texts. Because
(55) records show that it took nine months to produce the dress, scholars assumed it must have adorned the large statue. But by investigating the methods of production and the size of the looms used, researchers have ascertained that in fact a dress for the small statue
(60) would have taken nine months to produce.

1. Which one of the following most accurately expresses the main point of the passage?

(A) Archaeology is an expanding discipline that has transformed itself in response both to scientific advances and to changing cultural demands such as a recently increasing interest in women's history.

(B) A diversity of new approaches to the study of ancient textiles has enabled researchers to infer much about the history of textiles and their creators in the ancient world from the scant evidence that remains.

(C) Despite many obstacles, research into the textile production methods used by women in the ancient world has advanced over the past century to the point that archaeologists can now replicate ancient equipment and production techniques.

(D) Research into the history of textiles has spurred sweeping changes in the field of archaeology, from the application of advanced technology to the revaluation of ancient artifacts that were once deemed useless.

(E) Though researchers have verified certain theories about the history of textiles by using technological developments such as radiocarbon dating, most significant findings in this field have grown out of the reconstruction of ancient production techniques.

2. The author's attitude concerning the history of ancient textile production can most accurately be described as

(A) skeptical regarding the validity of some of the new hypotheses proposed by researchers
(B) doubtful that any additional useful knowledge can be generated given the nature of the evidence available
(C) impatient about the pace of research in light of the resources available
(D) optimistic that recent scholarly advances will attract increasing numbers of researchers
(E) satisfied that considerable progress is being made in this field

3. The passage indicates that the re-creation of ancient techniques was used in which one of the following?

(A) investigating the meanings of certain previously unintelligible technical terms in ancient texts
(B) tracing the sources of raw materials used in the production of certain fabrics
(C) constructing certain public museum displays concerning cloth-making
(D) verifying that a particular 5,000-year-old cloth was indeed a shirt
(E) exploring the issue of which of two statues of Athena was clothed with a particular garment

4. The author intends the term "traditional sources" (line 1) to exclude which one of the following?

(A) ancient clay objects that cannot be identified as pieces of pottery by the researchers who unearth them
(B) historically significant pieces of cloth discovered in the course of an excavation
(C) the oldest known complete garment, which was found among other pieces of cloth in a collection
(D) re-creations of looms from which inferences about ancient weaving techniques can be made
(E) ancient accounts of the adornment of a statue of Athena with a dress made by Athenian women

5. The passage as a whole functions primarily as

(A) a defense of the controversial methods adopted by certain researchers in a particular discipline
(B) a set of recommendations to guide future activities in a particular field of inquiry
(C) an account of how a particular branch of research has successfully coped with certain difficulties
(D) a rejection of some commonly held views about the methodologies of a certain discipline
(E) a summary of the hypotheses advanced by researchers who have used innovative methods of investigation

6. According to the passage, which one of the following was an element in the transformation of archaeology in the past century?

(A) an increased interest in the crafts practiced in the ancient world
(B) some archaeologists' adoption of textile conservation experts' preservation techniques
(C) innovative methods of restoring damaged artifacts
(D) the discovery of the oldest known complete garment
(E) archaeologists' policy of not discarding ancient objects that have no readily identifiable value

7. Which one of the following most accurately describes the function of the first paragraph in relation to the rest of the passage?

(A) A particularly difficult archaeological problem is described in order to underscore the significance of new methods used to resolve that problem, which are described in the following paragraphs.
(B) A previously neglected body of archaeological evidence is described in order to cast doubt on received views regarding ancient cultures developed from conventional sources of evidence, as described in the following paragraphs.
(C) The fruitfulness of new technologically based methods of analysis is described in order to support the subsequent argument that apparently insignificant archaeological remains ought to be preserved for possible future research.
(D) The findings of recent archaeological research are outlined as the foundation for a claim advanced in the following paragraphs that the role of women in ancient cultures has been underestimated by archaeologists.
(E) A recently developed branch of archaeological research is described as evidence for the subsequent argument that other, more established branches of archaeology should take advantage of new technologies in their research.

GO ON TO THE NEXT PAGE.

This passage was adapted from articles published in the 1990s.

The success that Nigerian-born computer scientist Philip Emeagwali (b. 1954) has had in designing computers that solve real-world problems has been fueled by his willingness to reach beyond established
(5) paradigms and draw inspiration for his designs from nature. In the 1980s, Emeagwali achieved breakthroughs in the design of parallel computer systems. Whereas single computers work sequentially, making one calculation at a time, computers
(10) connected in parallel can process calculations simultaneously. In 1989, Emeagwali pioneered the use of massively parallel computers that used a network of thousands of smaller computers to solve what is considered one of the most computationally difficult
(15) problems: predicting the flow of oil through the subterranean geologic formations that make up oil fields. Until that time, supercomputers had been used for oil field calculations, but because these supercomputers worked sequentially, they were too
(20) slow and inefficient to accurately predict such extremely complex movements.

To model oil field flow using a computer requires the simulation of the distribution of the oil at tens of thousands of locations throughout the field. At each
(25) location, hundreds of simultaneous calculations must be made at regular time intervals relating to such variables as temperature, direction of oil flow, viscosity, and pressure, as well as geologic properties of the basin holding the oil. In order to solve this
(30) problem, Emeagwali designed a massively parallel computer by using the Internet to connect to more than 65,000 smaller computers. One of the great difficulties of parallel computing is dividing up the tasks among the separate smaller computers so that
(35) they do not interfere with each other, and it was here that Emeagwali turned to natural processes for ideas, noting that tree species that survive today are those that, over the course of hundreds of millions of years, have developed branching patterns that have
(40) maximized the amount of sunlight gathered and the quantity of water and sap delivered. Emeagwali demonstrated that, for modeling certain phenomena such as subterranean oil flow, a network design based on the mathematical principle that underlies the
(45) branching structures of trees will enable a massively parallel computer to gather and broadcast the largest quantity of messages to its processing points in the shortest time.

In 1996 Emeagwali had another breakthrough
(50) when he presented the design for a massively parallel computer that he claims will be powerful enough to predict global weather patterns a century in advance. The computer's design is based on the geometry of bees' honeycombs, which use an extremely efficient
(55) three-dimensional spacing. Emeagwali believes that computer scientists in the future will increasingly look to nature for elegant solutions to complex technical problems. This paradigm shift, he asserts, will enable us to better understand the systems
(60) evolved by nature and, thereby, to facilitate the evolution of human technology.

8. Which one of the following most accurately expresses the main point of the passage?

(A) Emeagwali's establishment of new computational paradigms has enabled parallel computer systems to solve a wide array of real-world problems that supercomputers cannot solve.

(B) Emeagwali has shown that scientists' allegiance to established paradigms has until now prevented the solution of many real-world computational problems that could otherwise have been solved with little difficulty.

(C) Emeagwali's discovery of the basic mathematical principles underlying natural systems has led to a growing use of parallel computer systems to solve complex real-world computational problems.

(D) Emeagwali has designed parallel computer systems that are modeled on natural systems and that are aimed at solving real-world computational problems that would be difficult to solve with more traditional designs.

(E) The paradigm shift initiated by Emeagwali's computer designs has made it more likely that scientists will in the future look to systems evolved by nature to facilitate the evolution of human technology.

9. According to the passage, which one of the following is true?

(A) Emeagwali's breakthroughs in computer design have begun to make computers that work sequentially obsolete.

(B) Emeagwali's first breakthrough in computer design came in response to a request by an oil company.

(C) Emeagwali was the first to use a massively parallel computer to predict the flow of oil in oil fields.

(D) Emeagwali was the first computer scientist to use nature as a model for human technology.

(E) Emeagwali was the first to apply parallel processing to solving real-world problems.

10. The passage most strongly suggests that Emeagwali holds which one of the following views?

(A) Some natural systems have arrived at efficient solutions to problems that are analogous in significant ways to technical problems faced by computer scientists.
(B) Global weather is likely too complicated to be accurately predictable more than a few decades in advance.
(C) Most computer designs will in the future be inspired by natural systems.
(D) Massively parallel computers will eventually be practical enough to warrant their use even in relatively mundane computing tasks.
(E) The mathematical structure of branching trees is useful primarily for designing computer systems to predict the flow of oil through oil fields.

11. Which one of the following most accurately describes the function of the first two sentences of the second paragraph?

(A) They provide an example of an established paradigm that Emeagwali's work has challenged.
(B) They help explain why supercomputers are unable to accurately predict the movements of oil through underground geologic formations.
(C) They provide examples of a network design based on the mathematical principles underlying the branching structures of trees.
(D) They describe a mathematical model that Emeagwali used in order to understand a natural system.
(E) They provide specific examples of a paradigm shift that will help scientists understand certain systems evolved by nature.

12. Which one of the following, if true, would provide the most support for Emeagwali's prediction mentioned in lines 55–58?

(A) Until recently, computer scientists have had very limited awareness of many of the mathematical principles that have been shown to underlie a wide variety of natural processes.
(B) Some of the variables affecting global weather patterns have yet to be discovered by scientists who study these patterns.
(C) Computer designs for the prediction of natural phenomena tend to be more successful when those phenomena are not affected by human activities.
(D) Some of the mathematical principles underlying Emeagwali's model of oil field flow also underlie his designs for other massively parallel computer systems.
(E) Underlying the designs for many traditional technologies are mathematical principles of which the designers of those technologies were not explicitly aware.

13. It can be inferred from the passage that one of the reasons massively parallel computers had not been used to model oil field flow prior to 1989 is that

(A) supercomputers are sufficiently powerful to handle most computational problems, including most problems arising from oil production
(B) the possibility of using a network of smaller computers to solve computationally difficult problems had not yet been considered
(C) the general public was not yet aware of the existence or vast capabilities of the Internet
(D) oil companies had not yet perceived the need for modeling the flow of oil in subterranean fields
(E) smaller computers can interfere with one another when they are connected together in parallel to solve a computationally difficult problem

GO ON TO THE NEXT PAGE.

Proponents of the tangible-object theory of copyright argue that copyright and similar intellectual-property rights can be explained as logical extensions of the right to own concrete, tangible objects. This
(5) view depends on the claim that every copyrightable work can be manifested in some physical form, such as a manuscript or a videotape. It also accepts the premise that ownership of an object confers a number of rights on the owner, who may essentially do whatever he or
(10) she pleases with the object to the extent that this does not violate other people's rights. One may, for example, hide or display the object, copy it, or destroy it. One may also transfer ownership of it to another.

In creating a new and original object from
(15) materials that one owns, one becomes the owner of that object and thereby acquires all of the rights that ownership entails. But if the owner transfers ownership of the object, the full complement of rights is not necessarily transferred to the new owner; instead, the
(20) original owner may retain one or more of these rights. This notion of retained rights is common in many areas of law; for example, the seller of a piece of land may retain certain rights to the land in the form of easements or building restrictions. Applying the notion
(25) of retained rights to the domain of intellectual property, theorists argue that copyrighting a work secures official recognition of one's intention to retain certain rights to that work. Among the rights typically retained by the original producer of an object such as a literary
(30) manuscript or a musical score would be the right to copy the object for profit and the right to use it as a guide for the production of similar or analogous things—for example, a public performance of a musical score.
(35) According to proponents of the tangible-object theory, its chief advantage is that it justifies intellectual property rights without recourse to the widely accepted but problematic supposition that one can own abstract, intangible things such as ideas. But while this account
(40) seems plausible for copyrightable entities that do, in fact, have enduring tangible forms, it cannot accommodate the standard assumption that such evanescent things as live broadcasts of sporting events can be copyrighted. More importantly, it does not
(45) acknowledge that in many cases the work of conceiving ideas is more crucial and more valuable than that of putting them into tangible form. Suppose that a poet dictates a new poem to a friend, who writes it down on paper that the friend has supplied. The
(50) creator of the tangible object in this case is not the poet but the friend, and there would seem to be no ground for the poet's claiming copyright unless the poet can be said to already own the ideas expressed in the work.

14. Which one of the following most accurately expresses the main point of the passage?

(A) Copyright and other intellectual-property rights can be explained as logical extensions of the right to own concrete objects.
(B) Attempts to explain copyright and similar intellectual-property rights purely in terms of rights to ownership of physical objects are ultimately misguided.
(C) Copyrighting a work amounts to securing official recognition of one's intention to retain certain rights to that work.
(D) Explanations of copyright and other intellectual-property rights in terms of rights to ownership of tangible objects fail to consider the argument that ideas should be allowed to circulate freely.
(E) Under the tangible-object theory of intellectual property, rights of ownership are straightforwardly applicable to both ideas and physical objects.

15. According to the passage, the theory that copyright and other intellectual-property rights can be construed as logical extensions of the right to own concrete, tangible objects depends on the claim that

(A) any work entitled to intellectual-property protection can be expressed in physical form
(B) only the original creator of an intellectual work can hold the copyright for that work
(C) the work of putting ideas into tangible form is more crucial and more valuable than the work of conceiving those ideas
(D) in a few cases, it is necessary to recognize the right to own abstract, intangible things
(E) the owner of an item of intellectual property may legally destroy it

16. The passage most directly answers which one of the following questions?

(A) Do proponents of the tangible-object theory of intellectual property advocate any changes in existing laws relating to copyright?
(B) Do proponents of the tangible-object theory of intellectual property hold that ownership of anything besides real estate can involve retained rights?
(C) Has the tangible-object theory of intellectual property influenced the ways in which copyright cases or other cases involving issues of intellectual property are decided in the courts?
(D) Does existing copyright law provide protection against unauthorized copying of manuscripts and musical scores in cases in which their creators have not officially applied for copyright protection?
(E) Are there standard procedures governing the transfer of intellectual property that are common to most legal systems?

17. Suppose an inventor describes an innovative idea for an invention to an engineer, who volunteers to draft specifications for a prototype and then produces the prototype using the engineer's own materials. Which one of the following statements would apply to this case under the tangible-object theory of intellectual property, as the author describes that theory?

(A) Only the engineer is entitled to claim the invention as intellectual property.

(B) Only the inventor is entitled to claim the invention as intellectual property.

(C) The inventor and the engineer are equally entitled to claim the invention as intellectual property.

(D) The engineer is entitled to claim the invention as intellectual property, but only if the inventor retains the right to all profits generated by the invention.

(E) The inventor is entitled to claim the invention as intellectual property, but only if the engineer retains the right to all profits generated by the invention.

18. Legal theorists supporting the tangible-object theory of intellectual property are most likely to believe which one of the following?

(A) A literary work cannot receive copyright protection unless it exists in an edition produced by an established publisher.

(B) Most legal systems explicitly rely on the tangible-object theory of intellectual property in order to avoid asserting that one can own abstract things.

(C) Copyright protects the right to copy for profit, but not the right to copy for other reasons.

(D) Some works deserving of copyright protection simply cannot be manifested as concrete, tangible objects.

(E) To afford patent protection for inventions, the law need not invoke the notion of inventors' ownership of abstract ideas.

19. The passage provides the most support for inferring which one of the following statements?

(A) In most transactions involving the transfer of non-intellectual property, at least some rights of ownership are retained by the seller.

(B) The notion of retained rights of ownership is currently applied to only those areas of law that do not involve intellectual property.

(C) The idea that ownership of the right to copy an item for profit can be transferred is compatible with a tangible-object theory of intellectual property.

(D) Ownership of intellectual property is sufficiently protected by the provisions that, under many legal systems, apply to ownership of material things such as land.

(E) Protection of computer programs under intellectual-property law is justifiable only if the programs are likely to be used as a guide for the production of similar or analogous programs.

20. It can be inferred that the author of the passage is most likely to believe which one of the following?

(A) Theorists who suggest that the notion of retained rights is applicable to intellectual property do not fully understand what it means to transfer ownership of property.

(B) If a work does not exist in a concrete, tangible form, there is no valid theoretical basis for claiming that it should have copyright protection.

(C) Under existing statutes, creators of original tangible works that have intellectual or artistic significance generally do not have the legal right to own the abstract ideas embodied in those works.

(D) An adequate theoretical justification of copyright would likely presuppose that a work's creator originally owns the ideas embodied in that work.

(E) It is common, but incorrect, to assume that such evanescent things as live broadcasts of sporting events can be copyrighted.

GO ON TO THE NEXT PAGE.

Passage A

In music, a certain complexity of sounds can be expected to have a positive effect on the listener. A single, pure tone is not that interesting to explore; a measure of intricacy is required to excite human
(5) curiosity. Sounds that are too complex or disorganized, however, tend to be overwhelming. We prefer some sort of coherence, a principle that connects the various sounds and makes them comprehensible.

In this respect, music is like human language.
(10) Single sounds are in most cases not sufficient to convey meaning in speech, whereas when put together in a sequence they form words and sentences. Likewise, if the tones in music are not perceived to be tied together sequentially or rhythmically—for
(15) example, in what is commonly called melody— listeners are less likely to feel any emotional connection or to show appreciation.

Certain music can also have a relaxing effect. The fact that such music tends to be continuous and
(20) rhythmical suggests a possible explanation for this effect. In a natural environment, danger tends to be accompanied by sudden, unexpected sounds. Thus, a background of constant noise suggests peaceful conditions; discontinuous sounds demand more
(25) attention. Even soft discontinuous sounds that we consciously realize do not signal danger can be disturbing—for example, the erratic dripping of a leaky tap. A continuous sound, particularly one that is judged to be safe, relaxes the brain.

Passage B

(30) There are certain elements within music, such as a change of melodic line or rhythm, that create expectations about the future development of the music. The expectation the listener has about the further course of musical events is a key determinant
(35) for the experience of "musical emotions." Music creates expectations that, if not immediately satisfied, create tension. Emotion is experienced in relation to the buildup and release of tension. The more elaborate the buildup of tension, the more intense the emotions
(40) that will be experienced. When resolution occurs, relaxation follows.

The interruption of the expected musical course, depending on one's personal involvement, causes the search for an explanation. This results from a
(45) "mismatch" between one's musical expectation and the actual course of the music. Negative emotions will be the result of an extreme mismatch between expectations and experience. Positive emotions result if the converse happens.
(50) When we listen to music, we take into account factors such as the complexity and novelty of the music. The degree to which the music sounds familiar determines whether the music is experienced as pleasurable or uncomfortable. The pleasure
(55) experienced is minimal when the music is entirely new to the listener, increases with increasing familiarity, and decreases again when the music is totally known. Musical preference is based on one's desire to maintain a constant level of certain preferable
(60) emotions. As such, a trained listener will have a

greater preference for complex melodies than will a naive listener, as the threshold for experiencing emotion is higher.

21. Which one of the following concepts is linked to positive musical experiences in both passages?

   (A) continuous sound
   (B) tension
   (C) language
   (D) improvisation
   (E) complexity

22. The passages most strongly suggest that both are targeting an audience that is interested in which one of the following?

   (A) the theoretical underpinnings of how music is composed
   (B) the nature of the conceptual difference between music and discontinuous sound
   (C) the impact music can have on human emotional states
   (D) the most effective techniques for teaching novices to appreciate complex music
   (E) the influence music has had on the development of spoken language

23. Which one of the following describes a preference that is most analogous to the preference mentioned in the first paragraph of Passage A?

   (A) the preference of some people for falling asleep to white noise, such as the sound of an electric fan
   (B) the preference of many moviegoers for movies with plots that are clear and easy to follow
   (C) the preference of many diners for restaurants that serve large portions
   (D) the preference of many young listeners for fast music over slower music
   (E) the preference of most children for sweet foods over bitter foods

24. Which one of the following most accurately expresses the main point of Passage B?

(A) The type of musical emotion experienced by a listener is determined by the level to which the listener's expectations are satisfied.
(B) Trained listeners are more able to consciously manipulate their own emotional experiences of complex music than are naive listeners.
(C) If the development of a piece of music is greatly at odds with the listener's musical expectations, then the listener will experience negative emotions.
(D) Listeners can learn to appreciate changes in melodic line and other musical complexities.
(E) Music that is experienced by listeners as relaxing usually produces a buildup and release of tension in those listeners.

25. Which one of the following most undermines the explanation provided in Passage A for the relaxing effect that some music has on listeners?

(A) The musical traditions of different cultures vary greatly in terms of the complexity of the rhythms they employ.
(B) The rhythmic structure of a language is determined in part by the pattern of stressed syllables in the words and sentences of the language.
(C) Many people find the steady and rhythmic sound of a rocking chair to be very unnerving.
(D) The sudden interruption of the expected development of a melody tends to interfere with listeners' perception of the melody as coherent.
(E) Some of the most admired contemporary composers write music that is notably simpler than is most of the music written in previous centuries.

26. Which one of the following would be most appropriate as a title for each of the passages?

(A) "The Biological Underpinnings of Musical Emotions"
(B) "The Psychology of Listener Response to Music"
(C) "How Music Differs from Other Art Forms"
(D) "Cultural Patterns in Listeners' Responses to Music"
(E) "How Composers Convey Meaning Through Music"

27. It can be inferred that both authors would be likely to agree with which one of the following statements?

(A) The more complex a piece of music, the more it is likely to be enjoyed by most listeners.
(B) More knowledgeable listeners tend to prefer music that is discontinuous and unpredictable.
(C) The capacity of music to elicit strong emotional responses from listeners is the central determinant of its artistic value.
(D) Music that lacks a predictable course is unlikely to cause a listener to feel relaxed.
(E) Music that changes from soft to loud is perceived as disturbing and unpleasant by most listeners.

S T O P

IF YOU FINISH BEFORE TIME IS CALLED, YOU MAY CHECK YOUR WORK ON THIS
SECTION ONLY. DO NOT WORK ON ANY OTHER SECTION IN THE TEST.

1	B	Main Point
2	E	Attitude
3	E	Detail
4	D	Meaning
5	C	Purpose
6	E	Detail
7	A	Function of a Paragraph
8	D	Main Point
9	C	Existence
10	A	Viewpoint
11	B	Function of a Statement
12	A	Strengthen
13	E	Implication
14	B	Main Point

15	A	Detail
16	B	Evaluation
17	A	Implication
18	E	Viewpoint
19	C	Implication
20	D	Viewpoint
21	E	Comparative (Detail)
22	C	Comparative (Implication)
23	B	Comparative (Application)
24	A	Comparative (Main Point)
25	C	Comparative (Weaken)
26	B	Comparative (Main Point)
27	D	Agree/Disagree

Question Families	Question Types	Number of Incorrect Questions
Synthesis	Main Point	
	Structure	
	Purpose	
	Function of a Paragraph	
	Function of a Statement	
Information	Detail	
	Existence	
	Meaning	
Inference	Implication	
	Viewpoint	
	Attitude	
	Principle	
Process	Application	
	Strengthen	
	Weaken	
	Evaluation	
	Extension	
Comparative Reading	Relationship	
	Agree/Disagree	
	Comparative	

For Questions 1–7

Traditional sources of evidence about ancient history are archaeological remains and surviving texts. Those investigating the crafts practiced by women in ancient times, <u>however</u>, often derive little information

(5) from these sources, and the archaeological record is particularly unavailing for the study of ancient textile production, as researchers are thwarted by the perishable nature of cloth. What shreds persisted through millennia were, until recently, often discarded

(10) by excavators as useless, as were loom weights, which appeared to be nothing more than blobs of clay. Ancient texts, meanwhile, rarely mention the creation of textiles; moreover, those references that do exist use archaic, unrevealing terminology. <u>Yet despite these</u>

(15) <u>obstacles, researchers have learned a great deal about ancient textiles and those who made them, and also about how to piece together a whole picture from many disparate sources of evidence.</u>

Technological advances in the analysis of

(20) archaeological remains provide much more information than was previously available, especially about minute remains. Successful modern methods include radiocarbon dating, infrared photography for seeing through dirt without removing it, isotope

(25) "fingerprinting" for tracing sources of raw materials, and thin-layer chromatography for analyzing dyes. As if in preparation for such advances, the field of archaeology has also undergone an important philosophical revolution in the past century. Once little

(30) more than a self-serving quest for artifacts to stock museums and private collections, the field has transformed itself into a scientific pursuit of knowledge about past cultures. As part of this process, archaeologists adopted the fundamental precept of

(35) preserving all objects, even those that have no immediately discernible value. Thus in the 1970s two researchers found the oldest known complete garment, a 5,000-year-old linen shirt, among a tumbled heap of dirty linens that had been preserved as part of the well-

(40) known Petrie collection decades before anyone began to study the history of textiles.

The history of textiles and of the craftswomen who produced them has also advanced on a different front: recreating the actual production of cloth.

(45) Reconstructing and implementing ancient production methods provides a valuable way of generating and checking hypotheses. <u>For example</u>, these techniques made it possible to confirm that the excavated pieces of clay once considered useless in fact functioned as loom

(50) weights. <u>Similarly</u>, scholars have until recently been obliged to speculate as to which one of two statues of Athena, one large and one small, was adorned with a dress created by a group of Athenian women for a festival, as described in surviving texts. Because

(55) records show that it took nine months to produce the dress, scholars assumed it must have adorned the large statue. But by investigating the methods of production and the size of the looms used, researchers have ascertained that in fact a dress for the small statue

(60) would have taken nine months to produce.

Main Point

The main point is stated in the last sentence of the first paragraph. It is that, despite obstacles (lack of archeological remains and written records), researchers have learned much about ancient textiles and the people who made them.

Paragraph 1

This paragraph provides background information to explain why there is so little information about ancient textile production. The problem is that there are limited archeological remains, and many items that did survive were discarded. In addition, written records rarely mention the creation of textiles and use archaic terminology. The paragraph then states the main point of the passage.

Paragraph 2

This paragraph explains that technological advances have made it possible to get more information from limited remains. It provides some examples of technologies used to analyze items. It also explains a recent philosophical revolution in archaeology that has resulted in archaeologists preserving all objects. It then presents the example of a 5,000-year-old linen shirt that was preserved before anyone studied the history of textiles.

Paragraph 3

This paragraph describes how recreating the production of cloth advances the history of textiles and craftswomen. It states that reconstructing and implementing ancient methods is a good way to verify hypotheses. It then provides two examples. The first is the discovery of loom weights. The second is how understanding the method of production enabled researchers to determine which of two statues of Athena was adorned with a dress described in a text.

Identify Viewpoints

The author's viewpoint is not present. There are no other viewpoints in the passage.

Which one of the following most accurately expresses the main point of the passage?

This is an MP question. It is an Informational passage, so the author's viewpoint is absent. The main point is stated in the last sentence of the first paragraph. It is that despite the lack of archeological remains and written records, researchers have learned much about ancient textiles and the people who made them. We should anticipate a correct answer choice that expresses this descriptive statement.

(A) **Archaeology is an expanding discipline that has transformed itself in response both to scientific advances and to changing cultural demands such as a recently increasing interest in women's history.**

This answer choice includes incomplete information. It makes no reference to textiles. Instead, it is a general statement about archeology and women's history. This is a loser.

(B) **A diversity of new approaches to the study of ancient textiles has enabled researchers to infer much about the history of textiles and their creators in the ancient world from the scant evidence that remains.**

This matches our anticipated answer choice. Researchers have learned much about ancient textiles and their creators from the scant evidence remaining. The new approaches mentioned at the beginning of this answer choice are the new technologies and the reconstruction methods discussed later in the passage. This is a candidate.

(C) **Despite many obstacles, research into the textile production methods used by women in the ancient world has advanced over the past century to the point that archaeologists can now replicate ancient equipment and production techniques.**

This also matches our anticipated answer choice. It states that research into textiles has advanced despite obstacles, and it mentions the replication of ancient equipment and techniques that are discussed in the third paragraph of the passage. This is a candidate as well.

(D) **Research into the history of textiles has spurred sweeping changes in the field of archaeology, from the application of advanced technology to the revaluation of ancient artifacts that were once deemed useless.**

This answer choice makes too strong of a claim. The second paragraph states that research into textiles benefited from the use of new technologies in archaeology and from the practice of preserving all objects. However, there is no indication that textile history research spurred these changes. This is a loser.

(E) **Though researchers have verified certain theories about the history of textiles by using technological developments such as radiocarbon dating, most significant findings in this field have grown out of the reconstruction of ancient production techniques.**

This answer choice also makes too strong of a claim. The passage states that significant findings resulted from the reconstruction of ancient production techniques, but it does not state that most of the significant findings have grown out of this technique. This is also a loser.

We have two candidates, (B) and (C), so we need to eliminate one. Looking back at (C), we can see that it is the weaker candidate. It actually addresses the wrong task. The third paragraph presents the reconstruction and implementation of past production methods as one of the approaches used to learn more about the history of textiles. This information expands on the main point stated in paragraph one. Therefore, (B) is the correct answer choice.

2. Correct Answer (E). Difficulty Level: 1 / 4

The author's attitude concerning the history of ancient textile production can most accurately be described as

This is a rare example of an ATT question for an Informational passage. As the author's viewpoint is absent, there are no keywords in the passage that indicate the author's opinion. The information is presented in a neutral manner. In addition, the prompt does not reference a viewpoint or topic from a specific part of the passage. Therefore, we cannot anticipate a correct answer choice and must proceed directly to eliminating answer choices.

(A) skeptical regarding the validity of some of the new hypotheses proposed by researchers

This answer choice includes irrelevant information. The author does not make any claims about the hypotheses of researchers. This is a loser.

(B) doubtful that any additional useful knowledge can be generated given the nature of the evidence available

This answer choice includes contradictory information. The main point of the passage is that researchers have learned a great deal about ancient textiles from disparate sources of evidence. This is a loser.

(C) impatient about the pace of research in light of the resources available

This answer choice includes irrelevant information. There is nothing in the passage that indicates the author is impatient with the pace of research. This is a loser as well.

(D) optimistic that recent scholarly advances will attract increasing numbers of researchers

This answer choice also includes irrelevant information. There is no mention in the passage about attracting increasing number of researchers. This is a loser.

(E) satisfied that considerable progress is being made in this field

This answer choice seems to describe the author's attitude. The term *satisfied* here means *persuaded by evidence*. The author neutrally presents information that shows that considerable progress is being made in this field. At no point is there any indication that this information is debatable or that the author does not fully accept it. Therefore, the author seems convinced that progress is being made. This is the correct answer choice.

3. Correct Answer (E). Difficulty Level: 1 / 4

The passage indicates that the re-creation of ancient techniques was used in which one of the following?

This is a D question. The topic of the prompt is the re-creation of ancient techniques. Looking back at our analysis of the passage, we can see that this is discussed in the third paragraph. The third sentence of this paragraph states that the re-creation of ancient techniques was used to confirm that items were in fact loom weights. The last sentence of the passage states that researchers used the re-creation of ancient techniques to determine which statue of Athena was adorned by a dress described in texts. We should anticipate a correct answer choice that restates one of these details.

(A) investigating the meanings of certain previously unintelligible technical terms in ancient texts

This answer choice addresses the wrong part of the passage. Texts with archaic and unrevealing terminology are

Chapter 10

mentioned in the first paragraph as an obstacle to learning about ancient textiles. There is no indication that the re-creation of ancient techniques was used to address this problem. This is a loser.

(B) tracing the sources of raw materials used in the production of certain fabrics

This answer choice also includes information from the wrong part of the passage. Tracing sources of raw materials is discussed in the second paragraph in relation to a new technology. This is also a loser.

(C) constructing certain public museum displays concerning cloth-making

This answer choice also includes information from the wrong part of the passage. Museum displays are discussed in the second paragraph as an early motive for gathering archaeological items. This is a loser as well.

(D) verifying that a particular 5,000-year-old cloth was indeed a shirt

Again, this answer choice includes information from the wrong part of the passage. The 5,000-year-old shirt is presented in the second paragraph as an example of a positive result of archaeologists preserving all items. This is a loser.

(E) exploring the issue of which of two statues of Athena was clothed with a particular garment

This matches one of our anticipated answer choices. The re-creation of ancient techniques made it possible to determine which statue was clothed with a particular dress. This is the correct answer choice.

---

4. Correct Answer (D). Difficulty Level: 2 / 4

The author intends the term "traditional sources" (line 1) to exclude which one of the following?

This is an M EXCEPT question. The question asks us for something that is excluded from the term *traditional sources*, which is used in the passage in reference to archaeological remains and surviving texts. The incorrect answer choices will all include something that can be classified as archaeological remains and surviving texts. The correct answer choice will include something that cannot. It is difficult to anticipate a correct answer choice for an EXCEPT question, so we should proceed directly to eliminating answer choices.

(A) ancient clay objects that cannot be identified as pieces of pottery by the researchers who unearth them

This answer choice presents something that the author would consider a traditional source. Ancient clay objects would fall under the category of archaeological remains. This is a loser.

(B) historically significant pieces of cloth discovered in the course of an excavation

This answer choice also presents something that the author would consider a traditional source. Historically significant pieces of cloth would be considered archaeological remains. This is also a loser.

(C) the oldest known complete garment, which was found among other pieces of cloth in a collection

This answer choice presents something that the author would consider a traditional source as well. The oldest known complete garment would be considered archaeological remains. This is also a loser.

(D) re-creations of looms from which inferences about ancient weaving techniques can be made

This answer choice seems to present something that the author would not consider a traditional source. A recreation of a loom would not be archaeological remains (it is a newly built item) or a surviving text. This is a candidate.

(E) ancient accounts of the adornment of a statue of Athena with a dress made by Athenian women

This answer choice presents something that the author would consider a traditional source. Ancient accounts would be considered surviving texts. This is a loser.

As (D) is the only candidate, it is the correct answer choice.

5. **Correct Answer (C).** Difficulty Level: 3 / 4

The passage as a whole functions primarily as

This is an unusually worded P question. The author's viewpoint is absent. The main point of the passage is that despite the lack of archeological remains and written records, researchers have learned much about ancient textiles and the people who made them. We should anticipate a correct answer choice that describes this neutral summary of the key information in the passage. Given the atypical structure of the question, the answer choices begin with nouns rather than action verbs. However, these nouns serve the same function with regard to eliminating answer choices. For example, *a description* would be appropriate for a main point that is a descriptive statement, while *a claim* would be inappropriate. We should expect to see something along the lines of "a description of how a field of research has advanced despite obstacles."

(A) a defense of the controversial methods adopted by certain researchers in a particular discipline

Defense is an inappropriate term for a passage that does not make a claim. The author is not defending a particular method. In addition, there is no indication that any of the methods discussed in the passage are controversial. This is a loser.

(B) a set of recommendations to guide future activities in a particular field of inquiry

Set of recommendations is also an inappropriate term for a passage that does not make a claim. The author is not recommending anything in the passage. This is also a loser.

(C) an account of how a particular branch of research has successfully coped with certain difficulties

Account is an appropriate term for a passage that does not make a claim. In addition, the description of the main point is accurate. This is a candidate.

(D) a rejection of some commonly held views about the methodologies of a certain discipline

Rejection is an inappropriate term for a passage that does not make a claim. The author does not reject (or even express an opinion about) any of the methodologies discussed in the passage. This is a loser.

(E) a summary of the hypotheses advanced by researchers who have used innovative methods of investigation

Summary is an appropriate term for a passage that does not make a claim. However, the description of the main point is inaccurate. The author does not summarize any hypotheses in the passage. This is a loser as well.

As (C) is the only candidate, it is the correct answer choice.

6. Correct Answer (E). Difficulty Level: 2 / 4

According to the passage, which one of the following was an element in the transformation of archaeology in the past century?

This is a D question. The topic of the prompt is the transformation of archaeology in the past century. Looking back at our analysis of the passage, we can see that this topic is discussed in the second paragraph. The fourth sentence of this paragraph states that the field adopted the precept of preserving all objects, even those that have no immediately discernible value. We should anticipate a correct answer choice that restates this.

(A) an increased interest in the crafts practiced in the ancient world

This answer choice includes irrelevant information. The passage does not discuss an increased interest in ancient crafts. This is a loser.

(B) some archaeologists' adoption of textile conservation experts' preservation techniques

This answer choice also includes irrelevant information. There is no mention of archaeologists adopting the techniques of textile conservation experts. This is a loser as well.

(C) innovative methods of restoring damaged artifacts

Again, this answer choice includes irrelevant information. The passage does not mention innovative methods to restore damaged items. This is a loser.

(D) the discovery of the oldest known complete garment

The answer choice addresses the wrong task. The oldest known garment is mentioned in the second paragraph as an example of how the decision to preserve all archeological remains transformed society. It is an example of the detail requested in the prompt—not the detail itself. This is also a loser.

(E) archaeologists' policy of not discarding ancient objects that have no readily identifiable value

This matches our anticipated answer choice. The decision to not discard ancient objects that have no identifiable value was an element of the transformation of archaeology in the past century. This is the correct answer choice.

7. Correct Answer (A). Difficulty Level: 1 / 4

Which one of the following most accurately describes the function of the first paragraph in relation to the rest of the passage?

This is an FP question. The function of the first paragraph is to present a problem that researchers face (lack of archeological remains and surviving texts related to textiles) and explain that researchers have learned much despite this obstacle. We should anticipate a correct answer choice that includes an appropriate action verb and an accurate description of this function.

(A) A particularly difficult archaeological problem is described in order to underscore the significance of new methods used to resolve that problem, which are described in the following paragraphs.

This matches our anticipated answer choice. The first paragraph describes a problem and indicates that it is being resolved. The following paragraphs describe the methods used to resolve this problem. This is a candidate.

(B) A previously neglected body of archaeological evidence is described in order to cast doubt on received views regarding ancient cultures developed from conventional sources of evidence, as described in the following paragraphs.

This answer choice includes irrelevant information. The author does not cast doubt on received views from conventional sources of evidence anywhere in the passage. This is a loser.

(C) The fruitfulness of new technologically based methods of analysis is described in order to support the subsequent argument that apparently insignificant archaeological remains ought to be preserved for possible future research.

This answer choice addresses the wrong part of the passage. New technologies and the preservation of apparently insignificant archaeological remains are discussed in the second paragraph. This is a loser as well.

(D) The findings of recent archaeological research are outlined as the foundation for a claim advanced in the following paragraphs that the role of women in ancient cultures has been underestimated by archaeologists.

This answer choice includes irrelevant information. The passage does not claim that the role of women in ancient cultures has been underestimated. This is also a loser.

(E) A recently developed branch of archaeological research is described as evidence for the subsequent argument that other, more established branches of archaeology should take advantage of new technologies in their research.

This answer choice also includes irrelevant information. The passage does not compare branches of archaeological research or make suggestions for their future. This is a loser.

As (A) is the only candidate, it is the correct answer choice.

For Questions 8–13

This passage was adapted from articles published in the 1990s.

The success that Nigerian-born computer scientist Philip Emeagwali (b. 1954) has had in designing computers that solve real-world problems has been fueled by his willingness to reach beyond established
(5) paradigms and draw inspiration for his designs from nature. In the 1980s, Emeagwali achieved breakthroughs in the design of parallel computer systems. Whereas single computers work sequentially, making one calculation at a time, computers
(10) connected in parallel can process calculations simultaneously. In 1989, Emeagwali pioneered the use of massively parallel computers that used a network of thousands of smaller computers to solve what is considered one of the most computationally difficult
(15) problems: predicting the flow of oil through the subterranean geologic formations that make up oil fields. Until that time, supercomputers had been used for oil field calculations, but because these supercomputers worked sequentially, they were too
(20) slow and inefficient to accurately predict such extremely complex movements.

To model oil field flow using a computer requires the simulation of the distribution of the oil at tens of thousands of locations throughout the field. At each
(25) location, hundreds of simultaneous calculations must be made at regular time intervals relating to such variables as temperature, direction of oil flow, viscosity, and pressure, as well as geologic properties of the basin holding the oil. In order to solve this
(30) problem, Emeagwali designed a massively parallel computer by using the Internet to connect to more than 65,000 smaller computers. One of the great difficulties of parallel computing is dividing up the tasks among the separate smaller computers so that
(35) they do not interfere with each other, and it was here that Emeagwali turned to natural processes for ideas, noting that tree species that survive today are those that, over the course of hundreds of millions of years, have developed branching patterns that have
(40) maximized the amount of sunlight gathered and the quantity of water and sap delivered. Emeagwali demonstrated that, for modeling certain phenomena such as subterranean oil flow, a network design based on the mathematical principle that underlies the
(45) branching structures of trees will enable a massively parallel computer to gather and broadcast the largest quantity of messages to its processing points in the shortest time.

In 1996 Emeagwali had another breakthrough
(50) when he presented the design for a massively parallel computer that [A)]he claims will be powerful enough to predict global weather patterns a century in advance. The computer's design is based on the geometry of bees' honeycombs, which use an extremely efficient
(55) three-dimensional spacing. [A)]Emeagwali believes that computer scientists in the future will increasingly look to nature for elegant solutions to complex technical problems. This paradigm shift, he asserts, will enable us to better understand the systems
(60) evolved by nature and, thereby, to facilitate the evolution of human technology.

Main Point

The main point is stated in the first two sentences of the first paragraph. It is that Emeagwali drew inspiration from nature to achieve breakthroughs in the design of parallel computer systems that solved real world problems.

Paragraph 1

This paragraph states the main point of the paragraph and provides background information about Emeagwali. It also introduces Emeagwali's first breakthrough—the use of parallel computers to track the flow of oil in subterranean formations.

Paragraph 2

This paragraph provides additional details about Emeagwali's efforts to model oil flow. It explains why this is challenging. It also points out a difficulty with parallel computing—dividing up tasks among separate computers. It then discusses how this problem led Emeagwali to use the mathematic principle that underlies the branching structure of trees to design a parallel computing network capable of modeling oil flow.

Paragraph 3

The third paragraph discusses a second breakthrough Emeagwali achieved and introduces his viewpoint. He designed a parallel computing system based on the geometry of bees' honeycombs that he claims will be able to predict global weather patterns. He also believes that scientists will increasingly look towards nature to solve complex problems and this paradigm shift will help to facilitate the evolution of human technology.

Identify Viewpoints

The viewpoint of Emeagwali is presented in the third paragraph. The author's viewpoint is not present.

8. Correct Answer (D). Difficulty Level: 2 / 4

Which one of the following most accurately expresses the main point of the passage?

This is an MP question. It is an Informational passage, so the author's viewpoint is absent. The main point of the passage is stated in the first two sentences of the first paragraph. It is that Emeagwali drew inspiration from nature to achieve breakthroughs in the design of parallel computer systems to solve real world problems. We should anticipate a correct answer choice that expresses this descriptive statement.

(A) Emeagwali's establishment of new computational paradigms has enabled parallel computer systems to solve a wide array of real-world problems that supercomputers cannot solve.

This answer choice includes incomplete information. The fact that Emeagwali was inspired by nature is a key element of the main point. However, this answer choice does not make a reference to it. This is a loser.

(B) Emeagwali has shown that scientists' allegiance to established paradigms has until now prevented the solution of many real-world computational problems that could otherwise have been solved with little difficulty.

This answer choice includes irrelevant and incomplete information. The passage does not state that scientists have an allegiance to established paradigms. In addition, this answer choice makes no reference to Emeagwali's breakthroughs or the fact that he drew inspiration from nature. This is a loser.

(C) Emeagwali's discovery of the basic mathematical principles underlying natural systems has led to a growing use of parallel computer systems to solve complex real-world computational problems.

This answer choice includes irrelevant information. There is no indication in the passage that Emeagwali discovered the basic mathematical principles underlying natural systems—the passage simply states that he used them. In addition, the passage does not state that there is a growing use of parallel computer systems. This is a loser as well.

(D) Emeagwali has designed parallel computer systems that are modeled on natural systems and that are aimed at solving real-world computational problems that would be difficult to solve with more traditional designs.

This matches our anticipated answer choice. Emeagwali designed parallel computer systems based on natural ones to solve real-world problems. The additional detail that these problems are difficult to solve with more traditional designs is stated later in the last sentence of the first paragraph. This is a candidate.

(E) The paradigm shift initiated by Emeagwali's computer designs has made it more likely that scientists will in the future look to systems evolved by nature to facilitate the evolution of human technology.

This answer choice addresses the wrong viewpoint. This claim is made in the last two sentences of the third paragraph by Emeagwali. There is no indication in the other parts of the passage that this claim is accurate. This is a loser.

As (D) is the only candidate, it is the correct answer choice.

9. Correct Answer (C). Difficulty Level: 2 / 4

According to the passage, which one of the following is true?

This is an EX question. The prompt does not include a topic. Therefore, we cannot anticipate a correct answer choice and should proceed to eliminating answer choices.

(A) Emeagwali's breakthroughs in computer design have begun to make computers that work sequentially obsolete.

This answer choice includes irrelevant information. The passage does not claim that computers that work sequentially are becoming obsolete. This is a loser.

(B) Emeagwali's first breakthrough in computer design came in response to a request by an oil company.

This answer choice also includes irrelevant information. The passage does not state that Emeagwali's first breakthrough was a response to a request from an oil company. This is a loser as well.

(C) Emeagwali was the first to use a massively parallel computer to predict the flow of oil in oil fields.

This answer choice seems compatible with the information in the passage. The fourth sentence of the first paragraph states that Emeagwali pioneered the use of parallel computers to predict the flow of oil and that, until that time, supercomputers had been used for oil field calculations. This is a candidate.

(D) Emeagwali was the first computer scientist to use nature as a model for human technology.

This answer choice makes too strong of a claim. The passage indicates that Emeagwali was the first (or, at least, one of the first) to create parallel computer systems based on natural systems. However, this answer choice makes the much broader claim that he was the first to use nature as a model for technology in general. This is not supported by the passage. This is a loser.

(E) Emeagwali was the first to apply parallel processing to solving real-world problems.

Again, this answer choice makes too strong of a claim. The passage states that Emeagwali pioneered the use of parallel computers to solve a specific type of real-world problem. However, there is no indication that this was the first use of parallel computers to solve real-world problems in general. This is another loser.

As (C) is the only candidate, it is the correct answer choice.

10. Correct Answer (A). Difficulty Level: 3 / 4

The passage most strongly suggests that Emeagwali holds which one of the following views?

This is a V question. The prompt references a viewpoint from a specific part of the passage. Emeagwali's viewpoint is presented in the third paragraph. Emeagwali claims that his parallel computer design will be powerful enough to predict global weather patterns a century in advance. He also believes that computer scientists in the future will increasingly look to nature for solutions to complex technical problems and asserts that this paradigm shift will enable a better understanding of natural systems and facilitate the evolution of human technology. There are a couple of inferences that can be made here. We can infer that global weather patterns can be predicted far in advance by computers. Another logical inference of this is that natural systems have overcome problems that are similar to problems related to human technology. We should anticipate a correct answer choice that expresses one of these inferences or another one that is compatible with Emeagwali's viewpoint.

(A) **Some natural systems have arrived at efficient solutions to problems that are analogous in significant ways to technical problems faced by computer scientists.**

This matches one of our anticipated answer choices. If Emeagwali believes that computer scientists should look to nature for solutions to complex technical problems, then natural systems must have arrived at solutions for problems similar to the ones faced by computer scientists. This is a candidate.

(B) **Global weather is likely too complicated to be accurately predictable more than a few decades in advance.**

This answer choice includes contradictory information. The third paragraph of the passage clearly states that Emeagwali claims his design could be powerful enough to predict global weather patterns a century in advance. This is a loser.

(C) **Most computer designs will in the future be inspired by natural systems.**

This answer choice makes too strong of a claim. Emeagwali believes that computer scientists will increasingly look to nature for design inspiration, but we cannot say that most designs will be inspired by nature based on this claim. This is another loser.

(D) **Massively parallel computers will eventually be practical enough to warrant their use even in relatively mundane computing tasks.**

This answer choice includes irrelevant information. The practicality of parallel computers for use in mundane tasks is never discussed in the passage. This is a loser.

(E) **The mathematical structure of branching trees is useful primarily for designing computer systems to predict the flow of oil through oil fields.**

This answer choice also makes too strong of a claim. The second paragraph states that Emeagwali used the mathematical structure of the branching of trees to design a computer system to predict the flow of oil through oil fields. However, this does not mean that this is the primary use of this mathematical structure. In fact, the last sentence of the second paragraph states that this structure can be used to model certain phenomena, such as subterranean oil flow. This implies that there are other uses. This is a loser as well.

As (A) is the only candidate, it is the correct answer choice.

---

11. **Correct Answer (B).** Difficulty Level: 2 / 4

Which one of the following most accurately describes the function of the first two sentences of the second paragraph?

This is an FS question that asks about the first two sentences of the second paragraph. Therefore, we should read the referenced sentences and the ones that come before and after. The preceding sentence explains that supercomputers were too slow and inefficient to predict such complex movements (oil flow). The two referenced sentences explain that the modeling of oil field flow requires the simulation of the distribution of oil at many locations, and, at these locations, there are a variety of variables to calculate. The sentence that follows states that Emeagwali designed a parallel computer to solve this problem. There seem to be two possible functions of the referenced sentences. First, they explain why supercomputers are unable to predict oil flow. Second, they present a problem that Emeagwali attempted to solve. We should anticipate a correct answer choice that expresses one of these functions.

(A) **They provide an example of an established paradigm that Emeagwali's work has challenged.**

This answer choice includes contradictory information. The referenced sentences do not include an example of an established paradigm. This is a loser.

(B) They help explain why supercomputers are unable to accurately predict the movements of oil through underground geologic formations.

This matches one of our anticipated answer choices. The referenced sentences explain why supercomputers cannot predict the movements of oil. This is a candidate.

(C) They provide examples of a network design based on the mathematical principles underlying the branching structures of trees.

This answer choice includes contradictory information. The referenced sentences do not provide examples of a network design. This is a loser.

(D) They describe a mathematical model that Emeagwali used in order to understand a natural system.

This answer choice addresses the wrong part of the passage. The mathematical model is discussed at the end of the second paragraph, and it has no relation to the function of these sentences. This is also a loser.

(E) They provide specific examples of a paradigm shift that will help scientists understand certain systems evolved by nature.

This answer choice includes contradictory information. The referenced sentences do not provide examples of a paradigm shift. This is a loser.

As (B) is the only candidate, it is the correct answer choice.

12. **Correct Answer (A).** Difficulty Level: 3 / 4

Which one of the following, if true, would provide the most support for Emeagwali's prediction mentioned in lines 55–58?

This is an S question. The argument referenced in the prompt is Emeagwali's claim that computer scientists in the future will increasingly look to nature to solve complex technical problems. This is a difficult argument to identify a weakness for as it consists of a claim without any direct support in the immediate context. Therefore, we should proceed to eliminating answer choices.

(A) Until recently, computer scientists have had very limited awareness of many of the mathematical principles that have been shown to underlie a wide variety of natural processes.

This answer choice seems to strengthen the argument. In making the claim that scientists will increasingly look to nature for solutions in the future, Emeagwali is assuming that this is not already being widely done. He is also assuming that scientists have not already considered this approach and rejected it. This answer choice addresses both of these assumptions. This is a candidate.

(B) Some of the variables affecting global weather patterns have yet to be discovered by scientists who study these patterns.

This answer choice includes irrelevant information. The fact that variables affecting global weather patterns have not been discovered has no relevance to the argument. This is a loser.

(C) Computer designs for the prediction of natural phenomena tend to be more successful when those phenomena are not affected by human activities.

This answer choice also includes irrelevant information. Emeagwali's claim is that scientists will look to nature to solve technical problems. This answer choice is about a factor that affects computer predictions of natural phenomena. This is a loser.

(D) Some of the mathematical principles underlying Emeagwali's model of oil field flow also underlie his designs for other massively parallel computer systems.

This answer choice includes irrelevant information as well. Whether or not Emeagwali used the same mathematical principles in multiple designs neither strengthens nor weakens the argument. This is also a loser.

(E) Underlying the designs for many traditional technologies are mathematical principles of which the designers of those technologies were not explicitly aware.

Again, this answer choice includes irrelevant information. That designers were not aware of the mathematical principles that underlie their designs has no relevance to the argument. This is a loser.

As (A) is the only candidate, it is the correct answer choice.

---

13. **Correct Answer (E).** Difficulty Level: 3 / 4

It can be inferred from the passage that one of the reasons massively parallel computers had not been used to model oil field flow prior to 1989 is that

This is an IMP question. The topic of the prompt is a reason massively parallel computers had not been used to model oil field flow prior to 1989. Looking back at our analysis, we can see that the use of parallel computers to model oil field flows is discussed in the first and second paragraphs. The third sentence of the second paragraph states that a difficulty of parallel computers is dividing the tasks among the separate computers so that they do not interfere with each other. It then states that this problem caused Emeagwali to look to natural processes for ideas. It seems logical to infer that this problem was the reason that parallel computers had not been used to model oil field flow before Emeagwali did so in 1989. We should anticipate a correct answer choice that expresses this inference or another one that can be logically drawn from this section of the passage.

(A) supercomputers are sufficiently powerful to handle most computational problems, including most problems arising from oil production

This answer choice includes contradictory information. The last sentence of the first paragraph clearly indicates that supercomputers could not accurately predict oil field flows. This is a loser.

(B) the possibility of using a network of smaller computers to solve computationally difficult problems had not yet been considered

This answer choice makes too strong of a claim. The passage indicates that Emeagwali was one of the first to use parallel computer systems to solve complex problems. However, this does not mean that others did not consider this approach. This is a loser.

(C) the general public was not yet aware of the existence or vast capabilities of the Internet

This answer choice includes irrelevant information. There is no information in the passage about the general public's awareness of the Internet. This is also a loser.

(D) oil companies had not yet perceived the need for modeling the flow of oil in subterranean fields

This answer choice also includes contradictory information. The last sentence of the first paragraph states that supercomputers had been used for oil field calculations and to predict oil flow movements (albeit, unsuccessfully). This indicates that oil companies were aware of the need to model oil flow. This is another loser.

(E) smaller computers can interfere with one another when they are connected together in parallel to solve a computationally difficult problem

This matches our anticipated answer choice. The computers that make up a parallel system can interfere with each other. Emeagwali found a solution to this problem by looking at a natural system. This is the correct answer choice.

For Questions 14–20

[A)]Proponents of the tangible-object theory of copyright argue that copyright and similar intellectual-property rights can be explained as logical extensions of the right to own concrete, tangible objects. This

(5) view depends on the claim that every copyrightable work can be manifested in some physical form, such as a manuscript or a videotape. It also accepts the premise that ownership of an object confers a number of rights on the owner, who may essentially do whatever he or

(10) she pleases with the object to the extent that this does not violate other people's rights. One may, for example, hide or display the object, copy it, or destroy it. One may also transfer ownership of it to another.

In creating a new and original object from

(15) materials that one owns, one becomes the owner of that object and thereby acquires all of the rights that ownership entails. But if the owner transfers ownership of the object, the full complement of rights is not necessarily transferred to the new owner; instead, the

(20) original owner may retain one or more of these rights. This notion of retained rights is common in many areas of law; for example, the seller of a piece of land may retain certain rights to the land in the form of easements or building restrictions. Applying the notion

(25) of retained rights to the domain of intellectual property, [A)]theorists argue that copyrighting a work secures official recognition of one's intention to retain certain rights to that work. Among the rights typically retained by the original producer of an object such as a literary

(30) manuscript or a musical score would be the right to copy the object for profit and the right to use it as a guide for the production of similar or analogous things—for example, a public performance of a musical score.

(35) According to [A)]proponents of the tangible-object theory, its chief advantage is that it justifies intellectual property rights without recourse to the widely accepted but problematic supposition that one can own abstract, intangible things such as ideas. But while this account

(40) seems plausible for copyrightable entities that do, in fact, have enduring tangible forms, it cannot accommodate the standard assumption that such evanescent things as live broadcasts of sporting events can be copyrighted. More importantly, it does not

(45) acknowledge that in many cases the work of conceiving ideas is more crucial and more valuable than that of putting them into tangible form. Suppose that a poet dictates a new poem to a friend, who writes it down on paper that the friend has supplied. The

(50) creator of the tangible object in this case is not the poet but the friend, and there would seem to be no ground for the poet's claiming copyright unless the poet can be said to already own the ideas expressed in the work.

Main Point

The main point is stated in the second and third sentences of the third paragraph. It is that the tangible-object theory does not account for the assumption that some intellectual property is intangible and that the work of conceiving ideas is more valuable than putting them into tangible form.

Paragraph 1

The first paragraph presents the viewpoint of proponents of the tangible object theory—that intellectual property rights can be explained as logical extensions of the right to own tangible objects and that intellectual property is able to be manifested in some physical form.

Paragraph 2

This paragraph provides background information about property rights and retained rights. It then explains how tangible-object theorists apply these notions to intellectual property. They argue that copyrighting a work indicates an intention to retain certain rights to it. The paragraph then specifies a couple of retained rights—the right to copy a work and the right to use a work to produce similar works.

Paragraph 3

This paragraph states one additional advantage of the tangible-object theory—it justifies intellectual property rights without recourse to the idea of owning intangible things. The paragraph then states the main point, which is the author's conclusion that the tangible-object theory is flawed because it does not account for the fact that some intellectual property is intangible and that the work of conceiving ideas is more valuable than putting them in tangible form. An example of a poem is then given to support this claim.

Identify Viewpoints

The viewpoint of tangible-object theorists is presented throughout the passage. The author's viewpoint is present, and it appears in the last paragraph. The author critiques the tangible object theory.

14. Correct Answer (B). Difficulty Level: 2 / 4

Which one of the following most accurately expresses the main point of the passage?

This is an MP question. It is an Argumentative passage, so the author's viewpoint is present. The author's conclusion appears in the second and third sentences of the third paragraph. It is that the tangible-object theory does not account for the assumption that some intellectual property is intangible and that the work of conceiving ideas is more valuable than putting them into tangible form. We should anticipate a correct answer choice that accurately expresses this conclusion.

(A) Copyright and other intellectual-property rights can be explained as logical extensions of the right to own concrete objects.

This answer choice refers to the wrong viewpoint. This claim is related to the tangible-object theory, which the author criticizes. This is a loser.

(B) Attempts to explain copyright and similar intellectual-property rights purely in terms of rights to ownership of physical objects are ultimately misguided.

This matches our anticipated answer choice. The tangible-object theory explains intellectual property rights in terms of ownership of physical objects. The author points out two flaws in this theory. This is a candidate.

(C) Copyrighting a work amounts to securing official recognition of one's intention to retain certain rights to that work.

This answer choice refers to the wrong viewpoint. This is a claim made by proponents of the tangible-object theory. Even if the author agrees with this claim, it is not related to the main point of the passage. This is a loser.

(D) Explanations of copyright and other intellectual-property rights in terms of rights to ownership of tangible objects fail to consider the argument that ideas should be allowed to circulate freely.

The answer choice includes irrelevant information. The claim that ideas should be allowed to circulate freely is not made in the passage. This is a loser.

(E) Under the tangible-object theory of intellectual property, rights of ownership are straightforwardly applicable to both ideas and physical objects.

This answer choice includes contradictory information. The passage clearly indicates that under the tangible-object theory, rights of ownership are applicable to physical objects rather than ideas. This is a loser.

As (B) is the only candidate, it is the correct answer choice.

15. Correct Answer (A). Difficulty Level: 2 / 4

According to the passage, the theory that copyright and other intellectual-property rights can be construed as logical extensions of the right to own concrete, tangible objects depends on the claim that

This is a D question. The topic of the prompt is the theory that copyright and other intellectual-property rights can be construed as logical extensions of the right to own concrete, tangible objects. Although this is discussed throughout the passage, it is introduced in the first paragraph. The second sentence of this paragraph explicitly states that the theory depends on the claim that every copyrightable work can be manifested in some physical form.

We should anticipate a correct answer choice that restates this.

(A) any work entitled to intellectual-property protection can be expressed in physical form

This matches our anticipated answer choice. It accurately paraphrases the detail we located in the passage. This is a candidate.

(B) only the original creator of an intellectual work can hold the copyright for that work

This answer choice includes contradictory information. The last sentence of the first paragraph explicitly states that copyright can be transferred to another person. This is a loser.

(C) the work of putting ideas into tangible form is more crucial and more valuable than the work of conceiving those ideas

The answer choice addresses the wrong viewpoint. This is a claim made by the author in the third paragraph. It is presented as a shortcoming of the tangible-object theory. This is also a loser.

(D) in a few cases, it is necessary to recognize the right to own abstract, intangible things

The answer choice includes contradictory information. The tangible-object theory holds that every copyrightable work can be manifested into a physical form. This is a loser as well.

(E) the owner of an item of intellectual property may legally destroy it

This answer choice addresses the wrong part of the passage. This information is presented at the end of the first paragraph as an example of a right of a copyright holder. It is not a claim that the tangible-object theory depends on. This is a loser.

As (A) is the only candidate, it is the correct answer choice.

---

16. **Correct Answer (B).** Difficulty Level: 2 / 4

The passage most directly answers which one of the following questions?

This is an E question. The prompt references the passage in general. Therefore, we cannot anticipate a correct answer choice and must proceed directly to eliminating answer choices.

(A) Do proponents of the tangible-object theory of intellectual property advocate any changes in existing laws relating to copyright?

This answer choice includes irrelevant information. The passage does not discuss changing existing laws related to copyright. This is a loser.

(B) Do proponents of the tangible-object theory of intellectual property hold that ownership of anything besides real estate can involve retained rights?

This seems to be a question that is answered by the passage. The third sentence of the second paragraph states that a seller of a piece of land may retain certain rights. The fourth and fifth sentences of this paragraph state that the notion of retained rights can be applied to intellectual property and mention a literary manuscript and musical score as examples. This is a candidate.

(C) Has the tangible-object theory of intellectual property influenced the ways in which copyright

cases or other cases involving issues of intellectual property are decided in the courts?

This answer choice includes irrelevant information. There is no mention of court cases in the passage. This is a loser.

(D) Does existing copyright law provide protection against unauthorized copying of manuscripts and musical scores in cases in which their creators have not officially applied for copyright protection?

This answer choice also includes irrelevant information. The author does not discuss protection against unauthorized copying of works when creators have not applied for copyright protection. This is a loser.

(E) Are there standard procedures governing the transfer of intellectual property that are common to most legal systems?

Again, this answer choice includes irrelevant information. Standard procedures governing the transfer of intellectual property are not discussed in the passage. This is also a loser.

As (B) is the only candidate, it is the correct answer choice.

17. Correct Answer (A). Difficulty Level: 4 / 4

Suppose an inventor describes an innovative idea for an invention to an engineer, who volunteers to draft specifications for a prototype and then produces the prototype using the engineer's own materials. Which one of the following statements would apply to this case under the tangible-object theory of intellectual property, as the author describes that theory?

This is an IMP question that provides a hypothetical scenario for consideration and then asks for an inference based on this scenario and the information in the passage. Although the tangible-object theory is discussed throughout the passage rather than in a specific part, the information in the prompt is sufficient for us to anticipate a correct answer choice.

The prompt presents a scenario in which an inventor describes an idea for an invention to an engineer, and the engineer drafts the specifications and then produces the prototype using his or her own materials. The prompt asks us to determine which of the answer choices would apply to this case under the tangible-object theory. The first sentence of the second paragraph states that a person who creates an original object from his or her own materials acquires all rights to that object. In addition, in the example of the poem presented by the author in the last two sentences of the third paragraph, a poet dictates a poem to a friend, who writes it down on paper that the friend supplied. This results in the poet losing rights to the poem (and friend presumably gaining them).

Based on this information, we can infer that in the scenario described in the prompt, the engineer would gain the copyright to the invention under the tangible-object theory. We should anticipate a correct answer choice that expresses this inference or another one that can be logically drawn from the passage.

(A) Only the engineer is entitled to claim the invention as intellectual property.

This matches our anticipated answer choice. The engineer is entitled to claim the invention as intellectual property because he or she created the original object (the prototype). This is a candidate.

(B) Only the inventor is entitled to claim the invention as intellectual property.

This answer choice includes contradictory information. Under the tangible-object theory, it is only the person who manifests an idea into physical form that is the copyright holder. In the scenario presented in the prompt, the inventor does not do this. This is a loser.

(C) The inventor and the engineer are equally entitled to claim the invention as intellectual property.

This answer choice also includes contradictory information. Only the engineer is entitled to claim the invention as intellectual property. This is another loser.

(D) The engineer is entitled to claim the invention as intellectual property, but only if the inventor retains the right to all profits generated by the invention.

This answer choice also includes contradictory information. The last sentence of the second paragraph states that the right to the profits from copying an object is generally retained by the object's creator (in this case, the engineer). This is a loser as well.

(E) The inventor is entitled to claim the invention as intellectual property, but only if the engineer retains the right to all profits generated by the invention.

This answer choice also includes contradictory information. Only the engineer is entitled to claim the invention as intellectual property. This is another loser.

As (A) is the only candidate, it is the correct answer choice.

18. **Correct Answer (E).** Difficulty Level: 3 / 4

Legal theorists supporting the tangible-object theory of intellectual property are most likely to believe which one of the following?

This is a V question. The prompt does not reference a viewpoint or topic from a specific part of the passage. Therefore, we cannot anticipate a correct answer choice and must proceed directly to eliminating answer choices.

(A) A literary work cannot receive copyright protection unless it exists in an edition produced by an established publisher.

This answer choice includes irrelevant information. The passage does not mention established publishers. This is a loser.

(B) Most legal systems explicitly rely on the tangible-object theory of intellectual property in order to avoid asserting that one can own abstract things.

This answer choice also includes irrelevant information. Different legal systems are not discussed in the passage. This is a loser.

(C) Copyright protects the right to copy for profit, but not the right to copy for other reasons.

This answer choice includes contradictory information. The first paragraph specifies that the tangible-object theory holds that the producer of an object has the right to do whatever he or she pleases with it, including copying it. This is a loser.

(D) Some works deserving of copyright protection simply cannot be manifested as concrete, tangible objects.

This answer choice refers to the wrong viewpoint. This claim is made by the author in the third paragraph. This is a loser.

(E) To afford patent protection for inventions, the law need not invoke the notion of inventors' ownership of abstract ideas.

This seems like a statement proponents of the tangible-object theory would agree with based on the information in the passage. The first sentence of the third paragraph states that the chief advantage of this theory is that it justifies intellectual property rights without recourse to the supposition that one can own abstract ideas. This is the correct answer choice.

19. **Correct Answer (C).** Difficulty Level: 3 / 4

The passage provides the most support for inferring which one of the following statements?

This is an IMP question. The prompt does not reference a topic from a specific part of the passage. Therefore, we cannot anticipate a correct answer choice and must proceed directly to eliminating answer choices.

(A) In most transactions involving the transfer of non-intellectual property, at least some rights of ownership are retained by the seller.

This answer choice makes too strong of a claim. The second paragraph uses real estate as an example of a non-intellectual property for which at least some rights can be retained by the seller. However, this does not mean that rights are retained in most transactions involving the transfer of non-intellectual property. This is a loser.

(B) The notion of retained rights of ownership is currently applied to only those areas of law that do not involve intellectual property.

This answer choice also makes too strong of a claim. Real estate is presented as an example of a non-intellectual property for which ownership rights can be retained. However, we cannot say for certain that this means that the concept of retained rights is only applied to areas of law that do not involve intellectual property. This is also a loser.

(C) The idea that ownership of the right to copy an item for profit can be transferred is compatible with a tangible-object theory of intellectual property.

This seems like a logical inference based on the information in the passage. The second sentence of the second paragraph states that if the owner transfers ownership of an object, the full complement of rights is not necessarily transferred to the new owner. The use of *necessarily* implies that the owner may transfer the full complement of rights if he or she desires (including the right to copy an item for profit). This is a candidate.

(D) Ownership of intellectual property is sufficiently protected by the provisions that, under many legal systems, apply to ownership of material things such as land.

This answer choice includes irrelevant information. The passage does not discuss whether or not intellectual property is sufficiently protected by the provisions that apply to ownership of material things. This is a loser.

(E) Protection of computer programs under intellectual-property law is justifiable only if the programs are likely to be used as a guide for the production of similar or analogous programs.

This answer choice also includes irrelevant information. The topic of when protection of works under intellectual-property law is justified is not discussed in the passage. This is another loser.

As (C) is the only candidate, it is the correct answer choice.

It can be inferred that the author of the passage is most likely to believe which one of the following?

This is a V question. The author's viewpoint is introduced in the third paragraph. The author presents two critiques of the tangible-object theory. The first is that it does not address the assumption that some intellectual property is intangible. The second is that the theory does acknowledge that the work of conceiving ideas is more valuable than putting them into tangible form. There are many possible inferences that can be drawn from these critiques, making it difficult to anticipate a correct answer choice. Therefore, we should proceed directly to eliminating answer choices.

(A) Theorists who suggest that the notion of retained rights is applicable to intellectual property do not fully understand what it means to transfer ownership of property.

This answer choice includes information from the wrong part of the passage. Transfer of ownership and retained rights are discussed in the second paragraph. These concepts are unrelated to the author's critiques of the tangible-object theory. This is a loser.

(B) If a work does not exist in a concrete, tangible form, there is no valid theoretical basis for claiming that it should have copyright protection.

This answer choice refers to the wrong viewpoint. This is the position of the tangible-object theorists rather than of the author. This is another loser.

(C) Under existing statutes, creators of original tangible works that have intellectual or artistic significance generally do not have the legal right to own the abstract ideas embodied in those works.

This answer choice includes irrelevant information. The passage does not indicate whether or not existing statutes grant creators of tangible works the legal right to own the abstract ideas embodied in those works. This is also a loser.

(D) An adequate theoretical justification of copyright would likely presuppose that a work's creator originally owns the ideas embodied in that work.

This seems like a statement the author would agree with. The author criticizes the tangible-object theory because it does not acknowledge that the work of conceiving ideas is more valuable than putting them in tangible form. Therefore, the author would likely agree that a theoretical justification of copyright would assume that the work's creator owns the ideas embodied in that work. This is a candidate.

(E) It is common, but incorrect, to assume that such evanescent things as live broadcasts of sporting events can be copyrighted.

This answer choice includes contradictory information. The author criticizes the tangible-object theory because it does not account for the assumption that some intellectual property is intangible. Therefore, the author must not believe that this assumption is incorrect. This is a loser.

As (D) is the only candidate, it is the correct answer choice.

For Questions 21–27

Passage A

In music, a certain complexity of sounds can be expected to have a positive effect on the listener. A single, pure tone is not that interesting to explore; a measure of intricacy is required to excite human
(5) curiosity. Sounds that are too complex or disorganized, however, tend to be overwhelming. We prefer some sort of coherence, a principle that connects the various sounds and makes them comprehensible.

In this respect, music is like human language.
(10) Single sounds are in most cases not sufficient to convey meaning in speech, whereas when put together in a sequence they form words and sentences. Likewise, if the tones in music are not perceived to be tied together sequentially or rhythmically—for
(15) example, in what is commonly called melody— listeners are less likely to feel any emotional connection or to show appreciation.

Certain music can also have a relaxing effect. The fact that such music tends to be continuous and
(20) rhythmical suggests a possible explanation for this effect. In a natural environment, danger tends to be accompanied by sudden, unexpected sounds. Thus, a background of constant noise suggests peaceful conditions; discontinuous sounds demand more
(25) attention. Even soft discontinuous sounds that we consciously realize do not signal danger can be disturbing—for example, the erratic dripping of a leaky tap. A continuous sound, particularly one that is judged to be safe, relaxes the brain.

Passage B

(30) There are certain elements within music, such as a change of melodic line or rhythm, that create expectations about the future development of the music. The expectation the listener has about the further course of musical events is a key determinant
(35) for the experience of "musical emotions." Music creates expectations that, if not immediately satisfied, create tension. Emotion is experienced in relation to the buildup and release of tension. The more elaborate the buildup of tension, the more intense the emotions
(40) that will be experienced. When resolution occurs, relaxation follows.

The interruption of the expected musical course, depending on one's personal involvement, causes the search for an explanation. This results from a
(45) "mismatch" between one's musical expectation and the actual course of the music. Negative emotions will be the result of an extreme mismatch between expectations and experience. Positive emotions result if the converse happens.
(50) When we listen to music, we take into account factors such as the complexity and novelty of the music. The degree to which the music sounds familiar determines whether the music is experienced as pleasurable or uncomfortable. The pleasure
(55) experienced is minimal when the music is entirely new to the listener, increases with increasing familiarity, and decreases again when the music is totally known. Musical preference is based on one's desire to maintain a constant level of certain preferable

(60) emotions. As such, a trained listener will have a greater preference for complex melodies than will a naive listener, as the threshold for experiencing emotion is higher.

Main Point of Passage A

The main point is stated in the first and last sentences of the first paragraph. It is that, in music, a certain level of complexity and coherence has a positive effect on the listener.

Main Point of Passage B

The main point is stated in the first two sentences of the first paragraph. It is that a listener's expectations with regard to certain elements within music determine the experience of musical emotion.

Similarities Between Passages

Both passages discuss the emotional responses of listeners to music.
Both passages discuss the relationship between musical complexity and the positive emotional response of a listener.
Both passages suggest that music that follows a predictable pattern stimulates a positive emotional response from a listener.

Dissimilarities Between Passages

Passage A discusses both music and sounds in general, while Passage B focuses exclusively on music.
Passage B discusses the difference between trained listeners and naive listeners, while Passage A does not.

21. **Correct Answer (E).** Difficulty Level: 2 / 4

Which one of the following concepts is linked to positive musical experiences in both passages?

This is a C Detail question. The topic of the prompt is positive musical experiences. Looking at the similarities we noted, we can see that both passages discuss the relationship between musical complexity and the positive emotional response of a listener. We should anticipate a correct answer choice that restates this detail.

(A) continuous sound

This answer choice includes irrelevant information. Passage B does not discuss continuous sound. This is a loser.

(B) tension

This answer choice includes irrelevant information. Passage A does not discuss tension. This is a loser as well.

(C) language

This answer choice also includes irrelevant information. Although language is mentioned in Passage A, neither passage discusses this concept with regard to positive musical experiences. This is a loser.

(D) improvisation

Again, this answer choice includes irrelevant information. Neither passage discusses improvisation. This is another loser.

(E) complexity

This matches our anticipated answer choice. The first paragraph of Passage A states that a certain complexity of sounds can have a positive effect on the listener. The last paragraph of Passage B claims that a trained listener will have a greater preference for complex melodies as the threshold for experiencing emotion is higher. This is the correct answer choice.

22. **Correct Answer (C).** Difficulty Level: 2 / 4

The passages most strongly suggest that both are targeting an audience that is interested in which one of the following?

This is an unusually worded C Implication question. The prompt asks us to infer the target audience of both passages. Although the prompt does not include a specific topic, the correct answer choice will likely be related to an aspect of the main content of each passage that overlaps. Looking back at the similarities we identified, we can see that both passages discuss the emotional response of listeners to music. As this is related to the main topic of both passages, it is almost certainly the topic that the target audience is interested in. We should anticipate a correct answer choice that expresses this.

(A) the theoretical underpinnings of how music is composed

This answer choice includes irrelevant information. Although Passage B indirectly discusses musical composition, Passage A does not discuss it at all. This is a loser.

(B) the nature of the conceptual difference between music and discontinuous sound

This answer choice also includes irrelevant information. Passage B does not discuss the difference between music and discontinuous sound. This is a loser.

(C) the impact music can have on human emotional states

This matches our anticipated answer choice. Both passages discuss emotional responses to music. This is a candidate.

(D) the most effective techniques for teaching novices to appreciate complex music

This answer choice includes irrelevant information. Neither passage discusses teaching novices to appreciate music. This is a loser.

(E) the influence music has had on the development of spoken language

This answer choice includes irrelevant information. Passage A mentions language, but does not discuss the influence of music on language. Passage B does not discuss language at all. This is a loser.

As (C) is the only candidate, it is the correct answer choice.

---

23. **Correct Answer (B).** Difficulty Level: 3 / 4

Which one of the following describes a preference that is most analogous to the preference mentioned in the first paragraph of Passage A?

This is a C Application question. The prompt asks for a preference that is analogous to the preference mentioned in the first paragraph of Passage A. Therefore, we can ignore Passage B entirely. We are looking for an analogous situation. Rereading the first paragraph of Passage A, we can see that the referenced preference is for sounds with coherence, which is defined as a principle that connects the various sounds and makes them comprehensible. We can reframe this in general terms as a preference for something that includes an element that makes it comprehensible. We should anticipate a correct answer choice that describes a comparable situation.

(A) the preference of some people for falling asleep to white noise, such as the sound of an electric fan

This answer choice includes contradictory information. It describes a preference for something (white noise) that does not include an element that makes it comprehensible. This is a loser.

(B) the preference of many moviegoers for movies with plots that are clear and easy to follow

This matches our anticipated answer choice. It describes a preference for something (movies) that includes an element (clear plots) that makes it comprehensible. This is a candidate.

(C) the preference of many diners for restaurants that serve large portions

This answer choice includes irrelevant information. It discusses the quantity of something. This is also a loser.

(D) the preference of many young listeners for fast music over slower music

This answer choice includes irrelevant information. It compares one type to another type. This is a loser as well.

(E) the preference of most children for sweet foods over bitter foods

This answer choice also includes irrelevant information. Like (D), it compares one type to another type. This is a loser.

As (B) is the only candidate, it is the correct answer choice.

Which one of the following most accurately expresses the main point of Passage B?

This is a C Main Point question. The prompt asks for the main point of Passage B only. Therefore, we can ignore Passage A. The main point of Passage B is stated in the first two sentences of the first paragraph. It is that a listener's expectations with regard to certain elements within music determine the experience of musical emotion. We should anticipate a correct answer choice that accurately expresses this conclusion.

(A) The type of musical emotion experienced by a listener is determined by the level to which the listener's expectations are satisfied.

This matches our anticipated answer choice. The listener's expectations determine the experience of musical emotion. This is a candidate.

(B) Trained listeners are more able to consciously manipulate their own emotional experiences of complex music than are naive listeners.

This answer choice addresses the wrong task. It is an inference based on a supporting detail in the third paragraph of the passage. This is a loser.

(C) If the development of a piece of music is greatly at odds with the listener's musical expectations, then the listener will experience negative emotions.

This answer choice includes incomplete information. The passage is about emotions in general (positive and negative). This answer choice only mentions negative emotions. This is a loser as well.

(D) Listeners can learn to appreciate changes in melodic line and other musical complexities.

This answer choice also includes incomplete information. It only mentions a positive response to music. In addition, it does not discuss the role of a listener's expectations. This is another loser.

(E) Music that is experienced by listeners as relaxing usually produces a buildup and release of tension in those listeners.

This answer choice addresses the wrong task. The buildup and release of tension (and the resulting relaxation) is a supporting idea in Passage B, not the main point. This is a loser.

As (A) is the only candidate, it is the correct answer choice.

25. **Correct Answer (C).** Difficulty Level: 3 / 4

Which one of the following most undermines the explanation provided in Passage A for the relaxing effect that some music has on listeners?

This is a C Weaken question. The prompt asks about an argument in Passage A only. Therefore, we can ignore Passage B. The topic of the prompt is the explanation of the relaxing effect that some music has on listeners. This is discussed in the third paragraph of the passage. The author claims that some music that is continuous and rhythmic can be relaxing for listeners because danger tends to be accompanied by sudden and unexpected sounds in a natural environment. This argument does not have a clear weakness, so we will proceed to eliminating answer choices. We should anticipate a statement that either exposes a weakness in the argument or attacks the support for it.

(A) The musical traditions of different cultures vary greatly in terms of the complexity of the rhythms they employ.

This answer choice addresses the wrong part of the passage. Complexity is discussed in the first paragraph and is not part of the explanation of why some music relaxes people. In addition, the passage does not discuss the musical traditions of different cultures. This is a loser.

(B) The rhythmic structure of a language is determined in part by the pattern of stressed syllables in the words and sentences of the language.

This answer choice addresses the wrong part of the passage. Language is discussed in the second paragraph of the passage and is not part of the explanation of why some music relaxes people. This is a loser.

(C) Many people find the steady and rhythmic sound of a rocking chair to be very unnerving.

This answer choice seems to weaken the argument. If many people find the continuous and rhythmic noises of a rocking chair to be unnerving, then it is unlikely that music relaxes people because it is continuous and rhythmic. Another explanation for the relaxing effect may be needed. This is a candidate.

(D) The sudden interruption of the expected development of a melody tends to interfere with listeners' perception of the melody as coherent.

This answer choice strengthens the argument. If a sudden interruption of the development of a melody affects listeners' perception of the melody as coherent, then listeners would likely feel less relaxed when such an interruption occurs. This strengthens the author's claim that music is relaxing because it is continuous and rhythmic. This is a loser.

(E) Some of the most admired contemporary composers write music that is notably simpler than is most of the music written in previous centuries.

This answer choice includes irrelevant information. The passage does not compare the music written by contemporary composers with the music written in previous centuries. This is a loser.

As (C) is the only candidate, it is the correct answer choice.

---

26. Correct Answer (B). Difficulty Level: 2 / 4

Which one of the following would be most appropriate as a title for each of the passages?

This is a C Main Point title-variant question. The main point of Passage A is stated in the first and last sentences of the first paragraph. It is that, in music, a certain level of complexity and coherence has a positive effect on the listener. The main point of Passage B is stated in the first two sentences of the first paragraph. It is that a listener's expectations with regard to certain elements within music determine the experience of musical emotion. The overlap between these main points is the first similarity we identified between the two passages—both discuss the emotional response of listeners to music. We should anticipate a correct answer choice that accurately expresses the overlapping elements of the passages' main points.

(A) "The Biological Underpinnings of Musical Emotions"

This answer choice includes irrelevant information. Neither passage discusses the biological basis of musical emotion. This is a loser.

(B) "The Psychology of Listener Response to Music"

This matches our anticipated answer choices. Both passages are about the emotional responses of listeners to music. Emotional response is an aspect of psychology. This is a candidate.

(C) "How Music Differs from Other Art Forms"

This answer choice includes irrelevant information. Neither passage compares other art forms to music. This is a loser.

(D) "Cultural Patterns in Listeners' Responses to Music"

This answer choice also includes irrelevant information. Neither passage discusses cultural patterns. This is another loser.

(E) "How Composers Convey Meaning Through Music"

This answer choice includes irrelevant information as well. Neither passage discusses how composers convey meaning. This is also a loser.

As (B) is the only candidate, it is the correct answer choice.

---

27. Correct Answer (D). Difficulty Level: 3 / 4

It can be inferred that both authors would be likely to agree with which one of the following statements?

This is an A/D question. The prompt asks for a point of agreement between the two passages. Looking back at our analysis, we can see that both passages discuss the emotional response of listeners to music. In addition, both discuss the relationship between musical complexity and the positive emotional response of a listener. Finally, both suggest that music that follows a predictable pattern stimulates a positive emotional response from a listener. We should anticipate a correct answer choice that expresses one of these points of agreement.

(A) The more complex a piece of music, the more it is likely to be enjoyed by most listeners.

This answer choice includes contradictory information. Passage A claims that a certain level of complexity is preferable, but that sounds that are too complex are confusing. In addition, Passage B states that sophisticated listeners will enjoy more complex music than naive listeners. This suggests that at least some listeners will not enjoy very complex music. This is a loser.

(B) More knowledgeable listeners tend to prefer music that is discontinuous and unpredictable.

This answer choice includes irrelevant information. Passage A does not mention knowledgeable listeners. Passage B mentions trained listeners, but states that they prefer complex music—no mention is made of discontinuous and unpredictable music. This is also a loser.

(C) The capacity of music to elicit strong emotional responses from listeners is the central determinant of its artistic value.

This answer choice includes irrelevant information as well. Neither passage discusses the artistic value of music. This is another loser.

(D) Music that lacks a predictable course is unlikely to cause a listener to feel relaxed.

This answer choice seems to express a point of agreement between the two passages. It is related to our third anticipated answer choice. The third paragraph of Passage A states that continuous and rhythmic music has a relaxing effect and that discontinuous sounds demand more attention. The first paragraph of Passage B states that when musical expectations are not satisfied, the listener experiences tension. Relaxation occurs when this tension is resolved. Both passages link relaxation to music that is predictable. This is a candidate.

(E) Music that changes from soft to loud is perceived as disturbing and unpleasant by most listeners.

This answer choice includes irrelevant information as well. Passage A mentions soft sounds, but does not discuss music that changes from soft to loud. Passage B does not discuss soft or loud music at all. This is a loser.

As (D) is the only candidate, it is the correct answer choice.

HACKERS
LSAT *Reading Comprehension*

Chapter 11

Question Index

Question Index

Chapter 1 – Welcome to the LSAT

[Drill]

Page 18. December 2003. PT 42, Section 3, Passage 3

Chapter 2 – Deconstructing the Passage

[Drill]

Page 36. December 2008. PT 56, Section 4, Passage 4
Page 37. December 2004. PT 45, Section 2, Passage 3
Page 42. October 2005. PT 47, Section 2, Passage 2
Page 43. December 2007. PT 53, Section 4, Passage 4
Page 47. October 2004. PT 44, Section 1, Passage 1
Page 48. December 2005. PT 48, Section 3, Passage 2
Page 52. October 2008. PT 55, Section 2, Passage 2
Page 53. December 2009. PT 59, Section 4, Passage 1

Chapter 3 – Synthesis Family

[Example Passages and Questions]

Q1. October 2004. PT 44, Section 1, Passage 1, Question 1
Q2. October 2004. PT 44, Section 1, Passage 1, Question 4
Q3. October 2004. PT 44, Section 1, Passage 1, Question 2
Q4. October 2004. PT 44, Section 1, Passage 1, Question 7
Q5. October 2005. PT 47, Section 2, Passage 2, Question 6
Q6. October 2005. PT 47, Section 2, Passage 2, Question 10

[Practice Sets]

Q1. June 2006. PT 49, Section 3, Passage 3, Question 14
Q2. June 2006. PT 49, Section 3, Passage 3, Question 16
Q3. June 2006. PT 49, Section 3, Passage 3, Question 19
Q4. October 2005. PT 47, Section 2, Passage 3, Question 12
Q5. October 2005. PT 47, Section 2, Passage 3, Question 13
Q6. October 2005. PT 47, Section 2, Passage 3, Question 18
Q7. December 2003. PT 42, Section 3, Passage 2, Question 8
Q8. December 2003. PT 42, Section 3, Passage 2, Question 10
Q9. December 2003. PT 42, Section 3, Passage 2, Question 13
Q10. December 2004. PT 45, Section 2, Passage 2, Question 7
Q11. December 2004. PT 45, Section 2, Passage 2, Question 8
Q12. December 2004. PT 45, Section 2, Passage 2, Question 10
Q13. December 2004. PT 45, Section 2, Passage 2, Question 14
Q14. October 2005. PT 47, Section 2, Passage 4, Question 19
Q15. October 2005. PT 47, Section 2, Passage 4, Question 24
Q16. October 2005. PT 47, Section 2, Passage 4, Question 26

Chapter 4 – Information Family

[Example Passages and Questions]

Q1. December 2005. PT 48, Section 3, Passage 2, Question 10
Q2. December 2005. PT 48, Section 3, Passage 2, Question 11
Q3. December 2005. PT 48, Section 3, Passage 2, Question 8

[Practice Sets]

Q1. December 2008. PT 56, Section 4, Passage 1, Question 4
Q2. December 2008. PT 56, Section 4, Passage 1, Question 5
Q3. June 2005. PT 46, Section 1, Passage 3, Question 17
Q4. June 2005. PT 46, Section 1, Passage 3, Question 19
Q5. June 2005. PT 46, Section 1, Passage 3, Question 20
Q6. December 2005. PT 48, Section 3, Passage 4, Question 23
Q7. December 2005. PT 48, Section 3, Passage 4, Question 24
Q8. December 2005. PT 48, Section 3, Passage 4, Question 26
Q9. June 2007. PT 51.5, Section 4, Passage 3, Question 16
Q10. June 2007. PT 51.5, Section 4, Passage 3, Question 22
Q11. June 2006. PT 49, Section 3, Passage 2, Question 9
Q12. June 2006. PT 49, Section 3, Passage 2, Question 12
Q13. June 2006. PT 49, Section 3, Passage 2, Question 13

Chapter 5 – Inference Family

[Example Passages and Questions]

Q1. December 2003. PT 42, Section 3, Passage 2, Question 15
Q2. December 2003. PT 42, Section 3, Passage 2, Question 14
Q3. December 2003. PT 42, Section 3, Passage 2, Question 9
Q4. December 2007. PT 53, Section 4, Passage 4, Question 27
Q5. December 2007. PT 53, Section 4, Passage 4, Question 23
Q6. December 2007. PT 53, Section 4, Passage 4, Question 24
Q7. December 2007. PT 53, Section 4, Passage 4, Question 21

[Practice Sets]

Q1. December 2002. PT 39, Section 3, Passage 2, Question 11
Q2. December 2002. PT 39, Section 3, Passage 2, Question 12
Q3. December 2002. PT 39, Section 3, Passage 2, Question 13
Q4. December 2002. PT 39, Section 3, Passage 2, Question 15
Q5. December 2002. PT 39, Section 3, Passage 2, Question 16
Q6. June 2003. PT 40, Section 4, Passage 2, Question 10
Q7. June 2003. PT 40, Section 4, Passage 2, Question 11
Q8. June 2003. PT 40, Section 4, Passage 2, Question 12
Q9. October 2004. PT 44, Section 1, Passage 4, Question 23
Q10. October 2004. PT 44, Section 1, Passage 4, Question 24
Q11. December 2009. PT 59, Section 4, Passage 3, Question 18
Q12. December 2009. PT 59, Section 4, Passage 3, Question 20
Q13. December 2009. PT 59, Section 4, Passage 3, Question 21
Q14. December 2006. PT 51, Section 2, Passage 2, Question 9
Q15. December 2006. PT 51, Section 2, Passage 2, Question 11
Q16. December 2006. PT 51, Section 2, Passage 2, Question 12

Chapter 6 – Process Family

[Example Passages and Questions]

Q1. December 2008. PT 56, Section 4, Passage 1, Question 2
Q2. December 2009. PT 59, Section 4, Passage 3, Question 19
Q3. December 2009. PT 59, Section 4, Passage 3, Question 22
Q4. December 2009. PT 59, Section 4, Passage 3, Question 17
Q5. December 2009. PT 59, Section 4, Passage 4, Question 27
Q6. December 2009. PT 59, Section 4, Passage 4, Question 26